Nigerian Petroleum Industry, Policies and Conflict Relations

Annotated Articles and Bibliography

VOLUME 2

FUEL SUBSIDY REMOVAL DEBATE AND PROTEST

PETROLEUM INDUSTRY BILL (PIB)

REFINERIES AND THE OIL SECTOR

Nigerian Petroleum Industry, Policies and Conflict Relations

Annotated articles and Bibliography

Compiled by
Henrietta O. Otokunefor
and assisted by Helen Emasealu

malthouse MP

Malthouse Press Limited

Lagos, Benin, Ibadan, Jos, Port-Harcourt, Zaria

Published by
Malthouse Press Limited
43 Onitana Street, Off Stadium Hotel Road,
Surulere, Lagos, Lagos State
E-mail: malthouse_press@yahoo.com
malthouselagos@gmail.com
Tel: +234 (0)802 600 3203

First Published 2014
ISBN 978-978-51932-7-5

Dedication

To our late brothers:

Dr Eric Eboe Otobo
Engr Owomano Eboe Otobo

Acknowledgements

My first appreciation goes to God for making the production of this work possible; it is all by His Grace. Next, I thank members of my immediate family for bearing with me turning our living room to a production room with newspapers scattered all the over. My special thanks go my husband, Tosan, who formatted and Prince for the scanning. Ota, Ochuko, Kome and Oghale gave all necessary encouragement to complete the work.

Sotonye Orji spent days collating the section on Deregulation and was always checking on me to find out the progress of the work. Eghuan Okonny deserves special mention for his contribution and to say thank you. Mrs. Helen Emasealu's contribution in doing some of the annotation and also taking part in editing some of the entries is hereby acknowledged. Owajimam Job is appreciated for doing the secretarial work of the annotation. My University Librarian, Dr (Mrs) C.O. Nwodo, is appreciated for allowing me to do the finishing from home in the last four days. Uwem Ebong, Emma Onwuzuruike, Akpovoke Shaire, Glory Edet and others for holding brief in the Department during my absence for those four days is greatly appreciated. Professor Emman Emasealu's kind gesture of bringing Helen to join in the editorial work and encouragement is appreciated and acknowledged. Same goes to Dr. (Mrs.) Susan Umeozor. I appreciate all your contributions in one way or the other.

My profound gratitude goes to my publisher for the express service in producing the two volumes of this work. The editorial work was painstakingly done in good time. I wish to express my sincere appreciation to Professor Dafe Otobo for writing the Foreword. The work came out as planned because of his sacrifice of working round the clock.

All works used in the annotation and compilation are also acknowledged especially the two major newspapers (*The Guardian* and *THISDAY*), their reporters, columnists and contributors. We hope to improve upon the next edition and readers should bear with me for any errors.

Foreword

Dr Henrietta Otokunefor, in my careful estimation, has put together a book whose title is somewhat deceptive and, indeed, does not fully reflect the true measure of its breadth and coverage of the subject area chosen – and thus greatly understates its immense significance and contribution to existing literature or works on the oil and gas industry in Nigeria.

What passes for "annotated articles and bibliography" is in fact a comprehensive and exhaustive discussion of each and everything thing about the Nigerian petroleum industry by experts in and outside academia, research institutes and think tanks, top functionaries in relevant ministries, government departments and agencies, past and current heads of state/presidents, past and current ministers, prominent and knowledgeable legislators, politicians of all descriptions and at all levels, top newspaper columnists, discerning local and foreign critics, interviews and transcribed broadcasts and press releases by same, officials of non-governmental organisations and a host of those loosely referred to as civil society organisations, civil and political activists of all hues, so-called international development agencies, some diplomatic missions, and the dead-panned apologists for successive governments.

It is remarkable that concentrated in one source (but in two volumes) is most information one could possibly seek on the oil and gas industry in Nigeria: basic production statistics, nature and activities of operators, deregulation and other official policies, relevant laws and regulations, regulatory agencies, pricing of refined petroleum products, marketers and their challenges, consumer and community reactions, vandalisation of pipelines and other infrastructure, refineries and chequered privatisation efforts, place of law enforcement and intelligence agencies, involvement of the National Assembly and its relevant committees, strategic issues and other impacts of local and international politics, etc.

The "conflict relations" bring to the fore quite crucially, I would think, why the oil and gas industry is the most conflict-ridden one in Nigeria over the decades, dominated by dissension over policies in and out of legislative chambers, oppositional activities of some groups/communities (especially in the Niger Delta), oppositional activities of the two trade unions (Nupengassan) and of the central trade union organisations and their affiliates (NLC, TUC), flare ups between and among tanker drivers and against security agencies, periodic nationwide protests over increases of pump-prices of refined petroleum products, activities and protests of independent marketers, posturing and conflict-inducing activities of opposition political parties, and of other organised groups in society.

Nigerian Petroleum Industry, Policies and Conflict Relations; annotated articles and bibliography should prove an immensely invaluable documentary source-book, to the general reader, more especially to regulators, the NNPC group, policy makers, researchers and social scientists in tertiary institutions and public and private sector think tanks, local and foreign operators, observers and those with interest in the oil and gas industry in Nigeria.

My recommending this book to all is probably superfluous since the contents speak for themselves; but certainly Henrietta Otokunefor deserves to be commended for this well thought through compilation.

Dafe Otobo, DPhil (Oxford)
Professor & President of the Nigerian Industrial & Employment Relations Association
University of Lagos
12 June 2014

Preface

In Nigeria, the issue of fuel subsidy removal has remained a thorny one which in January, 2012 became a time bomb that exploded in the one week-long protest and strike nationwide. Nigerians in compliance with the directives of organised labour and its allies took to the streets to protest the removal of fuel subsidy by the Federal Government. Socio-economic and educational activities across the country were paralysed.

The Minimum Wage Act 2011 that fixed the minimum wage at ₦18, 000.00 was fingered to have precipitated the 2012 crisis of oil subsidy. The State Governors, according to reports, agreed reluctantly to pay the minimum wage on the condition that the fuel subsidy would be withdrawn and the proceeds shared by the three tiers of government. There was however the question of whether there was fuel subsidy with both the official argument and opposing viewpoints of civil society. While the government claimed that there was subsidy on imported petroleum products for domestic consumption, the opposition refuted the claim. Government claimed that the landing cost per litre of premium motor spirit (PMS) locally known as petrol was ₦131.66, to which was added a marketer's margin of ₦9.34K to make the selling price at ₦141 per litre the New Year Day's pump price increase from N65 that sparked off the nationwide protest.

The civil society and other informed oil experts, including a former Petroleum Minister, offered a different perspective on the subsidy debate. They argued that if it was true that the refineries were working at 38.2 per cent efficiency as was claimed by government, then only shipping and refining cost would be attracted by the non-export crude. Consequently, the cost of fuel per litre ought to be ₦34.03; therefore at ₦65 per litre, Nigerians were already subsidising government by ₦30.97. They further noted that government in the past adopted off-shore processing to meet shortfall in domestic demand. Some key oil companies were selected and given oil to refine and supply the shortfall to cushion the domestic consumption with proceeds from the residual products paid into the government coffers.

Both cases, fuel subsidy removal and national minimum wage, not only show the interrelatedness of various strands of government's socio-economic policies, but also provide a snap-shot of the engaging debates and conflict situations that have characterised the oil and gas industry for the past four and more decades.

The debates, claims, counter claims and divergent viewpoints on a range of subjects and attendant issues generated are veritable wealth of primary materials to be collected, organised and preserved for use and posterity.

Libraries in Nigeria, especially the university libraries that are expected to meet the research needs of their patrons, have experienced the problem of making both the annotated bibliography and the compilation of the articles available to their patrons.

Nigerian Petroleum Industry, Policies, and Conflict Relations in two volumes are an annotated bibliography and compilation of newspaper articles, interviews, press releases/statements, paid adverts, transcribed TV and radio broadcasts on the Nigerian oil and gas industry, including fuel subsidy removal and the more recent protests. Each of the volumes is divided into five sections covering the same subject. Section 1 is on Deregulation; Section 2 treats Fuel Subsidy Payment and Regime Probe; Section 3 covers Fuel Subsidy Removal; Section 4 focuses on Fuel Subsidy Removal Debate and Protest; while Section 5 covers Petroleum Industry Bill (PIB), Refineries and the Oil sector in general.

The good news about the book is that it is a complete reference work at the finger of the user. There is no need to go elsewhere in search of the required entry or article after retrieving the title from the annotation.

ENTRIES

Fuel Subsidy Removal Debate
Fuel Subsidy Conversation: Beyond the subsidy removal debate
By Akin Osuntokun
THE GUARDIAN, Sunday, January 15, 2012, pg. 13
The write-up is a Face book Forum post on the subsidy removal debate. It contains angry rhetoric taken as fairly logical, representative and valid by and large. The economic rationality of the subsidy removal is not contestable by the logic presented. It rather counter poses a context that makes it impossible for government to demand sacrifice from the governed by posing the same questions of the "conduct of governance".

Fuel Subsidy Conversation: Jonathan-The Judas Iscariot of our time...Analogous Tale from Achebe's Things Fall Apart
By Isidore Emaka Uzoatu
THE GUARDIAN, Sunday, January 15, 2012, pg. 14
After giving the analogy between Achebe's *Things Fall Apart* and the crossroad in which Nigeria finds herself, a possible solution is presented. The deregulation of the downstream sector of the petroleum industry leading to full commercialization is given as the possible solution.

Fuel Subsidy Conversation: 'Make relevant data public for scrutiny, arrest impunity'. Kalu Idika Kalu
THE GUARDIAN, Sunday, January 15, 2012, pg. 9
As part of the debate on the removal of fuel subsidy, Kalu Idika Kalu argues that the process must be gradual and transparent as recorded in an interview on AIT.

Fuel Subsidy Conversation: one week of fire and fury.
By Alabi Williams
THE GUARDIAN, Sunday, January 15, 2012, pg.7
The write-up gives accounts of the events of the first week after the announcement of the fuel subsidy removal.

Fuel Subsidy Conversation: Sanusi - Both Govt, Labour should reach a compromise fast.
THE GUARDIAN, Sunday, January 15, 2012, pg. 8, 12
The paper presents the argument for the removal of fuel subsidy by Sanusi Lamido Sanusi as recorded off live interview by the African Independent Television (AIT). He argues that the current level of subsidy cannot be sustained, that it was mischievous to say there is no subsidy; an economic matter should not be politicize, those who fleece the nation must be punished and Govt must allow NIMASA do its job.

Fuel Subsidy Conversation...Tell it to the President
By Nnimmo Bassey
THE GUARDIAN, Sunday, January 15, 2012, pg. 14
The write-up contains information the fuel price/litre (naira) of OPEC Member countries and minimum wage (in Naira).

Fuel Subsidy Conversation: "We have to first audit our actual fuel consumption"
THE GUARDIAN, Sunday, January 15, 2012, pg. 10
The piece records the suggestions by Olisa Agbakoba of possible solutions to the ongoing subsidy removal crisis in a telephone chat with Gbenga Salau.

Fuel Subsidy Conversation: Why Govt took the hard decision
By Minister of Finance, Dr. Ngozi Okonjo-Iweala
THE GUARDIAN, Sunday, January 15, 2012, pg. 11
The write-up gives the views of the Minister of Finance, Dr. Ngozi Okonjo-Iweala in one of her appearances on Television debate on the fuel subsidy removal. It was recorded off live interview on African Independent Television (AIT).

Fuel Subsidy Removal.....The IMF Is At Work Again OSUNDARE on State of the Nation, NEWSPEOPLE.
By Anote Ajeluorou
THE GUARDIAN, Sunday, January 1, 2012, pg. 42-43
The fuel subsidy removal issue is the concluding part of the interview of Professor Niyi Osundare by Anote Ajeluorou on the state of the nation. The excerpts concludes with a call on "President Jonathan not to further compound the hardship" currently being suffered by Nigerians through the removal of fuel subsidy. He posits that the IMF is at work again like what happened during the Babangida's administration.

Govt, Civil Society, differ still on fuel subsidy
By Marcel Mbamalu, Dele Fanimo, Armsfreo Ajanaku Onome, Obiora Adubu and Sulaimon Salau
THE GUARDIAN, Friday, December 23, 2011, pg. 1, 2
At the town hall meeting organised by the Newspaper Proprietors Association of Nigeria (NPAN) in Lagos both the proponents and opponents of the planned subsidy removal yielded no ground of a compromise according to this write-up.

The many ironies of fuel subsidy debate
By Kayode Komolafe
THISDAY, Wednesday, February 1, 2012, pg. 56
The paper takes a look at the fuel subsidy debate presenting all the sides of the argument and drawing the conclusion that "the fuel subsidy debate is replete with ironies that deregulation policy should be further examined".

Pains of premium price for petrol
By Nike Sotade
THE GUARDIAN, Monday, January 2, 2012, pg. 13
The article gives a vivid account of the events and activities including all the arguments for and against the removal of fuel subsidy.

The Popular Will
By El-Rufai
THISDAY, Friday, January 13, 2012, vol.16, no. 6108, pg. 56
The article takes a look at the economics as well as the politics of the fuel subsidy, the cost of governance especially the bloated overheads, the SURE programme and the popular will of the people.

Protest raises the bar of the people's power, resolve
By Taiwo Akintunde
THISDAY, Friday, January 13, 2012, vol. 16, no. 6108, pg. 7
The writer posits that with each passing day, the number of protesters continued to grow and expand comprising of people from all strata of the Nigerian Society. These include the disabled, rich and poor, young and old, artisans and professionals, religious leaders across all faiths.

Reflections on the subsidy struggle
By Simon Kolawole
THISDAY, Sunday, January 22, 2012, vol.17, no. 6117, pg. 111
The article highlights some of facts to come out the revelations at the ad-hoc probe of the House of Representative of the fuel regime. Its author posits that the debates and agitations were very fruitful when viewed from the larger picture perspective.

"Subsidy: a wrong way to run an economy".
By Ini Akpabio
THE GUARDIAN, Sunday, January 1, 2012, pg. 53
The author posits that our national debate of the fuel subsidy removal are being "swallowed up by sentiment" without analytical approach and lack of vision by all stakeholders.

Subsidy: the governance debate has just begun
By Bolaji Owasanoye
THISDAY, Tuesday, January 24, 2012, vol.17, no. 6119, pg. vi

The author argues that the governance debate has just started as there are many issues to be cleared around the assertion that the subsidy it has been paying on fuel consumption is no longer sustainable.

'Subsidy removal is good if Govt is sincere' Prof. Akin Iwayemi
By Bankole Shakirudeen Adeshina
THE GUARDIAN, Saturday, January 7, 2012, pg. 26
The 38th President of the Nigerian Economic Society (NES) in an interview by Bankole Shakirudeen Adeshina posits that the right pricing template for oil must be provided to help translate into physical and economic development. In his opinion, subsidy should be removed but the deregulation of the industry must also be done with governments providing the enabling environment and a level playing field for the operators.

FUEL SUBSIDY REMOVAL PROTEST

Anger, frustration, hallmark fuel subsidy protests
By Chiemelie Ezeobi, Taiwo Akintunde and Comfort Umoren
THISDAY, Friday, January 13, 2012, vol. 16, no 6108, pg. 42, 43
The paper gives a vivid account of the protesters, many of whom trekked long distance to the Freedom Square, Ojota, Lagos in show of solidarity with a cause they believe in.

Anger over fuel price spreads by reporters.
THE GUARDIAN, Friday, January 6, 2012, pg.1, 2
The report gives account of the continued protest against the removal of subsidy on petrol on some states even before the proposed labour strike began.

As we go on strike
By OlukayodeOguta
THISDAY, Wednesday, January 11, 2012, vol.16, no.6106, pg. 39
The author argues that the people working with both labour and the civil groups in unison make very clear demands as they proceed on the strike, they will only receive palliatives that would have the day of reckoning postponed.

At a time like this...
By 'Lola Adewoyin.
THISDAY, Friday, January 13, 2012, vol. 16, no. 6108, pg. 19
The author shares the experiences of some Nigerians in ways to survive the negative effects of the nationwide strike and protest.

Beyond Labour's Strike: what next?
By Linda Eroke
THISDAY, Tuesday, January 24, 2012, vol. 77, no. 6119, pg. 36

The paper looks at the decision to suspend the fuel subsidy removal nation-wide strike by the organised labour and its attendant criticisms from stakeholders. The way forward is given to conclude the write-up.

Court stops NLC, TUC from going ahead with strike.
By Ibe Uwaleke, Godwin Ijediogor, Lemmy Ughegbe and Collins Olayinka
THE GUARDIAN, Saturday, January 7, 2012, pg.1, 2
The write-up reports that the National Industrial Court (NIC) issued an interim order to the National Labour Congress (NLC) and the Trade Union Congress (TUC) restraining them from the proposed strike over the fuel subsidy removal.

Crowds increase as protest enters day 4
By THISDAY Correspondents
THISDAY, Thursday, January 12, 2012, vol.16, no. 6107, pg. 7
The reports give an account of day-four of the nation-wide strike over the removal of fuel subsidy.

Did labour buckle under the weight of executive?
By Tunde Rahman
THISDAY, Saturday, January 21, 2012, vol. 16, no. 6116, pg. 15
The paper critically looks at the question of labour's compromise by the calling off the fuel subsidy removal strike. The author opines that labour succeeded in shutting down the economy for five days with a colossal loss to the economy of the country.

Doctor, Catholic bishops, others decry fuel subsidy removal.
THE GUARDIAN, Thursday, January 5, 2012, pg.4
The report carries a jointly signed statement by the President, Dr. Omede Idris and Secretary General, Dr. Bala M. Audu, doctors under the aegis of the Nigerian Medical Association (NMA) opposing the removal of fuel subsidy.

Fuel subsidy and the civil society
OBE: Occupy Nigeria was most effective, but we need to move to next level
By Kamal Tayo Oropo
THE GUARDIAN, Sunday, January 15, 2012, pg. 56
The paper covers the interview with the former president of the Civil Liberty Organisation (CLO) on the role played in the fuel subsidy protest and what the next target should be.

Fuel subsidy and government's new thinking
By Davidson Iriekpen
THISDAY, Thursday, January 26, 2012, vol. 17, no. 6121, pg 22
The article takes a look at the useful lessons from the strike and protests over the removal of fuel subsidy from the government's perspective.

Fuel subsidy protest: the good, the bad and the ugly.
By Charles Ajunwa
THISDAY, Monday, January 16, 2012, vol. 16, no. 6111, pg. 16, 17
The write-up reviews the previous week's nationwide protest over the fuel subsidy removal.

Fuel subsidy removal: their strike, our gains.
By Emmanuel Ugwu
THISDAY, Tuesday, January 24, 2012, vol. 17, no, 6119, pg 21
The writer looks at the reasons why the fuel subsidy removal strike and protests are ineffective in some states in the Eastern part of the nation especially in Abia State.

How protesters shut down Ibadan
By Tunde Sanni
THISDAY, Friday, January 13, 2012, vol. 16, no. 6108, pg. 18
The write-up is on how the five-day protest against the fuel subsidy removal impacted on the Oyo State Capital, Ibadan.

How Public Protest Impact Jonathan's Government
By Charles Ajunwa
THISDAY, Monday, January 30, 2012, vol. no. 6125, pg. 21
The author posits that the fuel subsidy removal protests appear to be a blessing in disguise in many aspects impacting on President Jonathan's approach to governance.

How subsidy protest divided Nollywood
By Azuka Ogujuba
THISDAY, Saturday, January 21, 2012, vol. 16, no. 6116, pg. 18, 19
The paper examines the impact of the fuel subsidy removal protest on Nollywood.

INEC shifts Adamawa Governorship poll
By Chuks Okocha and Matthew Onah
THISDAY, Wednesday, January 11, 2012, vol. 16, no. 6106, pg. 9
The news item carries the announced suspension of the January 14 Adamawa State governorship election by INEC.

Interpreting the subsidy rage
By Chima Ibeneche
THE GUARDIAN, Wednesday, January 18, 2012, pg. 51
The writer argues that life in Nigeria has become increasingly painful, frustrating and hazardous more importantly hopeless for the teeming unemployed graduates and the masses. While at the other end of the pendulum are the political office holders growing fatter, with government getting bigger and bigger. The writer draws attention to the state of insecurity in Nigeria, where if kidnapping fails to get one, Boko Haram will, if both fail then the chances are that violet armed

robbery would. Yet murders and crimes are seldom solved. Thus, the removal of fuel subsidy was only the last straw that broke the camel's back already carrying the above loads.

Kaduna: how the subsidy removal protest turned bloody.
By John Shiklam
THISDAY, Wednesday, January 18, 2012, vol. 16, no. 6113, pg. 21
The article is an account by the author on how the fuel subsidy removal protest in Kaduna turned bloody after been taken over by hoodlums and street urchins.

Labour orders nationwide strike as new fuel price regime begins.
THE GUARDIAN, Tuesday, January 3, 2012, pg. 1, 2
The write-up gives account of petrol stations adjusting their pump price and the immediate impact on transportation as fares nationwide jumped up by 120 percent in most cities.

Labour played into the hands of enemies of the country- Ekweremadu
By Kunle Akogun
THISDAY, Saturday, January 21, 2012, vol. 16, no. 6116, pg 45, 46
The write-up covers the interview of the Deputy Senate President, Senator Ike Ekweremadu a key participant at all the meetings to broker a truce between government and labour during the face-off between the federal government and organised labour.

Labour strike shuts down Nigeria
By Ndubuisi Ugah
THISDAY, Tuesday, January 10, 2012, vol.16, no. 6105, pg. 9, 10
The article presents zone by zone account of the nationwide strike called by the organized labour as it entered the second day.

Labour threatens mass protests
By Linda Eroke and Damilola Oyedele
THISDAY, Monday, January 2, 2012, vol. 16, no. 6097, pg. 1, 6
The write-up carries the reaction of the Nigeria Labour Congress (NLC) and the Trade Union Congress (TUC) to the announced removal of fuel subsidy by the PPPRA in January 1, 2012. In their joint statement issued same January 1, 2012, their state councils were directed to take steps to resist any price above N65 per litre of PMS while they wait for a date to begin general strikes and mass protest across the nation.

A leap in people's power
By Tope Templer Olaiye
THE GUARDIAN, Sunday, January 22, 2012, pg. 14
The writer compares the 2010 first Save Nigeria Group (SNG) protest of the continued absence of late Umaru Yar'Adua from the country and the 2012 fuel subsidy removal protest. He argues that the use of social media to galvanise and

mobilise the citizens in the later makes it stand miles apart from the former. He enumerates all the civil organisations and cyber activists that joined efforts with SNG in the 2012 fuel subsidy removal protest.

Lessons from the Anti-Subsidy Removal
By Emeka Nwosu
THISDAY, Tuesday January 24, 2012, vol. 17, no. 6119, pg. 14
The write-up gives the background to the fuel subsidy removal strike and protests before presenting the lessons.

The many faces of subsidy protest survivors: how traders, artisans lived with the industrial action.
By Geoff Iyatse
THE GUARDIAN, Sunday, January 22, 2012, pg. 49
The paper narrates the experiences of the essential commodity market during the one weeklong fuel subsidy removal protest. A situation liken to a war situation or a typical abnormal market situation by some of the survivors.

The Monday that Nigeria failed to explode.
By Omololu Ogunmade
THISDAY, Wednesday, January 18, 2012, vol. 16, no. 6113, pg. 17
The article covers the events that led to the sit-at-home order given by the organised labour to protesters and the subsequent action by the military men to cordon off the popular Gani Fawehinmi Freedom Park in Ojota, Lagos.

NLC Strike: Security chiefs assure protesters, others of safety.
By Terhemba Daka.
THE GUARDIAN, Saturday, January 7, 2012, pg. 10
According to the writer, the Inspector General of Police, Hafiz Ringim on behalf of the service chiefs at the end of the meeting of heads of the Nigerian Security agencies "disclosed that medical services would be on hand for the protesters during the proposed strike by NLC & TUC.

Passengers stranded as Foreign Airlines cancel flights
By Chinedu Eze
THISDAY, Wednesday, January 11, 2012, vol. 16, no. 6106, pg. 9
The writer gives account of how over 500 passengers were stranded at the Murtala Muhammed International Airport, Lagos as a result of the nation-wide strike and protest.

People power and its prospects
By Kayode Komalafe
THISDAY, Wednesday, January 18, 2012, vol. 16, no. 6113, pg. 48
The article looks at the prospects that the mass action from the fuel subsidy removal protests hold for the Nigerian popular democracy.

Police battle citizens as subsidy protest spread
By Reporters
THE GUARDIAN, Wednesday, January 4, 2012, pg. 5, 9, 10, 12
The reports give the accounts of Nigerians protesting the announcement of subsidy removal across the nation for the second day running before the organised labour and allies called for a general strike.

Protests reign all over amid desperate search for truce.
By Oghogho Obaywnana and others.
THE GUARDIAN, Wednesday, January 11, 2012, pg. 1
The write-up gives the account of the face-off between organised labour and the Federal Government over the removal of fuel subsidy.

Protests suspended as FG cuts petrol price to N97
By Ahamefula Ogbu
THISDAY, Monday, January 16, 2012, vol.16, no.6111, pg. 1, 8
The write-up carries the news of the suspended fuel subsidy removal protest after President Jonathan in a nationwide TV address reduced the pump price of petrol to N97 from N141.

Public space, social media and coming revolution
By Bayo Olupohunda
THE GUARDIAN, Sunday, January 22, 2012, pg. 14
The article dwells on the role of the social media and its effective deployment in calling "thousands of protesters from the middle class to the lowly mass of the working people together in a massive protest that sent the government into a panic mode".

Senate Proposes April date for deregulation
By Kunle Akogun and Ahamefula Ogbu
THIDSAY, Wednesday, January 11, 2012, vol.16, no.6106, pg 1, 6
The write-up gives the day two account of the nation-wide anti-fuel subsidy removal strike and protest including the reactions from the Senate, the Attorney General, Rivers State Governor, Inspector General of Police among others.

STREETPULSE...Our verdict on the strike
By Ejiro Odoua
THE GUARDIAN, Sunday, January 22, 2012, pg. 15
The write-up is an excerpt of the opinion expressed by some Nigerians about the outcome of the strike action in a chat with The Guardian.

Subsidy protest: gains, abuse of technology tools.
By Emma Okonji
THISDAY, Thursday, January 19, 2012, vol. 16, no. 6114, pg. 26

The article looks at how the technology tools were used during the nationwide-protests over the removal of fuel subsidy.

Subsidy Protest: the winners and losers
By Ademola Adeyemo
THISDAY, Wednesday, January 18, 2012, vol. 16, no. 6113, pg. 16
The article is an attempt by the author to identify the winners and losers of the seven-day nationwide protests over the removal of fuel subsidy.

The thrills and frills of subsidy protests
By Olaolu Olusina, Paul Obi, Hammed Shittu and Ibrahim Shuaibu
THISDAY, Sunday, January 22, 2012, vol. 17, no. 6117, pg 14, 15, 16
The article highlights some comical and thrilling moments that took place during the national strike and protests that added colour and sustained the momentum of the exercise.

The week that changed Nigeria
By Chidi Odinkalu
THISDAY, Sunday, January 22, 2012, vol.17, no.6117, pg. 24
The paper reviews some of the issues raised at the just concluded one week protests and strike over removal of fuel subsidy. It argues that the strike was about much more than just the subsidy removal. It concludes with the presentation of the positive agenda for governance offered by the protests.

FUEL SUBSIDY SCAM AND STRIKE ECONOMIC IMPACT

CBN admits fraud in subsidy scheme, warns of pressure on foreign reserve
By Azimazi Momoh Jimoh and others
THE GUARDIAN, Wednesday, January 25, 2012, pg. 1, 2
The news report put the total amount of money withdrawn from the Central Bank of Nigeria (CBN) and spent on fuel subsidy by the Federal Government as N1.763 trillion as against the 1.38 trillion given by the Ministry of Finance. The presence of sharp practices in the implementation of refined petroleum products and the subsidy regime was acknowledged by the CBN boss. He stated that non-performing bank loans to petroleum product marketing companies and for stock market transactions were a major contributing factor in the distress suffered by some Nigerian banks in 2008/2009. The House of Representative Committee public hearing on subsidy fund management was also informed by the CBN boss that the Petroleum Support Fund (PSF) which had N673 billion in 2001 was left with only N6 billion. He also gave the CBN's understanding of PSF which is operated by the PPPRA (Petroleum Products Pricing Regulatory Agency) though domiciled in the CBN.

Cost, gain of fuel subsidy removal
By Bukola Olatunji, Uchechukwu Nnaike and Funmi Ogundare.
THISDAY, Wednesday, January 18, 2012, vol. 16, no. 6113, pg. 34, 35

The article looks at the views of stakeholders in the education sector in respect of the cost to education and the subsequent benefit from the fallout on the sector.

DPO arrested for kibbling protesters
By THISDAY Correspondents
THISDAY, Tuesday, January 10, 2012, vol.6, no. 6105, pg. 1, 8
The write-up gives the nationwide account of strike called by labour to protest the removal of fuel subsidy with two deaths on the first day in Lagos and Kano. The strike grounded local flights, hampered the lifting of crude oil and the volume of trading on the floor of the Nigerian Stock Exchange (NSE) falling by 82%.

Gains and Loss of subsidy strike
By Cosmas Odoemena
THISDAY, Friday, January 20, 2012, vol.16, no. 6115, pg. 15
The write-up discusses the gains and loss of the one-week strike and posits that Nigeria as a nation is the biggest winner of all the activities. This is followed by the middle class as the second group of winners.

Labour strike: artisans, traders recount tales of woes.
By Festus Akanbi and Malachy Agbo
THISDAY, Sunday, January 22, 2012, vol.17, no.6117, pg. 26
The article recounts the losses by artisans and traders whose source of income are tired to their daily activities. It also examines the effects on other sectors such as tourism and agriculture.

NNPC created room for subsidy scam, marketers allege.
By Azimazi Momoh Jimoh
THE GUARDIAN, Thursday, January 26, 2012, pg. 15
The report gives the defence of the marketing firms in the petroleum industry under the umbrella of the Independent Petroleum Marketing Association of Nigeria (IPMAN) at the House of Representatives Ad Hoc Committee probing the oil subsidy regime. Their defence includes the allegation that the Nigerian National Petroleum Corporation (NNPC) awarded fuel importation contracts to "portfolio importers" who have neither depot nor product retail outlets. Instead they operate as middlemen who in turn sell at premium price to IPMAN members.

Reps uncover eight billion litres fuel subsidy scam.
By Azimazi Momoh Jimoh and Kelvin Ebiri
THE GUARDIAN, Thursday, January 19, 2012, pg. 1
The report says that the House of Representatives Ad Hoc Committee investigating the management of subsidy on petrol discovered a gap between 59 million litres of the product on a daily basis and the daily consumption capacity of 35 million litres only in the whole year of 2011.

Strike causes N733b loss to economy
By David Ogah *et al.*
THE GUARDIAN, Tuesday, January 17, 2012, pg. 1
Major economic sectors recorded N733.5 billion loss with the banks topping the losses chart of about N400 billion with the Information Communication Technology (ICT) Companies coming second with N159.5 billion. The figure could have been more worrisome if the nation's oil operations were disrupted according to the reports.

Strike: Interbank market loses N400 bn in 1 week.
By Obinma Chima
THISDAY, Monday, January 16, 2012, vol. 16, no. 6111, pg 26, 27
The paper gives the impact of the nationwide strike and protests on the financial market and other related issues.

We called off anti-subsidy removal strike in national interest, says Esele
THE GUARDIAN, Tuesday, February 7, 2012, pg. 43, 47
Esele, the Trade Union Congress (TUC) President says the strike was effective as the plan to shut down the strategic areas of the economy especially the airports was achieved. He states that "strike protests are a means to an end and not an end in itself

PETROLEUM INDUSTRY BILL (PIB), REFINERIES AND THE OIL SECTOR

Industries Transparency Initiatives (NEITI)
Withheld NEITI report impeding Nigeria's oil sector's growth, say CSOs
By Obiora Aduba and SulaimonSalau
THE GUARDIAN, Wednesday, September 14, 2011, pg. 42
The report contains the concern expressed by a coalition of 24 civil society organisations abroad over the continuous withholding of the NEITI audit report covering 2006 to 2008 of the nation's oil sector. The delay in its release is affecting the sector's growth and encouraging graft.

NLC, TUC, PENGASSAN, Others Fault Oil Sector Reform
By Nkechi Onyedika
THE GUARDIAN, Friday, November 25, 2011, pg. 64
The write-up carries the submission of stakeholders in the petroleum industry at a Stakeholders National Consultation on Petroleum Subsidy organized by the Initiative for Peace and Industrial Harmony that took place on Thursday November 24, 2011 in Abuja.

Govt must refund debt to Nigerians
By Anthony Kola olusanya
THE GUARDIAN, Wednesday, January 11, 2012, pg. 51

The author presents what he terms fact of the figures being owed Nigerians by the Nigeria Federal Government of over ₦64,266,060,000,000 trillion in excess amount paid for fuel over the last 12 years by the present civilian dispensation. The figure calculated from the ₦2 per litre surcharge on every litre of petrol bought by Nigerians by the Abacha military regime when the pump price of fuel to ₦17 per litre that was fathom into ₦ 65 of the Obasanjo's administration. Also included in the ₦65 per litre calculation was the road tax of about ₦2.50.

Petrol subsidy removal: the facts, the farce and the fears
By Dele Fanimo, Obiora Aduba, RoselineOkere, YemiAdepetun and Salaimon Salau
THE GUARDIAN, Thursday, December 29, 2011, pg. 10, 11
The article traces the debate on fuel subsidy removal to General Babangida's administration a military regime through Obasanjo's democratic rule to the present President Jonathan's. In all the debates and actions, the protests from the opposition especially the organized labour and civil society groups have resulted in reduction. And in all of the regimes, promises made have never been fulfilled. The article explains what is referred to as "subsidy". The article also dwells extensively on the Domestic Supply Obligation (DSO). Current price of petrol in OPEC countries are given in the article.

REFINERIES

Audit report details graft in NNPC's handling of crude
By John-Abba Ogbodo, Collins Olayinka and Obiora Aduba
THE GUARDIAN, Monday, January 30, 2012, pg.1
The report gives the controversy trailing the recent choice of auditors for the nation's extractive industries. According to the report, NNPC denies losing N700b through Kaduna refinery, giving explanation for the shortage and importation of crude.

FG begins TAM contract with builders of refineries
By Chineme Okafor
THISDAY, Wednesday, January 11, 2012, vol. 16, no. 6106, pg. 1, 6
The paper carries the argument of the Minister of Petroleum Resources why the pump price for petrol in Nigeria cannot sell at N65 per litre when it is as much as N200 in Chad, N175 in Ghana and in Niger at N190. The signing of TAM contract with original builders of the refineries by FG was also revealed.

Govt moves to prevent emergencies, fix refineries
By Saxone Akhaine and others
THE GUARDIAN, Wednesday, January 11, 2012, pg. 4, 6
This piece of news item tells of the fresh attempt to fix the nation's refineries by the Nigerian National Petroleum Corporation (NNPC) as the protest enters its

second day. It also gives the reason advanced by the Minister of Petroleum Resources why Nigeria cannot sell petrol at N65.

Investors seek clarification of profit margin on new refineries.
By Collins Olayinka
THE GUARDIAN, Wednesday, April 6, 2011, pg. 46
Segun Akpata, the Executive Director, Corporate Services of Total asserts that building refineries is a high capital intensive venture hence investors want the government to make some commitment regarding the expected returns on the capital.

Local refineries contribute 20 percent of national need, says PPPRA.
By Sulaimon Salau
THE GUARDIAN, Wednesday, November 2, 2011, pg. 47
The debate on the proposed fuel subsidy removal hits up, Product Pricing and Regulatory Agency (PPPRA) presents its stand in the deregulation agenda. This is that all stakeholders should decide the right time when full deregulation should start and appropriate measures should be put in place before its commencement.

Local refining imperative to Nigeria's petroleum industry growth, says experts
By Sulaimon Salau
THE GUARDIAN, Wednesday, December 8, 2010, pg. 43
The paper presents the opinions of the industry experts on the current situation where the refineries only produce 12 million litres of the 30 million litres of premium motor spirit (PMS) per day consumes by the nation. The short fall of 18 million litres are imported at the landing cost of N93 a litre using the Petroleum Product Pricing Regulatory Agency (PPPRA) template.

Mini/mobile refinery for Nigeria's fuel solution
By Nat Cole
THE GUARDIAN, Monday, January 30, 2012, pg. 13
The author enumerates the advantages of building mini/mobile refineries, putting the cost of a 4,000-barrel per day mini-refinery at about $9millios as of 2006. This cost excludes tank farms, generators and the buildings.

Nigeria loses ₦700b on Kaduna refinery, pays N12b annually to idle workers.
By John-Abba Ogbodo
THE GUARDIAN, Thursday, January 26, 2012, pg. 80
The report reveals the findings of the Senate Committee on Petroleum (Downstream) on their visit to the Kaduna refinery. These include the obsolete facilities, inability to refine even 30, 00 bpd instead of capacity production of 110,000bpd and the production of drums for oil companies in place of refining petroleum products.

Nigeria needs perfect strategy to induce investment in refineries say experts.
By Sulaimon Salau
THE GUARDIAN, Wednesday, May 11, 2011, pg. 46
Foreign energy experts are of the opinion that investment in private refineries can only be possible in favourable conditions that guarantee return on investment. This is given as the reason why only two of the 14 private refineries' licenses' are forthcoming.

Nigeria sustains lead as top Africa's oil producer.
By Roseline Okere
THE GUARDIAN, Wednesday, January 10, 2011, pg.42
Nigeria oil and gas sector by 2015, would account for 8.97% of African regional oil demand as reported in this article.

Pangs of rots in the petroleum downstream sector on Nigeria's economy
By Sulaimon Salau
THE GUARDIAN, Wednesday, January, 18, 2012, pg. 46
The writer traces the origins of the four refineries noting that the inability of the Federal Government to maintain them for full capacity production and efficient distribution brought in petroleum marketers and haulages. However, instead of improving the economy, the rot as in inefficiencies, corruption, abuse of natural monopoly powers; mismanagement, smuggling and bureaucratic bottlenecks almost collapse the economy.

Private refineries' scheme not feasible without deregulation, says Oniwon.
By Saxone Akhaine.
THE GUARDIAN, Friday, November 25, 2011, pg. 15
The write-up covers the argument by Dr. Austin Oniwon, the Group Managing Director of the Nigerian National Petroleum Corporation (NNPC) of how the deregulation of petroleum downstream sector would attract private refineries' scheme.

Port Harcourt refineries to work at full capacity by November, say NNPC.
THE GUARDIAN, Monday, January 16, 2012, pg. 15
The two Port Harcourt refineries with capacities to process 60, 000 and 150,000 barrels per day for both old and new respectively known to be working at very low capacities are expected to work at full capacity by November. This is because NNPC says the Federal Government has engaged MaireTecnimont, the original contractors that built them for a Turn-Around Maintenance (TAM). The history of both refineries is also give.

Subsidy triggers concern over state of refineries
By Sulaimom Salau
THE GUARDIAN, Wednesday, January 18, 2012, pg. 47

The piece cited the example of Venezuela, an oil exporting country with a population of 28 million and a single refinery producing as much as 940, 000 barrels per day (bpd). Whereas Nigerian four refineries produce only about 133,000 bpd with a total installed capacity of 445,000bpd.

Why govt'll build new refineries
By Abiodun Fagbemi
THE GUARDIAN, Thursday, December 29, 2011, pg. 9
Three new refineries according to the government to be sited in an unnamed location in Kogi,
State, Oloibiri, Rivers State and an unnamed state in the North-East are to be built as measures to increase supply and mitigate the effects of subsidy removal.

SUBSIDY REMOVAL

Challenge of subsidy removal and the transformation agenda: a lawyer's perspective
By Tony Odiadi
THE GUARDIAN, Tuesday, January 17, 2012, pg. 58
In presenting matters arising from the subsidy removal saga, the author sees a golden opportunity for the achievement of a paradigm shift in the President's transformation agenda. Stating that the resistance force has given him the most relevant areas Nigerians are angry about.

The hoodwinking of Jeffery Sachs
By Olu Akanmu
THE GUARDIAN, Monday, February 6, 2012, pg. 51
The essay looks at Professors Jeffery Sachs and Paul Collier's defense of the removal of oil subsidy by the Nigerian government. He posits that they both situated their arguments on sound economic policy suggestions within Nigeria's weak institutional political context. Hence they failed to appreciate the citizens' skepticism and the actual protest of the removal of the fuel subsidy.

Pains, gains of subsidy removal by stakeholders
By Obiora Aduba and Sulaimon Salau
THE GUARDIAN, Wednesday, January 11, 2012, pg. 45
The paper states the various reactions, allegations and explanation of stakeholders in their attempts to provide a solution to the current crisis of subsidy removal. Stakeholders include President Jonathan, Labour leaders, human right activist, ministers and key players in the oil sector.

People power!
THE GUARDIAN, Tuesday, January 10, 2012, pg.2-10

THE *Guardian* reporters present the accounts of the people's response to the directive of organised labour and its allies to take to the streets to protest the removal of fuel subsidy by the Federal Government.

Removal of oil subsidy (3)
Editorial
THE GUARDIAN, Wednesday, January 11, 2012, pg. 14
The editorial gives the assumption of the issue of subsidy and the history of the refineries. It argues that the crisis has solution that requires government's political will to achieve. It goes to proffer solutions to the current situation.

Stockwatch
THE GUARDIAN, Monday, January 23, 2012, pg. 42
The paper defines subsidy and also presents the different types of subsidies.

Subsidy. Between economies and statesmanship
By Ayo Olukotun
THE GUARDIAN, Friday, January 6, 2012, pg. 51
The author posits that 'even the authors of harsh neo-liberal policies do say that timing, consensus building in addition to the legitimacy of government have a bearing on the introduction and reception of policies. Therefore, timing and conjunctures including statesmanship can make a lot of difference in the implementation of structural adjustment policies like the removal of the fuel subsidy described as a 'New Year Shocker' for the citizens.

Subsidy crisis through a creative theory
By Simon Emeje
THE GUARDIAN, Thursday, February 2, 2012, pg. 68
The article defines creative theory, arguing that "the development of Nigeria from pre-colonial time to date is the process of creative autolytic destruction". It state further that the present condition of the "deregulation of the downstream petroleum sector should be weighed on the platform of creative autolytic destruction".

The subsidy on our democracy
By Emmanuel Badejo
THE GUARDIAN, Monday, January 23, 2012, pg. 51
The author posits that President Jonathan did Nigerians and democracy a favour by his brusque reawakening of the patriotic Nigerians in most of the citizens. The President's conviction of doing Nigeria a world of good by removing fuel subsidy made him tough as a nail. His tough stand exposed the value of the citizens' stakes in the democratic project. Consequently, they were forced to speak in unison against endemic national ills and insisted on it. Thus the nationwide strike period saw more questions asked and answered than during the Jonathan administration's last ten months.

Subsidy outside the neoliberal box
By Ayo Olukotun
THE GUARDIAN, Monday, February 6, 2012, pg. 52
The paper argues that the example of Venezuela an oil producing country with left leaning government is boasting of close to 40 refineries and an exporter of crude to Nigeria's Kaduna refinery is a better one for Nigeria to follow. It recommends that Nigeria needs policies outside the 'controversial neoliberalism straitjacket'.

Subsidy removal! Again, promises trail passage of PIB
By Obiora Aduba and Sulaimon Salau
THE GUARDIAN, Wednesday, January 18, 2012, pg. 45
The write-up expresses skepticism about fresh promises from Mr. President on passage of the Petroleum Industry Bill (PIB). It notes that the industry has suffered deferred investments running into millions of dollars due to the delay in the passage of the bill.

Subsidy removal crisis in perspective (1)
By Bukar Usman
THE GUARDIAN, Wednesday, February 1, 2012, pg. 51
The article attempts to answer the question of what led to the subsidy removal crisis especially in view of the attendant accusation and counter accusation as to who was responsible for the policy.

Subsidy removal crisis in perspective (2)
By Bukar Usman
THE GUARDIAN, Thursday, February 2, 2012, pg. 68
Perspective (2) is a continuation of the previous day article. This segment dwells on the denials over accusations that government was merely implementing World Bank/IMF programme on the removal of the oil subsidy. The author cites the IMF Working Papers and giving the dates of the meetings where the G-20 Leaders, the IMF and World Bank pushed for the adoption of their fuel subsidy removal policies. The fact of using Nigeria as a test case in advancing their price-gap methodology campaign by IMF officials dating as far back as 2003 is revealed. The said paper developed policies "to stop any strong protest and social unrest after subsidy removal". The article points out that Mrs. Okonjo-Iweala's claim of no prior knowledge of the policy or the connection of the IMF to the policy appears hard to accept. The question begging for answer is why subsidy removal policy is not applied to farm products subsidies in those developed countries now pushing down the throats of OPEC member countries.

Subsidy Scam: How Saraki's motion opened Pandora box
By Davidson Iriekpe. THISDAY, Friday, January 27, 2012, vol. 17, no. 6122, pg.17
The report looks at the Senator Bukola Saraki's sponsored motion that opened the "damning secrets" of the petrol subsidy regime leading to the setting up of the ad-hoc committee of the House of Representatives to probe the fuel subsidy regime.

We've no position on subsidy removal, say Reps
By Reporters
THE GUARDIAN, Wednesday, January 4, 2012, pg. 2, 4
The news reports claim that the House of Representatives that proceeded on recess on 20th of December, 2011, affirmed that no definite decision on the subsidy matter was taken before their recess. This came after the Executive arm of government removed the fuel subsidy on the 1st of January, 2012.

Petroleum Industry Bill (PIB)
Expert tasks Govt. IOCs on passage of PIB
By Obiora Aduba
THE GUARDIAN, Wednesday, February 2, 2011, pg. 43, 44
The author converses the need for both the Federal Government and the International Oil Companies (IOCs) to work together and agree on a fiscal regime that will yield some benefits to the Nigerian people.

Former NUPENG President opposes proposed policy.
By Alemma – OzioruwaAliu.
THE GUARDIAN, Tuesday, October 11, 2011, pg. 48
The former president of the National Gas Workers (NUPENG) gives his reasons of opposing the proposed fuel subsidy removal. These include the full commercialization of NNPC that will make it competitive, the passage of the Petroleum Industry Bill to create an enabling environment.

Good fate for the PIB
By Charles Soeze
THE GUARDIAN, Thursday, January 19, 2012, pg. 52
The article gives the benefits of having the bill passed and its fundamental objectives. The paper concludes with an appeal for its passage without delay.

Imperative of incorporating costing capacity in subsidy re-investment
By Agele Alufohai
THISDAY, Wednesday, January 25, 2012, Vol.17, No. 6120, pg 37
The paper advocates the incorporation of the discipline of costing practices and standards into the monitoring and evaluation of the Subsidy Reinvestment and Empowerment (SURE) Programme

Legislators need courage to pass PIB, says expert
By Salaimon Salau
THE GUARDIAN, Wednesday, September 24, 2011 pg. 42
The write-up contains the appeal to the legislators to pass the Petroleum Industry Bill (PIB) into law in order to revive the stagnant petroleum sector.

Local refining imperative to Nigeria's petroleum industry growth, says experts
By Sulaimon Salau
THE GUARDIAN, Wednesday, December 8, 2010, pg. 43

The paper presents the opinions of the industry experts on the current situation where the refineries only produce 12 million litres of the 30 million litres of premium motor spirit (PMS) per day consumes by the nation. The short fall of 18 million litres are imported at the landing cost of N93 a litre using the Petroleum Product Pricing Regulatory Agency (PPPRA) template.

Jonathan's 100 days: no respite yet for petroleum sector
By Sulaimon Salau
THE GUARDIAN, Wednesday, September 7, 2011, pg. 47, 48
The write-up touches on the contentious issues that have made it impossible for the 7th National Assembly to pass the bill (PIB). Example is the refusal to scrap the Petroleum Product Price Regulatory Agency and the Petroleum Equalisation Fund (PEF)

Minister raises hope on speedy passage of PIB...civil societies laud reps on progress
By Obiora Aduba
THE GUARDIAN, Wednesday, March 23, 2011, pg. 46
The Minister of Petroleum Resources, Deziani Allison-Maduke, reveals that they had worked on various sectors of the Petroleum Industry Bill in spite of a few hiccups as there was fresh assurance of its quick passage by the national assembly.

Nigeria risks N 15tr investment over non-passage of PIB
By Obiora Aduba and Taiwo Hassan
THE GUARDIAN, Wednesday, July 13, 2011, pg. 45
The paper reports the fears expressed by stakeholders of the non-passage of the Petroleum Industry Bill (PIB) by the National Assembly. The effect among others is the salvation of over $100 billion oil investment in the petroleum industry by local operators.

Petroleum Industry Bill and Nigeria's Capital Market
By Goddy Egene
THISDAY, Wednesday, February 15, 2012, vol.17, no. 6141, pg. 29
The article looks at prospects of how the passage of the PIB will boost the capital market. It also covers the controversial issues of the PIB and its relationship with the capital market. Presents market operators' views and cites the Chinese example.

The petroleum industry: challenges and achievements in 2011
By Muhyideen Jimoh
THE GUARDIAN, Monday, January 16, 2012, pg.17
The government reasons for the fuel subsidy removal and deregulation are enumerated as well as the opposition's side. Serious economic challenges for the country were created by price instability and security threats in the Niger Delta in 2011.

PIB: Forum seeks scrapping of PEF, PPPRA
By Collins Olayinka
THE GUARDIAN, Tuesday, February 14, 2012, pg. 20
The article or write-up carries excerpts from a document by a group of civil society organization calling for the scrapping of the Petroleum Equalization Fund (PEF) and Petroleum Product Pricing Regulatory Agency (PPPRA) for the Petroleum Industry Bill (PIB) to be effective.

Reforming the petroleum industry in Nigeria through the Petroleum Industry Bill (PIB)
Stockwatch
THE GUARDIAN, Monday, January 30, 2012, pg. 52
The article gives a brief introduction of the recent happenings leading to the new interest in the Petroleum Industry Bill (PIB). It then states the reasons for the law, its key features, institutions, employment opportunities and reaction to the proposed law.

Senate panel assures on PIB.
By John – Abba Ogbodo and Bertram Nwannekanma
THE GUARDIAN, Wednesday, December 7, 2011, pg. 16
The report asserts that the PIB is not dead even though it is not in the National Assembly. It would be re-introduced as each committee would work the NNPC and others for its reintroduction.

Senate reviews acreage, bidding process in oil sector
By John – Abba Ogbodo
THE GUARDIAN, Wednesday March 23, 2011, pg. 1, 2
Clause 195 was inserted in part three of the PIB by the Senate based on the recommendation of its Committee on Petroleum Resources that worked on the bill.

Fuel Subsidy Conversation: Beyond the subsidy removal debate

By Akin Osuntokun

***The Guardian*, Sunday, January 15, 2012, pg. 13**

THIS has been a very educating and maturing moment for Nigerians. For instance I received the following post on the subsidy removal debate on a Facebook forum: "Is it not madness that every state must produce a minister"? Is it not madness that for every ministry of the federal government, there is a substantive minister and a minister of state? Is it not madness that each of these ministers and ministers of state burden the tax payer and our economy by subsidizing a retinue of unwanted personal assistants, special assistants, aides, staff and embark on frivolous trips at great costs? Is it not madness that government officials in Nigeria travel at great costs when government officials in the UK are entitled to a 3rd class train ticket for local travel and the Prime minister is entitled to a convoy of two cars?

This angry rhetoric can be taken as fairly representative and the logic, by and large is valid. The logic does not contest the economic rationality of the subsidy removal but counter poses a context that makes it untenable for government to demand sacrifice from the people by asking the same question of the conduct of governance. It laid bare a context that rebukes the conduct of government as the ethical equivalent of the wrong it purports to redress; of living the opposite of what it preaches. Before now, protest against fuel subsidy removal boils down to the assertion that subsidy was a privilege to which the citizenry of an oil producing country was titled. In a commendable departure from this tradition, protesters now seek to take on the government on its own terms and persuasion of economic rationality. What the government is saying and which argument can really not be faulted is as follows; given the competing and crying priorities of social and economic infrastructural investment, would we rather spend our resources on the immediate gratification of fuel consumption? It is a mark of he elevation of national debate that we are all agreed that this should not be the case; and that this rationality of prudence, discipline and rational allocation of limited resources should and must apply to the totality of governance in Nigeria.

IN exchange for the exacting sacrifice being demanded in the removal of fuel subsidy, Nigerians are requesting an equal measure of prior reformist zeal from the government. It begins to get sticky when, in consummation of the transaction, the question is asked, what is government bringing to the table? The proposed palliatives, by themselves, are tenable only to the extent that government has sufficient credibility for the people to believe and trust that it has the requisite will and capacity to deliver as promised. It is this currency of credibility that has been in short supply and on which the transaction is presently stuck. Why and how so?

There was never going to be any pleasant way the subsidy removal was going to take effect but there was something particularly bizarre and insensitive about the introduction of the new fuel price regime on the New Year anniversary day. The 2011 budget year runs out at the end of March and the presumption { encouraged by the government itself} was that deregulation policy would follow in the wake of the introduction of the 2012 budget in April. No better incendiary could have sparked the protest than this new year slap. Other reinforcing ammunition had also been provided by the government. How, for instance, did the subsidy catapult from below three hundred billion naira to over one trillion in 2011? If there is an innocent explanation for this as I believe, why is the government acting coy on getting public with it? Again the government itself had encouraged the notion (and used it to buttress the argument for deregulation) that oil marketers had beer perpetrating sundry abuses and fleecing Nigeria under the cover of the subsidy regime. We have also heard of an audit report corroborating these alleged misdeeds. What better instruction is there than to begin the oil sector reform with a crackdown on the worst perpetrators of this malfeasance?

We have had to endure the most criminal excesses of Boko Haram since the inception of this administration. As the experience or the most powerful country on earth illustrated, confronting and taming terrorism is easier said than done but the seeming incapacity of government against this menace is widely believed as attributable to a singular lack of will and resolute resolve. And then, of course, the government has been worsted in the raging propaganda warfare. This is made worse by the calculated assault of vested interests (cashing in on the quite popular resistance to the deregulation) to demonize Jonathan as the worst disease to ever afflict Nigeria. Yet there is hardly any elected government of Nigeria better invested with legitimacy than that of President Goodluck Jonathan to tackle the big and confounding issues of the day. Nigerians with their huge egos were massively attracted to the personality of Jonathan whose most identifiable quality is humility. Too much of a good quality can also be bad and so by the time Jonathan felt compelled to start defining himself as "…Am not a lion, am not an army general, am not a goliath…" people began reinterpreting his personality and style as humanity taken too far bordering on weakness and indecisiveness. In fairness however there is a sense in which Nigeria is inherently dysfunctional and harbours a self-destructive streak within its DNA. There cannot be any serious contention on the authenticity and credibility of the outcome of this year's Presidential election as handily won by Jonathan. What might happen and what did happen was a bitter and violent rejection of the outcome without regard to the credibility status of the election by General Mohammadu Buhari and the Congress for Progressive Change, CPC. This attitude became a big problem for Nigeria against the background of a sense of regional deprivation wrought by the disruptive effect of President Yaradua's death on the delicate geopolitical balancing of power succession in Nigeria. Nobody knows for sure whether Boko Haram operates autonomous of this sense of alienation but its activities have increasingly come to give a new unwholesome identity to Nigeria and truncated the positive momentum for social and economic development garnered from the globally acclaimed 2011 elections. This has had a destabilizing effect and done severe damage to the capacity of the Jonathan administration to grapple effectively with governance.

IN this standoff, President Jonathan has inherited the baggage of accumulated distrust and disenchantment with government that had piled on over the years. The problem here is that the longer the delay in addressing the question of economic rationality the greater the cost of postponing the evil day. Ironically it is now neither in the interest of the protesters and Nigerians nor of the government to revert back to the status quo ante of sixty five nairanot only for the fact that it is not sustainable in logic, but equally for the reason that haven bitten the bullet we might as well get on with the reality. That said, whatever the wisdom of government insistence on the once and for all subsidy removal, it would amount to an intransigence unbecoming of the democratic culture not to meet the protesters midway. What we have not said and needs to be said is how the present face off is rendered nugatory by the larger and enduring debate on the structural configuration that restores 'true' federalism to Nigeria. Amongst others, this will manifest in fiscal federalism and result inexorably in a situation whereby the oil producing states ie Niger Delta will own the resources and only pay royalty and taxes to the federal government What this means, in effect, is that the rest of Nigeria is compelled by dint of this restructuring to purchase fuel at the prevailing market price unless the states which are now largely deprived of their main source of revenue(oil) and to that extent impoverished if not rendered bankrupt decide to subsidize fuel consumption. The moral of this prospective eventuality is that, first and foremost, we urgently endeavour to rapidly diversify away from the present precarious mono cultural economy. Second is that it makes the argument of government on fuel subsidy removal more persuasive. Third is to factor this potential debate on the future of Nigeria

Fuel Subsidy Conversation: Jonathan-the Judas Iscariot of our time...Analogous Tale from Achebe's *Things Fall Apart*

By Isidore Emaka Uzoatu

***The Guardian*, Sunday, January 15, 2012, pg. 14**

Our underlying petroleum subidy debate has come to an end. You can quote me on that. Why, because a depth markpole in the river does not capsize a boat at low tide. The problem is now known and the solution cannot be farfetched. It could not have been less so ever since it turned to an egg and hen seniority puzzle between organised labour and government: while the egg cannot lay itself; a hen cannot emerge exnihilo. And now the cock has been brought into the fray...

First the given

The government and trumpeters of its monocle view have rhapsodized on end that we cannot afford to subsidize a consumable like petrol to the tune of 13 trillion Naira like in the previous year. This, they claim, being only way to avoid letting the prediction of an organ of the United States government on the lifespan of the Nigeria project coming true sooner. Those are not their words, though. Addedly, they argue that proceeds from the measure would be used to service the starving spheres of our national existence viz: roads, healthcare, railways and what have you.

Paraphrasing the view of Labour and the many more they managed to bring on the streets may not take longer. According to them, monies raised by this tourniquet on the windpipe of the nation's masses will only amount to more peculatory dividends for our master servants. A point they claim to be needless of buttress given how our politicians have proven that old habits die hard since all our democratic experimentations upon independence.

NOW that precedents have set, nothing remains but self-confession: I am willingly and truly a common man. Never mind that Frank Olize somehow missed me in his search of us in his News Line days. Thusly, I deem it fit to be guided by the street understanding of the issues at hand hence my summaries above. More so, by so doing I hope to avoid drawing their wrath which, as seen lately, can be catastrophic for any mortal be he high, mighty or both.

Arguably, to the average Nigerian the main job of their government is to supervise our common wealth. To them, therefore, these resources do not belong to these elected representatives — that is assuming they were freely and fairly chosen. This is why the running of government as if it were the private business concerns of these officials annoys them. If savings were made at the end of the day, they would ask, how would it be equitably snared? A pointer here remains the mounting illiteracy and innumeracy in the land following the exorbitant cost of deregulated education. In fact, part of the disparity between the government and the governed in this very debate is traceable to this. Most of us always smell rats when figures surpass a million!

But however one ends up looking at the issues raised, all the points are subsumed by the very tenet of democracy as expounded by its founding fathers: government of the people, for the people and by the people. Thus whatever actions any government worth its avoirdupois in votes carries out must tag us the people along. The present case comes off worse given the way and manner representatives are selected in this country. I believe and strongly at that that if the present decision of the government had the support of the people, our labour leaders would have been on their way to exile by now. Else, they would only stay behind to wallow in the mire or their folly.

While these play out, we should not in any circumstance be fooled by the actions of the two chambers of the federal legislature. They are only putting their mouth where their sinecures are. A critical observer even pointed out that they only acted as they did because the President jettisoned them for the governors. The latter, in part, saw this as their only avenue to more money to battle the Abuja intruders who would often battle them in their God given domains with their Ghana must go lobby loots.

AS these unfold, an analogy subsists: the killing of Ikemefuna in Achebe's Things Fall Apart. Thank God the venerable elder statesman who delineated The Trouble with Nigeria when his peers were yet chasing after escaping rats from our burning national hut has added his voice to current drama. Though he sets the tale in the imaginary rural Africa Village Umuofia around the time we made or the West made contact with us, themes from the tale still haunt our every move. Whoever said there are no modern-day prophecies.

As the tale goes, the people of Umofia are recompensed with the boy following a barter of heads with their neighbours who murdered a virgin of their land. The boy is handed to Okonkwo for safe keep in his household. As the boy ripens for sacrifice, the god he was appeased with wants his head literally and the elders take him for a stroll. As the first machete cut descended on the poor boy he had no other option than run to his surrogate father, Okonkwo. What followed is now part of world lore in so many languages: lest he be labelled trepid his greatest fear Okonkwo dealt the final blow on a boy that calls him father!

If Nigeria at this crossroads can be likened to Ikemefuna, the rusted wheel of our national politics has made GEJ our current rather. With the cabal on our jugulars via petroleum subsidies we had no one else to run to but our democratically elected President. And what does he do? To our greatest dismay he raised a macheteless hand our votes did not bequeath a machete You can only imagine what would have happened if he had one like once upon our military presidents of yore when there were no alternatives to nonsense. In his IMF-induced hallucination GEJ forgot that it is only a tree that does not remove long after a death sentence has been passed on it.

All the same, the President is at all only qualified for blame. He could well end up being God's arrow in the circumstances. After all, if Judas did not kiss Jesus Christ the teeming Christians in our number would never have been saved. As opined by even our Labour leaders, this is the time to get at the so called cabal as well as our government officials. A death knell has sounded for monkey de work, baboon de chop in all possible ramifications. And the time is apt as solutions to problems are not often as complex as its cause once properly deciphered.

A possible solution is the touted deregulation of the downstream of our petroleum industry. But we should not stop at that. The target should be for full commercialization. If we have PMS to sell to our numerous neighbours with very good mark-ups attached, only then would we have not only seen the light at the end of the channel but reached its very end as well.

Fuel Subsidy Conversation: make relevant data public for scrutiny, arrest impunity

By Kalu Idika Kalu

***The Guardian*, Sunday, January 15, 2012, pg. 9**

HOW did we get into this in the first place?

How sad for a nation to be thrown into many problems! Clearly, we need to look at structure of governance and the quality of the decision. We have major security situation that is still unfolding. That raises a question on why we allowed a situation that sends many people into the street to have arose. We seem to be held down with too many problems at the same time.

On the security situation, the government has responsibility to protect lives and property wherever lives are. That goes beyond mere pronouncement. You have to show a sign of responsibility. Those charged with the responsibility of security should make sure that measures are taken to prevent breaches. Of course, lately the President came out to say that there would be measure of infiltration within the administration and even within the security. That means we have a major question on why the ordinary citizen should trust government to do its responsibility.

We now have a situation like we did after the civil war when people are beginning to move back to their states. This is not to mention the carnage of people worshiping; people are being killed in other places. That alone is a major crisis. It is on this basis that we begin to question the policy that created the situation we are now. Obviously, I am sure it was not intended but that already underscores the issue.

Couldn't the situation have been properly studied to know how it could happen?

Let me say that the issue is not about deregulation. Deregulation has been going on for years all over the world. The argument is not solely on the opportunity cost of stopping subsidy or not stopping it. The real issue is how do you manage such a policy issue such so that it does not create disruption or dislocation? That points to how prices of commodities change every-day. Naturally, if you have been saving and building up an economy over the years, when issue like this arises people may complain that additional Nl or 50k has been added to bread. That happens all the time.

The issue is not deregulation; the issue is how it will be implemented. By definition, a developing country has fragile production, supply and demand structure. So, you have to measure the kind of shock you can apply to that system will not create problem. The solution, therefore, is whether all these things are being taken into account.

It is an anomaly to say members of cartel are fleecing the economy... people want to know who the people are. What action has been taken against them? What is the way forward to make sure that they are not in place to do what they are accused of doing? There is a major concern when we just say cartel or cabal. We have to make decision on how much could have been added to the pump price to cover the real cost of somebody who is producing locally or importing. We need to know the full amount involved in the process. Relevant data need to be properly andlysed in order to take a proper stand.

How would you go about the situation if you were directly in charge?

You can use subsidy for all kinds of things to encourage production or to put emphasise on particular area of production. It is how you manage it that is the issue. Any government coming into place has to see what is on ground and define whether he can make do with it without destroying the entire economy. Clearly, one issue, going forward, is that government has to go back and look at how the issue of subsidy could be better handle.

Go back to N65 per litre?

Within this period (four months to the end of 2011 budget), we could consider how much of it we can accommodate in the budget. If the government comes up to say because of what we are doing we are building infrastructure, reviving small scale industries, reviving agriculture it could be reasonable. But I don't know of any government that will take that once. That is too high. The argument should be — could deal with it in two, three or four years? You must make sure that the productive sector is not damaged; there is a way you can damage the productive sector, including exchange rate. By next year, you are dealing with much bigger problem because the impact it would have had this year. The issue of deregulation has been settled. The issue now is how do you deal with it in a way that it does not destroy the economy.

Maybe nobody wants to go back to history. You are bound to ask how come we have been spending so little. We have terrible statistics of women dying, shortage in infrastructure and many people dropping out of schools. This was why it was clear that in few years ago when we were leading other countries to debt forgiveness, by the standard we have in all these things, we should not have paid out such amount of money. That was a wrong choice.

Are you talking about infrastructure as problem?

If you try 25 per cent in some countries people will be in the streets. I Believe the government could go back, re-examine what it wants to do. Another issue on why people are out there is that people want to know those the government refers to as cartel. Of course, you cannot be mentioning names unless you are sure how much you over paid them. And the cartel could not have gone to the public purse top withdraw the money. So, you have to identify those in governance who are involved. Well, I heard some investigations are going. But it is high time we began to see results. This is really what I think is necessary.

Then, the issue is not removing 100 per cent but how much can you accommodate. And this must be related to what the economy can absorb at the point in time.

Then could you also examine this in relationship with the international organisations' (IMF and World Bank) agenda?

Some people argue that Nigerian government is executing IMF/World Bank, agenda with the removal of subsidy?

I listened to the question being raised by the Finance Minister; I think it is one of the wrong perceptions we have to get out ot our minds. I think it is a terrible misconception. I worked in the World Bank for eight years. The reason you do well or you are promoted is because your country is doing well. All the notions that they are suppose to do something negative are totally unfounded. There are lots of misconceptions.

Why are they still relevant; why are they still handed funds raised by advanced countries. Recently G20 gave IMF $200b and I know Nigerian journalists ran back home to say we should not touch it. There are lots of misconceptions. Lots of countries don't even know that they should be using resources that make sense for them. Borrowing only makes sense when the benefits outweigh the costs.

Have we been borrowing like that?

We have like that. We didn't manage what we borrowed well. This lend to exchange rate problem, delay in payment and things like that. For an economy of our size, we need a lot of funds. It is not enough to be talking about foreign investors though they are important. For foreign investors to come, the minimum domestic investments in infrastructure, health and others should be in place. That means you need to have people who can manage the resources.

Can you just abdicate responsibility and say some people took some money? The kind or impunity we have developed in all sectors is unimaginable. You can't say you don't want to borrow like some countries did. Those countries borrowed to build critical infrastructure, which makes them leading economies today. I think these are some of the things we need to reaffirm. A country of our size should be a major beneficiary of such facilities because our needs are very many. There is no way we can get all these things by assuming that some investors will come. We need to go out there and make sure that if you want to build a railway, you build the right one. That goes for every other sector.

What is your advice to the organised labour?

There are experts within government. If they need help, they can also bring other people outside the government to tackle the issue. We all Nigerians whether you are a security personnel or labour leader. I just feel that we reel there are so many divides. Whether you are a Police officer or not, we are all Nigerians. If anybody wants to express his grievance, let he do so. The assumption that anybody on the street is trying to destroy property and should be scared away is unfounded. For government to say it is not shifting its ground is unreasonable. The step is too high by all standards. The issue is not deregulation because that has been accepted in the world over.

Based on interview on AIT

You can use subsidy for all kinds of things — to encourage production or to put emphasise on particular area of production. It is how you manage it that is the issue. Any government coming into place has to see what is on ground and define whether he can make do with it without destroying the entire economy. Clearly, one issue, going forward, is that government has to go back and look at how the issue of subsidy could be better handle.

Fuel Subsidy Conversation: one week of fire and fury

By Alabi Williams

***The Guardian*, Sunday, January 15, 2012, pg.7**

BEFORE the federal government made real its plan to remove the subsidy allegedly paid on imported petroleum (PMS) and fully deregulate the downstream sector of the petroleum industry, the argument for and against the policy had been isolated, with government officials explaining why the subsidy had to go, and nonstate actors replying with same intensity of verbal resistance.

The only well articulated forum for the debate was the Lagos Town Hall meeting of December. That forum provided proponents ample time and space to explain their position. It gave equal amount of time and space for their arguments to be punctured by Nigerians who think otherwise. It was a beautiful gathering and the next thing to do was to sustain the debate and move it around.

But as the debate was gradually reaching a crescendo, government unplugged the rhythm. Like a joke, the federal government on January 1, 2012 jabbed at the country's most sensitive area, carelessly announcing a policy that raised the price of petrol from ₦65 to ₦138 and beyond.

For a moment, Nigerians were stranded and frozen on the same spot, lost in their tracks and confused about how to move forward. Then, there were frenzied, uncoordinated responses all over the country by Nigerians, trying to engage the New Year present from government. A lot of the people had not yet overcome the hangover of the long Christmas/New Year holidays, and the merriments that went with it. Many budgets were rudely overtaken too, because they had been benchmarked on the old pump price of ₦65.

The organised Labour was taken by surprise, and needed time to articulate a befitting response, which it came up with after meeting on Wednesday, January 4. By the next day, Labour told those who cared to listen that it would galvanize the workforce and other civil society groups for a showdown with government, beginning Monday, January 9.

Government was forced to then mount a more rigorous campaign on why subsidy must go, sending emissaries for media talk shows, while its supporters notably the Neighbour2Neighbour, ₦2N, and spending funds on advertorials, which did not convince Labour and many Nigerians. Government also tried a Joker: using the now too familiar and well abused ex parte order from the Industrial Arbitration Court, to compel Labour to return to the dialogue table, which government itself had rudely stopped. Labour turned deaf ears.

Sunday, January 8, members of the House of Representatives convened an emergency session, with a view to troubleshoot and compel the two warring parties to hold on. To follow up, the House set up an ad hoc committee to commence negotiation. Government did not heed the motion to revert to status quo ante, Labour also refused to suspend the impending strike action.

MONDAY, January 9, broke with Nigerians spilling on the streets, in an unprecedented civil action against government. The signs were very clear, that this was going to be the 'mother of all mass actions'.

The Senate caught the signs and by Tuesday, it commenced another reconciliation move. By Wednesday, the FEC was deeply shaken by the spread and dimension of the protest. But instead of backing out, government mounted more propaganda and explanations of why it took that action. Labour and the civil society had stopped listening. Thursday was tumultuous, even as the reconciliation by the Senate and others seemed to yield some fruits, but there was no good news yet. Friday was half day, but it was no less a huge successful outing for Labour

The whole of last week was consumed by the struggle for and against the removal of subsidy on petrol. Government got its fingers burnt and the mass action waxed strong, until a weekend break was announced.

Whether government would cease the break to save the country from total collapse would be seen at the end of yesterday's meeting between government, Labour and the mediators.

Fuel Subsidy Conversation: Sanusi; both Govt, labour should reach a compromise fast

***The Guardian*, Sunday, January 15, 2012, pg. 8, 12**

IT is argued that Subsidy is provided for in 2011 budget, which has been extended to March 2012...

What I said was that my understanding was that there was not enough provision anyway in the 2011 budget to cover what had already been spent on subsidy. So, if you had a provision of ₦250 billion or ₦300 billion and you already spent multi trillion, extending the budget doesn't mean there was a provision for it. The fiscal authority had already spent much more than what was budgeted in the year. So I'm not sure that that argument really is an argument for not implementing the policy in January.

Where is the hard proof to show that truly there exists subsidy somewhere; could you please break it down for Nigerians to see that there exists subsidy?

These things are very simple; and markets don't lie. If you go across the Republic of Benin or to Cameroun or to Ghana, which are basically geographically the same distance as Nigeria from the countries from which we import fuel, you will like to ask yourself how much do they pay per litre on oil.

If oil were ₦40 per litre as people say, why will it sell at ₦195 in those countries? And if they sell at ₦195 and you pay N65, who is paying the difference? Someone is paying the difference.

So, we don't have to go into technical and economic analysis. I think I've heard a lot of argument that is based on confusion between financial concept and economic concept.

The fact that you sell crude oil and import petroleum products does not mean that the cost of the refined product is different between what you earn from crude and what you get from refined product; they are different things.

The money that you earned from the sale of crude oil was available for you among competing economic choices. If you choose to use it to subsidise fuel, you have already chosen to take it away from infrastructure, from education, and from health; that is an economic cost.

So, I think people are talking like accountants and not like economists. It doesn't really make sense to say there is no subsidy.

We can debate whether the subsidy actually represents fuel brought and consumed in Nigeria; that is a debatable issue. You can also debate whether the template used by the PPPRA at any point in time exactly reflects what should be the case.

I don't think anyone can argue that they are selling fuel all around us at ₦180 or ₦190 and we are selling at ₦65 and there is no subsidy. Who is paying the difference; God Almighty?

What exactly has informed the removal of subsidy at this time? Is it because they want to raise more money for government or they are trying to deregulate, which one of the options?

The decision about timing is always one taken by the political authorities, not by us. I have been on record for a very long time as saying that fuel subsidy was unsustainable; there is no way you are going to continue running a deficit budget and then subsidising consumption—not on the scale we are doing it. And people need to understand that this is a country with 160 million people. The nearest country to us, in terms of population in OPEC, is Iran, which has 70 million people. Saudi Arabia has 24 million people. Saudi Arabia produces eight million barrels per day; we produce two million barrels per day.

Part of the problem we have is that we exaggerated this concept of being an oil rich country. We sell two million barrels per day; we have 160 million people; we have decaying infrastructure, very bad educational system, poor healthcare; no roads. And we simply decided that we are going to allocate resources to an area that, in my view, should be a lower economic priority. And it was time to change.

If we continue spending a trillion plus every year on debt to subsidise fuel for another three years; what will happen is that we run into huge sovereign debt.

Are we deregulating now?

Removal of subsidy is one component of the deregulation of the industry, and deregulation does not mean the absence of regulation. The oil industry will have to remain a regulated industry. Even if you remove the subsidy, you have to make sure that consumers are not being unduly exploited.

But certainly, if you want to attract investment, you have to pay the market price.

But for me and from the Central Banking position, the fundamental reason subsidy has to go is that it is unsustainable. We spent $8 billion in 2011, basically selling $8 billion out of the reserve to petroleum marketers. We paid another $8 billion equivalent as subsidy, which is $16 billion. $16 billion is 8 per cent of our GDP. It is 50 per cent of our federation reserves. There is no way any country can continue paying out that kind of money and survive.

Are you saying there should not be subsidy in an economy; or how much of it is necessary at this time?

I have been clear on this for many years. Ideologically, I'm a very strong supporter of subsidy; but the subsidy needs to be for production and the need to go to the poor and not middle men. If you have a subsidy that supports the construction of a refinery, I will support it because refinery will reduce dependence on imported fuel; refineries will create jobs; refineries will probably enhance our export earnings. If you have a subsidy on Agriculture providing training at low cost or Agric equipment at low cost, all of that I will support it. But for you to subsidise importation of petroleum products is to keep refineries in Europe and the Middle East open. They sell to you and make profit and you create the jobs out there; meanwhile, you are not creating jobs in Nigeria.

There is no reason a country that is producing crude oil should not invest in the construction ofits own refinery. This is the kind of support that government needs to provide support that creates productive capacity, creates employment opportunities, creates aggregate demand and leads to sustainable economic growth, not supporting the importation of goods from abroad.

The impression out there is that the way and manner that the government is pushing the subsidy issue suggests that the government is broke; is Nigeria broke?

I don't think the word broke is proper; broke is just a sensational term. I want to ask you a question; do we want Nigeria to be actually broke before we take the right policy decision. If we can see the warning signals in the horizon we have seen Greece, Italy, Spain, and Ireland. We have seen what sovereign debt can do to a country.

We have seen the Asian and Latin American financial crisis; and we are clearly heading towards that in the next few years. And that borrowing is not going into the development of infrastructure, and the right areas, as far as the economy is concerned, and that is the issue.

You didn't respond to the question, if we are broke or not.

No, we are not. The country is not broke, but a responsible government does not wait until the country gets broke before it acts, and that is the point. The signals are all over there, and we cannot continue borrowing and subsidising fuel consumption and that is the reality.

We can continue doing that for the next two years, but what would happen is that we would saddle the next government with a huge sovereign debt crisis. We have seen Ireland; we have seen the Latin American and Asian financial crisis; and that happened because usually, people do not want to be in the difficult position, and tnen it gets too late.

The fact that the government is acting now does not mean that Nigeria is broke. What it means is that if we don't do something, and continue at this rate, we are going to have a problem.

The $8 billion dollars figure you have talked about has been disputed, and people have said that if we did not spend that much, we are simply giving a dog a bad name in order to hang it..

Let me say that I was the first person, over a year ago, to alert this country to what I saw as fraud in the subsidy regime. I was before the House of Reps at a public hearing. I did say that I believe that some of the fuel.. .let me give you an example; if you create a situation in which you provide an incentive for greedy people to exploit, it will be very difficult for to you to stop corruption. Every time you go to the fuel station and fuel your car, what happens is that you pay ₦65 per litre, and the government pays ₦80 per litre, if you are looking at a price of ₦135 per litre.

For the oil marketer, all he needs to do is to produce documents that shows that he imported X number of litres, and then he can claim ₦80 per litre, and that is the problem. Now, that incentive that you have provided is one that allows people to go and exploit the system. So, I said over a year ago that I don t believe that all the importation that is coming into the country were delivered to the country because economics tells me that if you are selling at ₦65 per litre in Nigeria, and ₦170 in Benin, then they will take the fuel across the border to Benin and other parts of West Africa.

Based on the records from NIMASA talking about vessels being offloaded on the high sea, we suspect that some of the alleged importation never got into the country.

Nigerians will want to know why government is not thinking of downsizing and transfer power to the states so that they can generate more money internally and use efficiently...

First of all, there is question about our own Constitutional arrangement. And this is really not a thing for the President, the central authority and certainly not for the Central Bank. We do have a federation and that federation does lay out a framework and a guideline for how things are done.

I have personally believed that the presidential system is too big for us. We need an economic system that is suitable for our country.

I prefer the parliamentary system. I don't think we need a bicameral legislature. I have said this several times since 1990; I said it in 1997 that we don't need 36 states.

Many of these states are not viable. I don't think we need 778 local governments. Each of these local governments has chairman and councillors. We nave 36 states with permanent secretaries and directors, one Minister from every state. God knows how many ministries they have. It is not simply a structure that is suitable for a developing economy.

If you look at the budget of 2012, out of the N1.8trillion of the executive arm of government, ₦1.6trillion is actually personnel cost. How do you reduce that? You have to retrench workers; you have to reduce salaries; you have to stop paying pensions? How do you do that?

I personally think you can fire half of the workers of the Federal Government and the government will still work. But will Nigerians accept that? If I have my way, I will simply fire 50 per cent of the employees of the public service.

People are saying it is not the job of the Central Bank for you to be at the forefront of the subsidy removal. What do you think?

It is not about being at the forefront. It is about being honest and having proper correspondence about what should be done in the public sector and private sector. The National Economic Council (NEC), which is chaired by the Vice President has, for long recognised that this is what should be done. All the state governors are part of this decision. The fact that the governors are not coming out to say we were part of the decision and supported it does not mean that they were not part of it. That some of us are saying we are part of it does not mean we are at the forefront.

Besides, there are times in the life of a government when you take some decisions that are unpopular. Popularity is not the basis for assessing economic decision. If Jonathan wakes up today and says we are going to be paying every Nigerian ₦10,000 every month, everybody will be on the streets cheering him. That will be a popular decision; but it is a very terrible decision. If another person comes and says we are withdrawing that money; Nigerians will be on the streets demonstrating. That does not mean the decision is wrong. That is where we are.

You are simply telling Nigerians that no matter what the price of oil is, no matter what the exchange rate is; you will not pay anything above ₦65 (it doesn't matter whether a barrel is $100 or $200). Is that a sound economic policy?

A subsidy means the person subsidising is the poor changer. If the price is ₦130 and you pay ₦100 while the person subsidising pays ₦30, that is subsidy. But if you pay ₦65 while the person pays ₦80, that is no longer a subsidy, he is buying it and giving it to you for free.

At a town hall meeting you said three per cent increase in inflation is what we expect with prices sky rocking, should we still expect that?

I don't know; we haven't seen the numbers. The numbers, unfortunately, are going to be December numbers. We can only have January inflation numbers in February. But it doesn't mean that because the commodity you consume has gone up by 50 per cent; the inflation rate is 50 per cent. What I said was assumption based on my projection.

I looked at consumer price index; I looked at other indicators and I said if you have this situation as a result of this condition, this could be what we are expecting.

What we had was extreme second round effect. We might end up, maybe not in January but towards the middle of the year, getting inflation at 14 per cent or 15 per cent. But remember that in 2009, we were at 15.6%. If it gets to 14 per cent, it is not going to be a good thing, and we don't want it to get there. But if it does, it is something we can deal with and bring down.

Is it not possible to fix the refineries and make them work up to 90 per cent capacity before we eventually remove the fuel subsidy?

I don't think it is impossible. Decision as to what to do and how to do it is a function of terms agreed on. My understanding is that there is ongoing negotiation now; I don't know when the negotiation will end. My job is to see how much is brought from subsidy; see increased government's fiscal position and how to build reserve.

If you want to build up your reserve; if you want to build stable exchange rate; if you want to maintain stable rate of inflation; if you want to have sustainable debts, you have to do something. The negotiations of the timing and the amount are issues with the responsibility of the political authority.

If the government reverts to N65 temporarily, are we going to be in trouble?

The federal government can continue to pay subsidy at N65 per litre for a while. I am not saying it is economically impossible, but it is not wise. I will not want to comment on what the government can do because I am not part of the negotiation.

Speaking as a Nigerian, I will like to see a win win situation in which case the government shifts a little and remove it in one or two instalments.

Nigerians should also shift and understand that if we continue doing it today our children are going to pay for it. We have debt of ₦5.4trilion, and we are spending N13trillion in subsidy.

There is no way your children are going to have the right kind of lives if you don't build infrastructure for them but leave behind mounting debts for them. If we borrow money and build roads, power plants and factories, they will earn revenues to pay the debts. We don't have savings; that is our problem. If we have savings, if we are earning more than our immediate essential requirements, we could take some of those savings and go on holidays. If you don't have savings and you keep taking overdrafts for holidays, when you die, your children will find out that you don't even have a house because the banks will take over the house and sell it to recover their debts. By then, you would have helped them to build a lifestyle that they can no longer sustain.

Do you consider the CBN's AGO financing scheme and other similar funds as subsidies? If they are, what stops the government from ridding the oil sector of corruption and still sustain the fuel subsidy?

The difference is that the subsidies we provide are for production, not consumption. A company like Notore is a fertilizer producing company in Rivers State. When we started intervention, the company owed banks a lot of money. The rates of interest were high and the banks were about to foreclose the company.

Meanwhile, the government was providing subsidy for importation of fertiliser while only 11 per cent of the farmers were getting fertiliser. The company had bright prospects out the money they owed banks was a big challenge. The scheme gave them refinancing opportunity; it got money for 15 years at seven per cent.

Today, Notore is producing at 90 per cent capacity. It has created new jobs; it is producing and distributing fertiliser to farmers.

You have to be smart about how you subsidise. The United States government subsidises its cotton farmers; European governments subsidise their cattle farmers. So, nobody should come here ideologically to tell us not to subsidise. But what should we subsidise? We should subsidise production and make sure that the subsidies get to those who need them, not through middlemen. Why are we talking about cabal? It is because there has been a small group of people that benefited so much from this regime. And they are rich. Now there is a contradiction. Some say the subsidy is for cabal while another say it is for the people. The subsidy actually benefited the cabal more than the poor people

Is it wrong to adopt the same thing for the refineries that is, subsidizing local refineries?

Yes that's my view; that has always been my view. Instead of subsidising fuel import, we should subsidise local refineries. If I have my way, I will give them all the incentives the need starting from tax waivers…even cash contributions I will give to promote the establishment of refineries to help people get jobs and to move from the target PMS to full petrochemical companies in general; whether cheap power, cheap loans or whatever it is that they need to start, we should give them.

Some people wonder how we were able to pay our debts and achieve other things in the past under subsidy regime?

Remember that we got debt cancellation when oil price was $147 per barrel and producing about 2.5 million barrel per day. So, we took advantage of that opportunity to build our reserve to negotiate debt cancellation.

Whether after that we were able to set the economy on the path of sustainable growth is a different matter. I am saying that Obasanjo government did not perform but the started the power reform. If we had continued with the implementation of the power plan from 2007, we would have had improved power today.

We also have the Petroleum Industry Bill (PIB) that has been with the National Assembly and the executive for the past two and half years. If it were passed, we would have had the right investment in the sector. The real issue is not whether there was subsidy or not, the real issue is that we have continued to be very ineffective in terms of implementation of policies that were articulated. This is something we need to take responsibility for as public officers and start doing something different.

Is there no alternative way of going about the deregulation without hardship?

If you listened to the budget speech the President gave, there is tax relief for equipment in agriculture industry and it focuses on agricultural value chains. These are results of a very wide consultative and collaborative process aimed at addressing the long-term infrastructure needs of the economy. Structural change is long-term; retrenchment and fiscal consolidation is medium term, while monetary policy is short-term. It is very easy for us to increase interest rate overnight but it is less easy to reduce ₦500 billion from government's spending. And it is much less easy to move away from primary production to production of intermediate goods. It takes a longer period. Let us understand that that is how the economy works.

In terms of the options on the table, I think the discussion between the government and labour should move to that direction. I am not in anyway speaking for the government. I am speaking as one concerned about people dying unnecessarily.

I think the people have right to go out to the streets; they have the right to be protected. If we can debate issues without bloodshed, things will be much easier I think it is important that we find solution in the next 24 or 48 hours. If that solution means compromise, it is all right.

But I think going back to ₦65 will make a total mess of everything we have done so far. Let us reach a discussion that says this is where we will be today; this is where we will be in December with conditions. If the government will need to prosecute those involved in the subsidy, it is fine.

I have personally believed that the presidential system is too big for us. We need an economic system that is suitable for our country.

Fuel Subsidy Conversation: Tell it to the President

By Nnimmo Bassey

***The Guardian*, Sunday, January 15, 2012, pg. 14**

The nationwide strike in Nigeria against a I petrol price hike, enters Day Four as this is being written. Nigerians woke up at the dawn of the New Year to learn that price of a litre of petrol had been jerked up by about one hundred and twenty per cent. Petrol now costs 141 naira and 200 naira (about one US dollar) per litre in an economy where the minimum wage is 18,000 naira (about one hundred and ten US dollars). We note that even before the organised labour call outworkers on strike, citizens had already hit the streets in protest against what they see as an insensitive and unacceptable action by the government.

The response of government to the massive uprising has been rather worrisome. First of all the government presents a face that says there are no options to the move they have made. The speeches by the president and the many presentations by the governor of the Nigerian Central Bank, the ministers of Labour/Productivity, Petroleum Resources, Information and the Minister of Finance, remain persistently paternalistic and convey the message that they do not hear the dissensions across the nation. In moments of dramatic expression, the Minister of Petroleum Resources demonstrated on television how the government's hands are tied on the matter of fighting the rot in the petroleum sector. It would be interesting to know why the government allows itself to be bound hand and foot by thieves!

The major anchor on which the petrol price hike has been tethered is that government is spending a disproportionate amount of the national wealth on subsidizing the importation and circulation of petrol in Nigeria. The number one reason given by the Minister of Finance in her Brief on Fuel Subsidy is that from 2006 to 2011, about ₦3.7 trillion was spent on subsidy and that a whopping ₦1348 trillion was spent in the first ten months of 2011. She projected that the figure will reach ₦1.436 trillion by the end of that year. This figure is said to be 118percent of the nation's capital budget. The debates that run alongside with the protest show that a huge chunk of what was paid as subsidy in 2011 was actually "arrears from 2009 and 2010." Veteran activist lawyer Femi Falana raised this issue on a recent television debate (11/01/2012) and posed the critical question about the way and manner statistics are used by government in attempts to get Nigerians accept the huge leap in the pump price of petrol. The government has failed on this elementary point to use the figure of what was actually spent subsidizing the cost of petrol consumed in Nigeria in 2011. They prefer the bogus figure that includes arrears for 2009 and 2010. Nigerians are beginning to believe that the size of the cash doled out in "subsidies" in 2011 can be explained by the fact that this happened in an election year.

Nigerians are also told that the only way to stop the smuggling of petroleum products is to get Nigerians to pay higher price for the product. Really? One official even said that Nigeria's so vast that it cannot be policed and therefore smuggling will thrive without a price hike. Really? And who is supposed to watch the boarders, to protect the citizens?

We hear over and over again that the lower petrol costs do not benefit the poor. The reality on the ground just a few days into the new price regime has shown that this is not convincing argument. Smallscale entrepreneurs, for example those who run barbershops, depend on small petrolpowered electricity generators to stay in business. With huge public power deficits, many homes are powered with same type of generators. Nigerians buy potable water from suppliers who own water boreholes. Some of these citizens' waterworks are powered with the same type of generators. Because of absence of public goods and services we run autonomous or deregulated services at home and at work.

Another argument for the removal of subsidies on petrol in Nigeria is that in the league of oil producing countries the price in Nigeria is only higher than that of Brunei, Yemen, Oman, Algeria, Kuwait, Bahrain, Qatar, Saudi Arabia, Iran and Venezuela. Whereas Ghana recently increased the price of petrol by about 20 per cent, in Nigeria it is a minimum of 120 per cent. Do not forget also that the Ghanaian economy is not run on petrol powered electricity generators. Nigerians have seen that it is more helpful to extend the comparison to the minimum wage figures of the countries also. It is at that level that the hole in this argument becomes apparent.

OPEC Member countries	Fuel Price/litre (Naira)	Wage (in Naira)
1. Venezuela	3.61	95,639
2. Kuwait	34.54	161,461
3. Saudi Arabia	25.12	99,237
4. Iran	102.05	86,585
5. Qatar	34.54	101,250
6. UAE	78.18	
7 Algeria	63.55	55,957
8. Libya	26.69	23,813
9. Iraq	59.66	25,813
10. Nigeria	140.200	18,000
NON OPEC countries		
1. USA	157	197,296
2. UK	334.41	295,644
3. Oman	48.67	91,583

THE Nigerian government continues to talk tough while the number of protesters on the streets swell. In fact some of the spokespersons manage to hiss out their disdain for the protest without moving their lips. The SURE (Subsidy Reinvestment and Empowerment Programme) promises are taken with a pinch of salt by a populace who see these as the sort of political campaign talks they are used to hearing.

Nigerians are not opposed to making sacrifices that would put the nation on a sound economic footing. The government's effort at taxing citizens so as to generate more revenue should not be embarked on without showing seriousness about halting profligacy by public structures. Why can our political office holders (executive and legislative) not take a 50 per cent cut in their salaries and allowances? Why the retinue of advisers and ministers?

Nigerians have been bemused by the amounts in the 2012 national budget earmarked for expenditure on food, cutleries, newspapers and medical facilities for pets.

In and outside of government, immoral display of wealth is an indication of primitive accumulation through dispossession or the poor or some less than transparent means. We can keep pay attention to individuals celebrate birthdays within the range of 30 to 50 years who dominate pages of newspapers with birthday wishes that simple birthday cards can do. The same indicators are displayed through congratulatory messages for receiving political appointments, chieftaincy titles, honorary degrees and other things that bloat the ego of the fat cats in our midst.

Tensions need to be doused and one way will be for public officials to watch what they say. It will be helpful if they would say nothing when they do not have anything new to say. There is enough anger in the land!

Fuel Subsidy Conversation: "We have to first audit our actual fuel consumption"

***The Guardian*, Sunday, January 15, 2012, pg. 10**

Former President of the Nigeria Bar Association (NBA) and founder of the Nigerian Chamber of Shipping (NCS) Olisa Agbakoba (SAN), in a telephone chat with GBENGA SALAU, suggested possible solutions to the ongoing subsidy removal crisis.

What is the way forward?

I THINK the way forward, obviously, is for those in labour and government to have the best wisdom to decide how to resolve this crisis.

But I also think that this was a crisis that could have been avoided if government had carried everybody along. The people are not against deregulation but they are simply against how it was done in such a hurry.

For instance, when we met the president, I told him I was concerned that we were consuming as much as 35 million litres of PMS. And at the town hall meeting, the Central Bank Governor confirmed that the consumption level was not that quite high.

Also, the Director General of the NIMASA has confirmed that the figures are not that high. So, if we are consuming 13 million litres of "legal" petrol", it would mean that the "legal" subsidy would fall to about ₦200 to ₦300 billion a year, which the government can easily afford, if this calculation had been done properly before the announcement of January 1.

The responsibility to ensure that people do not bring illegal goods to Nigeria is vested in NIMASA and I have told government people, to give NIMASA the proper support so that they could do their work in a way that will make sure that not a single drop of illegal petrol comes in. But the problem is that, the so-called cartel has found a way to overwhelm government and government has had no response.

So, in my own single calculation, I said number one, if NIMASA did its work properly—and I know that the Director General of NIMASA has expressed willingness to enforce to the letter the Nigeria shipping laws (if he had been empowered to do this)—then, the arithmetic of what we consume would automatically fall.

So, this is the simple analysis I have proposed to government, that if they had this and cut down our consumption or determine our true consumption, the falsehood that we spent N13tril lion on subsidy would be revealed, it would not be more than ₦200 billion. The question would then be, can the government afford to or not afford to subsidise Nigerians by ₦200 billion every year? So, that is the simple argument.

Outside the recent port reforms, what other steps do you think government can take to remove some of the additional cost as a result of the inefficiency you have mentioned?

It is the responsibility of NIMASA to enforce the maritime laws; NIMASA will check to see that all our shipping is properly done, that is the job of NIMASA. But let me just take you through the crude oil production circle; what happens with crude oil is that, we have two markets. We have export and non-export markets.

For the export market, we are controlled by the Organisation of the Petroleum Exporting Countries (OPEC), which gives us a quota to export and that is about 2.4 million barrels per day. When we export that, we sell it at international price; so, if the price is $140 per barrel, we sell it at that price. And there is the non-export market; the government allows us 500,000 barrels of crude oil, so that we can drive our cars in Nigeria. We could only refine about 50 per cent of the 500,000 barrels. It means we can refine 250,000 barrels of crude oil in our local refineries.

The cost of refining and taking it to the pump, where the people buy it, is about #34. That is the reason I asked, where is the subsidy in the first 'Govt Must Allow NIMASA To Fully Implement Our Shipping Law' The Mafia Are Not The Otedolas, Tinubus... They Are the Unknown' place. If your total cost is ₦34 and you are selling at N67, then there is no subsidy; in fact, there is a big tax.

But now, you take it from ₦67 to ₦145, there is a further tax. What government cannot explain to us is, the simple arithmetic of how is it that it cost N67 at the filling station, the government fails to do this. But we have calculated ourselves, using people who have the scientific knowledge that it costs ₦34 to do everything from the crude — taking the crude from the ground, refining the crude, transporting it to filling stations anywhere in Nigeria; that it is ₦34.

But there is a problem, which is that only 50 per cent of the 500,000 barrels that we have reserved for Nigeria that are refined here. So, the remaining 50 per cent is sent abroad in what the government calls the crude oil swap.

It is now sent abroad and brought back to join the 50 per cent refined locally; that one costs N35, but where the oil cabals come in is that the government now pretends that the ones we sent abroad to refineries also attract international price, which is not possible.

A very simple example is: if my wife has a school where we bake bread for the children, and we need five bags of wheat to make the bread, and our bakery in the school can only bake for 50 per cent of the students, we have to take the remaining to a baker and tell him, 'please bake this bread for us. We would only pay him for the baking of the bread, not the wheat, because the wheat is our own already'.

So, when we send the crude oil for refining abroad, we do not pay for it because it already belongs to Nigerians. By the time we bring it back, the only cost is shipping and refining, but government goes to add tne international price to it; that is the problem. By the time it comes here, they tell us it is ₦170 plus.

The thing is so simple: All we would have done is sit down with government (those of us in the oil and gas, and civil societies). We can have a roundtable discussion. And that was why after the town hall meeting, I assumed that this is the first of the town hall meeting, that there would be many town hall meetings, where eventually the people can ask the question, what is the price of petrol at the pump? And I still challenge any government official to a debate on this.

If you watch all the television presentations by government ministers, nobody has ever answered that question. The challenge to them is, let us take a chalk and go to a chalkboard and determine the price of selling petrol at the pump, starting from taking the product from the ground to exploration, refining and transporting it to the filling stations and allowing the distributors to make their own profit, let us put that to a debate. I challenge the government that the price is ₦34 not ₦67, but if I am wrong, let the government now file in the correct figure.

However, the beauty of what has happened is, government cannot impose policy without our consent.

If the product is resold at international market price, where does the money go?

That is a good question. Which account does it go to? The fraud in this thing is plenty. The crude that they send abroad is not at international price but they now sell it to us at international price and we have no idea where the money goes to; they have not explained where it goes. The problem is now placed on us.

And that is why we are all insisting that the way to go is by deregulation. So, the government must understand that our objection to the price is not that it does not make economic sense; our objection is the way they imposed it. Because if government hands off from the business of oil and gas, and they say to us, the reason is because of this oil cartel, there is corruption, demurrage issues and these are the people that are benefiting, so rather than allowing few people to benefit, let it be determined by market forces, Nigerians will not say no.

They will agree because there is a lot of corruption in the petroleum sector caused by government control of the NNPC and that is why a lot of us had argued that, in order to clean up the market, the sector should be deregulated.

Also, if government can put the same energy, put into this subsidy removal into passing the Petroleum Industry Bill (PIB), that would nave made a big difference because the PIB would remove the government hands in the industry, just like when they passed the telecommunication reformed bill.

Even if the government returns the price to ₦65, should it end there, since the people's anger is also about the need to tame the so called mafia?

The government has a policy on anticorruption; the policy is that it will not tolerate any corrupt practices and that is why it has set up institutions to fight corruption, one being the EFCC. We have also set up laws to make sure that they work in the correct ways.

So, what I will expect government to do in order to convince us that its intention is well placed is to identify everyone who has taken part in stealing our natural resources, not just petroleum, and ensure they are severely punished.

Looking at the effort of Sanusi in cleaning the banks, the same could be done in this sector. We have the DPR, Marine Police and NIMASA, whose job is to make sure that anything irregular on our waters, is not allowed to happen and when it happens, they prosecute those involved.

If government allows all the agencies to work, I will expect that all those who have benefited wrongfully are identified and prosecuted.

Let me also say, the mafia is not Otedola; it is not Oando, these are people who are doing business genuinely. The mafia are those people who you do not even know, who have access to government agencies and can get allocation and when they get allocation, they sometimes do not even import, all they do is to produce document and hand it to the PPMC, NNPC and the PPPRA.

But Otedola is a genuine businessman. The mafias are people you do not know; they are not even in the business of importing anything, but they understand the process very well and use their connection to make a lot or money and those are the people I expect the government to have crushed.

Fuel Subsidy Conversation: Why government took the hard decision

Minister of Finance, Dr Ngozi Okonjolweala in one of her appearances on the Television (AIT)

***The Guardian*, Sunday, January 15, 2012, pg. 11**

On Recurrent expenditure?

IF there is corruption in it we have to stop it. We are going to audit these things. Government is not shying away from auditing. But while we are doing that, we don't want it to continue. When you talk about corruption, we are not only acting to stop it. But what do wee do about those who are involved? And government is not Shying from that. Remember when I just came, I said the cost of recurrent expenditure is too high. When I left the last time it was about 60 per cent of the budget; now it is 74 per cent. And that is even causing challenge for monetary policies. It is something we nave said not what we were told. And we said we were going to look at how we were going to reduce that. We said we would look at where the waste is and stop it. We want to do it in a systematic way;

we want to find out where linkages are in our pensions and salaries. We will investigate and act on the results.

The elements that account for increase in consumption include population. There is population dynamics. The larger you grow the more of product you consume. Between 2002 and 2010, crude was $51 per barrel. In 2011, it was ₦83. Of course that gap is an issue. There is also exchange rate difference between the Naira and dollar. There is the issue of the issue of fuel being hijacked because we are lower than neig bouring countries. Those are the elements.

The recurrent ejroenditure seems to be on the high side still Why can't we reduce the cost of governance in order to divert more funds to capital projects?

Last year, there was salary increase of 53 per cent, which includes minimum wage and general salary increase. Salary bills account for up to 80 per cent of recurrent expenditure. When you talk about reducing that, it means you have to lay off people. When people talk about recurrent they should understand that it is largely about salary cost of running government. Ir we wake tomorrow and say 40,000 people are laid off, that means 40,000 people are out in the streets. The same people who say we should cut cost will say "this is a wicked government" because each of those people supports eight or more people in his village. So you have to look carefully when you want o cut cost. You may cross check which agencies duplicate functions and all that. But it has to be done with common sense so that you will not throw people into the streets.

We have had experience of ghost workers and ghost pensioners. That means non-existing workers who earn who are paid. To get out of that, you have to do biometric exercise. We have started that, and we have been about to cut N1 from Police pensions. That is the first thing we are doing. We want to do that in the entire civil service so that we know the exact figure that we have. After that, we can go to the next stage, which is merging agencies, commissions and committees that have overlapping functions. This is a systematic process.

Diesel was deregulated some years ago. What have been the gains of deregulation of diesel? What is the guarantee that the deregulation of fuel will not go the same way, which takes us to the issue of trust?

I can't remember of we had this land of protest then. Diesel is used largely by manufacturers while PMS is used more by ordinary people. That is why everybody is so concerned about the subsidy removal, and that is why people are on the streets. We must be able to snow people that we are transparent. We must be able to convince them what we want to do. We have an estimated amount of money for subsidy, when that money comes in, we will publish it for everybody to see. You will see it and you will see where it is going. Everybody is working to ensure that the SUREP succeeds. This is because the issue is very sensitive. We will be transparent such that everybody will see how we spend what comes in.

You will remember when we started publishing the revenues of the three tiers of government. And for the fact that people could see what the Federal, their states and local governments earned, they began to question about the revenues. They will ask why is such and such projects not in place? They will know which governor is not doing his job. The same way we will publish the proceeds so that people will see where it is going. We cannot tell people that we have done what we have not done because social media are there. We will use the money on projects that are verifiable. If we say we are doing Lagos-Ibadan Expressway and you can't find what have say we nave done, then you will know that the government is not saying the truth. This will be different because the money will be used in line with our promise to Nigerians.

Most Nigerians believe that whatever will go to state and local governments will go the same way of federal allocation

We must not allow failure of the past to prevent us from planning for the future. The issue is how do we deal with the pains and address the issue of corruption. This is because we don't want Nigerians to suffer in vain.

Coming to the projects you articulated in the SURE documents, were they not captured in the 2012 budget?

I think we have two things on the table—the regular 2012 budget and additional provision that will capture the subsidy proceeds and other funds that are not in the budget. We should remember that Nigerian resources come on monthly basis based on our sale of crude and royalties paid to the government. Some of the projects are already in the budget but we don't want them to continue to drag on because of insufficient funding. We have about 6000 ongoing projects that have experienced unnecessary delay because of poor funding. What we want to do is to take the additional money and add into the regular budget to fast track the execution of the projects.

How is the execution of theses programmes going to affect an ordinary person at the grassroots?

The programmes are for the grassroots people not the elites. When you talk about job creation, it is in two categories. There are the skilled youths, which comprise graduates of universities and polytechnics. We have programme that will scale them. We will provide incentives to companies to train; we will help some of them who are very entrepreneurial to create jobs for themselves and employ their peers. We are going to launch a programme that will create 350,000 jobs in addition to YouWin programme, which we expect to create about 800,000 jobs yearly. These will help youths to find jobs and be more useful to themselves and the society. We will be working with states to make the programmes successful. We are also expecting the state governments to create their own programmes in addition top what the federal government is doing. Some of them have ongoing programmes. We will work with them to scale up those programmes. We are willing to partner with any state governor that is desirous and willing to create youth empowerment programme. We are already in touch with them.

When you talk about road construction, it is absolutely for the grassroots people. When you have good roads, you are talking about helping the people to bring their goods to the market faster and cheaper. A bus driver will no longer tell you that potholes on everywhere and as such charge you twice what he should have ordinarily charge you. The agro finance scheme we will develop is for farmers at the grassroots. That will increase availability of food items and makes them cheaper. These are grassroots projects.

The argument is that some of the programmes articulated are ordinary programmes that should have been carried out by the government some of which have been provided for by budget in the past years. Abuja-Lokoja road, for instance, was awarded around 2006 yet it has not been delivered. Why do we have to finance the projects from subsidy removal proceeds?

I think you should ask the contract about the history of payment. It has been stop and go system. Even when they have certificate, they are not still paid. The ideal is that we will be able to shorten the delivery time if there is additional funding.

We have a portfolio of 6000 projects, which drags on for several years because the resources are not enough. The estimate for infrastructure is put at Nl.6 trillion a year because we have not invested in infrastructure adequately for some years now. There were years we did not invest at all. I am talking about two to three decades ago. Now we need Nl.6 trillion yearly to gap created. With what we currently budget for infrastructure, it will take us so long to address the deficit. We need to get resources from everywhere to add to the regular budget; we even need to borrow some for productive purposes. By the time wedo this, during next Christmas when people go home, there will be material difference.

How does this fall in line with the NEEDS, SEEDS and LEEDS document, which you were part of the team that prepared? This is because people believe you are importing IMF doctrines to Nigeria.

I want to say once and for all that people should be fair to me because before I came I read that the governors wanted subsidy removed. It was published that the governors were supporting subsidy removal. It is not fair. Is it fair when people are not saying the truth? People should be very fair because this was a discussion that was on before I came. I can argue that for myself.

The NEEDS document was a medium term plan to put the economy on its feet. And if you look at alongside what is now called the Transformation Agenda and Vision 2020...

How consistent is it?

It is very consistent because it was aimed at transforming the economy, improving the living standards of the people, creating wealth and improving services. And we said that it would increase economic stability because if you don't do that you can't do any other thing. We channel resources to productive segment or the economy. Like Sanusi said, why should you subsidize corruption instead of production? We keep saying subsidy should be channelled to areas where it will have greater impact on the lives of the people. We should build roads and revive refineries. We will make sure that we refine our products here.

How sure do we expect the private refineries licensed by the Obasanjo administration come on bound?

Nigerians should be wondering why not one out of the 18 refineries that were licensed has not been built. The operators know that they could never recover their cost let alone make profit at ₦65 per litre. At that price, they will not be able to survive. That is why they have not built. What government will do is to partner with them because we have not developed the capacity to manage refineries. There are some who already have licences while anothers have given expression of interest to build.

From the information I got from the Petroleum Ministry and the NNPC, they have brought those who built the existing refineries. I am aware that within 15 to 24 months they will have been able to do the turn-around maintenance (TAM) properly and the refineries will be able to produce at 90 per cent capacity.

'Fuel Subsidy Removal...The IMF Is At Work Again' OSUNDARE on State of the Nation, NEWSPEOPLE.

By Anote Ajeluorou

***The Guardian*, Sunday, January 1, 2012, pg. 42-43**

Now government is talking about subsidy removal and we have the Minister of Finance, Okonjo-Iweala, who is the coordinating minister for the economy in her second coming to that position. She is coming with IMF and World Bank background, with a certain skewed orientation towards Africa. What do you make of this mix?

The subsidy issue is going to decide the fate of this country in year 2012, whether we are still going to have a country called Nigeria or whether there will be none at all. That we are talking about subsidy or no subsidy now takes me back to the point I made earlier on. We don't have rulers who think and feel; we don't have rulers who have the interest of the people of this country at heart. But we've been through all this before. Who can forget in a hurry the way the then President Babangida got the country debating whether we wanted the IMF or not, how the country roundly rejected the IMF's 'conditionalities', but Babangida and his group smuggled them in through a subterfuge called SAP (Structural Adjustment Policy). This was when the drastic devaluation of the naira began, and with it the devaluation of the Nigerian life. Nigeria is still reeling in the fever of that economic- fiscal fiasco.

IMF is at it again. Its new president, France's Christine Laggarde, has just visited Nigeria and has given a pass mark to the Jonathan administration. With Dr. Okonjo-Iweala, the IMF's Trojan horse at the helm in the finance ministry, that international task master and global finance police has a jolly good friend in a powerful place indeed. There is no country in the world that has swallowed the IMF pill without spinning into retching bouts and, at times, rigor mortis. For, as I said in one of the poems in Songs of the Season,

The IMF Is a doctor Who heals the patient By killing him first

Yes, those clinical undertakers of vulnerable economies are at it again, and the very life of every Nigerian is on the line Let us look at the 'subsidy conundrum. Is there a subsidy really? Then who, what, is being subsidized? We all need to go back to Prof. Tam David West's recent interview on this issue. If there is anybody who understands the oil and gas industry and how it works, it's David West, Nigeria's former Petroleum minister. Because Nigeria cannot run efficient refineries, and therefore it has to import the refined products, the government is now asking the Nigerian people to pay for its inefficiency and criminal mismanagement and corruption. The questions we should be asking are: who are the people responsible for the non-functioning of our refineries? Who are the beneficiaries from this dysfunction? Who are the lucky owners of oil blocks and instant billionaires from oil quotas?

If our rulers were people with a sense of shame, they wouldn't be talking about subsidy at all. They should cover their faces in shame and apologize to the Nigerian people; for if anything, it is the Nigerian people that need some form of hardship allowance from their incorrigibly incompetent government.

And our President and his officials have been going from church to church (have they called at the mosques yet?), asking for God's blessing for the kind of socio-economic mayhem they are about to unleash on the Nigerian people through the removal of the so-called subsidy; asking the pastors to pray to God to make Nigerians compliant to and accepting of their impoverished situation, begging Almighty God to soften the minds of Nigerians. But no one entered a plea for God to smash the incubus of corruption and mismanagement that has brought this country to its knees. Our President never asked God to grant him the courage and candour to make a public declaration of his assets as required by the constitution of the country he rules...

Nigeria is a country tottering on the precipice. Our rulers are doing everything to tip it to the abyss. As a student of history, I know that revolutions do not just happen. They are caused almost invariably by rulers that are blind, deaf, insensitive, and megalomaniacal. It is this insidious cocktail that produces the 'Distance of Power', that affliction that has always engaged my attention whenever I ponder the use and misuse of power. And I ask: President Jonathan, are you close enough to hear the heartbeats of those you rule? Can you hear the wailing in the land? Can you see the hunger in the streets? Can you see the protuberant stomachs of kwashiorkor-ravaged children? Can you see the hordes and hordes of our children who roam the streets because their parents are too poor to send them to school? Can you hear the unending screams from those face-to-face shacks where spouses tear each other into pieces over the non-availability of house-keeping money? Can you hear the interminable rat-a-tat of the sophisticated guns of armed robbers as they bloody our days and terrify our nights? President Jonathan, can you hear? Can you see? Can you feel? Your predecessors flogged us with whips; will you advance their various acts of cruelty by whipping us with scorpions? President Jonathan, do you still remember that young, ambitious boy from Otuoke who never had shoes until well into his teenage years? Well, now he is a King in the Marble Palace with a wardrobe large as a house. Look through the tinted windows of power. You will see millions of children whose shoeless feet embarrass our land. You will behold thousands that have no feet to call their own.

Some people say your government is under pressure to remove the 'subsidy because Nigeria is broke. Ask: who broke the country? Can you con-front corruption head-on? It is the giant monster responsible for all the holes through which the vital juice of Nigeria is leaking. The Nigerian people are not responsible for the heedless squander-mania and arrant improvidence that got us into this mess. Don't heave the burden on the backs of those already bent and bruised by the consequences of the foul actions of the powerful and well connected.

President Jonathan, our country would not be broke if our rulers stole less and served more, if our governments were not so bloated with redundancies, if we did not squander most of our resources on the maintenance of a parasitic political class of which you are an affluent member.

Mr President, please do not toy with the fate of this country. A still restive Niger Delta is simmering in the south; Boko Haram bombs make a mockery of your government's security system in the north Most of our people are poor (no, impoverished) and desperate and angry. They are like the savannah grass in the harmattan. Do not throw a flaming match into their fold.

Remember: the country over which you preside (just like the election that brought you into office) is fragile and frighteningly flawed. Tell the IMF and its Trojan Horse in your cabinet that you are not ready for the suicide which they are so heedlessly asking you to commit. Tell them you are not ready to commit Nigeriacide. A word, they say, is enough for the wise. For the wise, that is.

Govt, Civil Society, differ still on fuel subsidy

By Marcel Mbamalu, Dele Fanimo, Armsfreo Ajanaku Onome, Obiora Adubu and Sulaimon Salau

***The Guardian*, Friday, December 23, 2011, pg. 1, 2**

THE debate on the planned removal of fuel subsidy became keener yesterday as officials of government and leaders of civil society took their arguments to a public forum. At the end of almost five hours of a robust debate, the proponents and opponents yielded no ground for a compromise.

The town hall meeting was organised by the Newspaper Proprietors Association of Nigeria (NPAN) in Lagos. The Finance Minister, Dr. Ngozi Okonjo-Iweala and Minister of Petroleum Resources, Mrs. Deziani Alison-Madueke, articulated the position of the government while former President of the Nigerian Bar Association (NBA) and activist lawyer, Mr. Femi Falana, were among others that opposed the policy.

Okonjo-lweala agreed that citizens' cynicism and lack of trust in the government were the reasons for the elongated debate on subsidy removal, insisting that the government was sincere with its policies. While presenting facts on subsidies, Mrs. Okonjo- lweala, who is also the Co-ordinating Minister for the Economy, said that deregulation meant limited inter-vention in certain prices by the government as it would allow for more transparency in the sector.

She said: "It also allows for free entry and exit for those who want to operate in the sector, as we have examples of other sectors, which are deregulated and liberalised like the telecommunications sector. In 2000 and 2001, our telephone company, NITEL, has 450,000 phone lines that was supplying the entire country of 150 million people.

"Today, Nigeria can boast of 80 million GSM lines. So, if five years to cater for the roads from the $10 billion spent yearly, ₦500 billion intervention fund, another $500 million for the infrastructure and trucks.

Falana, who also totally objected to the policy, said similar policies had been made by previous governments, but the infrastructure were not there after Nigerians had made sacrifices. "We are here today hearing the same story," he said.

He, however, lauded the Minister of Petroleum for the re-organisation in the Petroleum Products Pricing and Regulatory Agency (PPPRA), noting that the number of importers had drastically reduced.

Besides, he said that there were laws that had taken care of the lapses which government was complaining about, but that the laws were not enforced. He therefore urged government to go back to those laws and make PPPRA do its job.

The Governor of Edo State, Adams Oshiomhole, who claimed to always stand on the part of the masses, urged government not to do what people could not afford.

"Let government move on the direction they have chosen but as a people, we have the right to insist that every naira gained from this policy should not be used for the comfort of the few. This government does not have any option, if it does not take this decision, Nigeria will crash and everybody will be in problem," he said.

Oshiomhole also condemned the role played by the local auditing firms in the subsidy saga. He urged the Federal Government to invite foreign auditing firms to intervene in the issue, since the local audit firms had lost credibility.

The former President of the NLC said government should investigate and arrest the gangs in the Nigerian National Petroleum Corporation (NNPC) who embezzled money meant for turnaround maintenance of refineries, and that the cabals in the petroleum sector should be punished.

The Trade Union President, Peter Esele, alleged that some people in government were behind the cabals, urging government to fish them out for proper prosecution.

He noted that there were loopholes in the PPPRA template due to some padded margins, while the Pipeline Product Marketing Company (PPMC), was another firm engrossed in auditing challenges.

Besides, the Petroleum and Natural Gas Senior Staff of Nigeria (PENGASSAN) has urged the Federal Government to institute a panel to probe the alleged fraudulent acts of some oil and gas companies, which illegally benefited from subsidy of the downstream sector.

Reacting to a report by the KPMG, an internationally- recognised accounting and auditing firm, the union said that all the firms involved and those behind them should be punished for committing the crime.

PENGASSAN President, Mr. Babatunde Ogun, said for the Federal Government to .gain the confidence and trust of the Nigerian people, it must embrace transparency by conducting further investigations with a view to bring those behind the fraud to book.

"If you do that, we have a deal and we will support subsidy removal," he said o been there to debunk the claims of government officials that there has been no subsidy of petrol but corruption.

The Many Ironies of Fuel Subsidy Debate

By Kayode Komolafe

***ThisDay*, Wednesday, February 1, 2012, pg. 56**

It was instructive that even after labour suspended the week-long strike that began on January 9, some eminent Nigerians still staged a protest march in Lagos to protest the deployment of soldiers. The march convened by septuagenarian lawyer and political activist, Mr. Tunji Braithwaite, attracted the participation of octogenarian constitutional lawyer, Professor Ben Nwabueze, former minister of finance, Dr. Kalu Idika Kalu, and a number of intellectuals and activists.

The protesters were sadly tear-gassed by the police. This act of the state would remain a stain on the democratic credentials of the administration of President Goodluck Jonathan. History would record it as one of the monumental mistakes made by the government in handling the popular protest. The moral of the action of the senior citizens who took part in that march on Lagos streets was that the culture of protest cannot be killed no matter the mutation the Nigerian state has undergone.

It has, of course, been widely acknowledged in many reviews of the events that the issue has transcended price of petrol. It has developed into a full-scale interrogation of the governance process with penetrating questions being asked about the workings of the system.

However, the incident referred to above has brought out a hidden irony in that episode of the subsidy struggle. Dr. Kalu, now a septuagenarian, was in his younger days in the 1980s the high priest in the temple of deregulation, liberalisation and privatisation and other capitalist drugs to Nigeria's economic ailments. Now, if the Jonathan administration had its way, the January 1 increase in fuel price would just be greeted with a mild academic debate on the merits of deregulation. After all, those who defend the government's policy hardly mention fuel price hike. They would rather regale you with the many gains of deregulation.

The profound irony should ordinarily have interested policymakers that a personality of Kalu's ideological orientation would join the protest. The protest against the deployment of soldiers was a derivative of the protest against fuel subsidy removal. We should be conscious of the history of the policy now presented as a new-found economic wisdom in this land. For Kalu to join the protest, it could probably mean that this is not the way he would go about the deregulation of the downstream sector of the petroleum industry when he was the oracle of Structural Adjustment Programme in the regime of President Ibrahim Babangida. Significantly, instead of a mere debate on the implementation of deregulation the focus has shifted to larger issues of governance and the management of the fuel subsidy is just one of them.

So while, for instance, some proponents of deregulation of the downstream sector of the oil industry claim that the policy is the panacea to corruption, the protesters insist that corruption, as an issue on its own, has to be tackled with or without deregulation. Take government out of it and the problem is solved, so goes the argument of our deregulators. But the tone of the protest is that this administration cannot abdicate its governance responsibility. Deregulation is no answer to the problems of governance including corruption and incompetence. The private sector, as the global crisis of capitalism has shown since 2008, is not immune to corruption anywhere. Contrary to the arguments here that there is an economic injunction which says that publicly owned refineries should not work there are successful state-owned oil companies including refineries in other countries. According to the last week's edition of *The Economist*, the world's ten biggest oil and gas firms, measured by reserves, are all state-owned". While policy makers here hold on to their rigid faith in market fundamentalism to solve all problems not minding the social consequences, those who once benefited from market forces are rethinking their systems. As the discussions at this year's economic forum in Davos, Switzerland, have shown even successful capitalists are now questioning why the system is incapable of tackling growing inequity to which the Occupy movement is a response. If you domesticate the matter, those who believe in deregulation here seem to underrate the magnitude of the pains that would arise from the policy.

This brings us to another huge irony in the debate. The same people that the officialdom pro-ject as the beneficiaries of deregulation were the ones who took to the streets unimpressed by the one thousand and one benefits of the policy as claimed by government. In a gross misreading of the situation, Oxford professor, Paul Collier, described the popular protest as "the power of the street" and likened the historic action of the Nigerian people to the "sad folly of the Tea Party" in his January 15, 2012 piece in the "Financial Times". Ironically, Collier is the author of the acclaimed book on economic development entitled "The Bottom Billion". According to him the youths should be demonstrating in support of the government for stopping the "squandering oil revenues" on subsidy. Collier could not see that the protest was against pushing more millions of Nigerians into the bottom billion of the global poor by a deregulation policy not well articulated. It is ironic that he has drawn a parallel between a progressive action of the Nigerian people and the ultra- conservative shenanigans of the Tea Party in the United States. The Yoruba have a saying that "a ki mo iya Oso ju Oso Id" (you cannot claim a greater knowledge of Oso's mother that Oso himself). But Collier is claiming to know the interests of the Nigerian people more than the same people who have been victims of the bitter consequences of anti-people policies for decades now. That is why Collier's professional colleague. Professor Joseph Stiglitz, the American Nobel Prize Winner in Economics, says we should be wary of technocrats and experts when they arrogantly dismiss people's resistance to their harsh policies as "populist".

Yet another irony is the insinuation that those who benefit from the big money-making of fuel importation were the sponsors of the protests. The battle cry of the protesters was that government should as a matter of policy promotes local refining of fuel so that the huge subsidy associated with fuel importation would disappear. The protest was, among other things, against the national shame of Nigeria being the only OPEC member lacking adequate internal refining capacity. How can the protest be in favour of those who have found a most profitable business in fuel importation?

It is precisely because the fuel subsidy debate is replete with ironies that deregulation policy should be further examined.

Pains of premium price for petrol

By Nike Sotade

***The Guardian*, Monday, January 2, 2012, pg. 13**

"After a protracted and heated debate over the highly sensitive issue of the removal of subsidy on petrol, the government finally dropped the bombshell on Nigerians yesterday the subsidy regime started yesterday, not April I, a move that is sure to be unpopular in an oil rich nation where citizens have come to expect cheap fuel as one of their few government benefits".

BEFORE dusk on Saturday, fuel marketers have stopped the sale of petrol at filling stations as they got wind of the imminent removal of the so called subsidy on the product The few stations that usually sell petrol late into the night armed robbers do not allow many filling stations to dispense fuel after 7.00 p.m. feigned lack of stock to stop selling, or if they sold at all, they employed one pump out of several in their stations. But apparently in a bid to stop the further spread of the rumour of its move, the fuel pricing regulatory agency, the Petroleum Products Pricing Regulatory Agency (PPPRA), went public yesterday with the official announcement: Effective today, it will stop the payment of subsidy to petroleum importers. The agency also assured customers that prices would be competitive. "The PPPRA wishes to inform all stakeholders of the commencement of the formal removal of the subsidy on Premium Motor Spirit," the letter signed by PPPRA executive director Reginald Stanley, said.

"Petroleum products marketers are to note that no one will be paid a subsidy on PMS discharges after 1st January 2012," it added.

The brilliant argument backed with facts and figures of Dr. Izilien Agbon, a former HOD, Petroleum Engineering Department and former ASUU Chairman, University of Ibadan, now resident in Dallas, United States that imported fuel in Nigeria should not sell above ₦39.30 a litre and locally refined, ₦34.36, published by *The Guardian* on December 28, 2011, seemed not to have swayed government with yesterday's action. With the removal of petrol subsidy, the new pump price of petrol has increased from ₦65 a litre to ₦143.56. The move could also see gas prices increase dramatically in the next few days.

The government estimated it could save $8 billion by phasing out subsidies, and planned to use that money to help the poor.

This surprise move by the Federal Government was not expected so soon by Nigerians, especially after the widely broadcast and prolonged town hall meeting organised by the Newspapers Proprietors Association of Nigeria (NPAN) last week in Lagos that brought all stakeholders together to debate the issue.

During the debate, Finance Minister, Dr. Ngozi Okonjo-Iweala, Minister of Petroleum Resources Deziani AlisonMadueke and Central Bank Governor, Malam Sanusi Lamido Sanusi, went on the offensive to defend unpopular plans to remove a petrol subsidy they said was wasteful and would bankrupt future governments if not tackled. The three key government officials tried to persuade Labour and transport unions, civil rights groups, market women and a lawyers' association all bitterly opposed to the subsidy removal that Africa s second biggest economy had no choice.

Letting markets determine the pump price of petrol in Nigeria would push it up to N120 a litre, Mrs. OkonjoIweala said, from ₦65, but it would save over Ni trillion in subsidies this year.

President Goodluck Jonathan had been planning to phase out the subsidy as soon as possible this year, but previous attempts have been caught up in rancorous debate.

The government had said that deregulation start on January l and later changed it to April 1. Bu OkonjoIweala told the nation later that government was still consulting and was yet to fix a date.

But last week at the town hall meeting, Sanusi drew applause when he said Nigeria spent $16 billion of its foreign exchange on costly imported fuel in the first 11 months last year $8 billion sold by the bank to petroleum importers and a further $8 billion spent by the Treasury on the subsidy itself.

"Removing the fuel subsidy is not some magic silver bullet that can solve all the problems of Nigeria... but the burden is unsustainable on the government's finances," he had argued.

"We can keep paying the subsidy into 2015, but the next government will be saddled with the debt."

He acknowledged the move was likely to prove unpopular, but asked: "Is it our responsibility to pursue the popular policy or the policy that is right for Nigeria?"

Responding to that charge, OkonjoIweala said: "There's a lot of cynicism about everything the government says and does. What we are saying is: Give us a chance to rebuild that confidence. You have a government that is correcting things."

She added that any increase in the cost of goods would soon be offset by economic reforms, such as more efficient customs clearance at ports that would reduce the cost of imports.

It is likely to be a bitter pill to swallow, although the government has promised to ameliorate it by providing safety nets to the poor to compensate them for higher fuel costs.

"The price of transport could double... The poor man cannot afford that," said Mr. Ben Murray Bruce, Chief Executive Officer of Silverbird Group.

"If you remove the subsidy, this is what you have to do: Subsidise transport for the poor folks trying to go to work."

Previous attempts by governments to remove the subsidy have been so unpopular they prompted strike action and street protests. But Sanusi urged unions to accept it, saying the system of fuel procurement was hugely corrupt and that removing it also removed one major avenue to corruption.

Jonathan, his economic team and the 36 states governors have all agreed the subsidy should go.

A common argument put forward by Nigerians against the subsidy removal is that they do not trust the government to spend the money they save wisely, instead of pocketing it.

Nigeria produces almost three million barrels of oil daily but a lack of investment in refineries and infrastructure means almost all of this is exported, while refined fuel products such as petrol have to be imported at great cost, making the subsidy a huge drain on public finances.

Some Nigerians have argued that there is nothing like fuel subsidy that what they are removing is merely the cost of administrative incompetence and inefficiency by the Nigerian National Petroleum Corporation (NNPC). Audit report of the NNPC, prepared by KPMG and SS Afemikhe & Co, had disclosed untidy accounting procedure.

Meanwhile, organised Labour rose from their meeting with President Jonathan recently in Abuja, affirming readiness to ground the nation's economic activities with an indefinite strike if the Federal Government goes ahead to remove the controversial petrol subsidy.

Nigeria Labour Congress (NLC) President, Abdulwaheed Omar, said the Labour has started mobilising the congress's affiliate unions and state councils for action in case the government eventually removed the subsidy.

He said Labour told the Presidency that if non-oil producing nations can refine petroleum products, they did not see why a big oil producing country like Nigeria would be importdependent in respect of the product God has blessed it with.

According to him, the government was reminded of its basic responsibilities to the populace, explaining that it ought not take externally driven prescriptions by the World Bank/International Monetary Fund (IMF) as others did on the Structural Adjustment Programme under the Babangida military regime.

At the meeting attended by Vice President Namadi Sambo, OkonjoIweala, Alison Madueke, President Jonathan presented a document titled: "Subsidy Reinvestment and Empowerment Programme (SURE)," under which it listed among other projects, the construction or completion of eight major roads and two bridges, provision of healthcare for three million pregnant women, six railway projects, youth employment, mass transit, 19 irrigation projects, and rural and urban water supply.

Ghana a few days ago also swallowed the World Bank/IMF pill by removing fuel subsidy. Petrol now sells for the equivalent of about ₦148 a litre

"Omar said Labour told the Presidency that if non-oil producing nations can refine petroleum products, they did not see why a big oil producing country like Nigeria would be import-dependent in respect of the product God has blessed it with."

The Popular Will

By El-Rufai

***ThisDay*, Friday, January 13, 2012, vol.16, no. 6108, pg. 56**

Any discerning reader that is familiar with this column will have by now been able to see a common trend that runs through this column in the past 30 weeks or so. This week's column must of necessity be on a subject of popular will with respect to the political turmoil with which the country is currently bedevilled. Let me first commend and salute the people of Nigeria young, old, middle aged, labour, civil society, employed, unemployed, market women, and youths for summoning the courage to do that which is perhaps unprecedented in the struggle to make Nigeria better and greater during our lifetime.

It was only a few weeks ago that President Goodluck Jonathan dared Nigerians by publicly boasting that he was ready to confront mass revolt rather than defer the removal of subsidy on petrol. It is self-evident that no well-meaning government would affront us all that way when the foundation for the legitimacy for governance derives from the people.

It was George Bernard Shaw that aptly stated that "Power corrupts and absolute power corrupts absolutely". Most people only know this much about this popular quotation but for those who are able to dig deeper, the above represents, at best, only half of the full quotation which ends with "Except for those who learn from lessons of history" and is read in conjunction with the first part of the quotation.

Thus President Jonathan would not have allowed power to get to his head if he had learned anything from the lessons of history. Some have argued that Nigeria is different and as such the Arab Spring has no place in Nigeria. Do they still think so? To be sure, the ongoing struggle between the executive arm of President Jonathan's administration and the people is, in the view of this column, for all intents and purposes the Nigerian equivalent of the Arab spring. It is the popular will which shall and must prevail at the end of the day.

So what really is at stake? Is this just about the removal of the fuel subsidy, when to remove it or is it about what a good government should be?

First, let us examine the economics as well as the politics of the fuel subsidy. As stated in one of our previous articles on this column on the subject of the petroleum industry, there are two schools of thought: (1) That of 'Buhari and Tam David-West' that believes there is no subsidy if actual cost of exploration, local refining and transportation are the constituents of the pump price for refined petroleum products, and (2) The 'government' school that is based on the opportunity cost, i.e., the international quoted price for petroleum products.

Clearly, if domestic refineries are functional and producing enough to meet domestic demand, as the seventh largest exporter of crude oil should do, the difference between the two schools of thought would narrow as it is simply because the actual cost of delivering a litre of petrol to the pump head would have been about N40 that no one in the executive arm of government has yet been able to refute or disprove. Therefore the fact that the government has to resort to the opportunity cost basis as a rationale for justifying the existence of an "import-based" subsidy is indeed a self-induced burden that the Nigerian people are being forced to bear.

This brings to mind a fundmental principle of common law that no one should profit from his or her wrong, which when applied should preclude the government from seeking to pass the inefficiency and incompetence on its part in failing to ensure that our domestic refineries work and jobs are created. Indeed the economic cost to the nation is not just a subsidy element that the Nigerian people are having to suffer but also foreign exchange, well paying jobs and skills that have gone down the drain with importation of refined petroleum products. We can therefore conclude that the economic justification for the withdrawal of the fuel subsidy is self-induced and should not stand.

Secondly, even if the Nigerian people should decide that refined petroleum products should be sold at the opportunity cost which is the international benchmark price, the popular will remains that the cost and size of government today is unwieldy and unacceptable. In 2011 nearly 75 per cent of the entire budget was spent on recurrent expenditure. The people have complained time and again that the salaries and allowances of the executive and legislative arms of government are neither affordable nor sustainable. Why has the government shied away from tackling 75 per cent of the problem whilst devoting energy to the remaining 25 per cent?

The bloated overheads are not only real but have been carried forward into the 2012 budget proposal such that only ₦13 trillion out of the toted budget of ₦4.75 trillion is available for capital expenditure. Meanwhile, the presidency is budgeting ₦1.8 billion to maintain 'existing furniture, office and residential quarters', ₦1.7 billion for travel (₦724 million domestic, ₦951 million international), a ministry has budgeted ₦2.5 billion for 'citizens call centres' whilst the ministry of agriculture has budgeted ₦1.2 billion to incorporate commodity marketing companies. Stationery, refreshments and snacks in the Presidency will consume about ₦2 billion, miscellaneous spending by the Presidential Villa alone totals about ₦1.7 billion for food, honorarium and something called welfare packages. The SGF and head of service will also receive over ₦2.5 billion for miscellaneous expenses including about ₦300 million for welfare and ₦270 million for security votes. These are nothing but misplaced spending priorities!

Moving on to the components of the so called ₦1.3tr fuel subsidy (by end of October 2011) the government is bent on removing, we can ignore the fact that no one in government has been able to analyse and substantiate how the amount of the subsidy ballooned or skyrocketed from the earmarked amount of N240 billion or between of ₦300-₦500 billion in the last four years, to the ₦1.3 trillion now and focus on the fact that both the government and the people have agreed that the process and system of subsidy payments are corrupt and fraught with fraud. So the question is why this government is not as anxious to investigate and charge all those found to have abused the system as it is determined to remove the subsidy.

Meanwhile, government has also budgeted about ₦1,147 billion (not ₦922 billion!) for the security sector. Ordinarily, given that security of lives and property is arguably the most important function of government, no one will quarrel with the magnitude of this provision for national security per se but for the fact that like everything handled by this administration, it is riddled with secrecy, lack of transparency and corruption. People are demanding the so called security votes to be made more transparent and for competitive bidding to be the norm for all national procurements in accordance with the Public Procurement Act. So at a time when the entire country is under siege from attacks by insurgents, religious fanatics, armed robbers, kidnappers and militants alike, including the unfortunate and condemnable massacre of innocent citizens in sacred places of worship, the government chose to worsen the mood of the nation by unilaterally removing the fuel subsidy.

In response to the widespread anger, the government in yet another show of insensitivity and incompetence, announced a so called 'SURE' package to ostensibly alleviate the suffering of the citizens but if truth be told, the so called 'SURE' package is founded on unsure, unsound and uncertain grounds. But for the fact that it may not be politically correct to accuse the government of embarking on a grand 419 scheme, the SURE programme is close to being a mirage if only because not a single naira provision has been made in the 2012 budget for the programme in its entirety. So it is bad enough that the government blatantly violated our constitution by admittedly expending more than ₦1.3 trillion on fuel subsidy without legislative approval or appropriation, but it is taken to the point of absurdity that the government will now openly announce and publish an elaborate programme of spending as detailed in the SURE programme without any appropriation whatsoever.

This is why the people must see the Jonathan administration for what it is. The excuse that the government plans to submit a supplementary budget is clearly an afterthought that should be out rightly dismissed.

In any case, the 2012 revenue projections already assume zero deductions for subsidy and still contains nearly ₦1 trillion as deficit, so where will SURE get the revenues to fund it? We should cross that bridge if and when we get there if only because a bird in hand is worth 10 in the bush.

For the government to offer a so called palliative that has not even been submitted as a budget proposal is as deceptive as it is a case of medicine after death given that the people's suffering started as far back as the 1st of January when those that travelled for the holidays were and are probably still stranded. The unaffordable price increases that were occasioned by the removal of the subsidy with which necessities such as transport and food were immediately affected are present and continuing and no one knows how many will not be alive to benefit from the so-called palliatives.

The government needs to apologise to Nigerians and go back to the drawing board. Nigerians, including this writer, are not against deregulation *per se* and if any example of shoddy government is needed, it is to be found in this current impasse of subsidy removal. Deregulation is a package of transition from public monopoly to competitive market. Necessary ingredients for this transition include at the barest minimum; (1) well articulated policy review; (2) enabling legislation to de-monopolise the sector; (3) a regulatory agency that will supervise the sector and implement the programme; (4) attracting and licensing of private sector providers in the sector. That is what we did in the BPE with the telecommunications sector, and now the electricity industry.

Clearly when the Jonathan administration's approach to this issue is measured against the foregoing minimum for ingredients, it is glaring obvious that what we have is, at best, a knee approach rather than a well thought out deregulation programme. If not, who is the regulatory agency for the deregulated downstream petroleum sector? If the answer is PPPRA, is the agency well equipped and ready for this task? And where are its programme? And why was the petroleum industry bill not enacted prior to the subsidy removal? Who are the private sector competitors that will replace or augment the moribund publicly owned refineries? Are we to continue to depend on the imported refined products as a substitute for local value addition and job creation?

These and more are the reasons why the people have embarked on the peaceful protest against subsidy removal.

As can be summarised from the foregoing points, there can be no rational economic justification for the subsidy removal until the wastages in government have been curtailed if not eliminated, those that abuse the system have been penalised or sanctioned; just as there can be no political or social justification until a consensus has been reached by the people that petroleum products should be priced at the opportunity cost. It only remains to also state that the legal issue of whether or not the ongoing protest is legal is an issue of semantics simply because the injunction that the government procured from the National Industrial Court (NIC) is only to preclude organised labour from calling for or embarking on a national strike. It is submitted that this is not just a strike but a peaceful protest that goes beyond organised labour.

This in essence is the thesis of this submission that the right to protest in support of the popular will is an inalienable, fundamental human right that can never be abridged or abrogated by any court; such that were organised labour to recall their members from the national strike, this nationwide peaceful protest will continue unabated. The government is duty bound to protect its citizens and see that no protester is harmed, so a situation where thugs are attacking and vandalising the NLC offices or attacking unarmed youths in Abuja should be looked into by the government. Overwhelming majority of Nigerians are not just protesting against the removal of the fuel subsidy but against bad governance that manifests itself in the pervasive insecurity of lives and property, widespread corruption and unacceptable huge cost of running the government.

In conclusion, both houses of the National Assembly have called on the executive arm of government to respect the popular will and not only reverse its position on removal of fuel subsidy but to also begin to address itself to the urgent pressing issues of corruption, insecurity and bloated cost of governance. This is the popular will that cannot be wished away. President Jonathan was wrong to have dared the people's resolve. Now that he has been confronted with mass protests, it is in the collective best interest for him to begin to show that he is a democrat and a leader by respecting the popular will. The sooner the better. Or worse still, the government sought to save about $7 billion from subsidy removal whilst the country is losing between $1 - $2 billion daily by way of lost GDP from the nationwide protests. Is this not a case of penny wise pound foolish? The answer is President Jonathan's call and not that of his cabinet and advisers.

Protest Raises the Bar of the People's Power, Resolve

By Taiwo Akintunde

***ThisDay*, Friday, January 13, 2012, vol. 16, no. 6108, pg. 7**

On an uncommon resolve and rare show of tenacity, hundreds of thousands of protesters seem to have doubled their commitment to continue the strike as a way of forcing government to revert its policy on the deregulation of the petroleum downstream sector.

With each passing day, the swirl of opposition has continued to grow and expand, so much that the park no longer accommodates the bourgeoning crowd at Gani Fawehinmi Freedom Park, Ojota, Lagos.

Hosting all strata of persons, including the fit and the disabled, rich and poor, young and old, artisans and professionals, religious leaders across the faiths, the strike which was called by the Nigeria Labour Congress (NLC) and Trade Union Congress (TUC) has long grown beyond the prism of those two bodies. Nigerians from all walks of life have been on the throng of the mass protest which is being coordinated by the Save Nigeria Group (SNG) and other civil society organisations in Lagos.

Day four of the strike and mass protest yesterday seemed to be an improvement on the previous three days as more people from different parts of Lagos State were seen trooping to the venue to listen to the leaders and speakers at the rally. Even an element of the mystique got introduced to die protest, when some dreary "native doctors" dressed in some weird regalia were also at the park, claiming to be conjuring the spiritual elements to soften the heart of President Goodluck Jonathan to change his mind and spare Nigerians more deaths and hardship. They came with their tools of trade: a mall old bag, with tired strap, and a broken zip by the side, a small hand bell and some cowries and even a small hand mirror, to complete the weird apparatus of the trade. They explained it was their own contribution to the struggle as they were neither hired nor were they expecting any monetary reward.

The speakers have continued to encourage and educate Nigerians on the need for them to resist the decision of the Federal Government on the removal of petroleum subsidy, which has raised the price of petrol from ₦65 per litre to between ₦138 and ₦150 in several parts of the country.

Convener of the SNG, Pastor Tunde Bakare, urged Nigerians not to get tired of the protest, adding that the massive turnout every day was a proof that the people are tired of the sundry deceits of government.

I want you all to know that the future of Nigeria lies in our hands and it is time that we all must fight together for this cause. There is no gainsaying that corruption has eaten deep in the system of government but we have every right to say no to bad and wasteful governance

"Remember that today's crowd is more than yesterday and this is how the number will continue to rise from thousands to millions until the government bows to the will of the people. I urge you all not to get tired because we will not stop until victory is ours," he said.

Speaking to *ThisDay* on arrival, wife of late Gani Fawehinmi, Mrs. Ganiyat Bukola Fawehinmi, and son, Muhammed, said the government would only regret at the end of the day if they refused to grant the demand of Nigerians, saying that the people have been woken up from their slumber and their voices must be heard.

Muhammed said: "I only pity President Goodluck Jonathan who has today lost the support of Nigerians in the cause of his governance.

"The ongoing strike is a demonstration against a government that was once getting the support of the people and that is a big shame to the presidency.

"He must listen to Nigerians and reverse his decision, allow fuel to be sold for N65 per litre and then seek for negotiations from Nigerians."

An activist, Mr. Felix Morgan, urged Nigerians to continue to fight for their rights while the strike is still on, adding that this is only the moment Nigerians who have the power to exercise their franchise during election also have the right to resist any form of maltreatment and injustice from the government.

"I want you all to know that the future of Nigeria lies in our hands and it is time that we all must fight together for this cause. There is no gainsaying that corruption has eaten deep in the system of government but we have every right to say no to bad and wasteful governance," he said.

Also addressing the crowd, were executives of the Nigerian Union of Local Government Employees (NULGE), The Academy, a nongovernmental organisation based in Lagos, and both speakers insisted that no worker would resume unless the government reverts to the old price.

The teeming army of people at the rally had no dull moments as they sang and danced to the music of popular Nigerian artistes railing at government policies.

They insisted that the demonstration would continue until a favourable response comes from the Federal Government.

Reflections On The Subsidy Struggle

By Simon Kolawole

***ThisDay*, Sunday, January 22, 2012, vol.17, no. 6117, pg. 111**

Senator Bukola Saraki, former governor of Kwara State, wanted to move a motion on the floor of the senate last year. He wanted a probe of the fuel subsidy regime.

How was ₦240 billion budgeted for subsidy for the whole of 2011 and nearly N1 trillion had been spent by September without appropriation? For months, the senate leadership re' touch the motion. The media piled pressure on them. Eventually, it was tabled and passed. An ad hoc committee, headed by Senator Magnus Abbe, was set up to probe the subsidy saga. What Saraki started a few months ago has now snowballed into something of international interest. But while the senate probe seems to have lost momentum, the House of Representatives' version is yielding revelations upon revelations, in excess of what we expected.

Now we know that while we consume 35 million litres of petrol everyday, we actually imported 59 million litres and under the subsidy is a difference of 24 every blessed day. At the rate of roughly ₦76 subsidy per litre, that comes to ₦667 billion worth of subsidy paid on what we most likely did not consume or was most probably not imported at all. The Nigerian National Petroleum Corporation (NNPC), we now know, used to import petroleum products without proper documentation, according to the testimony of Nigeria Customs Service. In other words, NNPC could do anything with the products since there was no record. They could divert the products to neighbouring countries. In fact, they could claim 200 million litres for 20 million litres. NNPC's regular excuse, according to Customs, was that it was a matter of "urgent national importance"—as it were—and Customs should not constitute a stumbling block that could lead to fuel crisis.

We also know now that the quoted subsidy figure of ₦1.3 trillion was not for petrol alone. We never knew this before. When government was campaigning to increase the price of petrol, we were only told that the ₦1.3 trillion spent on subsidy would now go into infra-structural development. But now we are being told the amount included kerosene as well. And there was no plan to remove kerosene subsidy all along, in essence, ₦1.3 trillion "savings" was just propaganda. The "savings" would be less; which reminds us once again about the lack of transparency in the whole business. Whose figures are these? Who verified them? The Coordinating Minister of the Economy and Minister of Finance, Dr. Ngozi Okonjo-Iweala, finally told us that nobody authorises NNPC to deduct subsidy before federal allocations are shared. She said it was just a practice. NNPC sells crude, collects tne proceeds, decides how much subsidy is, deducts it and then hands over the balance to the Federation Account Allocation Committee (FAAC). Wonderful.

In the whole debate, the Governor of the Central Bank of Nigeria (CBN), Mallam Sanusi Lamido Sanusi, also stimulated my thinking. He was the first and only government official to openly canvass a compromise as the strikes and demonstrations brought the economy to a halt. I don't know if he was sent to do so by the government to douse the tension (he said he spoke in a private capacity), but it struck a chord in me immediately. However, I am more interested in the perspectives that he brought forward. As someone who had been canvassing the removal of subsidy long before the latest round of fuel price hike, Sanusi made his points quite clearly, even if I didn't agree with him on some issues.

Being the one largely responsible for maintaining macro-economic stability, he had raised the alarm on the increasing demand for dollars to import fuel. This was hurting the economy and piling pressure on the exchange rate. Even before he became CBN governor, Sanusi had been canvassing the removal of fuel subsidy. Last year alone, CBN sold $8 billion to fuel importers. There are several implications that go with that.

One, with the increasing demand for dollars, CBN had to dip hands into our foreign reserve to fund the forex market; if not, the naira would have gone on a free-fall. It would probably have been ₦250 to $1 today if CBN had failed to intervene and left everything to market forces. You can guess the effects of a fallen naira on the economy and on the public. Already, because defending the naira affected our reserve position, we are being told somebody has "stolen" or "mismanaged" the savings.

Two, because of the subsidy there were spurious demands to import fuel. We now know that not all those who claimed to have imported fuel actually did. Unfortunately, the "importer" would have bought dollars on the pretext of bringing in petrol; the capital then flies to some foreign account somewhere, hurting the local economy badly. Sanusi, I believe, was privy to a lot of data on this fraud. This must have informed his rigorous campaign for the removal of the subsidy. His position was: if subsidy was removed, the true level of demand for fuel and forex (for fuel import purposes) would be established; the demand for $8 billion would fall and reduce pressure on our reserve.

For somebody who had a history for the "*talakawa*" (the masses), he seems have fallen out with his "constituency" over his unending justification of the removal of fuel subsidy. He said recently that he was not against subsidy for the poor. What he is against is subsidising consumption "which benefits only the elite'. He advocated subsiding production which he said he was already executing in agriculture through the Nigerian Incentive Base Reach Sharing for Agricultural Lending (NIRSAL). Subsidising consumption, he said, creates jobs in other countries from where Nigeria imports goods we ought to be producing locally.

Now, I disagree with Sanusi on the issue of "subsidising production, not consumption". I do not quarrel with the fundamentals of his argument, but the failings are glaring a bit. If we want to subsidise production, should we then not return to diesel subsidy since most factories run on it? Shouldn't we subsidise electricity for factories instead of increasing tariffs as we are now doing? As my senior colleague, Kayode Komolafe, pointed out to me last week, if I fuel my car on my way to office, is that production or consumption? The barber who fuels his generator with petrol, is that consumption or production? The salon operator who uses petrol for her generator, is that consumption? The tomato grinder who uses petrol to power her machine, is that production or consumption? On these grounds, I disagree with Sanusi.

I agree that subsidy has to be targeted at the poor so that it can be effective. For instance, why should Aliko Dangote and Ado John Sule buy petrol at the same price? Unfortunately, some of these things are beyond what we can control. Agriculture is heavily subsidised in Europe. Every farmer gets financial incentives to keep farming. As a farmer, Prince Charles of England gets subsidy payments! He is not a poor man, I suppose. When agriculture is subsidised, the produce is cheaper. Everybody who goes to the market to buy carrots or milk enjoys the same low prices. It doesn't matter if the buyer is rich or poor. The market cannot discriminate. The seller will not ask if you're rich before putting the price tag on it. And, mind you, that is consumption. When citizens are paid dole, social security, unemployment allowances, etc., is that consumption or production that government is subsidising? I don't think Sanusi can push this argument too far really, even if he has the interest of the poor at heart.

However, Sanusi made one of the most telling contributions to the debate with his take on the size of government. Do we need all these expenditure centres? Do we need 36 states and 774 councils? Do we need all these ministers? Long ago, he alerted us to the huge budget allocated to the recurrent expenditure, and also what the National Assembly is consuming as overhead. They wanted to chop off his head then, but the reality is biting us harder now.

By and large, I enjoyed the debates and agitations that the last fuel price hike generated. I don't think we've had anything that fruitful in years. Those who think the people lost out because petrol price was not reverted to ₦65 per litre are not seeing the larger picture. What I am sensing in my spirit now is that if we keep the momentum going, we would end up cutting the huge waste in government and also having more transparency in the oil sector. That's not a bad bargain.

Kami Attacks Foretold

On December 19, 2011, *ThisDay* ran a story on impending attacks on Kano. We quoted an e-mailed statement from Boko Haram's spiritual head, Muhammad Abubakar Shekau, who vouched to "launch endless and violent attacks" on the city. Shekau said the group had earlier released an open letter to the people of Kano, including the Emir of Kano, Alhaji Ado Bayero, and Governor Rabiu Kwankwaso. He said: "The message here is that everybody knows that a lot of our people were killed in Kano State, especially in Wudil town. We had perfected plans to take revenge but some notable scholars intervened by pleading with us. They also assured that our members would never be persecuted again and we took them by their words. Unfortunately, however, about five months ago, security agencies began trailing and arresting our members who are carrying out their legitimate businesses, alleging that they were thieves and armed robbers.' Last Friday, Boko Haram launched massive attacks on Kano. So far, 143 deaths have been recorded, including that of Channels TV's Enenche Akogwu. Hmmm...

Escapist Response

Where did the rumour originate from that President Goodluck Jonathan gave Inspector General of Police Hafiz Ringim 24 hours to produce die runaway Christmas Day bombing suspect, Kabiru Sokoto, or be sacked? To the best of my knowledge, what the Police Affairs Minister Caleb Olubolade said was that the IG had been queried to explain Sokoto's escape from police custody. There was no question of sack in 24 hours. I don't think President Jonathan is interested in sacking anybody. If not, the entire security apparatus would have been overhauled since the country came under heavy bombardment from Boko Haram, especially with the successful attack on police headquarters in Abuja last year. I don't need any expert to tell me that something is seriously not working in the way we are prosecuting the war. Neither do I need anybody to tell me that a change in personnel is urgently needed. Unfortunately, silent Jonathan would do anything but tamper with his security chiefs who are presumed to be his loyalists. So it goes.

Unknown Soldiers

While Nigerians have been facing a serious threat from Boko Haram militants who have unleashed unprecedented terrorism on the country, the most urgent priority now, it would seem, is to militarise Lagos State over a very peaceful demonstration. The misuse of troops should be condemned by all reasonable Nigerians. Those who are rejoicing over it today should realise that they would have no justifiable reason to protest tomorrow if the guns are turned in their direction. The most disingenuous explanation came from the Defence Headquarters which claimed that it was Lagos Governor Babatunde Fashola who requested for the troops in... 2010! Of course, there was a joint police/military arrangement in place with Lagos long ago, renewable from time to time; but it was purely to fight crime not to stop peaceful protesters.

One More Resolution

I have thoroughly been impressed with the role the National Assembly has been playing in this subsidy crisis. Senate President David Mark acted as a good mediator and seasoned crisis manager, while the House hearings have exposed a lot of rot in the petroleum sector. We are hearing so many disgusting things. However, I could not but comment on the House resolution two weeks ago that petrol price should revert to ₦65. Good one. We also need another resolution: the federal lawmakers should revert to the allowances they were collecting before jacking them up two years ago. That would be a great sacrifice and a sign of sincerity on their part as they go through the 2012 budget.

"Subsidy: a wrong way to run an economy."

By Ini Akpabio

***The Guardian*, Sunday, January 1, 2012, pg. 53**

Fuel subsidy is a symptom of an underlying dysfunction in our society. The dysfunction to start with, is a corrupt and inefficient political set-up. I am saying that because our neighbour – Niger Republic – was wise enough to open a refinery close to our borders. You do not need to go to school to know what they want to achieve. Now you will ask yourself – what is happening to Nigeria? Why can't we build a refinery? I think the major problem of our inability to do quite a number of things is corruption. The result of our corrupt culture is something like subsidy, which will always come in. until we address the real disease, we will continue talking about the symptoms.

The current situation is what I call between the frying pot and the fire; each is hot in its own way. The current government did not start fuel subsidy. They only want to see if they can end it; hence, they are trying to see if they can go from the symptom and probably trace the main disease and find a way of curing it. What they have been trying to say, which is logical, is that they cannot cure our malaria when our temperature is still very high.

What every doctor does during a medical case is to firstly stabilise the patients temperature, reduce the headache and attempt to attack the main sickness. We, as Nigerians, must show a lot of understanding. This is because it is not the problem of Dr. Goodluck Jonathan that we are discussing; it is not the problem of the government at the moment but our problem.

But what the people are saying is that they no longer trust the government since it doesn't keep to the terms...

For that reason, we need greater and better communication approach in order to address the problem. The Federal Government should be able to tell us, in clear terms, what the issues regarding fuel subsidy are all about. We need transparency on its part. They also need humility by telling us where they have failed. They should be able to explain to us how they have failed to make our refineries work; they have failed to ensure that subsidies are transparently documented and paid for.

They should be able to explain to us how they have failed to engage us properly apart from rhetoric on the benefits of the removal of fuel subsidy.

I will also blame the masses, including the Nigerian Labour Congress (NLC), who have failed to understand that the problem is our problem which we, as a people, can as well solve in no time. If you keep hitting your head against the wall, chances are that your head gets broken at a point. What we are doing, regarding fuel subsidy as a people, is like we are hitting our heads on the wall. Even the Nigerian Labour Congress and other civil societies, royal fathers and the national assembly should engage the federal government and get a clear-cut documented assurance that subsidy is the answer to the problem that bedevilled us economically.

Why don't we translate it to an irrevocable contract with either China or USA and whoever that shows us irrevocable assurance that roads would be built. If you go to borrow money from the bank or finance house, sometimes, you are told to write a post-dated cheque. That is the understanding I'm talking about. I feel in our haste to play to the gallery, we have not been able to to sit down to look whether there are alternative options as regards the issue of fuel subsidy? We must engage ourselves.

If we say our refineries should commence work, where are thos templates that can be utilised for this purpose? If there are no proofs, then we need to look for another alternative. I have realised that most of our national discussions are often swallowed by sentiment, which is really not good for us as a country; it is not just on the issue of subsidy. They are mostly swallowed by lack of analytical approach and lack of vision by all the parties involved.

Are you saying that the government is right after all?

My take is that subsidising fuel is not a proper way to run a country, especially if the country lacks the capacity to continue to subsidise fuel. I used to tell my friends this; don't come to me and say I should assist you because you want to go to an orphanage to donate free clothes. If you don't have a personal capacity to give, then sort out your problem first before you think of giving. If you don't have three square meals, you lack the capacity to give others food. What the government is telling us is that we are not eating three meals, so why would we continue to give? So it is either you make the government capable of eating three meals and continue feeding us or stop them from feeding us since they lack the capacity.

Subsidy: the Governance Debate Has Just Begun

By Bolaji Owasanoye

***ThisDay*, Tuesday, January 24, 2012, vol.17, no. 6119, pg. vi**

The Federal Government triggered early this year a most unanticipated crisis or perhaps if anticipated, it underestimated the reaction and underrated the pain, tension and frustration of Nigerians from long years of corrupt and irresponsible governance where the leadership has disconnected itself from the reality of everyday life in different parts of Nigeria.

The government is struggling to convince Nigerians that the subsidy it has been paying on fuel consumption is no longer sustainable. But there are many issues yet to be cleared around that assertion.

First we need to establish whether or not there is subsidy and if so, how much and its quantum. The government has so far failed to debunk the arguments of those who say there is no subsidy, or if there is, that it is not up to ₦1.3trillion being claimed by the government going by appropriations from immediate preceding years. Government needs to use data at its disposal to convince Nigerians that local fuel consumption doubled in 12 to 24 months necessitating an astronomical jump in subsidy. The credible way to achieve this objective is to allow robust debate that will throw up ideas from which government can benefit.

Secondly, government has not been able to justify why it lumped the pump price for local production with the pump price of imported products. Surely, fuel refined locally ought to be cheaper than imported one because some of the additional components in imports are cost of shipment, demurrage etc. which do not feature in local production. Government has failed to articulate clearly its policy or program on pricing of locally produced fuel as opposed to pricing of imported fuel. Any argument that locally produced and imported fuel should sell at same price will be a hard sell to Nigerians because one cannot imagine how a farmer who plants and harvests abundant yield of yam from his farm goes to sell all the yam to outsiders in the market and then asks his children to go to the market to buy yam at prevailing market for a price that they cannot afford. The children are likely to ask, why is my father a successful yam farmer? As pedestrian as the analogy may seem, the farmer must have a credible response otherwise he will have a mutiny on his hands.

Rather than trying to beat or drive a good idea underground, government must counter these arguments with superior arguments. Government cannot afford to be imperial in this regard because Nigerians are not idiots. If government's argument is sound it will enjoy popular support the croons of apologists with self -serving agenda.

The third point to be made is that subsidy though bad for business is not inherently abhorrent in socio-economic development agenda. Every government decides what it will subsidise. If this government does not wish to subsidise PMS or any petroleum products it must explain to the people what it will subsidise - education, health, agriculture, critical infrastructure, road transportation, social welfare, unemployment benefit, etc. It is widely known that developed countries in Europe and America subsidise agriculture as part of their development agenda. Therefore, any argument directly or indirectly from these quarters for wholesale elimination of subsidy in the development agenda of Nigeria should be taken with huge doses of suspicion.

More important, is that no subsidy removal or subsidy implementation regime will succeed under the present atmosphere of chronic corruption. Government is trying to segment issues as if they are not related. Subsidy implementation or subsidy removal outcome is linked with corruption which is linked with the style of governance which is linked with government's capacity to deliver on promises no matter how juicy those promises may sound now. The same cancer of corruption that brought has brought the nation to its knees now will eat away at whatever savings, if any, from subsidy removal or implementation. This is the critical issue the government is not willing to address. The dilemma of the government is that its key allies and functionaries are either deeply enmeshed in the corruption plaguing the nation or they are direct beneficiaries of it or both. Bearing in mind years of failed promises no one should fault the current level of cynicism against government.

Aside these, there are too many afterthoughts in government's reaction which indicate lack of focus and direction, further accentuating fears of misuse or misapplication of anticipated subsidy savings. Government suddenly announced the Subsidy Reinvestment Programme and establishment of the Kolade-led Committee when opposition to subsidy removal became widespread. More fundamental is that the Kolade Committee really has no resource to manage. If fuel subsidy has been removed and was not budgeted for in 2012 budget, it implies that all government capital projects for 2012 are captured in the proposals of MDAs. The question begging an answer is, "Will those MDAs hand over their capital allocations to the Kolade Committee or what"?

Government would have availed itself better if it decided that pending the total deregulation of the downstream sector, the subsidy regime for the intervening period will be overseen by a team of credible and incorruptible Nigerians led by Kolade. This would mean that while the debate went on for the best palliatives and subsidy continued, the regime would at least be monitored by credible people to ensure that the country pays for what it gets and is consumed. Inherent in this approach however, would be tacit admission of the failure of institutions like NNPC and PPRA that had for years pretended that they were managing the situation.

The wider issues as other commentators have said is that we must look beyond subsidy to style of governance and the cost of governance. In a recent short piece on the cost of governance which I did last year, I noted that a single issue like the biometric data of Nigerians is being budgeted for by different government agencies all collecting money from the same budget for the same issue. INEC for voter register, Nigeria Communications Commission through the telecoms companies, National Identity Management Commission, Immigration and more recently the Federal Road Safety Commission are all collecting biometrics at huge sums of money either directly from government budget or by taxing the citizens like FRSC and Immigration.

Right now we are not interrogating these issues just as we are not interrogating many other issues. The mind-boggling remuneration of political appointees, the legislature and use of generous budgetary allocation to the judiciary are all part of the wider debate. As we interrogate the federal level we must interrogate the state governments and the local government level. Gradually, we will get to these issues because they are no longer remote. All said and done, petrol subsidy is merely a trigger for a wider debate that will culminate in a critical decision on the future of governance in Nigeria. The government will be myopic to think that it has successfully broken the strike and that life goes on and it's business as usual. The vituperations of speaker after speaker against government at the rallies of the one-week national fuel strike in opposition to the sudden removal of subsidy serves as barometer for the true feelings of Nigerians who acting in unison chose to break their silence publicly.

One of the most significant indicators that this is the beginning or a marathon race for the soul of the nation is the active role played by the hitherto taciturn middle class who came out in large numbers, individually and through their professional associations to berate government's method of doing the right thing the wrong way or for its strong headed justification of an intrinsically wrong thing as right.

Owasanoye is Research Professor and Director of Research, Nigerian Institute of Advanced Legal Studies.

'Subsidy removal is good if govt is sincere' Prof. Akin iwayemi

By Bankole Shakirudeen Adeshina

***The Guardian*, Saturday, January 7, 2012, pg. 26**

As the newly elected president of NES, what are the statutory obligations expected of you?

The Nigerian Economic Society represents the interest of economists in Nigeria. The society, since inception, has strived to professionally represent the members of the organization and the public, especially in terms of economic issues like policy implementation, programmes and so on. Our contributions and impacts thereafter prompted President Goodluck Jonathan to include the incumbent president of the society in his economic management team.

What is the position of NES on the controversy over fuel subsidy removal?

I am going to speak as the president of the society. My views are personal on this issue. The society would make its position known officially soon. As a professor of economics, any good has what we call the real price, which needs to be paid. For example, I am the seller of a product and I would want to sell my product where I can derive maximum value for it. So that I can continue with my production and the necessary investment I need to do. At the end of the day, my utmost interest is in arriving at a win-win situation for myself, as a producer of the product, and for the consumer, who depends on the product.

Economic progress is about producing goods and services that people would value, in terms of what they pay for it, which would encourage the producer to sustain the production with better quality. Under this arrangement, the producer sells all needed to be sold, and the consumer gets all needed and derives maximum value for the consumption.

Everybody is happy. But if you don't allow that product to be priced in a way that would promote a win-win situation, you are going to have problem.

Interestingly, oil is a peculiar product because it is depleteable. When you produce and consume a litre or barrel of oil today, it is gone forever. It is not replaceable. Therefore, its pricing is different from the way you price other products such as yam, milk and even beer, which could be reproduced. Yes, it's a natural resource and belongs to every Nigerians, but we must get the right pricing template for oil which would help in translating into physical and economic development. Besides an effective pricing template, we must also provide for effective infrastructural, industrial and economic structures that would sustain us thereafter when oil would no longer be marketable or be exhausted.

So, you think things would be better when the subsidy is removed?

From my viewpoint, yes. The subsidy should be removed. But what needs to be done is that the industry should be deregulated and let government hands off and provide the enabling environment and level playing field for the operators to thrive.

Besides, the government should also comply with the International practice, which requires that palliative measures be established to absorb the shockwaves that could come with such a process. And in doing this, adequate compensation should be put in place, especially for the low-income earn remember there was a time when SIM card was very expensive. But now, it does not cost more than a ₦100.00 or so. That is the beauty of a competitive and independent market.

So, if you allow a more competitive market structure, where government just plays a regulatory role and does not support any party (by giving them money for importation), things would improve. That is why we are talking of corruption in the system. Even the government has discovered that there is a cartel behind what is happening. And anywhere there is a cartel, they try to skim rent from people and the consumers end up paying for it.

How about the direct and indirect impact of the removal of subsidy on the masses, especially as regards inflation?

If government deregulates the market, which I support, the refineries would be privatized and capable hands would be allowed to run it. And a marketing environment that would allow investors to earn reasonable returns in the sector would be guaranteed.

It would just be a matter of time before we experience a boom, like that of the telecommunications industry, in the nation's oil and gas sector.

It is shameful that Nigeria, over time, has been having stunted growth in the sector. By virtue of its potentials, it is supposed to be producing and refining in large quantity for consumption, even across the Sub- Sahara Africa. But instead of doing that, we are importing from Cote d'Voire, Cameroun and others.

Our compares, like Indonesia, which is also a member of the Organisation of Petroleum Exporting Countries (OPEC), are steadily exporting refined oil products on regular basis, unlike Nigeria.

The public sector, except for few exceptions, has not been able to run any commercial enterprise properly because of the geo-political interests. That is why we expend so much on turn-around maintenance for our refineries and sooner or later, they are back to square one or even worse.

There is no country in the world where refinery is being run the way Nigeria's are. Imagine a refinery being run where capacity utilization is awful and below 50 per cent and sometimes below 30 per cent and we keep pouring billions of naira into it? And the refineries work for some time and pack up because of various interests at stake? Never! It can only happen in Nigeria.

Because it is very expensive to build a new refinery, we have to adopt a more cost- effective measure to get things to work. It is because of the bottlenecks. It is because of the environment, which bores down on framework for the right pricing, a critical issue to every investor. With the global financial crisis, banks are more hesitant to give loans and many of these Nigerians firms can not get the type of loan needed to set up a working factory and the stringent environmental condition imposed on them appear insurmountable.

Are you saying political interference has slowed the pace of development in the nation's energy sector?

Sincerely, political interference or what I call political economy has made the energy sector to underperform. And that is why we are saying government should just play the role of regulatory agency that would allow the interest of both consumers and producers to be taken care of. By that, things would be a lot better in Nigeria and everybody will be happy.

If the alleged ₦1.3trillion annual subsidy is eventually removed, how are we sure it would be judiciously expended on developmental projects?

That is part of the political economy I was talking about. You say something and the other party takes you for your word. And if you are consistent with it, then we build a formidable mutual trust between us. Thereafter, our trust leads to reputation. I think that is the core of what is happening in this case. Over the years, the government has promised to do so many things, but people have not seen those promises fulfilled.

To resolve this, there must be targeted compensation scheme in place, especially for the low-income household, like I have said. Government could create jobs, free education and free meal for primary and secondary school students across the country.

Anger, frustration, hallmark fuel subsidy protests

By Chiemelie Ezeobi, Taiwo Akintunde and Comfort Umoren

***ThisDay*, Friday, January 13, 2012, vol. 16, no 6108, pg. 42, 43**

At the Gani Fawehinmi Freedom Park, Ojota, Lagos, anger and discontent best describe the mood of the unprecedented crowd that has been trooping there since Monday when the nationwide strike declared by the Nigeria Labour Congress (NLC) began. An unrepentant critic of government policies until he breathed his last, many reckon that the naming of the Park after the late fiery senior advocate, Chief Gani Fawehinmi, was a fitting tribute to his beloved memory. If he was alive, Gani, as he was fondly called, would be at the head of the activists that have been addressing the tumultuous crowd of opponents of the petroleum subsidy removal by the Federal Government. However, his successors in the struggle have been acquitting themselves creditably and that probably explains why the people have been trooping there in large numbers. Each day's attendance was an improvement of the previous day.

In the absence of public transport, many trekked long distances to the Freedom Square to show solidarity with the cause at great risks to their health. A good number of the people believe that if the policy is not reversed, the poor masses would be finally emasculated and that is why they braved all the odds to be present to show solidarity with labour and civil society organisations. Once there, anger, frustration and outpouring of emotions coupled with outright cursing of presumed enemies of Nigeria overwhelm them. However, simmered tempers visibly, reduced as one of Nigeria's foremost comedians, Tee Mac led the teeming crowd of protesters on the rendition of the National Anthem on Monday, January 8, 2012, the first day of the nationwide strike. Despite the pains and sufferings that was written on the faces of the protesters, it was however a touching moment when Tee A, the comedian, asked them to reaffirm their commitment to the country by singing the national anthem.

While the anthem was on, even the hardest of hearts were seen wiping tears from the comers of their eyes. The crowd sang with nostalgia for a country they hope Nigeria would become. The voices were raised in one accord in prayers for the country. The crowd shared three things in common; pain, suffering and agony. The protest was spearheaded by the Save Nigerian Group (SNG), as well as the Nigerian Labour Congress (NLC) and the Trade Union Congress (TUC), under the aegis of the Joint Action Front (JAF).

Other civil society organisations present were the Occupy Nigeria Protest Group, Education Rights Campaign, Academic Staff Union of Universities, Nigerian Medical Association, Know your Rights International (KnoRights) among others.

The nationwide strike to protest fuel subsidy removal was strictly adhered to by the citizenry in Lagos as shown by closed shops and deserted roads. The first day of the strike also saw protesters trooping to Ojota from five cardinal points; Ikeja, Iyana-Ipaja, NLC secretariat in Yaba, Alaguntan, Idi Iroko and the old Toll Gate.

The protesters had placards, which read: 'Stop Killing Nigerians,' 'Let our children wear shoes to school,' '25 per cent pay cut is not enough,' 'Tackle corruption not fuel subsidy,' 'Nigerian Youths say no to fuel subsidy removal,' 'Jonathan, stop breeding criminals,' 'Nigeria is not for sale,' 'Black man's spring' and 'Egypt and Libya's spirit of solidarity has arrived Nigeria,'' amongst others.

According to the Save Nigerian Group (SNG), Nigerian leaders must and should lead by examples. Accordingly, they stated that there must be no removal of fuel subsidies until the leaders' extravagant lifestyles are no longer subsidised by the masses.

In its demands, the group said there must be a law in place that makes stealing public funds an offence punishable with a minimum sentence of life imprisonment. They also said the immunity clause at the federal and state levels must go. While they declared that henceforth, all government contracts must be by open tender, they restated their desire to see that the presidency's overheads must not exceed 35 per cent of the budget as against the current 72.2%. For the legislators, they stated that they should not earn more than a permanent secretary (salary and allowances inclusive).

The group demanded that the president's salary and allowances must not exceed ₦25 million per annum, adding that feeding in the president and vice-president's lodges (outside of official functions) should be paid for by the consumer.

Flaying the conventional numerous convoys used by public officers, the group said no government official must have more than one official car neither should they be enticed to any foreign medical treatment. Also, the office of the first lady at the federal, state and local government levels, they posited, must be scrapped as it is unconstitutional. To this end, they also called for the reduction of special advisers and special assistants.

Speaking to the teeming crowd, Convener, Save Nigerian Group (SNG), Pastor Tunde Bakare, said the masses would not budge until the government rescinds its unfavourable decision on fuel subsidy removal. He said universally, sovereignty belongs to the people of the nation and as such, power is in their hands. To this end, he posited that if the masses should ask the present administration to vacate the State House, he would have no option but to comply.

He urged the crowd not to relent in their efforts to flush out the present administration from power, adding that the fight would only be successful if persistence and determination is applied. He condemned the state of insecurity in the country, adding that the government has failed in one of its primary responsibilities in securing the citizenry.

"Jonathan has not been able to secure the country as shown by the extent Boko Haram has infiltrated the nation, wrecking destruction in its wake. If the president has not been able to secure himself, how can he secure the entire country?" he asked.

Bakare said any government that is incompetent does not deserve the vote of the people and as such the sitting president should be fired along with his ministers. "Let's leave religion out of this and address the real issue at hand and that is the fight for good governance.

He lamented what he called the lackadaisical attitude of the presidency towards the strike. According to him: "The president said he is ready for our protest but he has forgotten so soon that we risked our lives so that he will be acting president. The truth of the matter is that we are not just fighting against the removal of fuel subsidy, we want good governance and anti-corruption war to be carried out."

Speaking to *ThisDay*, 11-year old Kehinde Alabi, a Junior Secondary School (JSS1) student of Oregun High School, Lagos, passionately pleaded with President Goodluck Jonathan to reduce the price of fuel. Even with his limited knowledge of what the real situation is, the young lad showed a surprising grasp of what poverty and what it portends for his family with the removal of fuel subsidy. Not surprising, because as soon as he drops his school bag after school he hawks sachet water to augment the family's income.

With his father's meagre income as a mechanic and the mother an agbo (a Yoruba traditional medicine) seller, Kehinde said he and his five siblings have to pitch in and augment the income through sales.

He, however, lamented that with the removal of fuel subsidy, the future looks bleak for his little business of sachet water. Buttressing, the lanky lad disclosed that a bag of sachet water that was formerly sold at ₦60 has jumped to ₦150. He said he makes little gain at the end of the day as sometimes people refuse to buy a sachet of water for ₦10 as against the former price of ₦5. In his plea he said, "President Jonathan, please help my family and rescue us from hunger. We are hungry in our house.

"The problem of fuel subsidy has caused the increase in prices of everything in the market and my parents cannot afford it. Hunger wants to kill us at home. I want to grow up too to become somebody in life." When he finished his passionate appeal, there was not a cheek without a tear.

Speaking to the crowd, matriarch of the late Fawehinmi family, Mrs. Ganiyat, flayed the insensitivity of the government to the plight of the masses. According to her, removing fuel subsidy was the height of wickedness. While urging the masses not to give up, Mrs. Fawehinmi urged the Federal Government to revert the price of fuel to its former rate as it inadvertently affects the cost of other commodities.

In his speech, Fawehinmi's first son, Mohammed, who was brought to the square on his wheelchair, said the masses are tired of suffering and would want to enjoy the dividends of democracy. According to him, the removal of fuel subsidy was a stab in the back for the teeming Nigerians that voted in him into power. He said: "Jonathan appealed to the conscience of the people when he said he had no shoes and they unanimously voted him in but today, it is indeed regrettable that he has betrayed them.

"All we are asking is that they revert the fuel price to ₦65 and there will be peace. There is yet time for him to listen at this stage, when we are ready to listen but it will come to a point where we would not hear his reasons."

Also speaking to the protesters at the park were officials of the the NLC, headed by the Vice Chairman, Comrade Isa Aremu. Chairperson of JAF, Dr. Dipo Fashina and Secretary JAF, Comrade Abiodun Aremu.

They emphasised the need for the government to reverse its decision on the removal of fuel subsidy as well as ensure that the refineries are working so that the petroleum industry can be able to produce fuel locally.

"We still maintain our demand that the government re-appraise its decision made on the first of January this year to increase the price of fuel," Aremu said. Reiterating tot the mass protest is the beginning of the struggle for attainment of justice for suffering Nigerians, they said action continues until the government yields to their demands.

Charging the crowd with different songs, scion of the late Afrobeat musician, Femi Kuti, said the struggle must continue till the goal is achieved. According to him, the struggle is not new to him as his father, the late legend, Fela fought his own share of the battle.

Foremost activist and legal counsel, Femi Falana in his speech condemned attempts to use ethnicity to cause distractions for the protesters. He said: "We made Goodluck Jonathan president and he came back to betray us, telling us that we do not matter."

Corroborating Bakare's position, Falana said section 14(2) of the constitution provided that the authority of any government to rule resided in the people. He called on Nigerians to exercise the power in rejecting the fuel subsidy removal, noting that the Jonathan administration had failed to live up to the constitutional provisions that the welfare of the people "shall be the primary responsibility of the government."

Falana said: "They have told us that Chad is selling petrol at ₦205 per litre. That means they are not going to stop at ₦141. They are still going to ₦205. Nigerians have to exercise their power to reject the removal of fuel subsidy. Nigeria is the only country which has oil in the world and sells petroleum products at international price."

While calling on religious leaders to spearhead the protest for their different bodies, Afro beat singer, Dede Mabiaku, said: "We are not here because of the removal of fuel subsidy rather to preach the fight against corruption. They are preaching sacrifice when they are not ready to make one."

The protest despite the peaceful manner in which it was conducted was not without hitches. Due to the ban on movement, some of the protesters who lived in far away areas of the state had difficulty in marching to Ojota, the centre point.

In many parts of Lagos, they registered their grievances by burning tyres and harassing motorists who were plying the roads to part with money. On roads like Itire, Mushin, Fadeyi, Onipanu, Palm Groove, Ogunlana Drive, Ilasa, Bartlet and some parts of Surulere amongst others, witnessed burning tyres. However, the hoodlums had a field day at places like Mushin, Fadeyi and Onipanu as warring factions took their fight to the streets. The warring faction's unleashed mayhem on the residents and passers-by alike as they sprayed hails of bullets.

Also, the Divisional Police Officer of Pen Cinema Police Station, Olubunmi Segun, a Chief Superintendent of Police, shot 26 year-old Ademola Aderinto to death at the Ogba area of the state even as he injured four others.

The injured in the gun fire were; Christian Amadi, Alimi Abubakar, Egbijo Samuel and Joy Monday. They were taken to County Hospital, Ogba, for treatment after which they were transferred to the Lagos State University Teaching Hospital, Ikeja.

On Tuesday, January 10, 2012, the protest saw to the death of three persons along the Ikorodu Expressway. At Ketu Bus stop, along the Ikorodu expressway, a motorcyclist who was simply identified as Ahmed, was burnt to death while another was crushed to death by a commercial bus. The deceased was only identified through his belt, his jeans and his almost burnt stripped shirt by a relative and a friend.

Also at the Mile 12 area of the state, one of the hoodlums who were trying to stop a commercial bus was crushed to death. According to reports, the hoodlums had blocked the road and were extorting money from motorists .The strike has caused a heavy shut down of the nation as the commercial capital of Nigeria has been grounded. Many Lagosians, either part or not actively involved in the protest have been complaining bitterly 'about the 'negligence' of the government saying that they have refused to listen to the voice of the masses.

Government establishments like the sea ports, airports, and railway completely shut while other commercial activities were firmly stagnated.

While sharing her experience with *ThisDay*, Mrs. Rukayat Ajiroba, 38, a trader at Ojuwoye Market in Mushin who lives at Lawanson area of Lagos, said the strike has not been helping her in anyway because she earns income daily to feed her three children whom the eldest one is just 16 years old.

"We understand that the people are fighting the government with this demonstration but I want the government to consider the demand of the people so that everyone can go back to their businesses and fend for their various families. If this continues for a long time, am sure there will be more chaos and even the government will no longer be in safety," she said in her local dialect.

Another trader, Mrs. Felicia Chinyere Adams, who sells building materials along Fadeyi Bus-stop, said many of her supplies are stalled at the Tin Can Island Port in Apapa and that is because the port is currently not functioning. "I need to make supplies to my customers but I can't because my goods are stalled in Apapa port which is currently shut down due to the strike.

This is where I make money to support my husband in financial expenses in the family but for three days now, I am unable to do that because of the strike. My husband is a civil servant working at the Lagos State Ministry of Works. I don't know why it has to take this long and yet the government has refused to listen to the people. Though I heard it on the news that the Senate President, David Mark is in talks with officials of the NLC but how long will that take before the masses stop suffering," she said.

He also accused government of planting the story in the media to divert attention from the actual issue of the removal of subsidy.

Lakemfa explained that Labour leaders across the country were currently busy mobilising workers for the industrial action.

The statement read in part: "This is an absolute falsehood. Labour leaders are busy mobilising for the indefinite strike action and mass protests, which commence on Monday January 9th 2012, and have no time for frivolous, unsustainable and unproductive 'dialogue' with the Presidency or any of its Dialogue Committees.

"We see these stories of 'meetings' with the Federal Government as mischievous and part of government's strategy to break the fuel hike protest." Lakemfa stressed that the Labour movement was not interested in any kind of meeting with government officials until the prices of petrol was reverted to the N65 per litre.

He added: "we call on workers and the Nigerian people to ignore all such stories and remain focused and committed to participating actively in the general strikes, mass rallies and street protests starting on Monday January 9th, 2012."

The NLC also faulted government's claim of importing 1,600 buses, saying the buses were being imported by the Trade Union Congress (TUC) through a loan obtained from the Urban Development Bank of Nigeria.

It posited that the imported buses would still be inadequate as only two would be available for each local council.The NLC added: "One would have thought that the Presidency would put these 'cushioning effects' in place before the unreasonable hike in petrol price."

But, the Financial Controller of the Calabar-based Niger Mills Company, Ogban Ekpei, yesterday in Calabar, Cross River, charged labour unions in the country to prudent utilisation of proceeds from the subsidy on infrastructure development so as to bring down commodity prices and reduce the sufferings of Nigerians.

He said: "I agree that the removal of subsidy in one fell swoop affects Nigerians nega-tively. Maybe it should have been done in phases 'but I do not see government going back on its position. It has been done, it nas been done. I do not see the strike as a solution to the problem.'

"I think Labour should instead emphasise the use of gains from the subsidy on provision of infrastructure. If the savings are invested in infrastructure, and manufacturers produce at reduced costs, then the effects of the subsidy removal would be countered by low cost of production."

Meanwhile, fresh violence erupted in Ilorin, Kwara State capital yesterday, as the oil subsidy protest, continued. According to sources, butchers in the town counting their losses during the earlier protests, had allegedly resolved to shun the abattoirs at Ipata Market and cattle ranch at Sango area of the town until when they would have exhausted their stock.

As we go on strike

By Olukayode Oguta

***ThisDay*, Wednesday, January 11, 2012, vol.16, no.6106, pg. 39**

I have watched with amazement the ongoing debate about fuel subsidy and the reactions of people. Social media is involved and hot, I am happy that the populace has taken a position to mimic the events that swept the Arab world recently, but my fear is that would the change that occurred in the Arab spring also happen in Nigeria. Can Nigerians fight for six months to effect a change?

I need to remind you that labour union that has called this strike does have positive integrity in Nigeria. I remember the events of the June 12 crisis and the role that the labour leaders especially Pascal Bafyau played to scuttle the popular uprising by the citizenry, thereby giving us five years of draconian rule by the late Sani Abacha- events that wouldn't have happened if the labour leaders didn't fail the uprising. I am also concerned about the role of double speaks like Femi Falana, who kept silent when the people of Lekki Peninsula were fighting the illegal toll gates at Tinubu's admiralty hotel doorstep (ACN), virtually kept silent in this- (politicians are united in corruption). The question is what really is the issue at hand? How can this be sorted out? What should be the goals of the resistance movements? What should we do that we didn't do before?

The issue of the removal of oil subsidy is simply the failure of governance in Nigeria. The arguments made by the government ministers are one that says we have given up the fight- citizens bear the costs. It's a shame that the government would advance an argument that there are few people monopolizing the subsidy and that we cant face them and so we give up. But a critical look at the issue is that the last thirteen years, no single achievement can be tied to the Federal Government despite the huge revenues that has accrued to them in the period.

The Federal Government that has been led by at least three different men in this period have combined together to give a genius status to a man, Gideon Orkar called barely literate person. We have the results of the Petroleum Trust Funds (PTF) still available but not federal government. A lot of the pharmaceutical companies are competing because of what PTF did, what has the government done? It's a shame that despite his failings, Nigeria seems to prefer a Sani Abacha to a PhD holder, the ironies of a potentially great country called Nigeria.

I once sat down with a federal minister who happens to share my faith, so I asked him why he and his colleagues couldn't make a difference, for the citizen's. This guy had a first class in school, was trained in one of the world's best consulting firm so knows strategy and change management, his response is one that shocked me, he blamed not politicians but the civil service as a cesspool of endemic corruption, that change was so difficult it needed structural reorganization, it was virtually impossible for them. In all the analysis, nobody is talking about the civil service, we have only faced the politicians, hence my fear. With deep apologies, any known saint would be stained in governance, (No wonder the late Alex Ibru advised Reuben Abati to refuse his appointment) hence the need to understand the forces involved and fight this time once and for all.

Why do we have 73% of revenue spent on recurrent expenditure? Why does the presidential wing have 11 aircrafts? Are we asking why government is budgeting ₦3m daily for feeding for the president and his vice? Is it that they would be feasting everyday for one year and still have capacity to govern? Why do ministers have 20 cars in their convoys? Why does the senate president who takes a pension of at least four hundred thousand monthly as an ex-general, take home 600 million yearly? Can we trust wasters with savings? Has any one asked a single road project that has been successfully completed in 13 years and they all have road completion certificates? Are we going to continue with "patch-patch" projects? No one has asked that despite the falling price of crude oil in the international market and a global recession that Nigeria wasn't immune to, that subsidy jumped from 300 million to 1.3 trillion? No questions asked? Why do we think the government is giving up? It's only the citizens that they can face. They have given up on the rest? Have we asked why there are over 34,000 Nigerians (paying an average sum of 10,000 pounds translated to 85 billion naira yearly) in UK universities studying despite huge allocations to federal universities? Has anybody asked why Emirates and Qatar airlines operates three flights out of Nigeria daily and are full with a large percentage going to India for medical treatment?

The answer is very simple - until we face the politicians, (both executive and the legislature), and the civil service, we are not going to get anything resolved. Let's not let labour be the final arbiter of the demands we are making. We sure need them, but they must work with the civil groups in unison. We must make our demands very clear otherwise we are going to have palliatives that would postpone the day of reckoning. We need an intervention in governance. Let the labour union for once shut down the economy, and let's negotiate to have an economic emergency in place.

During this period, the civil service would be limited to regulation, salaries and allowances of politicians be capped to the highest paid civil servant, and the intervention committee can intervene in education, health, agriculture and power. Trust me, only with that would you see a change in the country. The funds that have accrued can be used to promote clusters of industries, so that not only tiw industry but also supporting industries would work. With the liberalization of the telecom industries, there were also service providers that were also birth. We need to create clusters of industries in education (Canada, Britain, the US and even Ghana would stop treating your citizens with disdain), health (why not all the sick people in Western Africa coming to Nigeria?), Agriculture (what are we doing to our land - from the swamps of Bayelsa that can surely feed the entire country in rice to the deserts of the North - that can handle our dietary needs), tourism, the petroleum industry and in power; then and only then would we see a change? Once this change comes, elite Nigerians running to fan ethnic and religious tension to fight for power and divide the people would be shamed.

We need an economic emergency like that of PTF (it was the civil servants that found a willing ally in Gen Obasanjo to end the programme they weren't benefiting from it) but with wider scope so that we can get out of this woods-otherwise, surely Libya would be a child's play. Oguta writes from Lagos

At A Time Like This…

By 'Lola Adewoyin.

***ThisDay*, Friday, January 13, 2012, vol. 16, no. 6108, pg. 19**

There is time for everything under the sun, so says one of the good books. The period Nigerians are passing through at the moment is not the best of times. To say the New Year started on an unpleasant note may not be too far from the truth. What with the sky-rocketing prices of goods, services and other essential services that trailed the removal of subsidy on petrol which caught most unaware and made life unbearable to many. Most Nigerians who travelled to various parts of the country for the yuletide are stranded, and have become a bore to their hitherto elated hosts, because they have overstayed their welcome. At times like this, one needs to have sober reflection and figure out what the right step should be in the quest to minimise the effect of the current crisis and make the situation as bearable as possible.

Folks, getting angry alone will not solve the problem, instead, get angry, yes, but think outside the box and devise a means of surviving the effects of the strike. Know that most of those with whom you jump and shout have been wise enough to devise a means of survival so that they can live to fight another day.

Since the beginning of the strike called by the labour and civil society organisations, the hardship faced by the masses has become manifold. It is a known fact that before the subsidy removal crisis, most Nigerians have been living from hand to mouth, with most living by the day. Therefore, with the crisis reaching almost a week now, whatever had been saved in preparation for the crisis must have been exhausted by now.

As the saying goes in Yoruba, *agbajo owo ni a fi n so aya*, meaning, united we stand, an individual cannot opt out of the strike called by labour, but a wise individual could devise his or her own means of survival so that the negative effect of the strike will be minimally felt.

Some Nigerians have devised their own means of survival and they shared this with *ThisDay*.

Catherine Afegbua is a nurse. She lives in Abule-Egba, a suburb of Lagos, while her place of work is in Oshodi. Because she provides essential service, she has to be at her duty post whether there is strike or not. On a good day, she resumes by 9a.m. and closes by 6p.m., therefore, she leaves home by 7:30a.m; but the ongoing strike has changed her normal routine.

To get to work since the strike started, Kate, as she is fondly called leaves home by 5:30, because by 7:30, there would be no vehicle on the road to convey her to her destination and she gets to the office on a good time to enable the night nurse have enough time to get home before the strike starts. Kate said, "With fewer jobs available, I have to devise the means of keeping mine as well as prove to my co-workers that I am responsible and that I am not selfish. When I leave home by 5:30am, with fewer vehicle on the road, I get to work latest by 6a.m and so the night nurse has enough time to get to her own house and rest well enough to come back in the night. "By this, the hospital owner is not put under any unnecessary stress, he is rest assured that competent hands are on hand to take care of the patients and there is no unnecessary pressure on any member of staff, with everyone aware that if some could find their ways to the office, others should be able to do so too. Although it is not easy, but with the hope that the sacrifice will be temporary, I am ready to bear it for as long as it takes," she said.

Mrs. Funke Ajibose, owner of Faith Healing Home in Sango Ota, Ogun State, said "as the date for the commencement of the strike was approaching, she held a meeting with her staff on their coping strategy and some of the nurses whose homes are far from the clinic were implored to take a few things they'll need and move over to the hospital. Some of them obliged, although not without some compromise on our parts."

She said with the arrangement, patients in the home are not in danger of not being taken care of, in fact, the arrangement has been lauded by some of the patients who have their favourite nurses attend to them round the clock, because they are always on hand.

Another Nigerian, a career woman who doesn't want her name in print, said before the commencement of the strike, she had thought that at the end of the second day, the zeal would have waned and so, did not really prepare fully for a long stay at home. She said on the discovery that it would run for almost one week, she knew that in the evenings, the agitation would have mellowed down, so she went to the nearest ATM and withdrew some money with which she went to the market and get some of the things that had been exhausted. She said she is happy that the strike had inadvertently given her time to relax with her family, with enough opportunity to shake off the stress that had accumulated over a period of time.

She said since she discovered that markets open in the evenings, she goes out to replenish most of the essential commodities that have been exhausted and so the struggle continues. She said her husband goes out in the morning to join the protest and returns home in the evening by which time she would have gone to the market and return home to prepare the evening meal.

For 24-year-old James Adigun, his day starts by 6a.m when he leaves home to join other protesters at a designated point. He said himself and other colleagues have taken it upon themselves to educate some of the protesters not to resort to violence, because whoever property is destroyed is also a Nigerian who is also feeling the pinch of the subsidy removal. Adigun said his team are of the opinion that after the protests, stakeholders are still going to meet at a round table and talk the country out of the problem and so whatever anybody could do to make the protest peaceful should be done, so that the bitterness will not be too unbearable when everything has been resolved.

Asked about how he is coping with the strike, he said being self-employed, he returns in good time after the protest to open his office and display his wares. He said he has taken care of the lost times by extending his closing time, which instead of 6p.m., he closes by 10p.m, so that at the end of the time, nothing is lost in terms of revenue as his patrons by the second day, have become aware that he now opens shop in the evenings.

Talk about the survival of the fittest and don't forget to add that where fools die as a result of lack of knowledge, the wise will definitely survive, no matter the odds.

Beyond Labour's Strike: What next?

By Linda Eroke

***ThisDay*, Tuesday, January 24, 2012, vol. 77, no. 6119, pg. 36**

Not a few individuals and groups have expressed displeasure over the decision by the organised labour to suspend the nationwide strike and mass protests against the removal of fuel subsidy by the Federal Government.

Expectedly, many feel let down by the unions for agreeing to call off the strike without the subsidy being fully restored. They believed that the leaders of the Nigeria Labour Congress (NLC) and Trade Union Congress of Nigeria (TUC) - the organisers of the strike and mass protest - may have compromised the interest of the Nigerian masses in a bid to satisfy their own selfish interest.

They have continued to ask why the organised labour should at a time vhen the mass action was getting more intense suddenly suspend the strike; contrary to its initial demand for a reversal of fuel price to ₦65 per litre.

Their scepticism is understandable, given the high level of expectations from the labour leaders who many Nigerians look up to as defender of the rights of the masses. Unfortunately, the labour leaders were not prepared for a long-drawn battle as an indefinite strike ultimately poses the question of power, of who runs the country.

The joint labour and civil society team had been subjected to psychological warfare, and were constantly harassed by government and its agencies while the strike lasted.

Labour's Stance on Suspension

After series of meeting with the government and its representatives, the organised labour and its civil society allies bowed to pressure from government and suspended the weeklong strike and mass protest which had paralysed both economic and commercial activities across the country.

The suspension of the strike was jointly announced by the NLC and TUC hours after President Goodluck Jonathan reversed the price of fuel to ₦97 per litre last during a nationwide broadcast, though labour claimed that the new pump price was a unilateral decision by government.

NLC President, Comrade Abdulwaheed Omar and his TUC counterpart, Comrade Esele, in a statement said the decision to suspend the strike was taken after due consideration of the President's intervention, at which he cited security issues and willingness to tackle the cabal with Economic and Financial Crimes Commission (EFCC) and review the hard stance on timing and modality for deregulation.

Against popular belief, the labour leaders had explained that the decision to suspend the strike was taken in the interest of the overall economy as they view the suspension as an interim option to save lives and the few organisations from being destroyed. They were told that the security situation had deteriorated and that troops will have to be deployed.

They however hinged the success of the strike to efforts made to get government adopt the policy to drastically reduce the cost of governance, address accountability issues and current lapses in the oil sector, as well as ensure the speedy passage of the Petroleum Industry Bill (PIB).

"We note the major successes Nigerians scored in these past days in which they rose courageously as a people to take their destiny in their hands. First, the Federal Government that chorused continuously that its decision to increase petrol (PMS) price to ₦141 is irreversible and irreducible, was forced to announce a price reduction to ₦97. We however state categorically that this new price was a unilateral one by the Government.

"Secondly, Government has been made to adopt the policy to drastically reduce the cost of governance. A third major success Nigerians recorded was to get the Federal Government to decisively move against the massive and crippling corruption in the oil sector.

"While until now Government has seemed helpless to tackle corruption, the mass action of the people has compelled it to address accountability issues in the sector. In this wise, President Goodluck Jonathan has told the nation that the forensic audit report on the NftPC will be studied and proven acts of corruption will be sanctioned.

"He also promised that accountability issues and current lapses in the oil sector will be speedily addressed including the passage of the Petroleum Industry Bill (PIB). A related success of the mass action by Nigerians is the vow of Government to bring to justice all those who have contributed in one way or another to the economic adversity of the country. In view of the foregoing, Labour and its allies formally announce the suspension of strikes, mass rallies and protests across the country," the statement explained.

Opposition against Labour's Action

However, stakeholders have continued to react to the suspension of the mass action by Labour. Some have agreed that the action by the NLC and TUC is not so much about compromise, which is not unconnected, but that the trade union centres lack the programme, strategy and tactics to sustain the struggle, let alone win the struggle.

Others have commended Labour for the peaceful conduct and its doggedness during the strike. They are of the view that the gains from the protest outweighed the grievances people may have against the action of the labour leaders.

Those who have strongly opposed the suspension of the strike include the Joint Action Front (JAF) umbrella body for pro-labour md civil society groups in the country which described the action of labour leaders as a betrayal of the legitimate demand by Nigerians. The group rejected the ₦97 fuel price and described it as imposition which fell short of ₦65 being demanded by Nigerians.

In like manner, the Democratic Socialist Movement (DSM) also faulted labour's decision to suspend the strike stating that the action underscores the deep-seated illusion of the Labour leaders of influencing the capitalist government to act in the interests of working people.

According to the group, while labour leaders want Nigerians to believe that the new price was a unilateral decision of the government, the sequence of events in the 24 hours before the strike was suspended, as well as the statement jointly issued by the two trade union federations calling off the strike, indicates that they had made a rotten deal with the government.

It maintained that if Labour had offered a clear lead, the struggle could not only have forced back the price hike but also laid the basis for a complete transformation of the country.

Also, the Campaign for Democratic Workers' Right (CDWR) maintained that the decision to suspend the strike was unilaterally taken by the NLC and TUC, noting that civil society organisations which played a major role in the struggle were never consulted before the decision was taken.

The group, in a statement by its Publicity Secretary, Chinedu Bosah, maintained that the announcement by the TUC and NLC respectively, to the effect that they consulted with pro-people organisations/civil society organisations before agreeing to suspend the strike, was a lie.

"The suspension of the strike by the NLC, apparently agreeing to the ₦97 per litre when the working masses are still struggling for reversal to ₦65 per litre of fuel is a betrayal. It has shown that the labour leaders, with a historical mandate to lead the suffering working masses of the country out of misery, oppression and dictatorship, is shying away from this responsibility.

"This is simply because they do not have an alternative socio-eco-nomic and political agenda different from neo-liberal capitalist policies. That explains why the labour leaders are in strategic partnership with the ruling elite," it explained.

Also rejecting the new pump price, Save Nigeria Group (SNG) Convener, Pastor Tunde Bakare, faulted the decision of labour to unilaterally accept the new fuel price.

Bakare, in a statement said: "We have equally reviewed the broadcast of President Goodluck Jonathan where he unilaterally offered to reduce the pump price of petrol to ₦97 per litre. This tokenism shows that the display of people power in the last few days has not been in vain but it is far little to be acceptable.

"We demand a reversal to the pre-Jan 1 pump price of ₦65 per litre as a basis for a conducive atmosphere for a national conversation on the oil sector and how to deal with the corruption that has brought this needless crisis on the seventh largest producer of crude oil in the world that has been made to depend on import for it's refined product consumption," he added.

Also, the Campaign for Democracy (CD) expressed disappointment over labour's suspension of the strike. In a statement by its President, Dr Joe Okei-

Odumakin, CD said, "By suspending the strike, labour has dealt the hopes and aspirations of Nigerians for affordable fuel, and the movement for accountable and corruption-free governance, a huge blow."

Stakeholders' Commendation

Despite the criticisms among some stakeholders, the last general strike and mass protest has been described as quite historic and unprecedented in the history of the nation.

Firstly, it was the first time that the labour and its civil society allies have sustained a general strike for a whole week; secondly, it was the first time the country had experienced a truly nationwide mass action with mass protests taking place right across the country in more than 50 cities and town, which was sustained for over a week.

While analysts acknowledged that some gains had been made in the weeklong struggle, it is a known fact that the people's resistance had compelled the Federal Government to amend its stance that "there is no going back on the ₦141."

As a process too, the Occupy Nigeria protests did a lot to cement national unity, rebuild trust among Nigerians, and contributed more in seven days of joint action on the streets to nation building than government policies have contributed in the last 10 years.

Among the most active participants in the protests were youths and students who in places like Lagos organised street protests and rallies at their own expense.

Indeed, it will not be out of place to state that the one week general strike and the mass protests were the biggest movements of such scale so far in the history of Nigeria. The strike was total even in Northern parts of the country where state of emergencies had been declared as a result of the state of insecurity created by Boko Haram's terroristic activities.

According to the Financial Times, the protests have emboldened ordinary Nigerians and raised new awareness of wasteful expenditure.

Also, the Nigerian Bar Association (NBA) has aligned with organised labour's decision to suspend the strike in the hope that normalcy in the nation's economy, which the suspension will engender, will pave way for genuine negotiations on the issue.

Similarly, the Nigeria Employers' Consultative Association (NECA) commended Labour for yielding to its call to suspend the strike and dialogue with the Belgore Committee to deliberate and identify further palliative'measures that will cushion the impact of the policy on the citizenry.

Director General of the Nigeria Fmployers' Consultative Association (NECA), Dr. Segun Oshinowo, maintained that national strike or protest cannot effectively resolve the issues on ground.

According to him, the strike and mass protest called by labour and the civil society group had already disrupted economic activities in the country, with the economy losing a staggering ₦794.5 billion in the last five working days on account of the strike.

Speaking in defence of the organised labour, the Assistant General Secretary of the NLC, Comrade Denja Yaqub, argued that, contrary to the popular belief, labour leaders did not in any way compromise the interest of Nigerians but were blackmailed by government.

He urged Nigerians not to lose hope as the ₦97 announced by Jonathan was not the outcome of negotiations with labour. He hinted that the NLC and TUC are resuming negotiations to actualise the demand for the return of petrol pump price to N65.

"I want to remind us all that the trade unions in Nigeria are entities created by law and operate strictly, for now, within the operational guides of industrial relations. Under this premise, the unions make demands, which are presented before employers/government; they go into negotiations, and when negotiations fail, the unions proceed on strike. That is the tradition imposed by law on the unions. Here in Nigeria, the unions have tried several times to break out of this legal bondage and on each occasion, the state blackmails them.

"In this recent case, the demand by the unions was just on fuel price increase, and nothing more. And as the strike progressed, the unions were called for dialogue and presented with different price options but the leaderships of both the NLC and TUC consistently said No, government must return to ₦65 per litre before any negotiation.

"That was praiseworthy and they stood on this point, until the blackmail that the strike has been hijacked by some people for political advantage. The unions certainly faced a strong handicap on this because, for the unions to advance further, they need a strong movement of strongly visioned civil society activists, under one strong national platform that can keep cany on, as massively as possible on all other demands that are unrelated to labour's demands," he said.

Way Forward

The strike and mass protest have come and gone, however lessons must be learnt by all the groups that have actively participated in the mass action. There is therefore need for labour to strengthen its partnership with other civil society groups in order to build a strong movement of visionary civil society activists, under one strong national platform that can keep on with the struggle.

Denja, who clearly identified the need to build a strong movement that would be able to speak with one voice, said the platform was absent in Nigeria.

According to him, each time attempts were made to build one, it doesn't work because a lot of people, though very angry at the situation in Nigeria, lack organisational discipline to survive within such movements.

"Everyone wants his own organisation. Everyone wants his own platform. Everyone wants his own protests. Everyone wants his own street. And that way, we will lose the much needed common voice. We will lose the common purpose. And that's the problem. No rev-olution has ever succeeded under such circumstances," he said.

He maintained that the formation of the Labour and Civil Society Coalition (LASCO) with three constituents - NLC, TUC, and the JAF, has not fully grown to maturity, even though no one would be willing to wait until then before challenging oppression.

Court stops NLC, TUC from going ahead with strike.

By Ibe Uwaleke, Godwin Ijediogor, Lemmy Ughegbe and Collins Olayinka

***The Guardian*, Saturday, January 7, 2012, pg.1, 2**

THE National Industrial Court (NIC) yesterday issued an interim order restraining the Nigeria Labour Congress (NLC) and the Trade Union Congress (TUC) from embarking on a nationwide strike next Monday in protest of the withdrawal of fuel subsidy.

Meanwhile, the NLC and TUC have faulted the injunctions, insisting on the planned strike on Monday. In Abuja yesterday, apparently to drum support for the removal of the fuel subsidy, some besieged the Labour House headquarters of the NLC, which the union described as invasion sponsored by government.

In his reaction, the former President of the Nigerian Bar Association (NBA), Mr. Olisa Agbakoba Agbakoba, (SAN) said he was just studying the order, which is subject to several interpretations. He however said that the order was made against the Nigerian Labour Congress (NLC) and the Trade Union Congress (TUC) and not the Nigerian Bar Association (NBA) or other human rights groups and associations.

When asked if it would not be proper for NLC and TUC to suspend the Monday strike in obedience ot the court order and in the spirit of the rule of law, Agbakoba answered that 'it would be the ideal thing to do if only government can use the period of suspension of the strike iron out the very issues it supposed have addressed before announcing the removal of the fuel subsidy.

President of the court (NIC), Justice Babaamde Adejumo made the order following an expaite application brought on behalf government by the Attorney General of the Federation (AGF), Mohammed Bello Adoke (SAN) praying the court to restrain NLC and TUC from embarking on the mass protest / strike action.

In his ruling, Adejumo granted an order restraining the defendants from embarking or inciting the general public to embark on general strikes, street protests, mass rallies or any other action that would be inimical to the economic affairs of the Federal Republic of Nigeria pending the determination of the motion on Notice. The court therefore adjourned till January 12 for hearing of the motion on notice. It also granted an order of substituted service of the process on the respondent through national dailies.

The claimant had through their counsel, Fabian Ajogwu (SAN) prayed the court for an order restraining the defendants from embarking or compelling other persons to embark on a strike action or general strikes, mass rallies and street protest across Nigeria pending the determination of the Motion on Notice.

It further prayed for an order restraining the defendants from interfering with the exercise of the constitutional powers of the executive arm of the Federal Government of Nigeria in the allocation and use of scarce resources of the Federal

Republic of Nigeria, including but not limited to the transfer of resources previously allocatedto the subsidy of premium motor spirit among others for the medium and longterm socio-economic benefit of present and future generations or Nigerians.

Also, the claimant wants an order restraining the defendants from interfering in any way with the executive implementation of the 2012 Appropriation Act and other connected duties of the Executive Arm of the Federal Government of Nigeria in the management of the economic affairs of the Federal Republic of Nigeria.

The Federal Government also wants the court to restrain the defendants from embarking and/or inciting the Nigerian citizenry and the general public to embark on general strikes, street protests, mass rallies or any other action that would be inimical to the economic affairs of the Federal Republic of Nigeria pending the determination of the Motion on Notice. Moreover, the claimant wants an order granting leave to the claimant to serve the respondents with the originating processes in the matter vide substituted means.

In a 30-paragraph affidavit of urgency deposed to by one Yusuf Mok, a counsel in the office of the Attorney General of the Federation AGF averred that the removal of subsidy is not a dispute of right of the defendants or their members adding that the defendants did not also raise any dispute arising from a collective and the application is granted, the respondents have nothing to lose stating that the claimant has everything to lose if the prayer is not granted. He added that if the prayer were not allowed, it would affect the nation adding that it will be in the interest and stability of the country if the prayer is granted. He there prayed the court to grant the application.

TUC president general, Peter Esele, after much pressure, said: "Is the court telling us that we don't have the right to withdraw their services.

"Under the Nigeria Constitution, that right is guaranteed and if Nigerian workers are unanimous in withdrawing their services, I don't see anybody questioning that right."

NLC, in a press statement signed by its Acting General Secretary, Owei Lakemfa, urged Nigerians to ignore the injunction.

The statement read: "The NLC is not aware of any such injunction, we were not served any paper of court appearance. We were not present in court, nor were we represented in any capacity.

"Also, the NLC was not served any court summons, nor were we served any court order.

"The cretins in the administration imagine that by seeking to drag the judiciary in the mud, they can avert the general strikes, rallies and mass protests that will begin on Monday, January.

"They cannot make the simple analysis that the whole populace is angry and that Nigerians do not need any group to ask them to protest an evil policy that seeks to impoverish them."

It added: "The NLC asks Nigerians to ignore this ploy and rumour;

Crowds increase as protest enters day 4

By *ThisDay* Correspondentsl

***ThisDay*, Thursday, January 12, 2012, vol.16, no. 6107, pg. 7**

The ongoing strike called by the Nigeria Labour Congress (NIX) and the Trade Union Congress (TUC) to protest the removal of fuel subsidy by the Federal Government was bolstered yesterday by large crowds in some states and the Federal Capital Territory (FCT), Abuja. The protesters marched through the popular Nnamdi Azikiwe Express Way and converged on Area 1, Garki Junction.

Buoyed by the mammoth crowd, some of the key figures of the struggle warned the Federal Government to heed the voice of reason and reverse its decision on fuel subsidy. Speaking at the venue, the Country Director; ActionAid in Nigeria, Dr. Hussaini Abdu, echoed the message that they would not give up until the government reverts to the status quo.

However, both human and vehicular traffic also increased in most parts of the city at Zuba, Kubwa, Gwarimpa, Mabushi, Jabi and Beiger areas.

In Kano, two top Kano politicians, Gen. Lawal Jafaru Isa and the immediate past Deputy Governor of the state, Abdullahi Tijjani Muhammad Gwarzo, joined a mammoth crowd at the historic Groundnut Pyramid venue of yesterday's rally to protest in the state.

The Federal Government Secretariat along Katsina Road remained locked, while other government establishments complied with labour's appeal for them to stay away from duty.

But in a spirited move to shore up support for President Goodluck Jonathan, a non-government organisation, Ijaw Youth Congress (IYC), organised a rally at the Samson Siasia Sport Complex Yenagoa, Bayelsa State, and marched to the secretariat of the Nigeria Union of Journalists (NUJ).

The IYC asked labour leaders in the state to prevail on the national leadership of the NLC and TUC to negotiate with the Federal Government on palliatives and stop the wanton destruction of lives and properties in the country.

While Kaduna State Governor Patrick Yakowa equally accused those he called "overzealous elements" for cajoling underage children in Kaduna metropolis to hijack the protest against the removal of fuel subsidy.

In a broadcast to the citizens of the state, Yakowa said it was unfortunate that the good intentions of the labour unions regarding the removal of fuel subsidy were taken over by those with a hidden agenda.

In Oyo State, the anger against the removal of fuel subsidy in Ibadan has deepened with the take-over of several flash points in the mass rally by miscreants.

The organised labour and civil rights groups however continued their march on Ibadan streets with a rally at Idi-Odo Challenge, where speakers after another urged the people of the state to be united in their opposition to the subsidy removal.

But Ogun State Governor, Senator Ibikunle Amosun, has advised youths to eschew violence while expressing their grievances against the removal of fuel subsidy.

He said: "If you burn tyres on the road, the road will be destroyed and government will have to use your money to repair them again."

His Imo State counterpart, Rochas Okorocha, insisted that the people of the state would strengthen their doggedness and entrepreneurship to survive the pains of the hike in fuel price occasioned by the fuel subsidy removal.

He said this while addressing commercial transport operators, bus and taxi drivers at the Hero's Square, New Owerri yesterday.

The development in Delta State was different as hoodlums infiltrated the procession of protesters by running ahead of the procession to harass unsuspecting passersby and dis-possessing some people of their GSM handsets and other valuables. At least four of the hoodlums were arrested by security personnel on patrol along the Warri-Effurun-Sapele Road after they were caught by the mob and were about to be lynched.

Although, government and many private offices, schools as well as numerous business outlets remained under lock and key, human and vehicular traffic had generally increased steadily in Warn and adjoining areas like Effurun, Udu, Sapele and Okpe.

Protesters in some locations in Ado-Ekiti, Ekiti State resorted to extorting money from members of the public. But the protest attracted more participation of the people than the previous days, just as more barricades were erected and more bonfires made as the protesters trooped out in large numbers.

In Edo State, Governor Adams Oshiomhole vowed to deal with politicians and criminals who hide under the guise of the removal of fuel subsidy to foment trouble in the state.

Oshiomhole issued the threat when he addressed the Arewa community at Aduwawa, Eyean and Esigie in Benin City yesterday. Reacting to the violent protests and attacks on some innocent people in the state capital, Governor Oshiomhole said: "You don't have to be afraid. We are ready to deal with any criminal. Anybody who is planning to foment trouble will be dealt with squarely, because politicians have hijacked this protest. They want to create problems."

Reports from Enugu State indicate that members of organised labour and civil society organisations who attempted to protest clashed with the police at the entrance of the state secretariat of the NLC.

In Abia State, organised labour was thrown into disarray following an attempt by the state chairman of the NLC, Comrade Sylvanus Eye, to call off the planned rally against the removal of fuel subsidy. He managed to escape being lynched by irate workers who accused him of selling out to government. Eye had on Tuesday after a series of meetings with leaders of trade unions and market unions in the state announced that the rally would hold on the third day of the national strike but when the workers assembled at the Urban Primary School along School Road Umuahia the labour leader changed tune.

A number of patients at the Braithwaite Memorial Hospital (BMH), Port Harcourt, owned by the Rivers State Government, were discharged from the hospital just as the Emergency, Casualty and Labour wards of the hospital were shut. *ThisDay* gathered that the entrance to the hospital was locked as the state chapter of the TUC and the NLC directed all their affiliates in the state to continue to enforce the strike and monitor compliance.

Protesters in Kwara State have vowed to press on with their action until the Federal Government reverts to the ₦65 per litre.

And workers in Sokoto State remained at home yesterday, despite the threat by the Federal Government to implement its 'no work, no pay' policy on its workforce. *ThisDay* checks in the Sokoto metropolis revealed that virtually all public and private offices were closed.

However, the protest in Lokoja, Kogi State turned violent as protesters clashed with the police, leaving a boy and a police officer badly injured. Trouble started when tribal sentiment was introduced with some of the protesters alleging that Igbo traders were beginning to open and operate their shops at the detriment of the indigenes that kept on with the protest.

Did labour buckle under the weight of executive?

By Tunde Rahman.

***ThisDay*, Saturday, January 21, 2012, vol. 16, no. 6116, pg. 15**

Since labour suspended its five and a half days industrial action against the removal of fuel subsidy by the federal government some Nigerians have dressed NLC and TUC officials in all kinds of garbs. The suspension of the strike was greeted with shock and disbelief. Labour officials were openly lambasted by some Nigerians, some of who insists that labour had compromised. Some others simply called the officials sell-outs.

Labour's case was not helped by the appointment of the TUC President Peter Esele as a member of the government's committee to work towards a quick passage of the long-winding Petroleum Industry Bill. Some conveniently forgot that Esele is a former PENGASSAN president, works with an oil company and has a remarkable understanding of the oil and gas sector. In dealing with all of these, let us step back and recall how the protest started and the way and manner it was called off.

Recall that it was the civil society group that first began the protest against the removal of fuel subsidy before labour officially called out Nigerians to commence the strike and street protest penultimate Monday. So by the time Nigerians fully began the strike in response to the call oflabour, civil society groups had virtually taken the centre stage in the protest, directing affairs, dictating the pace particularly in Lagos, and the intensity was growing. Lagos, Eko for show, added a new high to protests. There was intense entertainment. Popular musicians and Nollywood artistes were falling heads over heels to be part of the protest at the Gani Fawehmmi Park, now Freedom Park. There were fiery speeches particularly by members of the Save Nigeria Groups led by Pastor Tunde Bakare, some or them calling for regime change.

The government in Abuja was getting restive. There was panic at Aso Rock But it was the organized labour that government recognized and that it negotiated with, it indeed there was anything called negotiation. Government's plan was to conveniently take out labour and ostracize it from the civil society groups (and I think it worked), before the strike was eventually suspended, government was in discussions with labour. Before labour eventually called off the strike last Monday, you would recall that it had in the early nours of that day first suspended the street protest ostensibly because information got to it that government would deploy soldiers to quell the protest in areas where it was taking place particularly in Lagos. The civil society groups were peeved by labour's suspension of the strike. This should be understandable. But whereas civil society groups are always rigid and uncompromising members of the civil society forgot that in trade negotiations, labour often shift grounds. In most of the negotiations with government over fuel price increase, labour often take a flexible approach, they were never hell bent on the old price. They always moved no matter how small. The problem in the extant situation though is labour, perhaps buoyed by the civil society groups, failed to snift ground. At another round of talks with government last Saturday, labour stood oy ₦65 per litre; it said it had no mandate to discuss a new price. Labour failed to have a new bargaining price which it would force on government. However, when it eventually buckled, labour made the point that the new price was government's unilateral decision and that it was not a negotiated price.

Did labour buckle under the weight of the executive? Did labour cave in underpressure? Did it lose the steam when it mattered most? I doubt it. I think after it had succeeded in shutting down the economy for five days and the colossal loss to the country in economic terms (some analysts estimated that we were losing between £800 million each day.

Those who think the strike by labour and civil society groups over fuel subsidy removal yielded no concrete gain given the fact the government failed to return the petrol price to ₦65 per litre have actually misjudged the situation. I think the nation, sorry the people, made giant strides with the almost six days industrial action. The gains recorded are both in general and specific terms. In general terms, the people have demonstrated their power. They have shown they can rise against an unpopular decision of government and the government has seen the wrath of the people. Never again will the people be taken for granted the way the Jonathan administration did by withdrawing fuel subsidy on New Year day with scant regard for the feelings of the people, forgetting that with subsidy removal comes astronomical rise in pump price of petrol (and its concomitant effects of of the strike), labour knew it had made its point sufficiently.

Labour had forced the bitter pill down government's throat as government had been forced to temporarily halt its' ill-timed much-trumpeted deregulation of Premium Motor Spirit. Government had been forced to partly restore the subsidy it had so brusquely and harshly removed. It moved from the ₦141 per litre it had imposed on us all with the sudden removal of the subsidy to ₦97 per litre. Having done all that labour knew the game was up. More so, the protest was taking a new dimension as some politicians masquerading as members of the civil society groups were taking advantage of the crisis to make other political demands. Labour knew the protest was adorning a different toga as some people were calling for regime change. The nation which was already virtually on its' knees was now tottering at the edge of the precipice. Any attempt to move it further would have been disastrous. And the government was getting panicky and desperate. Part or the desperate moves was the deployment of troops in Lagos. Under that situation, labour had to throw in the towel. It had to make it dear that regime change was not part of its agenda. It had to take the government's bait that it continues further negotiations on fuel pricing with the Belgore Committee.

Doctor, Catholic bishops, others decry fuel subsidy removal.

***The Guardian*, Thursday, January 5, 2012, pg.4**

The opposition to the removal of subsidy on fuel swelled yesterday with medical doctors, Catholic bishops and other groups threatening to protest against the policy. In a statement jointly signed by the President, Dr. Omede Idris, and Secretary General, Dr. Bala M. Audu, doctors under the aegis of the Nigerian Medical Association (NMA) rejected "this criminal increase in the pump price of fuel in the midst of increasing unemployment, red-alert insecurity, exponential poverty, increasing ill-health and diseases, collapsed educational systems, escalating anger and frustration in the land."

The NMA said it "will join the millions of Nigerians to resist this evil. State branches and affiliates of the NMA are directed to be ever ready for directives on the next line of action. Where democracy thrives, power belongs to the people, with the elected leader's istening to the yearnings of the people. This has not been so in this country, where government rules with impunity."

The doctors said government should in the first instance curb its waste, make the refineries functional and ensure accountability with verifiable audit in petroleum sector, tackle monu-mental corruption in the downstream sector of oil and gas operations and other sectors of the economy, stop frivolous foreign trips, and use the savings from these to begin to address the palliatives in the subsidy reinvestment empowerment programme.

The Conference of Catholic Bishops in Ibadan Province comprising Oyo, Ondo, Ilorin, Ekiti and Osogbo described the government's position as inappropriate.

The Catholic priests maintained that public interest and moral implications of government's action ought to have been considered first.

In a statement made available to reporters in Ibadan and signed by Most Rev. Felix Alaba Job, the group said before removing the subsidy, the government should have addressed the problems of huge irregularities and corruption associated with the provision of petroleum products in the country.

A coalition of civil society groups yesterday urged President Goodluck Jonathan in Kaduna to immediately reverse the decision to remove oil subsidy in order to avoid political turmoil and protests by Nigerians all over the country, which may derail the nascent democracy.

The coalition, led by the Executive Director of Human Rights Monitor (HRM), Mr. Festus Okoye, met in Kaduna yesterday, during an emergency meeting, accusing President Jonathan that after failure to deal with the massive corruption in government and bring to book the cabals that have held the nation hostage, he decided to embark on the removal of oil subsidy to further inflict hardship on the people and subject the economy to collapse.

The senator representing Ekiti North Senatorial District, Olubunmi Adetumbi, has said that the sudden removal of the subsidy on petroleum by the Federal Government was to prevent the Senate from probing the fraud discovered in the subsidy management by the Nigerian National Petroleum Corporation (NNPC).

He said that the policy was an affront to the National Assembly that was yet to complete deliberation on the proposal. Adetumbi, who said this in a statement yesterday in Ado Ekiti, Ekiti State capital said it would be wrong on the part of President Jonathan to think that the NASS would send a representative to the Christopher Kolade-led committee set up to manage the funds from the subsidy.

OBE: Occupy Nigeria was most effective, but we need to move to next level

By Kamal TayoOropo

***The Guardian*, Sunday, January 15, 2012, pg. 56**

Mrs. Ayo Obe, lawyer and foremost human rights activist and crusader, is former president of the Civil Liberty Organisation, (CLO). She spoke with

KAMALTAYO OROPO on the role civil society groups played in the last demonstration and what the next target should be.

Are you satisfied with the role played by the civil society in the recent mass action against fuel subsidy removal?

I am very satisfied with the role the civil society has played in the crisis. The civil society groups have been able to largely articulate what the people feel under the prevailing circumstances. I think the civil society have done very well, and in particular have taken the issue beyond the mere bread and butter of the politics of doubling or tripling of the price of fuel. They have made the people to understand that this was a matter of showing that there has been no attempt by the government at curbing it's waste and corrupt practices.

There is the feeling that the civil society relied heavily on the organised Labour, without which action could not De called?

I think that is a big mistake. One could say that the civil society, having been in this position many times before, ought to have known that when the time comes Labour would compromise. But you must also understand that demonstration started in the country on January 2, immediately the increment was announced by the government, without anybody waiting for the Labour.

In fact, Labour had to come up saying it was consulting to declare a general strike. Now, you may say they always declare a general strike, out actually it is the federal government that should be going to the Labour; Labour just pulled its chest-nut out of the fire. If not for Labour, government would have had no one to even negotiate with. The government would just have to face mounting opposition from the people on the streets.

We had the protest led by the Labour movement, we had the protest led by the civil organisations, and we have the protested by the ordinary young people, who I must say, put the protest on the map.

'Occupy Nigeria' was by far the most effective platform of actually getting the people to demonstrate their opposition to the government's step. Labour called its people out too; that means government could not function as well, but what many people would agree with is that from January 2ndthe protest was well and alive. People did not return to work on the 3rd of January, it was actually when Labour came out eventually to declare the strike you find people coming out on Friday and Saturday getting ready for the strike, other-wise the demonstration would just have continued.

My trade association, the Nigeria Bar Association, had already made proposals to the federal government on how to deal with this matter.

However, I think the Jonathan-led administration is really trying to fool itself, because before the end of 2011 Jonathan had had meeting with the civil society leaders in Abuja and they told him all these things. 'You first of all lead by examples. You first of all cut your waste and expenditures'. We have all seen the budget; it's disgusting and really very annoying. In fact, I will say the parallel between this protest and the way the government was throwing money all over the place for itself is best likened to the expenses scandal you had in Great Britain when people said, 'ah na, we are paying taxes so that parliament members can renovate their dog nouses? What kind of nonsense is that?'

In the same that the fuel increment is like tax on them; we have had enough evidence on the actual cost of petrol, the government people coming brandishing Nl.2 trillion. They are simply not telling the truth to the Nigerian people. So, when you add all of that together, you will realise that the people are merely saying, 'so, you will be buying two more bullet-proof cars, you will be renovating the chalet at the Nnamdi Azikiwe Airport, Abuja. You will be doing all these things for your own comfort, telling us that they could not be cut over-night but we the people will paying for all of these over-night. We don't think so' The outrage had come by the people, not necessarily by Labour. The civil society had met with President Jonathan and we said what again are going to say to Justice Belgore that Jonathan did not hear directly himself? If Labour wants to talk to Justice Belgore, very good. But Labour should know that it would take inputs from the civil society and the National Assembly when it comes to scrutinizing the budget the Jonathan's administration presented.

You said, you had a meeting with President

Excuse me, I didn't use that phrase (Fuel Subsidy Removal); you will never see me using that phrase. Instead, I insist on using Fuel Price Increase, okay? When you said Removal of Subsidy, we would have to start debating whether, or not, there was subsidy in the first place. So, it's best if we just use a new two terms. I can say it was a tax, you may say it was a subsidy given by government to those people who should reel lucky for whatever they can get. I will call it a 'tax', which means government becomes accountable. But in real sure term it was a new fuel price increase, which was what actually what happened.

Going back to the question, I want you to elaborate more the meeting the civil society had with President Jonathan

The Civil Society had a meeting with President Jonathan in December 2011, they raised all these issues. The government was expected to show a more great deal of seriousness and urgency in cutting down waste and general expenditures of government, before asking the Nigerian people to pay out more from their pockets.

Was this meeting at the request of the federal government or that of the civil society?

I believe the Jonathan administration, which had been fiddling with the desire to increase fuel price was aware that there were series of oppositions and resentments to that plan simply because they were saying that we will increase it and then we will cushiontheeffect. The civil society position was that 'if you have any cushion, throw it down first before you throw us out of the window.'

The Jonathan-led administration tried to convince the civil society that, "you can trust us, you should believe us. If we say we are going to do something, you should believe it'.

I don't know how it went, but if you leave in Lagos, you may have seen how residents of Lekki had behaved to the issue of the road, which they can already see part of it had been built. They had also seen that the Tinubu's administration and its offshoot Fashola administration have built other roads all over Lagos, and they still say, we don't want to pay a toll tor this road that has been built and even the ones we can see are being built.' Now, the Jonathan administration cannot even say we are building roads or we have built roads. I don't think the Jonathan administration needed to be told to put in the cushion first; but that is what they told him.

People feel that moment the NLC capitulated; the whole idea 'Occupy Nigeria' protest seemed to die a natural death. Could this be a coincidence or weakness of the civil society?

I believe the problem was that Civil Society allowed NLC to use them. NLC itself actually confessed that the people were so angry after January l, but we actually stepped in to channel the anger present it from turning into something different.

Now it may be that if Government does not perform very seriously in the next few months, regardless of anything they try to do, the people will not wait for NLC and the Trade Union Congress to react.

As they say revolution is not an overnight affair; the problem would either go away or the call for revolution will still be there. And if the government doesn't remove the course, then all this nonsense of occupying Lagos with armed soldiers would end up backfiring.

You put yourself in a situation where you have made nonsense of Labour, and you will fall back to dealing with the informal sectors. And believe me, most of these people outside the organized Labour movements are young and freshly coming up and organising things. They are not the activists of yesteryears, like myself.

Government may love to delude itself that the protest was organised by people or persons who lost in the last presidential election. Was it that they didn't understand what was going on or the president is spreading rumours away from the reality of what is happening in the country or what are they mistaking the whole thing for? But looking at civil society inspired protests in the country and comparing them with what is obtainable in other countries, will you say the Nigerian attempt has met with acceptable global standard and tradition?

We don't really have a big tradition of public demonstration, but we are developing one. That is why you found people talking about the Aba Women Riot; protests about the oppressions of the colonial master. But we have internalised that mistake that a protest must be a riot to the extent that we also call it Aba Women riot. Our culture of demonstrating is not what it was.

And on top of: this, you will remember that prior to this, the biggest demonstration you might talk about in Nigeria was the one in opposition of Ibrahim Babangida annulment of the June 12 presidential election. And what happened then was that General Sani Abacha just came out and shot to death two hundred people on the streets of Lagos. The reaction then was instead putting people In arms' way; we had stay at home protest. That is you sit at home and then you strike.

We progressed a bit more when Sani Abacha was having demonstrations organised to come in as civilian president. He started organising demonstrations to pretend that people are clamouring for his installation as a civilian president.

So, civil society then said if you have a pro demonstration, then we would have a counter demonstration. That was why his 2 million-man march in Abuja was met with 5 million man march in Lagos. When we had a pro-Abacha in Ibadan, people also came out and saying, Veil, we can as well nave anti-Abacha demonstration. At that stage the government responded with bullets.

Unfortunately, by the time Abacha was ready to die, the people had ceased to be afraid of government's bullets. And that is a problem. The point is that if people seemed not to be afraid of your bullets, what else do you have or can bring out? Jonathan has decided, so far, that instead of bringing out good government and performance, he will bring out depression and oppression. Getting so uncomfortable with some mild criticism anybody in government should not feel bad about.

I know you are not too comfortable with the ₦97 fuel price regime, what do you think can still be done?

I can observe that, of course, the people are definitely not happy with ₦97 as the cost of fuel. But I think that the gain of this is that whether you call it subsidy or tax, people have recognized tnat they are paying for this government. That if, government is collecting fuel subsidy out of their (the people) pockets, they may want to see what the government is doing with the money. That budget with its ridiculous contents of furniture, cutlery, newspaper and over-priced electrical equipment. All of that should be scrutinised.

And of course, the National Assembly should not think they have escaped scrutiny, because the people are paying for all of these. Constituency Allowance and all those nonsense. You will remember that the Governor of Central Bank told us that over 25 per cent of the federal budget is expended on the National Assembly.

It was before there was the feeling that money spent on the economy was coming from oil. But people are now recognising that actually it is coming from our own pockets. They have to account for how they spend money and to me that's the biggest gain.

As far as I am concerned the Kolade's committee is an unnecessarily waste of time and resources. You have ministries and if they can't over-see the implementation of the budget, what are they doing there? If Jonathan doesn't trust his ministers why appoint them? The Kolade Committee is not the issue, but to the extent that these things need a lot of over-sight, the civil society should be there, monitoring, firstly, the budget as it is passed and secondly in preparing for next year's budget. The Civil Society should be up and bold, saying we don't want to see 25 per cent going to the National Assembly, we want to see this percentage going to education, that percentage going into health and so, so and so going to rail and so on in order for the parameters of the budget, which the National Planning ministry ought to have done a lot work on, will be clear. That, we don't have issues of people drawing budgets over the top of their heads, without any coordination. That's why we have so many missing access or of people throwing up budget just on top of their needs.

I think the Ministry of Works should be able to over-see the construction of road project. Why do we need to add Kolade to the list?

Fuel subsidy and government's new thinking

By Davidson Iriekpen

***ThisDay*, Thursday, January 26, 2012, vol. 17, no. 6121, pg 22**

As the dust of the upheavals generated by the recently strike organised by the Nigeria Labour Congress (NLC), Trade Union Congress (TUC) and the civil society organisations dies down, it is perhaps to engage in a post-mortem reflection on the outcome of the unfortunate saga with a view to extriuseful lessons.

The nationwide strike, which witnessed street protests of a disturbing kind, was primarily intended to register the workers' displeasure over the removal of subsidy on Premium Motor Spirit (PMS) otherwise known as petrol. From the pump price of ₦65 per litre, the commodity officially sold at ₦141 per litre while Nigerians in some parts of the country spent between ₦250 and ₦300 to buy a litre of petrol on account of the artificial scarcity created by marketers.

To many analysts, the deregulation of the downstream sector by any government is a positive step towards conserving national reserves, re-channelling excess funds towards infrastructural development and above all, put to work existing refineries. Such projections according to them, are also meant to attract direct foreign investments, enhance construction of new refineries, create more jobs, widen the productive sector, and help raise the value of the Naira against the Dollar and other currencies.

Convinced that it was the germane thing to do, President Goodluck Jonathan, after extensive consultations with and endorsement by the Federal Executive Council (FEC), the National Economic Advisory Council (NEAC), the Nigeria Governors' Forum (NGF), the leadership of the National Assembly, and indeed, other stakeholders, announced the removal of subsidy on petrol, January 1, 2012, through the Petroleum Products Pricing and Regulatory Agency (PPPRA).

Even though the review ought not come to many Nigerians as a surprise since it was clear, prior to that announcement, that the 2012 Budget which had already been presented to the National Assembly made no provision for subsidy, the measure triggered spiralling effect on transport fares across the country, and ignited what could go as a national fury, with many demanding immediate reversal to the status quo ante. Labour's major argument was hinged on the fact that appropriate palliatives were not yet in place, to prompt increase in fuel price.

Another is the request that all those found to have mismanaged the subsidy funds in the past be brought to book and efforts made to resuscitate Nigeria's four ailing refineries. But beyond labour's genuine protests

With the return to reason as demanded by many well-meaning Nigerians, both labour and the Federal Government finally arrived at a meeting point, resulting in the reduction of pump price from ₦141 to ₦97 per litre of petrol.

To many observers, the success or otherwise of the just suspended strike does not lie in the concession labour was able to secure from government which had to climb down from ₦141 to ₦97 per litre but the exposition of the high level corruption and sleaze that characterised the operations of the oil and gas industry in Nigeria. Following the expositions and demands of labour, government has committed itself to probing the monumental fraud unearthed in the fuel subsidy regime and sanitising the oil and gas sector to ensure probity and transparency in the management of the industry.

With this development, Nigerians are eagerly looking forward to a forensic investigation of the subsidy fraud and the entire gamut of the oil and gas sector as promised by President Jonathan and the prosecution of members of the cartel that fed fat on the nation. Indeed, the one week strike by labour and civil society groups have thrown up many issues which must be squarely tackled for Nigeria to make any headway as a nation.

The week-long protests over fuel prices has put Nigeria's government under more pressure than ever before to make good on long-unfulfilled promises to reform its inefficient and corrupt energy sector. These include the assurance to implement the KPMG audit report engineered by the Minister of Petroleum Resources, Diezani Alison-Madueke.

For many Nigerians, one issue that kept reverberating during the protests by Nigerians against the removal of fuel subsidy was the need for the Federal Government to tackle the menace of corruption headlong if the country is to ever move forward. For them, they don't understand why the Jonathan-led administration lacks the courage or political will to tackle the hydra-headed malaise that has eaten deep into the country's foundation.

Speaker after speaker who mounted the podium to speak at the various rallies held across the country either lambasted the President of lacking the courage to arrest and prosecute those who have been looting the country blind or accused it of connivance. Most of the speakers, particularly those at the Lagos rallies all adorned T-shirt with the inscription: "Kill Corruption Not Nigerians."

Even the ordinary man on the street knows that nothing works in the country because of the corruption in high places. To them, that these people still walk the length and breadth of the country displaying their ill-gotten wealth is baffling.

What really fuelled the protests was the revelation that the government spent ₦13trillion on fuel subsidy in 2011 when ₦240 billion was the actual amount budgeted for project in the 2011 Appropriation Act. The difference would have gone a long way in fixing the country's dilapidated infrastructure. And yet, nobody was told how this came to be.

Apparently sensitive to this, Jonathan and oil Minister Allison-Madueke promised prompt action in the implementation of the long-delayed reforms to the oil sector. She promised to investigate corruption in the sector and this week Nigeria's corruption watchdog on her orders launched an investigation into the subsidy system, sending agents to the state oil company and petroleum pricing regulator.

It was against this background that government directed the EFCC to review all payments made in respect of subsidies on PMS and Kerosene, and to take all necessary steps prosecute any incidence of malfeasance, fraud, over-invoicing, and related illegalities in an open and transparent manner. So far, this is ongoing.

The minister also explained how the removal of fuel subsidy by the Federal Government would help curb the widely reported incidence of corruption in the downstream sector of Nigeria's oil and gas industry. She noted that apart from providing the flexibility for re-invest-ment of key funds into the provision of critical social infrastructure, the removal of subsidy on premium motor spirit (PMS) would help erase corruption which has trailed subsidy claims and counter-claims.

According to her, it is impracticable for anybody to expect government to stop the incidence of corruption in the downstream sector which is largely due to the subsidy regime and yet expect government to do so without removing the incidence of subsidy which is the biggest incentive for corruption in the sub-sector in the first instance.

The Minister further noted that she has set up a unit within her Ministry to be headed by an independent auditor to review the KPMG and other audit reports on the Nigerian National Petroleum Corporation, NNPC, and other parastatals and to immediately begin implementation of their findings.

"We have put in place a much more robust and aggressive transformation in the regulatory agencies of the downstream sector. PPPRA and DPR are being reformed as we speak. Sweeping changes are beginning to go across them as we speak. We have done this so as to tighten the regulatory indices in the oil and gas sector," she said.

Another key lesson was the promise by the government to ensure that the Petroleum Industry Bill (PIB) is passed. This it has followed with a committee headed by Udo Udoma to fine-tune and harmonise the bill.

Many analysts believe that there is a good fate for the PIB, which would be for the benefits of all Nigerians if the bill is passed into law. In the past, the bill suffered from legislative delays and special attention from the relevant authorities to make it a reality.

The analysts believe that the bill will inject new vigour in the NNPC by reforming its opaque, octopus-like structure to create discrete units to handle essential tasks based on training, professionalism and experience such as exploration and production, regulation and research.

The bill which combines 16 different Nigerian petroleum laws like the existing legislations as the Petroleum Act 1969; the Petroleum Profits Act 1959 and the Nigerian Petroleum Corporation Act of 1977, will restructure joint ventures between the NNPC and western majors to allow them to raise private capital, rather than rely on a notoriously unreliable injection of cash from Nigerian government at the expense of the poor Nigerians who live under hard economic conditions and abject poverty.

The analysts posited that the bill will make the government to increase its stake from a growing number of deep-water developments, review of the royalties on gas by creating a new fiscal regime separate from rules governing oil, changes to the way tax breaks are applied for new developments. Even companies will be encouraged to refine at least 50 per cent of their production in Nigeria by the end of the decade, and in addition, new rules to boost employment of Nigerians in the oil industry will take effect.

One of the most frequently asked questions during the protests was why are the refineries not working in spite of the billions of naira so far expended on it? They wondered why there are no functional refineries in the country as a way out of petroleum products' importation. The government was able to listen to this. By now, the Ministry of Petroleum Resources and the Nigerian National Petroleum Corporation (NNPC) have signed a formal contract for the turn-around maintenance (TAM) of the four refineries with their original builders with a commitment that it would not be like other TAM signed by previous governments.

The four refineries have a combined installed capacity of 445,000 barrels per day (bpd) and a comprehensive network of pipelines and depots are strategically located throughout Nigeria to link them.

The ogetrovemment assured Nigerians that within the next 24 months Nigeria would become a net exporter of petroleum products adding that with the removal of fuel subsidy, several investors an ready to invest in the nation's economy.

"In order to ensure that we get our refineries to 90 per cent utili sation and to show Nigerians that government is serious this timi around, we actually went back and brought the original contractor that built the nation's refineries in Warri, Port Harcourt and Kaduna Already, government has given an aggressive timetable and assure* that within 24 months all three major refineries will be producing u] to 90 per cent capacity utilisation," she said.

Another lesson was the promise by the organised labour and othe key stakeholders to engage the Justice Alfa Belgore committee. Th body was set up to douse public anger and dialogue with the group and accept the fuel subsidy policy.

Members of the committee, including Governors Chibuike Amaechi, Babangida Aliyu, Adams Oshiomhole, Sule Lamidi Peter Obi, are perhaps expected to douse tension in their states. It expected that labour will embrace the committee with the aim at permanently laying the issue to rest.

Fuel subsidy protest: the good, the bad and the ugly.

By Charles Ajunwa

***ThisDay*, Monday, January 16, 2012, vol. 16, no. 6111, pg. 16, 17**

The protest action ordered by the organised labour in protest of the controversial removal of fuel subsidy by the Federal Government commenced on January 9, 2012. Virtually all social and economic spheres in most states of the country including the Federal Capital Territory (FCT), Abuja, were brought to a halt. Apart from schools, markets, filling stations, banks and other institutions that remained under locks and keys, the streets were also deserted as commercial and private vehicles stayed out of the roads. However, the protest turned bloody in some states as some protesters fell to the bullets of the policemen. The ugly incidents later led to arson and lootings as miscreants hijacked the labour's peaceful protest to unleash mayhem on the people. Many properties were destroyed and in order to nip the incident in the bud, some state governments had to impose curfew in the affected states. However, last week, the protest took different shapes in the states of the federation.

Abia

In Abia State, the protest failed to take place as people in major cities went about their normal business. In Aba, the commercial nerve-centre of the state, the Ariaria International Market was opened for business and vehicular movement was normal as commercial vehicles and motorcycles were in full operation. Social and economic activities were also normal in Umuahia, the state capital, even as government workers stayed away from their offices.

On the second day of the strike, the state governor, Theodore Orji appealed to the labour leaders to go into negotiations with the Federal Government to resolve some of the issues raised by the removal of fuel subsidy. Oiji also asked workers in the state to resume work since there was no dispute between the state government and its workers. He also assured workers of their security as they returned to work.

Taking steps to cushion the effects of the removal of fuel subsidy, the governor on the third day of the strike announced that he had purchased 17 new buses to subsidize transportation cost in the state. Orji who declared that this is the first phase of the Mass Transit Scheme which would cater for the 17 local governments in the state, said he embarked on the scheme to mitigate the pains being experienced by Abians as a result of the removal of fuel subsidy by the Federal Government. The Governor said that the second phase of the Mass Transit Scheme would be launched in few months' time noting that his government will always go the extra mile to address the welfare of its citizens.

Adamawa

The protest failed to commence in Adamawa State last week Monday as it was the day the ruling Peoples Democratic Party (PDP) was holding its governorship election grand finale rally in Yola in a bid to return Governor Muritala Nyako in office for a second. However, the January 14 election was not to be as the Independent National Electoral Commission (INEC) announced its suspension. INEC's Chairman, Professor Attahiru Jega, said the election would now take place next Saturday.

Akwa Ibom

However, in Akwa Ibom State, the protest was effective last week as workers stayed away from offices in compliance with the instruction of the organised labour. The state government had to appeal to labour to embrace dialogue with the Federal Government in order to resolve the issues of fuel subsidy in the country. The state's deputy governor, Mr. Nsima Ekere, who made the appeal when he received a group of workers protesting the subsidy removal, on behalf of Governor Godswill Akpabio, said that rather than go on strike, it was better for labour to dialogue with the Federal Government to find lasting solution to the problem. He described the subsidy removal as "a sacrifice today to safeguard our tomorrow," he added that the unpalatable impact on the people was only temporary. So far, the protest had been peaceful in Akwa Ibom State as there was not any report of violence.

Anambra

Anambra State witnessed normal activities last week as commercial premises were opened for business except banks. The anti-subsidy removal protest however gave way for a pro-subsidy demonstration in major towns of Awka, Onitsha and Nnewi. The placards carrying demonstrators marched through the major streets of Onitsha, Awka and Nnewi describing President Goodluck Jonathan as "a courageous leader who should be supported by all Nigerians." The leader of the group, Comrade Raluchukwu Umeh, described the removal of subsidy as a temporary sacrifice for a better future and urged every discerning Nigerian to support the policy which he noted was a move made by the government to bail Nigeria out of her economic doldrums.

An elated Governor Peter Obi, thanked the people of Anambra State for their understanding over fuel subsidy removal, appealing to them to continue to go about their normal businesses.

He assured them that the initial hardship occasioned by subsidy removal was manageable instead of the havoc it would have caused the nation in future. He called for the people to be vigilant to ensure that proceeds from subsidy removal were judiciously utilised.

Bauchi

In Bauchi State, the protest action was effective as people trooped out to the streets to protest the removal of fuel subsidy. Government business and commercial activities were shut down and major streets across the state were cordoned off by angry protesters. Security was however tight.

Bayelsa

Bayelsa State which happens to be the home state of President Jonathan was calm during the five-day nationwide protest last week. The people in all the local govememnt areas in the state went about their normal activities. Even, there was a solidarity rally organised to shore up supports for President Jonathan. The rally, which was organised by the Ijaw Youth Congress (IYC) and supported by the security agents paraded the streets of Yenagoa from the Samson Siasia Sport Complex to the secretariat of the Nigeria Union of Journalists, asking labour leaders in the state to prevail on the national leadership of the NLC and the TUC to negotiate with the Federal Government on the palliatives and stop wanton destruction of lives and properties in the country.

However, some labour leaders were said to be threatened by the prosubsidy removal elements in the state.

Benue

Markudi, the Benue State capital and other major cities in the state also witnessed peaceful protests against the removal of fuel subsidy. Government workers stayed away from their offices while protesters took to the streets in Makurdi. However, Benue State Governor Gabriel Suswam praised members of the organised labour in the state for staging peaceful demonstration against the oil subsidy removal.

In a statement by his Special Adviser on Media and Public Affairs, Dr Cletus Akwaya, the governor said the decision to remove the fuel subsidy was a painful one but necessary for the development of the nation.

He said: "Mr President would ordinarily not delight in imposing pains on the people who elected him; neither would the governors agree to a new policy that would just impose hardship on people. But all of us, as political leaders, agreed that for this country to make progress, the oil industry has to be deregulated - which is what some people have termed oil subsidy removal." Suswam urged the organised labour to call off the strike to avoid further dislocation of the nation's economy.

"I believe that labour has made the point and Nigerians have registered their feelings. But we need to settle down quickly to confront the challenges occasioned by this policy," he said.

Borno

The 24-hour curfew declared in the state by the Bomo Stale Government following killings of some people by Boko Haram sect members took shine out of the anti-subsidy removal protest organised by the labour in the state. The state NLC Chairman, Mr. Titus Abana, said that the strike action would not involve any kind of street protest noting that all aspects of the strike would continue as scheduled. However, economic activities remained paralysed as the anti-subsidy strike entered the second day. In the state capital, all markets were closed and their gates were under lock and key.

Cross River

In Cross River State, the protest was not effective as workers defied the directives of their leaders in the state threatening to sanction members who failed to join the strike to protest fuel subsidy removal. The state's labour chairman, Mr. Nyambi Njom while reacting to the development said that the market union, taxi drivers and owners of fuel stations failed to join the strike.

Delta

Last week Monday, workers in Delta State came out en-masse to protest the removal of fuel subsidy, bringing commercial activities to a halt in the metropolis. As early as 7.30am, members of the NLC, other trade unions trooped out en-masse in a procession blocking popular streets in the state. As the strike entered the second day, the state was generally calm as the volume of vehicular traffic rose appreciably even as most social and economic activities were still at a low ebb.

Ebonyi

On the first day of the protest, workers in Ebonyi State, public workers ignored the directives of the labour leaders and reported for duties.

In Abakaliki, the state capital, virtually all the ministries and parastatals opened for work.

According to the workers, Governor Martin Elechi's state-wide broadcast on Sunday night, warning that the removal of the petrol subsidy was irrevocable and irreversible gave them the forewarning that observing the protest could cause them their jobs. Accordingly, all the markets in the state capital, including Ihe main market, Abakpa, were opened and traders were seen transacting their businesses.

Edo

The protest recorded a high level of success in Edo State as many people turned out to join the protest. However, three hoodlums were reportedly killed in the state capital by the police while attempting to loot shops. The state Commissioner of Police, David Omojola, confirmed the killings. On the second day of the protest, labour leaders suspended the protest and advised the residents to observe the protest from their houses. This development was as a result of the report that miscreants had hijacked the protest. A mosque in the city was burnt while two people were killed. Governor Adams Oshiomhole in his reaction vowed to deal with politicians and criminals who hid under the guise of the removal of fuel subsidy to foment trouble in the state. He issued the threat when he addressed the Arewa community at Aduwawa, Eyean and Esigie in Benin-City.

Reacting to the violent protests and attacks on some innocent people in the state capital, Oshiomhole said: "You don't have to be afraid. We are ready to deal with any criminal. Anybody who is planning to foment trouble will be dealt with squarely, because politicians have hijacked this protest. They want to create problems "

Ekiti

The protest was effective in Ekiti State as the Catholic Bishop of Ekiti Diocese, Bishop Felix Ajakaye, led thousands of residents of Ekiti State and leaders of oiganised labour and civil societies to protest the removal of fuel subsidy by the Federal Government. On the second day, the protest took a different dimension as youths displayed a mock coffin with an inscription: "RIP Oil Subsidy"

Enugu

The protest directive was ignored in Enugu as the state government announced the ban on public assemblies, meetings or processions in any part of the state until further notice. Governor Sullivan Chime, said he decided to ban the protest because it could lead to a breakdown of law and order. A labour leader in Enugu State, Comrade Festus Ozoeze, who was said to be attempting to enforce the nationwide strike was reportedly arrested by the police, tried by a mobile court and remanded at Enugu prisons.

Gombe

The strike was however successful in Gombe State when economic and vehicular activities were brought to a halt. Armed mobile policemen and other security men were deployed to strategic places, such as banks, offices and roundabouts to contain any outbreak of violence. The NLC Chairman in the state, Comrade Ahmed Maisakala, said that the union and other stakeholders would meet to appraise Monday's protest before taking the next step. The protests in the state had been peaceful.

Imo

Workers in Imo State joined the protest last week. Governor Rochas Okorochajiad insisted that the people of the state would strengthen their doggedness and entrepreneurship to survive die pains of the hike in fuel price occasioned by the fuel subsidy removal. He said this while addressing commercial transport operators, bus and taxi drivers at the Hero's Square, New Owerri last Wednesday.

Jigawa

Commercial motorcyclists in Jigawa State adorned their motorcycles with leaves as a sign of solidarity with the nationwide strike last week.

In Dutse, the state capital, youths in their hundreds on the first day of the protest matched on the streets protesting the subsidy removal .Offices, markets, banks and motor parks were shut.

Kaduna

The protest was effective in Kaduna as shops and markets were closed with the residents of the city remained indoors for fear of being attacked. However, the protest turned violent as hoodlums attacked innocent people and looted shops. The state government however moved swiftly and imposed a 24-hour curfew in Kaduna metropolis and its environs to forestall the breakdown of law and order.

The state government in justifying the curfew said the decision to impose the curfew was to check the activities of those who have hijacked the protest. In a statement by the state Commissioner of Police, Gala Nasarawa, he said that since the commencement of the nationwide strike against the removal of fuel subsidy on Monday, activities of hoodlums and street urchins have raised serious security concern in the state.

The statement issued after an emergency security council meeting presided over by Governor Patrick Yakowa, said: "We have realised that the strike over the removal of subsidy has been hijacked by persons other than those committed to the cause. Demonstration which began yesterday peacefully, today turned violent. People were harassed, intimidated, and installations vandalised. In view of this unfortunate situation, the Kaduna State Security Council had no choice than to impose a 24 hour curfew in Kaduna metropolis and it environs.

'This measure becomes imperative in order to safeguard lives and property of innocent citizens. Government is uiging all citizens of the state to remain calm, lawful and stay at home until further notice." However, the Coalition of Civil Societies, labour unions and the Nigerian Bar Association (NBA) had to suspend street protests and directed all residents of the state and protesters to remain at home and await further directives."

Kano

To avert the breakdown of law and order in Kano State, the state government had to impose a curfew following the violence that attended the protest in the state. The action organised by labour was hijacked by hoodlums. Four people were reportedly killed during the mayhem. Two top Kano politicians, Gen. Lawal Jafaru Isa and the immediate past Deputy Governor of the state, Abdullahi Hjjani Muhammad Gwarzo, also joined a mammoth crowd at the historic Groundnut Pyramid venue of a rally to protest the subsidy removal.

Katsina

Human and vehicular activities in Katsina State were brought to a halt last week in Katsina State. There were reports that hundreds of irate youths eager to turn the protest into violent action, broke loose from the crowd and led a demonstration to GRA Roundabout, barely 500 metres to Government House.

But a combined team of police, civil defence corps and soldiers at the strategic road intersection, however, stopped the aggrieved youths with tear gas as they were about to make bonfire with used tyres.

Kebbi

People came out in their thousands to protest the removal of fuel subsidy by the Federal Government. All shops, schools were closed. The protest was well organised and peaceful.

Kogi

Last week's protest against the removal of fuel subsidy was successful in Kogi State. Offices, schools and markets were closed following the labour directive to workers. But the peaceful protest turned violent in Lokoja the state capital as angry youths and security agents engage one another in a battle to prevent hoodlums from blocking the high ways and preventing travellers from passing through the city. Government offices and businesses were shut in total compliance with the industrial action.

Kwara

The protest was also successful in Kwara State, paralysing social and economic lives of the State capital, Borin. However, the senator representing Kwara Central in the National Assembly, Dr Bukola Saraki, said Federal Government and labour should dialogue to resolve the current impasse. In a statement by his media aide, Akintoba Fatigun, he said the removal of subsidy would remove corruption and graft in the down stream sector.

Lagos

Lagos was the hotbed of the protest against the removal of subsidy on fuel. The state had recorded the highest number of protesters, paralysing economic and social lives of the state. The Lagos protest however recorded some causalities .The Gani Fawehinmi Park in Ojota, became the rallying point for protesters with thousands of people converging at the park daily to register their anger against the increament in fuel price. Meanwhile, Governor Babatunde Fashola while addressing members of the Nigeria Bar Association (NBA), Lagos branch, who took the antifuel subsidy removal protest to the governor's house in Marina, said protesters should avoid violence during the protest, advising that vandalism of government property would not resolve the issue.

Nasarawa

From the first day of the strike action, social and economic activities in Lafia, the capital of Nasarawa State were paralysed. Banks, markets, shops, restaurants were shut down, market women, including petty traders all took to the streets, protesting against the removal of the subsidy on fuel.

The state chairman of Nigeria Labour Congress (NLC) , Asoloko Maku and his counterpart in the Trade Union Congress (TUC), Gabriel Agbashi, both went round Lafia, the state capital, to monitor the strike after a meeting of the organised labour at the Labour House.

Niger

In Niger State, the protest turned violent as the office of the Independent National Electoral Commission (INEC) was set ablaze by angry protesters. The campaign office of the governor, Muazu Babangida Aliyu, was not spared as it was burnt down. The same fate befell the office of the state Chairman of the PDP, Tanko Beji. Also, the irate mob did not spare the residence of Senator Dalhatu Awasu Kuta. Efforts by the police to quell the riot yielded little effort as the protesters attempted to bum the residence of Governor Aliyu's mother. The office of Hajiya Jumai Jafaru, a member of the Niger State House of Assembly was also burnt.

A police Inspector lost his life in the melee as rioters clash with men of the police. It took a combined team of police and soldiers to disperse them. The state government had to impose a 24-hour curfew in Minna in order to prevent further breakdown of law and order.

Ogun

During the last week protest, two persons were confirmed dead in Ogun State. One of the two victims, simply identified as Kaola, a dieselseller at Kara, Ibafo in Obafemi Owode Local Government Area of Ogun State, was, according to a witness, allegedly shot on the upper and left chest by the police. The other victim's identity was still shrouded in Ogun State governor, Senator Ibikunle Amosun, had to advise youths to eschew violence while expressing their grievances against the removal of fuel subsidy by the Federal Government. Amosun who said this while visiting major streets in Abeokuta to inspect the level of damage done in the state capital as a result of the labour and civil society's protests, expressed his displeasure with the protesters for burning disused tyres on some roads, complaining that die effect of the action was injurious to the lifespan of such roads.

Ondo

In Ondo State, protesters last week converged on the City Centre in Akure, the state capital from where they marched to other parts of the town. Protesters as early as 730am trooped to the major streets , Adesida/Oyemekun roads in Akure carrying various placards and a mock coffin demanding the resignation of President Goodluck Jonathan.

Osun

For five days last week, major roads in Osun State were occupied by protesters who were protesting the removal of fuel subsidy. Shops and offices remained shut and commercial motorcyclists did not operate. However, two persons reportedly lost their lives during the anti-subsidy protest in Osogbo.

Oyo

In Ibadan, Oyo State capital, thousands of protesters trooped out to participate in the last week's protest against the removal of fuel subsidy. Some of government property in Ibadan North West Local Government was destroyed by some miscreants who hijacked the protest.

Fuel subsidy removal: their strike, our gains.

By Emmanuel Ugwu

***ThisDay*, Tuesday, January 24, 2012, vol. 17, no, 6119, pg 21**

The removal of fuel subsidy is a vexed issue, which generated heated arguments in the past and will continue to be a source of debate for sometime to come because of its sensitivity to the socio-economic existence of Nigerians. Speakers have argued, especially against the background that those who insist on the removal have been accused of not doing enough to show transparency in their dealings with those who elected them to power.

While there was conflagration in many parts of the country, observers that have shown keen interest in the happenings in Abia State have described the strange departure of the organised labour unions and its affiliates as something worth looking into, to determine what informed this. Aside from the industrial action embarked upon by the members of Academic Staff Union of Universities, ASUU last year which paralysed the education sector, the last strike that has been witnessed in the state since then has been the one embarked on by the South East arm of the ASUU insisting on receiving the same pay packet as their contemporaries in the federal universities. Soon as a rapprochement was reached between the union and the state government towards the end of last year, strike had become a thing of the past.

In fact, it is very important to point out that since the enthronement of the present administration for a second and final tenure last May 29, the state has never witnessed any industrial unrest of whatever kind. While the entire country' was engulfed in strike over the New Minimum Wage introduced by the federal government to cushion the perceived suffering of the masses, Abia State remained largely free of such strike, with the leaders of the organised labour unions insisting that they will not embark on any strike over the minimum wage issue based on the agreements reached with Governor Theodore Orji and his promise to pay the new wage without delay as soon as the details were worked out by the bodies saddled with that duty.

In the just ended strike occasioned by the removal of fuel subsidy by the Federal Government, the organised labour unions though in support of the matter based on the orders from their various national leadership, yet it has been observed that street protests and mass demonstration had been seriously downplayed with workers remaining in the comfort of their homes and reading about the mayhem that has been unleashed in other parts of the country. Before the commencement of the strike, the union led by Sylvanus Eye had meet with other unions and affiliate bodies to intimate them of the strike and the need to ensure that all directives issued by the national leadership were carried out to its letters. He had also assured them shortly after the kick-off of the protest that mass protest on the streets was an option on the table which would be discussed on the second day of the event to get the feelings of all and sundry.

However on the second day of the strike and perhaps following a meeting between the union leaders and Governor Theodore Oiji, the groups decided to once again downplay embarking on mass protests on the streets of Umuahia and Aba, its commercial nerve centre, pushing the issue to another day. Though the decision was received with mixed feeling as those opposed to it sought the head of the leadership with the chairman escaping by the whiskers, yet the impact of the decision not to engage the members on a mass demonstration along the streets of Umuahia was not lost on political analysts, who see the entire event to mean that a new chapter has opened for the people of the state with the final agreement to jaw-jaw and not to war-war at every event.

According to analysts, the fact that the commercial city of Aba, noted for its notoriety when it comes to anti-government decisions chose to remain quiet and not only embark on its usual business as the days of the strike spread, but to also remain adamant to the issues at stake speaks volume and a lesson in leadership and statesmanship. Aba, the commercial nerve centre is a mixture of all the tribes in the country, majority of them largely limited in their education, whose major concern is buying and selling.

It also has handftil of entrepreneurs for whom the city is often called the Japan of Africa as these local and national entrepreneurs can match the products of their peers across the globe with ingenuity and wisdom. These group has always spoken out in matters of national discuss and champion several protests in time past including poor infrastructure in the area, insensitivity on the part of government towards the governed, insecurity and such other issues as the removal of fuel subsidy. In fact, so long as a demonstration had been called whether real or imagined, the occupants of the Enyimba City had never been left out.

The analysts explained that in the early days of the insecurity in Abia State, when kidnappers and armed bandits turned the city into a haven of disorder and brigandage, the entrepreneurs not only spoke out and demonstrated, but started relocating their businesses from the commercial hub of the state and asking the Federal Government to declare a State of Emergency in the area. Though this was not to be, yet it once again showed the resilience of the people to take issues as they come and remain resolute in their determination to achieve their set goals. The demand for a state of emergency was not called off until soldiers from the 82nd Division Enugu stormed the commercial city and its environs on September 30 last year and brought relief and a new song on the mouth of the people.

When the issue of infrastructural decay, especially the hardship on all the federal and state roads became unbearable for them, the traders came out in their hordes to demand for attention and insisted that if nothing was done early to give them a sense of belonging, they would turn the area into one big mess. Before this time, the government of Abia State had embarked on the rehabilitation of the Aba/Oweni road and the Port Harcourt Road, all federal roads in the commercial city. It also embarked on the reconstruction of state roads and therefore doused the tension that had already been generated.

Hence, the analysts insist that for the same people to remain cool in the face of the happenings in other parts of the country is worthy of investigation in order to perhaps, fashion a new way of dealing with issues or nipping such issues in the bud before they get out of hand. In the same vein, the stand of the organised labour in the early days of strike to remain in doors and preclude mass street demonstration is another event that is worthy of investigating.

Dr. James Ukachukwu, a university don insists that "the significance of what is happening in Abia State must be seen as a departure from the natural, where events would have been concluded to have taken place even before it started. This is because Abia, especially Aba, the commercial city is a different ball stadium or congregation, where the people are not moved by reason in the time past but by emotion. But this time around, it is no longer there; the people are no longer who they are said to be. They have become a different species of what I would call a New Nigeria where reason and facts tend to over-ride emotion and make beliefs. I see a new turn of events in Aba and Abia State and the only conclusion I have reached so far is that there is a strange departure from the style of governance in the state, which in turn has ushered in a new style of doing things."

According to him "I remember that when insecurity was high in the state, these people took the bull by the hom and told government the truth about the matter on ground. I have also observed that in the past, even without prompting, the residents of Aba had taken to the streets in support of whatever decisions had been taken by labour and its affiliates. I can tell you authoritatively that during the strike action by ASUU in the South East universities, the help of the residents of

Aba had been solicited in order to give the strike an unprecedented hype. It would have become a reality if government in its wisdom had not quickly stepped in and done our bidding. So for them to choose to go about their businesses and not demonstrate on the streets is an indication that they have seen something different from the past and are happy now."

Dr. Ukachukwu explained that from the point of view of analysts, the present leadership in Abia State led by Theodore Orji has done enough and needed not to roughshod the people just like it is happening in some states in the country where governors had to ban street demonstrations as a way of keeping people in their homes. "What we have observed is that Nigerians are not difficult people. All they want are the basic necessities of life and also to be told the truth and carried along in the scheme of things.

In all major decisions that the present administration has taken, consultations have been very broad and stakeholders allowed to make their inputs. Once you enjoy H the confidence of the people and carry them along in the scheme of things, then you can be rest assured that when you speak, the people will listen but if you chose to become a tyrant, of course the people of Enyimba city will rise to say no.

"In conclusion, let me say that the massive road reconstruction and rehabilitation, the return of shops to the deserving owners and the turning of the state into one big construction site is largely responsible for the followership the Governor enjoys today and it will remain so as long as he does not depart to the left or to the right. If he maintains the tempo of the delivery of democracy dividends embarks on constant interaction with the people and put his cards on the table for all to see, I see him not losing the confidence of the people in whatever issue he needs them," the university teacher said.

As the people count their losses and the dead are buried in some parts of the country, Abia is far removed from all these as the people remain in the comforts of their homes praying for either the Federal Government to shift grounds on the ftiel subsidy removal and for labour to understand the spirit behind the removal of the subsidy so that life can once again move on. In all, it is safe to conclude that you pat my back, I pat your back is the reason for the peace that now pervades in the state.

The government has patted the people on the back with good governance and consultation and the people are now patting the government on the back with not only maintenance of the peace, but also sustaining it because who knows what would have happened had street demonstrations been engaged. Perhaps as in time past, hoodlums and miscreants would have taken over and then mayhem unleashed on the people. That was the only way his supposed good intentions could come to fruition.

How protesters shut down Ibadan

By Tunde Sanni

***ThisDay*, Friday, January 13, 2012, vol. 16, no. 6108, pg. 18**

Apart from the protest that greeted the June 12, 1993 annulment of presidential poll believed to have been won by Basorun Moshood Abiola, the South west has never erupted with one voice in protest against the federal government's removal of fuel subsidy as announced by the Petroleum Pricing Regulation Agency {PPRA} on January 1,2012.

The revolt against the fuel subsidy since its announcement has rekindled the fire in the people of the region to stand up against injustice and unpopular policies. The march against the subsidy took up late in the Oyo State capital, Ibadan but when it eventually commenced, there appears to be no going back.

Ahead of the nationwide protest declared by the Labour Congress (NLC) and coalition of civil society groups under the aegis of Joint Action Forum {JAF}; there have been pockets of uncoordinated protests in the two states.

In Ibadan, there were isolated cases of protests occasioned by setting up of bonfires in some major areas like University of Ibadan [U.I], Sango, Mokola and Oke-Bola areas. The rallies were backed by various students' group, especially the Students' Union Government of the University of Ibadan. All the rallies had been peaceful with zero reports of police maximum intervention, though there was a case where the anti-crime joint military/police/SSS/NSCDC patrol codenamed 'Operation Burst' had burst the protesters and disperse their bonfires, especially in Oke Bola area last week Wednesday.

The chairman of the NLC in the state, Bashiru Olanrewaju and the JAF coordinator, Demola Aremu in outlining the Monday's protest had told thugs and overzealous police to steer clear of their protests as they would not tolerate the protest being hijacked or allow any police to display its overzealousness with either teargas or gun.

Following the announcement of the nationwide strike for Monday, all categories of people in the ancient city became restive, patiently counting days for the protest to take off. When the day rolled in, it was apparent that the ancient city would be under siege while the days of the protest lasted. For example, Oja Oke-Ado, one of the flashpoints of struggle in the town, as early as 7am on the day had been literally taken over by residents of the area who set bonfire on the all the roads linking the area to other parts of the city, demanding for cogent reason before any vehicular passage. A police pick up van brimming with policemen had attempted to disperse the protesters but the mob had stood their ground. The police sensing danger quickly beat a retreat.

The organized protest took off at the NLC secretariat at Gate area Ibadan around 8.15am with the protesters marching through some of the ancient parts like Oje, chanting anti President Goodluck Jonathan songs. The protesters carried placards bearing various inscriptions such as 'We don't want Badluck,' 'This is not the Nigeria of our dream,' 'Jonathan, you have failed the people'" fuel subsidy Jonathan's weapons of mass destruction and others. Banks, shops, filling stations and markets were shut down in all the towns as was the case in Ibadan. No life was, however, reported lost in the protest .The rally first berthed at Mapo with various leaders as former President of the Nigeria bar Association, {NBA} Rotimi Akeredolu {SAN}, chairman of JAF in the state, Dr Ademola Aremu NLC Chairman in the state, Comrade Bashir Olanrewaju and other union leaders taking turns to address the protesting masses to press on with the struggle until their demand was met.

According to them, the idea of subsidy removal is false and unacceptable. The protest against the subsidy removal, they said, would be total and con- tinous. Akeredolu, in his remarks, regretted that President Jonathan had quickly forgotten the promise that he made to the Nigerian masses. He lamented, "Our leaders indulged in taking us for granted. But this time we are saying 'No.' we must call the bluff of this government. President Jonathan is not a man of integrity. We want the government to do our bidding not us doing their bidding."

Aremu, said: "We shall continue to protest until the Federal Government reviews the removal of oil subsidy. We are here to let the 'looters' know that we are against the so-called subsidy removal. If not, the masses wouldn't have been out to protest the unpopular move by President Goodluck Jonathan. We elected him based on our trust. But, unfortunately, he has let us down. He once told us that he went to school without shoes. Now he has forgotten the experience."

He recalled that between 1999 and 2007, former President Olusegun Obasanjo increased the petrol pump price five times. This, to him, reflected the fact that the FG had failed the people. Therefore, he said that the people had lost confidence in the government. "They told us that they would use the money to improve on infrastructures but we don't trust them anymore. They should shut illegal refineries and fire the boys engaging in illegal refining to work at the refineries. Jonathan, David Mark and the Governors have failed us. It is either they reverse the price of petrol, resign or reverse the so-called removal of fuel subsidy."

Fuel Subsidy Conversation: How Public Protests Impact Jonathan's Government

By Charles Ajunwa

***ThisDay*, Monday, January 30, 2012, vol. no. 6125, pg. 21**

Charles Ajunwa writes that following his recent decisions especially the removal of petrol subsidy as well as the drop in his public ratings among Nigerians, President Goodluck Jonathan seems to have started to change his approach to governance

The recent nationwide strike called by the Nigeria Labour Congress (NLC) and Trade Union Congress (TUC) in collaboration with civil society organisations over the removal of petrol subsidy by the Federal Government appears to a blessing in disguise in many respects. To avert the sixday strike and protest that brought the entire country to a halt, President Goodluck Jonathan quickly made a national broadcast on January 7, 2012, where he announced among other things a reduction in the cost of governance.

Apparently to assuage many angry Nigerians who took to the streets at the heat of the recent nationwide strike, Jonathan had announced measures which he said were parts of the sacrifices being made to cushion the effects of removal of petrol subsidy on Nigerians.

Hear him: 'To save Nigeria, we must all be prepared to make sacrifices. On the part of government, we are taking several measures aimed at cutting the size and cost of governance including the ongoing and continuous effort to reduce the size of our recurrent expenditure and increase capital spending. In this regard, I have directed that overseas travels by all political office holders, including the President, should be reduced to the barest minimum. The size of delegations on foreign trips will also be drastically reduced; only trips that are absolutely necessary will be approved.

"For the year 2012, the basic salaries of all political office holders in the executive arm of government will be reduced by 25 per cent. Government is also currently reviewing the number of committees, commissions and parastatals with overlapping responsibilities. The report on this will be submitted shortly and the recommendations will be promptly implemented. In the meantime, all Ministries, Departments and Agencies must reduce their overhead expenses.

"We are all greatly concerned about the issue of corruption. The deregulation policy is the strongest measure to tackle this challenge in the downstream sector. In addition, government is taking other steps to further sanitise the oil industry. To ensure that the funds from petroleum subsidy removal are spent prudently on projects that will build a greater Nigeria, I have established a committee to oversee the implementation of the Subsidy Reinvestment and Empowerment Programme. I sincerely believe that the reinvestment of the petroleum subsidy funds, to ensure improvement in national infrastructure, power supply, transportation, irrigation and agriculture, education, healthcare and other social services, is in the best interest of our people," Jonathan had declared.

From what seems to be a new step to confidence building aimed at winning the hearts of many Nigerians who had lost confidence in him and his government, Jonathan started by doing the talk instead of engaging opposition political parties in the war of words.

On his promise to cut down foreign trips of government ^functionaries and the number of the usual large entourage which accompanies them while on trips, Jonathan who was invited to attend the ceremony marking African National Congress' (ANC) 100 years df existence in South Africa, cancelled the official trip at the heat of the nationwide strike over the removal of petrol subsidy.

Special Adviser to the President on Media and Publication, Dr. Reuben Abati, who announced the cancellation had expressed disappointment on rumours making the rounds that Jonathan left the country with two presidential Jets for South Africa. According to him, the President was in Nigeria, attending to matters of national interests. Jonathan on the said day attended the Armed Forces Remembrance Service at the National Christian Centre. Later, he was at the Eagle

Square, Abuja, to commission a national mass transit programme as promised in his national broadcast.

Also in keeping his promise to reduce frequent foreign trips by government officials, Jonathan had to put off an already scheduled trip to Davos, Switzerland for this year's edition of the annual World Economic Forum (WEF). Jonathan who was said to have sent an initial team to Switzerland was to leave Abuja for Davos last Wednesday evening after attending the weekly Federal Executive Council (FEC) meeting, but decided to cancel the trip because of the Kano mayhem. Jonathan was said to have immediately directed the team already in Davos to return home while another advance team that was scheduled to leave Abuja that evening aboard a Lufthansa flight was asked to return to base. The president also cancelled an African Union (AU) scheduled meeting in Addis Ababa, Ethiopia.

Besides, as part of steps aimed at checking the increasing level of insecurity in the country especially the menace of Boko Haram, Jonathan had last Wednesday approved the appointment of Mr. Mohammed Dikko. Abubakar as Acting Inspector General of Police. He said the move was aimed at repositioning the Nigeria Police Force to make it more effective and capable of meeting emerging internal security challenges. Abubakar who was until his elevation an Assistant Inspector General of Police replaced Mr. Hafiz Ringim who proceeded on terminal leave on January 25, 2012.

Presidential spokesman, Abati, who made the announcement said Jonathan also approved the retirement of all Deputy Inspectors General of Police with immediate effect. The retired DIGs included Mrs. Ivy Uche Okoronkwo, who was DIG POL 2i/c Force Headquarters, Abuja, Mr. Azubuko J. Udah, DIG Administration ("A" Dept), Mr. Sardauna Abubukar, DIG Training ("E" Dept.); Mr. Audu Abubakar, DIG Operations ("B" Dept); Mr. Saleh Abubakar, DIG Works ("C" Dept.) and Mr. Mohammed A. Yesufu, DIG Planning and InfoTech ("F" Dept.).

The president who also disclosed the establishment of a special committee to oversee the urgent reorganisation of the Nigeria Police Force to be led by the Chairman of the Police Service Commission, Mr. Parry B.O Osayande, a retired DIG, outlined the following terms of reference, viz: To identify the challenges and factors militating against effective performance in the Nigeria Police Force and make recommendations for addressing the challenges; t o examine the scope and standard of training and other personnel development activities in the Police to determine their adequacy or otherwise; to determine the general and specific causes of the collapse of public confidence in the Police and recommend ways of restoring public trust in the institution; to examine records of performance of officers and men of the Nigeria Police Force with a view to identifying those that can no longer fit into the system due to declining productivity, age, indiscipline, corruption and/or disloyalty and to make any other recommendations for the improvement of the Nigeria Police Force.

The committee's recommendations are to be implemented along with those by previous committees set up by government on the reform of the Nigeria Police Force.

Jonathan's reform agenda on governance issues has also not spared ministers who are beginning to take their duties seriously. The Minister of Petroleum, Mrs. Diezani Alison Madueke, had immediately after the nationwide strike was called off, ordered the Economic and Financial Crimes Commission (EFCC) to investigate activities of the Nigerian National Petroleum Corporation (NNPC) and Petroleum Pricing Products Regulating Agency (PPPRA) believed to be enmeshed in fraudulent practices. EFCC had since swooped on the two agencies.

However, the opposition Action Congress of Nigeria (ACN) recently challenged Jonathan to lead by example by reducing the high cost of governance, which the party said was eating deep into the country's resources and leaving little or nothing for developmental projects. ACN through its National Publicity Secretary, Alhaji Lai Mohammed, said the President had so far sent out conflicting signals over this issue and urged him to be consistent and firm.

"In one breath, Jonathan is giving an impression that he wants to run a lean and effective government by asking his ministers to drastically cut the number of their aides to two, as widely reported in the media and so far not refuted. In another, the same President has raised the cost of governance by appointing a retinue of personal aides and at least 40 ministers, even when the constitution prescribes one minister per state which should have pegged the total number at 36, creating additional ministries when he could have streamlined the existing ones and by also asking for higher pay for some of his aides.

"A President who is seeking higher pay for his aides and creating additional ministries can definitely not have the moral authority to lead the ongoing campaign to get federal lawmakers to slash their jumbo pay in the interest of the country," ACN said.

The party said however, that it was not too late for the President to retrace his steps and show leadership example, saying the achievements of any administration are not directly proportional to the number of ministers or presidential aides appointed by such administration. It added that the 'transformational agenda' of the present administration would remain a cliche, just like the sevenpoint agenda of his predecessor, Umaru Yar'Adua, "unless the President can match his rhetoric with action, take hard decisions and stop pandering to the whims and caprices of his sponsors or his directionless party.

"This week will mark the third month of the Jonathan administration, but Nigerians are yet to see any sign of the lofty ideals espoused by the President in his inauguration speech. But we are prepared to hold our fire and give the President the benefit of the doubt for now. But if the saying that morning shows the day is anything to go by, then we are afraid that the signs so far are not promising," ACN said.

It urged the President to routinely look at himself in the mirror by monitoring what Nigerians are saying through the independent media, instead of listening to fawning aides.

"For example, the country's evercreative newspaper cartoonists are already having a field day: In place of the President's lamentation that he went to school without shoes, Nigerian children are now crying they have no food on their tables; in response to the President's statement that the youth should emulate him, all we see are more youth donning bowler (or is it fedora) hats and the president's trademark attire; and whereas a few fat cat politicians and government appointees are savouring their newfound wealth, Nigerians are being crushed by rising costs of living. We hope the President is paying attention," the party said.

But with Jonathan beginning to shelve his old style of government which had done more harm than good to his administration, expectations are now high that he should sustain the momentum as that was the only way his supposed good intentions could come to fruition.

How subsidy protest divided Nollywood

By Azuka Ogujuba

***ThisDay*, Saturday, January 21, 2012, vol. 16, no. 6116, pg. 18, 19**

As Special Adviser on Strategy to the President, Oronto Douglas, certainly pulled a major one with the goodwill he helped secure for his boss from showbiz personalities. Such support was crucial as evident in last year's general election where the celebrities' star power helped rally votes for Jonathan.

Relying on the existing goodwill, Douglas convened a dialogue session at the Eko Hotel & Suites, in Victoria Island, Lagos, with the artistes. This is however disputed by some who allege the December 30 session was sponsored by the Actors' Guild. The premise for the allegation that Douglas sponsored the session was mat artistes reportedly got honorarium for speaking at the roundtable dubbed "Understanding Deregulation."

So, counting on the effect that the endorsement of actors like Segun Arinze, Rita Dominic, Genevieve Nnaji and Stephanie Okereke will confer on the case for subsidy withdrawal, Douglas reportedly hit the road. But he didn't reckon with the searing dichotomy in the movie industry. Artistes from the Yoruba and Hausa blocs were said to have been left out. "There is no problem with anyone organising a meeting or a roundtable parley. It is only if the intentions are not well articulated. I mean you can't be inviting people to come and see how you all can understand deregulation only for it to turn out mat it is some meeting to endorse fuel subsidy removal and not only that you gave the impression that it was a decision that was taken by the entire industry," a yoruba artiste who asked not to be identified said.

An old discord

Some however argued that the roots of the discordant tune go much deeper. There is a simmering resentment that only a group of people seems to be getting the exclusive deals. The recent national awards in 2011 did raise eye brows in the industry. Many artistes wondered how awards panel arrived at some of the individuals that were honoured and the criteria for conferring such honour. Criticism greeted the nomination of younger players like Stephanie Okereke with

Del York Film School (a company she has an interest in) allegedly handling Jonathan's presidential campaign commercials, Chinedu Ikedieze, a.k.a Aki, Kanayo O. Kanayo (KOK) and Genevieve Nnaji.

To these critics, the choice seems influenced by those who "worked for the president's campaign". "The awards were also unfairly skewed to just an ethnic section of the industry as well, are they saying that the Yoruba (apart from Olu Jacobs)or Hausa or even Edo actors are not worthy of the awards? Equity and fair play were missing in the criteria, if you ask me but that is water under a bridge," a producer, Charles Novia, said.

Talking subsidy

Present at the second session were movie producers, script writers, actors and actresses, heads of different guilds and journalists. Among prominent Nollywood greats were actors Paul Obazele, Zack Orji and Segun Arinze, the president of Association of Movie Producers, Zik Zulu Okafor, Paul Obazele the chairman of Actors' Guild board of trustees, Prince Ifeanyi Dike, president of directors Guild of Nigerian and CEO Abuja International Film Festival, Fidelis Duker. Others include director, Bond Emeruah, Segun Aina- Padonu, Nobert Anyanwu, Chike Bryan, Lilian Amah-Aluko, Zeb Ejiro, Chico Ejiro, Charles Novia, Monalisa Chinda, Ernest Azuzu, Charles Enozie, Ikechukwu Onyeka, Emmem Isone, Benita Nzeribe and several other Nollywood top-notch.

A meeting was convened at the National Arts Theatre, in Lagos after the subsidy had been removed and it was a no-holds- barred. According to Zack Orji, who presided, "fuel subsidy removal is not a problem. Rather, the fear that the proceeds from the removal will not be judiciously used is the headache the people have. While the federal government has shown us a blueprint of what they intend to do with the proceeds from the subsidy removal, it is yet to be known what the state and local governments intend to do with theirs. This is where our problem lies. There is a trust issue; can we really trust the government to be sincere injudiciously utilising the funds from the removal for the benefit of Nigerians?"

Nobert Adaewgu, a movie producer shared a similar sentiment. "The proceeds from the fuel subsidy removal (about N1.3 trillion) should be put into the foreign reserve to better the lots of Nigerians. I do not have a problem with the removal but we should give the president a chance to implement his policies but we will hold him solely responsible should he fail us eventually," he said.

For Novia, the removal was not exactly an issue. The manner of removal was "The manner and approach the president took to remove the fuel subsidy is suicidal. It was so impromptu and he didn't consider the people first. Ideally, the people should come first and. he should have created a sound public awareness campaign because this economic decision he took will benefit Nigerians but it's a long term project."

Orji's "No Pain No Gain" speech on the benefit of the removal apparently sought to set the tone for the discourse: "Before we can have the joy of a baby, a woman must first go through a nine-month period of pain. I see the removal as a temporary pain for Nigerians but we shall enjoy its long term benefits."

Segun Arinze believes that if subsidy was removed, the burden should be evenly borne by slashing the salaries of public office holders by a generous percentage, a view shared by the veteran producer, Zeb Ejiro, who posited that fuel subsidy removal is not a problem and the deregulation of the downstream sector will be very advantageous to Nigerians. "It was extremely expensive to get a SIM card then (I think it was around ₦22,000) when they first came to Nigeria but now, some 10 years after, you can get a SIM for as low as N100! It was because it was deregulated then. We should do the same in the oil sector for our long term benefit."

Duker observed that Nigerians are not angry that the subsidy was removed but that they are rather peeved by the rate of corruption in the country and the wrong time of the subsidy removal. Emeruah's comment was particularly scathing. "Was there anything like subsidy in the first place? When the fuel price was N65 per litre, there were promises that the government will do this, the government will do that. Nothing has been done so far. The promise of electricity is still a mirage. There were promises that roads will be renovated and built, security, water, manpower etc but till today nothing has been done. If Jonathan had given Nigerians steady light for at least six months and now comes out to remove subsidy on fuel as a way to continue the enjoyment of the light, it would have made a lot of sense. The only way for ward is to revert to the status quo ante." He got a resounding applause.

No industry-wide consensus

Actress Ayo Adesanya's take was rather dramatic. "Capital No! I don't support the removal of subsidy, because when fuel was at 65 naira per litre, cost of living was very high let alone when there's increase in fuel price. It is only God that can save us now." Adesanya took a swipe at artistes who had endorsed the removal. "How can one or two people from a group be spokespersons without even consulting everyone? We are in it together so we have to deliberate and come to a conclusion before such decisions should be taken on such delicate matters and on behalf of others."

In the words of Ibinabo Fiberesima, "Everybody is entitled to hold an opinion and the opinion should be respected, but to speak for a whole industry must be by consensus and some can represent that consensus." On whether she supports the removal of oil subsidy, she said, "I support the president and the masses because really they are saying the same thing, which to me is simply about the progress or Nigeria and I believe we all nave that as our top-most priority. Mr President sees from a global view and knows what's best for the country, so we must support him in his transformation agenda."

Practising what they preach

Some artistes like Bimbo Akintola gave action to their rhetoric. She was at the Gani Fawehinmi Freedom Park, in Lagos, to support the protest as well as speak to her teeming fans said. "I'm a Nigerian and I'm affected. At ₦140 per litre, what happens is that instantly prices of everything go up, transportation, food, everything. How on earth do you think we will survive? How many jobs do you do in a year as an artiste, as an actress that you will still be able to keep your standard of living if you buy petrol at ₦140? I'm here for my mum, my dad, my brothers and sisters, my cousins, my unborn chil dren, because we won't be able to live in this country if this continues It's saa that we have a government that doesn't care about the people. The people are supposed to be the government but in Nigeria it is the reverse; it's a select few and the citizenry suffer daily," she said.

Actor and Glo ambassador, Kunle Afolayan, described the initial removal as suicidal. "It's killing and a lot of us cannot afford it, which is why we all need to come together with one voice to plead with the government. We're not even fighting the government; we're pleading so that they can look at other ways in which this can be resolved. Look at the calibre of people who came out for the Occupy Nigeria protest, you have middle class, low class, upper class and all sorts of people because people are angry and upset. This is not just for our own future but for the future of our children as well."

Toeing the same path, actress Bimbo Thomas said she would rather be on the side of the masses. "I stay on the side of the masses any day, anytime. However, nobody has the right to speak for Nollywood practitioners without convening a meeting, what for? Let me quickly say this I'm sure we are the citizens of this same country where the "removal ot subsidy" caused a mass protest and affecting people's daily activities for five working days. I just want to give a peace of advice as a citizen of this country and so also as a member of Nollywood that whoever the group of people that might be thinking of endorsing or have endorsed the removal of subsidy in Nollyhood should do a re-think and stop the idea because there are so many problems in our sector and so many ways to proffer solutions with different approach other than removal of Subsidy."

Additional reports by Gbenga Bada and Amaka Eze

INEC shifts Adamawa Governorship poll

By Chuks Okocha and Matthew Onah

***ThisDay*, Wednesday, January 11, 2012, vol. 16, no. 6106, pg. 9**

The first major casualty of the Nigeria Labour Congress (NLC) and Trade Union Congress (TUC) national strike occurred yesterday, as the Independent National Electoral Commission (INEC) announced the suspension of the January 14 Adamawa State governorship election. Consequently, INEC said the governorship election would now take place on January 21.

INEC also said the decision to postpone the election was due to the prevailing situation in the state as well as the nation-wide strike. Governor Muritala Nyako had last week imposed a curfew in the state and pledged a N25 million to any one that would give information of the killers of some people in the state last week

Just on Monday, the ruling Peeples Democratic Party (PDP) concluded it grand finale rally in the state capital, Yola. But a statement signed by the Chairman of INEC, Professor Attahiru Jega, said the governorship election would no longer take place as scheduled

Jega said the election would take place in another week's time, stressing: "In view of the prevailing situation in Adamawa State, and after consultations with relevant stakeholders in the state, the Independent National Electoral Commission (INEC) has decided to postpone the governorship election in the state by one week. The governorship election will now hold on Saturday, January 21, 2012, instead of January 14, 2012 as earlier scheduled."

The commission reassures all Nigerians and Adamawa State residents in particular of its determination to conduct free, fair and credible election in the state. Jega said Commission was working very closely with all stakeholders, including security agencies, to ensure a conducive environment for the conduct of the election.

Confirming INEC's postponement of the election, the state Resident Electoral Commissioner (REC), Mr. Kassim Gaidam, told *ThisDay* that he got a directive from the national headquarters of the commission to inform all the relevant stakeholders about the postponement. Speaking further, he said he had called a meeting of the various stakeholders and passed on to them the relevant information about the re-scheduling of the election.

It would be recalled that *ThisDay* had reported about four days ago, that the governorship election might be postponed, considering the effect of the nationwide strike action embarked upon by the organised labour, which has totally crippled the state.

Interpreting the Subsidy Rage

By Chima Ibeneche

***The Guardian*, Wednesday, January 18, 2012, pg. 51**

WHAT has been remarkable during the weeklong strike called by the labour unions to protest the petroleum subsidy removal is the spontaneous support it received across the nation. It has been a convulsive explosion of popular sentiment and anger from people of all walks of life. Apparently, labour has drilled into some strong artesian aquifer that just burst into a tall geyser. My take is that what we have so far seen is indeed the proverbial last straw that broke the camel's back. And it begs the question: "what other loads was the camel carrying before the last straw was added?"

To conclude that the popular response to the subsidy removal was all about the increase in the pump price of petrol is to miss the point; to miss the whole point. Granted that the timing of the removal of the subsidy on New Year 's Day was awful considering that many ordinary people are usually broke after the festivities. Granted that an increase of the price of petrol from 65 to 140 naira per litre could lead to some inflation in the economy, the decision to remove the subsidy makes eminent sense and is in the long term interest of Nigeria. Even some of the labour leaders and some members of the National Assembly who oppose the subsidy removal agree that the subsidy, as currently practised, is not sustainable and bad for the economy on the long run.

Labour says it would support subsidy removal if the government first rehabilitates the existing refineries, builds new refineries, ensures local refining of all petroleum products needs, fights corruption, build roads and the railways before removal of subsidy. Of course this does not make sense. If the government can suddenly get the refineries to work at the instance of Labour, why has it railed to do so in the last 40 years? The refineries in Port Harcourt, Warri and Kaduna will not work any better now than they have so far unless there is a structural change in the way they are managed and governed. Organised private sector is right when they say that the refineries will have to be privatised and sold to capable private sector. If the issue is about fighting corruption, why would Labour and their cohorts oppose the plugging of this largest of corruption pipelines that sucks money directly from our national revenue, even before the governors can get a look in, and sends it straight into the pockets of corrupt bureaucrats and their conniving business people? Yes, the subsidy removal will plug a major corruption pipeline and should be supported if we want to right corruption. So these arguments against subsidy removal are fine as they go but they do not explain the popular opposition to the subsidy removal.

One argument that Nigerians have made which is irrefutable is that Nigerians do not trust the Federal Government, not just the Jonathan government, but its predecessors as well, to be prudent and accountable in the spending of public funds in the interest of society. The track record of our governments in governance and economic management has simply been woeful in the last 20 odd years. Therefore government has lost the right and authority to demand sacrifice from Nigerians on the promise of a better future. Rightfully, the people demand to see a demonstration of some of the future benefits before the imposition of additional pain. Still, this alone does not explain the popular uprising against the subsidy removal.

There remains the underlying fact that life in Nigeria has increasingly become painful, frustrating and hazardous; bereft of hope. Among those who poured out unto the streets are representatives of the millions of young Nigerian graduates who have no hope of finding jobs even some five years after graduation. Among those who demonstrated are some who carry the scars of police brutality and the daily extortion of the ordinary Nigerian by the police at every checkpoint on our roads. Above all, every Nigerian knows that no one is now secure in Nigeria. Recently, very recently, the entire South-East and South-South region was blighted by militancy and kidnapping. Just as this was abating, it was replaced by the more devastating terror of the Boko Haram sect in the North. In today s Nigeria, if kidnapping does not get you, Boko Haram will; if both fail to get you, you have the prospect of violent armed robbery. And we all know that murders and crimes are seldom solved. To rub salt into these wounds, while the quality of life is being drained from Nigerians: while hope is being denied the school leavers, politi- caloffice holders are growing fatter and fatter and government is getting bigger and bigger. It is this absurd state of affairs that Nigerians poured into the street to protest.

Since 1966 when the military had their misadventure into Nigerian politics, power and resources have been taken away from the regions and monopolised by the central government. With the seizure by the central government of all resources and all power, it has created the illusion that the federal government is omnipotent and can provide all the needs of Nigerians. Unfortunately, the unitary government and its monopoly has resulted primarily in bigger government, corruption and the replacement of the noble work ethics of Nigerians with rent seeking. The corrupt unitary government foisted on Nigeria by the military morphed into the constitutional democracy we have today with the added burden that the machinery of gov-ernment has grown astronomically. This is the structure Jonathan inherited; the structure he needs to change with the help of Mark and Tambuwal.

The pains that Nigerians feel that found expression in the popular protests is evidence that the concentration of power and resources at the centre has not been justified whatsoever by the delivery from that centre by successive administrations. Recent performance by the state governments in Lagos, Rivers and many other states shows that regional governments are proving better than the federal government at solving the economic and social problems of Nigerians. Federal roads in Lagos and Port Harcourt are eyesores relative to state roads. The Federal owned National Stadium in Lagos is inferior to the state owned stadium in Lagos, etc.

Yes the demand to fight corruption and to deliver more tangible economic benefits to Nigerians is also a cry for a return of more power and more resources to the federating units. Some call it fiscal federalism; others true federalism. Why should the Federal Constitution deny states the right to generate and distribute power in their states? Why should the federal government establish a central and easily corruptible organisation just to issue driving and vehicle licences? The over-concentration of power in the centre is the root of corruption and the only explanation of the absence of development in our economy.

The measured success that Obasanjo, an ex-soldier, achieved as president was primarily through the removal of some of the monopolies enjoyed by the centre. It was only when Obasanjo removed the NITEL monopoly that Nigerians joined the telecommunications world. By removing the monopoly of the National Provident Fund and the self-management or public sector pensions, Obasanjo gave Nigerians the hope to retire with any pensions. Jonathan, a civilian, should go further and faster. In addition to removing the monopolies in the economic sector, Jonathan should reduce the size of the federal government, reduce the obscene remuneration package of the National Assembly and devolve more powers to the regions.

The mass popularity of the strike called by Labour is a signal that Nigerians want significant positive change. Nigerians love Nigeria and are passionate about being Naija. Nigerians want a united, but federal Nigeria. So the best way forward is to produce change through incremental constitutional amendments, British style, towards a more balanced federal Nigeria. What the protest signals is that if the federal government - the executive and the legislature - is incapable of delivering incremental changes fast enough, there is the prospect that the people could rise in a popular demand for better conditions. We do not have to go that way! We should not allow the future of Nigeria to be determined by the passion of trade unionists and the frustration of the masses which could lead to unpredictable outcomes. To prevent that will require this present government - executive and legislature - to begin to deliver results now both in the economic sphere and more importantly also in the area of true federalism. Ibeneche, the author, is thesoon to be retired MD/CEO of NLNG.

Kaduna: how the subsidy removal protest turned bloody.

By John Shiklam

***ThisDay*, Wednesday, January 18, 2012, vol. 16, no. 6113, pg. 21**

From Monday's commencement of the nationwide protest against the removal of fuel subsidy by the Federal Government, it was obvious that the street protest in Kaduna was likely to be hijacked by hoodlums and miscreants. Besides, Kaduna is very fragile, and at the slightest provocation goes up in flames. It was for this reason that the labour unions in the state, organisers of the street protest, including the Nigerian Bar Association (NBA) and civil society organisations took adequate steps to ensure that mischief makers will not capitalise on the protest to foment trouble.

At the commencement of the protest, the labour unions were very strictly on their members joining the procession. The lawyers were dressed in their black suits while the Members of the Nigerian Labour Congress (NLC) and Trade Union Congress (TUC) were dressed in their uniforms all in an effort to ensure that their procession was not hijack my mischief makers.

The labour leaders, including the former governor of Kaduna State, Alhaji Balarabe Musa, former military administrator of Kaduna State, Col. Hamid Ali, human rights activist, Mallam Shehu Sani, among several others led the NLC/TUC procession that Monday from the NLC state secretariat, along Independence Way to Lugard Hall Roundabout and back to the NLC secretariat peacefully with police accompanying them.

The NBA group was led by some of its officials, including the Executive Director of the Human Rights Monitor, Mr. Festus Okoye among others. Their procession also started from the NLC secretariat through to Warf Road up to NEPA Roundabout. However on reaching the NEPA roundabout, thousands of youths, including the Almajiris who were carrying sticks, leafs and placards and chanting "Chanji" and moving like locust almost'over run the lawyers. Attempts by the lawyers to prevent this group from joining them proved abortive, leaving the lawyers with no option than to divert their procession through Kanta Road and back of the state Secretariat of the NLC.

By 12:00 noon or thereabout that Monday, the NLC/TUC, the NBA/ Coalition of civil societies had rounded up their protest with a press conference at the NLC state secretariat. That was the beginning of the build-up to lawlessness as the youth, some of who were driving and riding dangerously on trucks, cars and motorbikes took over the entire Ahmadu Bello Way, down to the Katsina Roundabout area, chanting "*Ba mu so cire talifi*" (we don't want removal of subsidy) and "Chanji mu ke so " (we want change).

Some of them took over the road leading to the Government House and were forcing people to mention the name of a particular politician before they were allowed to pass. The daring and hostile nature of some of the youths was a clear indication that unless something was done, their actions may lead to the breakdown of law and order.

For instance, they attempted to vandalise the Jonathan/ Sambo Campaign office and the large Billboard with the portraits of Jonathan, Sambo and Yakowa located by the NEPA Roundabout, opposite the New Nigerian newspapers office, but some of their leaders promptly stopped them.

Innocent people were equally harassed as they marched from the Ahmadu Bello Way to other adjourning streets like Warf and Kanta roads chanting their slogans and brandishing sticks and branches of trees.

They also called President Goodluck Jonathan and his Vice, Alhaji Namadi Sambo unprintable names, saying that the duo was the real Boko Haram.

While this drama was going on, another group stormed the Government House, Kaduna and wanted to force its way in, but the security men at the gate resisted them. The situation at the Government House soon turned into open confrontation as the Police; in attempt to disperse the crowd threw canisters of tear gas at them. But the group remained adamant as they merely retreated just a few metres away from the Government House Gate to the nearby Roundabout.

For about five hours or thereabout, the mob prevented anybody going in or coming out of the Government House, including top government functionaries and the Kaduna State Police Commissioner, Alhaji Bala Nasarawa, who was said to have been turned back from entering the Government House by them. The mob was said to have rebuffed the Kaduna State Chairman of the NLC, Mr. Adamu Ango who was said to have gone to appeal to them to suspend the protest, urging them to be peaceful. Posters and Billboards of Governor Patrick Yakowa, President Jonathan and the Vice President Namadi Sambo as well as PDP signboards within the Government House vicinity were not spared by the rampaging youths as they destroyed them.

Surprisingly, amidst all the provocation, the police and other security agents, kept their cool until at about 5:00pm when they were forcefully dislodged by a combined team of soldiers and the police. Although there was no protest on Tuesday, residents stayed indoors while business and commercial activities remained grounded. The city centre was deserted. Only a few private vehicles could be seen on the roads. However, on Tuesday the hoodlums and streets urchins who took over the streets turned violent when they started harassing innocent people and became provocative in their actions in an obvious attempt to find avenues for causing crisis.

The Nigerian Labour Congress (NLC), the Trade Union Congress (TUC), the Coalition of Civil Societies and the Nigerian Bar Association (NBA) had earlier in the day expressed displeasure with the activities of the hoodlums and quickly came out to dissociate themselves from them.

They also announced the suspension of street protest against the removal of fuel subsidy and directed their members and members of the public to stay home and await further directives. The NLC Chairman, Comrade Adamu Ango, while addressing newsmen said the decision to suspend the street protest was taken to avoid the breakdown of law and order.

"We don't want a breakdown of law and order in the state and that is why we decided to suspend street protests for now. We have meet at the level of Nigeria Labour of Congress and other civil society groups and the NBA and have agreed to suspend street protests. We want to plead with people that are protesting on the streets to go back to their houses. It is only the people that are saddled with the responsibility of monitoring the strike that are to come to the NLC secretariat daily.

"The NLC, TUC, NBA and civil society groups will be addressing press conferences at every point in time when the need arises. We want to seize this opportunity to plead with our teaming youths who are supporting this strike not to take the laws into their hand. They should not continue to protest where security agencies are trying to stop them. If they are asked to go back, please, in the interest of peace, obey and go back. The issues of this fuel subsidy are already known worldwide and we will continue to make our case known and so, we don't want a situation where we have casualties.

"We started this protest peacefully and we want to end it peacefully," the NLC chairman said at a news conference before the imposition of the curfew.

Also speaking during the press conference, the Chairman of TUC in the state, Comrade Shehu Mohammed appealed to members of the public to be calm as the message has been sent across the globe and to the presidency, stressing that "there should be no more street protest until the people of Kaduna State hear from us.

"We called for the protest in the first place and we are now saying that in order to maintain law and order in the state, the protest should be suspended until the people hear from us. We really appreciate the cooperation given to us and hope that the issue will be resolved very soon," he said.

Also speaking on behalf of the civil society groups, Mr. Festus Okoye said the strike in Kaduna was handled in a special way because of the peculiar security challenge in the state, stressing that with the present activities of some people, it was better for people to stay at home for the sake of peace and stability."

By 5:30 pm the streets were completely deserted. People were rushing home at a neck breaking speed as if the town was under siege as the hoodlums went about molesting people, prompting an emergency security meeting by the state government to decide on the next line of action to take in order to forestall the breakdown of law and order in the city.

The imposition of the 24-hour curfew on the metropolis and its environs was announced at about 7:30pm at the end of the security meeting, which was presided over by Governor Patrick Yakowa. In a statement signed by the Kaduna

State Commissioner of Police, Alhaji Bala Nasarawa, government said since the commencement of the nationwide strike against the removal of fuel subsidy on Monday, the activities of hoodlums and street urchins have raised serious security concern in theacity.

According to the statement "we have realised that the strike over the removal of subsidy has been hijacked by persons other than those committed to the cause. Demonstration which began yesterday peacefully, today turned violent. People were harassed, intimidated, and installations vandalised. In view of these unfortunate situations, the Kaduna State Security Council has no choice than to impose a 24-hour curfew in Kaduna.metropolis and its environs with effect from 9pm today (Tuesday) January 10, 2012. This measure becomes imperative in order to safeguard ^^s and properties of innocent citizens. Government is urging all citizens of the state to remain calm, lawful and stay at home until further notice."

Before the strike, some groups, notably the youth wing of the Christian Association of Nigeria had warned against mass protest in Kaduna in view of the volatile nature of the city and appealed to the labour unions to ask their members to stay home instead of coming out to protest on the streets as such protest may likely be hijacked by trouble makers.

News of the imposition of curfew was welcomed by residents, some of who said it was the right step in the right direction as it will prevent hoodlums from a repeat of the post election violence and the destruction and looting of their shops and businesses.

Labour orders nationwide strike as new fuel price regime begins

***The Guardian*, Tuesday, January 3, 2012, pg 1, 2**

ALTHOUGH it is still early tionofthe downstream sector days, Nigerians yesterday of the oil industry as pump gotatasteofthefullderegula- price differentiation was the order of the day in filling stations across the country.

Also, condemnation and commendation continued to trail the government's decision to remove the subsidy on petrol.

Meanwhile, a coalition of labour, civil society groups and others has said it would start a nationwide strike today over the removal of fuel subsidy that has pushed the price of petrol to at least ₦138 a litre from ₦65.

Apparently seeking a way to profit from the sudden inauguration of the regime, petroleum marketers in Lagos at first shut their outlets to motorists, which engendered queues at these stations.

Sensing a kill as exasperation lacked in on the public, the filling stations began to open one after the other, hiking their pump price to between N139 and N185 a litre.

However, if the filling stations had hoped to have a field day, they were mistaken as the queues soon dried up, with motorists choosing to buy products where the price was lowest. In what appears to be their reaction to this, price fluctuation kicked in as some of the stations brought their pump prices to retain patronage.

The roads in Lagos were free though, as residents kept indoors observing the holiday.Lagosians who ventured out contended with the expected hike in transportation cost of up 100 per cent. Curiously though, *The Guardian* noticed that some diesel-powered commercial vehicles tried to beat the competition by keeping to their usual fares. Any fear of fuel scarcity was also doused as depot operators in Lagos continued to load products. The depot price for petrol ranged between ₦129 and ₦130.

Petrol price in Abuja yesterday hovered between ₦138 and ₦141. The development had caused a soaring of public transport costs. From Kubwa to the city centre, which hitherto attracted ₦100 now costs N200 while fare from Lugbe area on the airport road was ₦250 from ₦100.

Also, hitherto comatose filling stations in Dutse, Jigawa ed up petrol at be-₦150 a litre.

Some of filling the stations opened in the early hours of yesterday and sold the product at ₦140 but changed the prices to ₦150 a litre after realising that the National National Petroleum Corporation (NNPC) mega station was selling at ₦138 a litre. At Dutse's motor parks, transportation fares jumped up by 120 per cent; Passengers from Dutse to Kano paid ₦1,000 as against ₦400. Many of them were stranded following this development.

One of them, Dantiye Dauda, said: "It is really unfortunate that the current administration is not sensitive to the plight of the common man."

In Markudi, Benue State, the few filling stations that opened for business sold petrol at ₦150 per litre while black marketers sold the product at ₦200. Several out- of-pocket travellers making for their stations preparatory to today's work were stranded as transport fares went up at all the motor parks. Bus drivers who usually collected ₦30 per drop charged ₦50. At the Pleasure Travels Park, a trip to Abuja now costs ₦3,000 as against ₦1,200 before now while a trip to Lagos now costs ₦5000 instead of ₦2500.

Also, a trip to Otukpo now costs ₦800 as against ₦350 while Gboko by bus which used to cost ₦200 now goes for between ₦500 and ₦600. Some commuters who spoke with The Guardian decried the sudden removal of subsidy on fuel and urged the Federal Government to have a rethink and rescind its decision on the issue.

In Plateau, filling stations sold a litre of petrol for ₦145. In the popular black market, the price of a quarter of a litre of the commodity ranges from ₦400 to N700. As a result, transport fares shot up in Jos. For example, from Angwan Rukuba to Jos Terminus, which used to be ₦50 is now ₦100, which was a common development across the city.

Opinions were divided though on the appropriateness or otherwise of the petrol subsidy removal. "Governments decision is very hasty and callous. Government does not have the feelings of the masses at heart. Government is just wicked," says Martin Gijo, a taxi driver.

But the National President of Indigbo Democratic Forum (IDF), Chidi Ndu, welcomed the removal saying that the removal will boost the industries.

Petrol has suddenly disappeared from most filling stations in Benin City, Edo State while those opened for business sold the product at between ₦138 and ₦145 a litre.

The NNPC Mega Stations, which were the only stations selling for ₦138 in the state capital suddenly stopped selling the product at about l p.m. and this led to long queues building in the few tnat were selling.

Filling Stations in Ado Ekiti, Ekiti State capital that hurriedly stopped selling and locked up their station on Sunday afternoon yesterday opened for business with new price regime, selling petrol at etween ₦146 and ₦150 per litre. But the NNPC Mega station and its subsidiary stations yesterday sold at ₦138 a litre.

The pump price hike has increased the cost of transportation in the state by 100 per cent. The commercial motorcyclist that charged ₦40 per drop yesterday charged ₦80.

Chaos broke out in Awka, the Anambra State capital yesterday when it dawned on residents that a 131 per cent increase in the price of petrol had crept on them. Commercial bus drivers and their customers engage themselves in bitter arguments, and even fisticuffs before the situation sunk in as the day wore on, the commuters realised that the situation was the same everywhere.

A survey of the situation in Onitsha, Nnewi, Ekwulobia, Awka and even Enugu revealed that the pump price petrol was between ₦150 and ₦180 a litre. Many commuters were forced back home, as short distances that hitherto cost ₦30 became ₦50, and destinations that were before now ₦100 turned ₦300. Awka to Enugu, which used to be ₦250 is now ₦1, 000.

Also, most filling stations within the Enugu metropolis refused.to open for business, while the very few that opened sold at between ₦180 and ₦200 a litre.

Transport operators at the busy old Park, Market Road and Holy Ghost areas made brisk business as they increased transport fares. Travellers from Enugu to Lagos paid ₦5,000 as against the tide celebrations. Also, transport fares to nearby places like Enugu to Onitsha, Enugu to Umuania, Aba, or Port Harcourt tripled. Most of the travellers, some of who were trying to return to their bases in order to be at work today but could not afford to part with the high fares, had to return home, hoping that the costs might crash soon. Residents of Kaduna State woke up yesterday to the increase in pump price of fuel in most of the filling stations that had locked their doors the previous day. Pump price of petrol ranged from ₦138 to ₦145 a litre.

At the black market where motorists bought petrol for convenience before the removal of the subsidy, a litre was ₦250 yesterday. Cost of intra-state and interstate transportation has also gone up by between 50 and 100 per cent in the state. Taxi fare from Kaduna to Abuja now cost ₦1,500 from ₦1,000; Kaduna-Kano is now ₦1,200 from ₦800; Kaduna to Jos is now ₦2,000 as against N1,300.

A market woman, Mrs. Hannah Mark, said a crate of soft drinks that used to be ₦1, 000 now cost ₦1,300.

believe mat this has been further reinforced by the issues that came up during this trying period. No doubt, we cannot sustain what we are doing presently in terms of cost of governance. It is very imperative that we have to cut our coat according to our size. The number of government agencies need to be trimmed down; the number of government employees need to be trimmed down; the number of political appointees need to be trimmed down; the amount payable to all these government officials and public servants also need to be trimmed down. Everybody needs to make a sacrifice if we don't expect our country to become a failed state. So, if we are going to deal with our infrastructural requirement, everybody needs to pay a price, everybody needs to make sacrifice. It is important that this be addressed. The issue of true federalism, of course we have been advocating that. But as you rightly pointed out these are constitutional reforms that cannot just be addressed by just switch of the button. So, when they are asking the president to do this, it is not the president alone. The issue of constitutional reform is basically the business of everybody: the National Assembly, the state assemblies and all the people who are going to contribute ideas are also involved. So, I believe this is the time for national reformation. We all need to be committed to it and be firm as we do this reform so that our children will have a better society. So, I believe that we need to deal with the issue of national security more than anything now. And in dealing with security issues, we also need to overhaul our security system. I have always contended that this is the only federal system of government with a unitary security system. This cannot be sustained for a long time. We need to decentralize our political system so that we can have local police and state police. I believe that is the best way we can begin to deal with peculiar security challenges in different parts of the country. It is only when you have policemen trained to deal with those types of challenges in their respective areas now we can begin to see some major changes in our security challenges, because no doubt if a policeman who is in Enugu for example is posted to Maiduguri, he is going to find it extremely difficult to cope with what is going on there. But the man who is alreaay in Maiduguri is already used to the security challenges there. Further training can enhance his performance there. And of course, the federal govern-ment is overburdened, so, there is need for us to look at the issue of devolution of power so that the federal government can be given slim powers; so that more powers will now devolve to states. And of course the states would need more resources to deal with that with federal agencies coordinating these things. And I believe we are going to have a better society if we do that.

How do you assess the roles played by certain interest groups during the crisis, especially some ethnic based groups which tended to ethnicize the issues at stake?

We had very unfortunate statements from some well respected leaders at this moment of our trial. And I didn't expect some of these things because those were things that helped to heighten tension in the country, creating fears in the minds of our people all over the country. People were beginning to move back to their areas of origin and so on. This was quite unfortunate. Because of the threats issued from different directions, people began to see the whole thing as ethnic issues, tribal issues, and sectional issues. That was why I said that labour had played into the hands of the enemies of the country. And so they were making all kinds of unguarded statements. Even labour would have found itself in a situation it never bargained for. So, it was at that point that the President, who was sworn in to defend the unity of the country came in to do something. I believe that he saw the way the country was drifting and as president of the country he needed to do something. That was why that broadcast came up. So, if labour is saying it didn't agree with the president before he announced the new price, I don't think the president needed to agree with any person before he made that broadcast. What was proper at that point was to save Nigeria from the hands of those who were trying to divide us.

Another issue thrown up by the crisis was the issue of the undue delay in the passage of the Petroleum Industry Bill. The crisis now made it very clear that the PIB is very crucial towards a true reform of the oil industry. So, what is the status of the PIB now, as some lawmakers have said the Bill is no longer with the National Assembly as the old one that was not passed by the last session of the Assembly has been withdrawn?

Let me say that technically there is no PIB with the National Assembly as we speak. We received in the last National Assembly the PIB. At some point, it was alleged, and I believe this was rieht, that there were different versions of this PIB. What they were discussing in the House of Representatives appeared to be different from what we were discussing in the Senate. And what the committee was dealing with appeared to be different from what we all had as members of the National Assembly. So, at a point we were supposed to discuss it when it came out from the committee, but there was serious issue over which version we are now looking at. So this was the argument until the end of the tenure of the last National Assembly. And technically, the Bill elapsed. And in accordance with the constitution, we expect the executive to re-send the Bill. But up till now, the executive has not resent it. I believe they are still working on it. And we hope they are going to bring something that is more straight-forward; that will be more engaging and that will cover the issues which the contemporary circumstance has raised. So, as I speak to you the Bill has not been sent to the National Assembly. But we are committed to the quick passage of the Bill as soon as it comes. It is a basic complement to the issue of deregulation. Without the Bill being passed, all talks about deregulation will come to naught because there will be no legal basis for some of the issues that are part and parcel of the deregulation.

One other issue that was thrown up by the crisis was the issue of transparency and accountability in the management of funds accruing from the nation's petroleum resources. Towards this end, the EFCC has launched an investigation into the affairs of the oil sector. At the same time, both chambers of the National Assembly are already conducting various investigations into this same sector. How do you mink these probes can best complement one another?

I like the word 'complement' because weaw (the legislature) are not going to do the job of the EFCC. The EFCC is to investigate and prosecute offenders. Ours stops with investigation under Section 88 of the constitution. Already our committee has done a lot of work. As soon as the committee completes its work, they will bring it to plenary and it will be fully discussed. When resolutions are taken we send it to the presidency who will now take appropriate action. I believe that at that point EFCC will now take advantage of some of the findings of our committee and then they can begin to do follow-ups with regards to the recommendations that would come with the investigation. For me, I believe that the EFCC can continue with what it is doing in terms of doing their job, arresting those they believe have issues to iron out and questioning them. But I have to state clearly that for now, they are still mere allegations and I believe in the rule of law and people should not be made to suffer unjustly. So, I guess that the EFCC should just question people and if they see a lead they can begin to investigate along that line. No doubt some people have been supplying fuel to this country, otherwise we won't be having fuel anywhere. So, I don't believe people are just putting the money in their pocket. But the problem is that there have been some sharp practices in the sector. There were over-invoicing, round tripping, collusions and all that. These are the areas I will like the EFCC to train their searchlight but not trying to make a scapegoat of innocent businessmen. I think it is important that whatever investigation they are going to conduct would not amount to witch hunting, it will be transparent and Nigerians would be able to know facts available to them and that all those who are found to be culpable would be made to face the music. And I believe that the difference between what they are doing and what we are doing is that by the time we conclude our work in the Senate, we are going to get the correct figures because all the areas of wastages would have been revealed. So while the EFCC is looking at the prosecution side, we are looking at the more enduring, long term solution to the issue of pricing. So, we hope that our findings would also help the NNPC and Ministry of Petroleum to carry out a major reform in that sector and help Nigerians to begin to see areas where we have wastages as a way of plugging those wastages and leakages. So, what we are doing and what the EFCC is doing, as you said, complement each other for the overall benefit of good governance and democracy to thrive.

In the aftermath of the nation-wide protest, the federal government deployed soldiers to the streets of some major cities, especially Lagos and this has been condemned by a cross section of Nigerians as out of tune with democratic ethos. How do you react to this?

You see, the trend in Lagos during the strike was creating tension in the land. There was fear in the minds of the people, there were issues of robbery; there were issues of molestations. So, it was important to reassure the people because where your right stops that is where the right of another person begins. Yes, you have the right to protest but you don't have the right to molest any person who doesn't want to be part of it. So, it is important that those segments of the society also have to be protected. We don't need to have soldiers on our streets when things are normal, but when things become abnormal it is also important that we have to restore order. If there is no order nobody can thrive. So, we don't want this country to go down in crisis and then everybody will suffer. So, it is important that we avoid any type of situation that will bring anarchy to our country. But the use of soldiers as a matter of fact should be a last resort. But if it is necessary, that is the instrument of coercion which the country needs to ensure that there is order, there is peace and that everybody is protected. I am not aware that those soldiers molested any person.

Labour strike shuts down Nigeria

By Ndubuisi Ugah

***ThisDay*, Tuesday, January 10, 2012, vol.16, no. 6105, pg. 9, 10**

As the nationwide strike declared by the Nigeria Labour Congress (NLC) took off yesterday, members of civil society organisations, politicians, political activists, actors and musicians have said the much canvassed revolution had finally commenced. It was successful in Lagos State as the massive protest rally held at Gani Fawehinmi Park, Ojota, featured 76-year old politician and political activist, Dr. Tunji Braithwaite, who said the current event in Nigeria showed that the appointed time to rescue the soul of Nigeria from those who held it captive had finally come.

"There's something called an appointed time. We are here today on this podium to announce to our children and rulers that the appointed time has arrived. There's no going back. With the power of the Almighty with us, we are taking over our nation and the entire black race and freeing ourselves," Braithwaite said.

It was also successful in Ekiti State as the Catholic Bishop of Ekiti Diocese, Bishop Felix Ajakaye, led thousands of residents of Ekiti State and leaders of several organised labour and civil societies to protest the removal of the oil subsidy by the Federal Government. The protest however came on a day the state government allayed the fears of non-indigenes, particularly members of the Hausa community of their safety in the state during and after the ongoing strike. But the protest, which grounded commercial, social and economic activities of the state to a halt, also witnessed several bonfires made by some hoodlums, across the major streets of Adebayo, Odo-Ado, Ajilosun on Akure road and other areas.

Another successful outing was recorded by labour and its allies as social and economic activities were paralysed in Ondo State as residents both in public and private sectors complied with the strike called by the NLC, Trade Union Congress (JVC) and other civil society groups over the protest. Protesters as early as 730am trooped to the major Adesida/Oyemekun Road in the Akure metropolis with placards bearing inscriptions condemning the action of the government, which they said would further impoverish Nigerians. Markets, banks, government offices, filling stations and shops were under lock and key just as streets remain deserted as commercial vehicle operators, taxi and commercial motorcyclists popularly called okada abandoned their tools of trade.

In another successful outing, at least two persons were injured during the anti-fuel subsidy peaceful protest in Osogbo, the Osun State capital by an unknown politician's vehicle in an attempt to flee from the protesters. The injured persons whose identities could not be ascertained as at the time of filing this report were allegedly hit by the politician driving along Gbongan -Ibadan express road while the protest lasted. The victims who were among hundreds of protesters who gathered at the popular Ola-Iya junction, Osogbo were later rushed to a private hospital in the town.

The strike was also a blissful outing in Oyo State, but policemen bravely repelled the vandalism of the state office of the Peoples Democratic Party (PDP). A toddler named Baraka, who rode piggyback on her mother who was on the protesting procession, cheated death as the Chief Security Officer (CSO) of the state governor, Abiola Ajimobi, allegedly fired two canisters of teargas to disperse the peaceful protesters as they advanced towards the state secretariat where Ajimobi wanted to address the protesters.

A mob which was trailing the peaceful procession of the JAF/NLC coordinated anti-fuel subsidy rally threw stones at the electronic signboard of the party at its secretariat along Queen Elizabeth Road, Ibadan.

SOUTH-SOUTH

Taking a cue from the South-west states, the protest recorded a high level of success in Edo State. But three suspected hoodlums were reportedly killed in Benin-City by the Police while attempting to loot during the protest staged by the organised labour against the removal of fuel subsidy in the state. The state Commissioner of Police, David Omojola, when contacted would neither deny nor confirm the incident as he was said to be attending a security meeting.

However, the protest was not successful in River State as shops, human and vehicular movement was recorded in the state unhindered. The management of Port Harcourt International Airport, Omagwa, near Port Harcourt said normal operations went on at the airport, in spite of the strike. Manager of the airport, Mr. Henry Anyanwu, told the News Agency of Nigeria (NAN) that operations at the airport were not disrupted by anybody.

The action was less successful in Cross River State as workers defied the directive of their leaders on the strike as the NLC and TUC in the state threatened to sanction members who failed to join the ongoing strike to protest fuel subsidy removal. The chairman of the State NLC, Mr. Nyambi Njom, told the News Agency of Nigeria (NAN) shortly after monitoring compliance in Calabar that market union, taxi drivers and owners of petrol stations failed to join in the strike.

Similarly, all was quiet in all fronts in Bayelsa State as residents of the state went about their duties as if the strike was never called. Civil society groups which called the protest quietly called it off as they were told by labour unions in the state that they didn't want to antagonise President Goodluck Jonathan.

Workers in Delta State responded to the call by the NLC to come out en-mass to protest the removal of fuel subsidy, as commercial activities were grounded in the metropolis. It was a successful protest in the state. As early as 7:30am, members of the NLC, other trade unions and okoda riders trooped out en-masse in a procession blocking the popular Inter Bau junction, a road linking

Government House, Delta State House of Assembly and the police headquarters and other streets in the metropolis.

SOUTH-EAST

However, the protest against the subsidy removal recorded a low turn-out in the South-east.

In Enugu, the directive of labour was not heeded as the State Government had banned public assemblies, meetings or processions in any part of the state until further notice. A statement issued by Governor Sullivan Chime yesterday, according to the News Agency ofNigera (NAN), said he banned the protests because such meetings could lead to a breakdown of law and order.

"The holding of any public assemblies, meetings or public procession in Enugu State of Nigeria is hereby prohibited until further notice," he said.

In Aba, the commercial nerve-centre of Abia State, the Ariaria International Market opened for business while people went about their normal business. Vehicular movement was normal as commercial vehicles and motorcycles operated. The Commissioner of Police in Abia State, Mr. Bala Hassan, said there was no form of strike in the state. In a telephone interview with the News Agency of Nigeria (NAN), Bala said: "I have monitored the situation in the state and reports from my field officers in Abia show there is not strike in the state.

"The area is calm. People are going about their normal businesses," he said, adding, "the main markets in Umuahia and Aba are open."

Similarly, the Onitsha Main Market in Anambra State, opened for normal business and life in the city was normal but banks were shut. Also in Imo State, a less successful outing was recorded, although public institutions such as government offices, banks, filling stations were under lock and key, while a handful of protesters mainly labour leaders were seen chanting solidarity songs with placards in some streets in the metropolis.

NORTH-EAST

It was less successful in Maiduguri as the NLC said it had shelved street protest in the ongoing fuel subsidy strike following appeal by security agencies in the state. The Borno State NLC Chairman, Mr. Titus Abana, told NAN in Maiduguri that the strike would not involve any kind of street protest, saying, all other aspects of the strike would continue as scheduled.

Government offices, business and commercial enterprises were shut down in Bauchi State in another successful, but peaceful protest just as major roads across the state capital were cordoned off by angry protesters against the removal of the fuel subsidy, amidst tight security in the state. *ThisDay* checks reports that as early as 7am in the morning, Civil servants, youths, public servants, carried placards with various inscriptions, such as: ".. .we have suffered enough, subsidy must be reversed", among others as they joined the organised labour in the state and led a procession to the Emir's Palace, as the starting point of the rally.

NORTHWEST

Thousands of people living in Kebbi State yesterday protested against the fuel hike announced by President Goodluck Jonathan last week. The protest was led by the state chairman of NLC, Comrade Sadiq Kaoje. The protest was very effective in all the nooks and crannies of the state especially in Bimin Kebbi Argungu, Jega, Yauri, and Zuru among other areas. Some of the placards of the demonstrators read "*Bamuso a kara kudin mai*", "we oppose to fuel hike" and "we don't want subsidy removed."

In Kano, the state government put in place a 6pm to 8 am curfew as a measure to avert breakdown of law and order, following the disturbance which followed the on-going strike, which was allegedly hijacked by miscreants. The protesters also torched and vandalised the office of the secretary to the state government, vandalised the fence wall of government house, while over 18 cars also set ablaze at the SSG office. Residence of Senator Bashir Garba Lado of Kano central residence at Wharf Road in Kano was also destroyed, his cars were also vandalised by the suspected hoodlums during the protests.

Sokoto State Police Commissioner, Mr. Baba Adisa Bolanta, said about 5000 policemen were deployed in the state to maintain security during the strike. Speaking to journalists in Sokoto yesterday, Bolanta said the command took the measure in order to avert the breakdown of law and order in a protest which completely shut down commercial and government activities.

In Kaduna, the crowd that responded to the nationwide strike was unprecedented. Hundreds of thousands of youths, including the Almajiris stormed in support of the labour unions.

Shops and markets were closed while residents of the city remained indoors for fear of the unknown, leaving the city centre deserted. The youths were daring in their protest over the removal of fuel subsidy as they marched round some parts of the city singing solidarity songs, carrying placards and saying all sort of unprintable words about President Goodluck Jonathan and his deputy, Alhaji Namadi Sambo.

NORTH CENTRAL

Workers yesterday shunned the strike called by labour due to the 'security situation' in the state. The union however said it was in total support of the nation-wide strike called by its national body, and it was fully complied within Plateau State.

The state Chairman of the union, Comrade Jibrin Bancir, who announced the suspension of the protest, while addressing journalists and the unionists at the NUJ Press Centre in Jos, said: "The immediate negative impact of the price increase on transportation, food items, drugs, school fees, rents, indicates that government is insensitive to the hardship experienced by Nigerians." Bancir said: "It is disheartening to note that while the country is facing a great challenge of insecurity; lives and properties are lost every day without a solution at hand, the government has decided to add more pains to Nigerians through this inhuman policy."

In Ilorin, it was a glorious outing for the organisers as workers in both private and public service, students, civil societies, markets women, artisans among others in Kwara State came out in large numbers to comply with the order of the NLC to protest the removal of petroleum subsidy by the Federal Government in the country. Offices, shops, kiosiks, business premises were also closed down and thereby halting buying and selling in Ilorin, the state capital and other towns in the state, *ThisDay* investigations revealed that, the situation in other major towns in the state were the same as all shops and business activities were also shut.

The affected towns include Offa, Ajase-Ipo, Oro, Omuaran, Share, Patigi, Lafiajifrinle and Shonga. Although the state capital experienced heavy presence of policemen who were armed to the teeth, an Air force aircraft also hovered around Ilorin.

In Lokoja, Kogi State, no gunshot was fired, no tear-gas canister was released, no arrest was made and no injury whatsoever was recorded but there was graveyard calm yesterday in the entire area with the ever busy Lokoja-Abuja road deserted when protesters held the state to ransom for about five hours. Labour leaders, comprised of the Chairmen, NLC, Comrade James Odaudu, his TUC counterpart, Comrade Abdulazeez Ganiyu, and other leaders of Civil Liberty Organisations (CLO) and NGOs were gathered at the Paparanda Junction as early as 7am where youths carrying anti-subsidy and anti-President Jonathan inscriptions converged to start the mass protest against subsidy removal by the Federal Government. The multitude of protesters, mostly youths marched from their Paparanda convergence point through IBB Way and Lord Lugard road where they arrived at the Kogi State Government House where the protest almost went out of hands. It took the persuasive efforts of the NLC and TUC leadership to avert the outbreak of lawlessness.

One of the organisers of the protests and Kogi State Coordinator, Centre for Human Rights and Conflict Resolution (CCHRCR), Comrade Idris Miliki, said the protest in the State was successful. "For two reasons, the protest is a victory protest. Since we went out and came back safely. Secondly, because our message has been passed. Nobody can hold us responsible for any violence or lawlessness and yet, our objective has been achieved. We also thank the police, since they stood by their words that if we are not violent, they will not be violent too," he recounted. Similarly, the NLC Chairman, Odaudu commended the protesters for conducting themselves in an orderly manner that was devoid of violence. He blamed breakdown in communication for the skirmishes that occurred at the government house.

At the Federal Capital Territory (FCT), Abuja, in an apparent obedience to the call for an industrial action, most streets of the city, were virtually empt. Though, the heavy presence of Police and armed military personnel contributed in keeping many residents of the city off from the streets. Apart from the empty streets, the banks, the hotels, various shopping malls and plazas including the famous Wuse and Garki markets were under lock and key. From the MKO Abiola Street which stretched from Area One to the International Conference Centre near the Radio House by Area Eleven was empty, the situation was the same as the other parts of the city. Workers did not come to work at the Federal Secretariat housing all the offices of the federal ministries and agencies. Though, the NLC and the TUC rallies did not get near to the Eagle Square, as it was blocked by Armoured Personnel Carriers (APC) Vehicles manned by the Police, Army and members of the Nigeria Security and Civil Defence Corps (NSCDC) officials cordoned off the square. Both the striking NLC and TUC officials and workers of the Federal Secretariats were not allowed to get nearer the secretariat. From the Agonyi Ironsi street housing the Transcorp hotel to the *ThisDay* Dome, Federal High Court Complex and adjoining streets were all cordoned off by security officials. Also at the junction of the Louis Edet House (Force Headquarter) to the Federal Ministry of Finance Office Complex were all cordoned off. It was therefore difficult to say whether the absence of workers from their respective offices was either in obedience to the NLC TUC induced strike or due to the fact that they were not allowed into their offices by the presence of security officials guarding the place. But a petrol station that dispensed the petroleum product was the AP station located opposite Transcorp Hilton Hotel. As usual, the station had a long queue as vehicles used the opportunity make a quick buy of the PMS.

Labour threatens mass protests

By Linda Eroke and Damilola Oyedele

***ThisDay*, Monday, January 2, 2012, Vol. 16, No. 6097, pg 1, 6**

The Nigeria Labour Congress (NLC) and the Trade Union Congress (TUC) have declared a showdown with the Federal Government through mass protests and strikes until the price of petrol is reversed to N65 per litre.

The leadership of the labour movements in a joint statement issued yesterday directed their state councils to take steps to resist any price above N65 per litre of PMS, and await a date for the commencement of general strikes and mass protests across the country. Nigerians were also urged to begin mobilisation for the commencement of the protests.

In the statement signed by the NLC's Acting General Secretary, Comrade Owei Lakemfa, and his TUC counterpart, Comrade John Kolawole, the congresses said the action of the Presidency at this period when Nigerians were mourning the victims of recent bomb blasts showed "insensitivity and callousness".

The Federal Government was also accused of thriving on falsehood as it had recently told Nigerians that consultations were still going on with various stakeholders including organised labour and if any fuel subsidy was being contemplated, it would be with effect from April 1, 2012.

"We also have information that it intends to make a litre of PMS ₦150.00 and then ask the NNPC to reduce the price at its fuel stations by a few naira. Nigerians must defeat whatever are the schemes of this government,"the statement read.

While expressing the readiness of organised labour to engage in a long drawn battle, the statement called on the National Assembly and governors to side with the people over the matter.

The labour unions urged the police and other security personnel not to accept any order to shoot protesting Nigerians or attack them, noting that there would be insistence that any officer who does so will be brought to justice.

"We also put the Jonathan Presidency and its surrogates on notice that we shall ensure that they are prosecuted up to the International Criminal Court if they, by acts of commission or omission spill the blood of any Nigerian over the protests that follow their inhuman acts against the people," the congresses warned.

The statement added that the leadership of the NLC and TUC would jointly issue directives in the next few days on the date the organised national strikes, street demonstrations and mass protests would commence.

President General of TUC, Comrade Peter Esele, viewed the latest development as "a stab in the back" by the Federal Government who only last week entered into a dialogue with the organised labour in a bid to forestall a looming anarchy.

He explained that the action of government was a total declaration of war on the "poor masses who are being punished by an inefficient system that is anchored on few corrupt oil thieves who are major sponsors and backers of government".

He disclosed that the National Executive Council (NEC) of TUC would meet in the next few days to take a firm decision on the issue.

"The Trade Union Congress of Nigeria (TUC) rejects without reservation the reported removal of petroleum subsidy by the Federal Government as announced by the Petroleum Products Pricing Regulatory Agency (PPPRA) executive secretary Reginald Stanley, which ushered in an anti-people based price of ₦141 per litre. This is unacceptable to us and to the Nigerian masses who have been ambushed by a government they expressively gave a popular mandate to represent them some few months back.

"We are surprised that the government could proceed to implement the removal without recourse to the National Assembly who all available indices indicate that they have not given it any legislative backing neither was it mentioned in the 2012 national budget.

"This action by President Goodluck Jonathan is therefore dictatorial, undemocratic and a total declaration of war on the poor masses of this country who are being punished by an inefficient system that is anchored on few corrupt oil thieves who are major sponsors and backers of government. This is why the government cannot muster enough political will to arrest and prosecute them. What we expect the Federal Government through the PPPRA to do is to tackle the corruption in the system first before this present action.

"For the avoidance of doubt, TUC insists that until new refineries are built and the old or existing ones are made to function optimally, there cannot be a removal of petroleum subsidy. Therefore, TUC on behalf of the Nigerian workers and the masses have declared a dispute of interest with the Federal Government," he said.

Also, a civil society group, the Joint Action Front (JAF), has called for civil disobedience to force the Federal Government to rescind its pronouncement.

The statement jointly signed by the group's Chairman and Secretary, Dr. Dipo Fashina and Comrade Abiodun Aremu, respectively, urged Nigerians to turn up en-mass for the protest.

Fuel Subsidy Conversation: A leap in people's power

By Tope Templer Olaiya

***The Guardian*, Sunday, January 22, 2012, pg. 14**

WHILE the eightday strike lasted, it was not strange hearing two friends exchanging pleasantries. While one hails his mend 'Save Nigeria', the other replies 'Enough is enough.' Among the Yorubas, who are famous for having a particular greeting for several occasions, the salutation during the strike was Eku subsidy Happy subsidy), which goes with the response, Reversal a ba wa laiye, meaning we would live to enjoy subsidy reversal.

These were some of the telltale signs of the mass action that swept through most parts of Lagos, particularly at the Gani Fawehinmi Park, Ojota.

Exactly two years ago, human rights activists under the umbrella of Save Nigeria Group (SNG) had stormed the seat of power at Abuja and the nation's commercial capital, Lagos, to protest the continued absence of late Umaru Yar'Adua from the country. The then president had been abroad for weeks for medical reasons. However modest, movement spearheaded by General Overseer of the Latter Rain Assembly, Pastor Tunde Bakare, was able to make its voice heard in the corridors of power.

On the first day of the strike action called by the organised Labour, it was a different SNG and vituperated Bakare that amassed thousands of youths and marshalled the Lagos rally at Ojota. Apart from the changes in time and circumstances, one remarkable feature, which made the two events stand miles apart, was the use of social media to galvanise and mobilize, while heaping fire and brimstone on their perceived enemies Goodluck Jonathan and his cabinet for inflicting so much pain on the nation with the New Year day withdrawal of fuel subsidy.

In this year's episode, SNG was not the only actor on stage. The group was joined by other civil organisation and cyber activists, which greatly employed the instrumentality of the social media to midwife a successful rally. Other collaborators included #Occupy Nigeria, Enough is Enough Nigeria coalition (EiE), Joint Action Forum (JAF), Restoration Nigeria Group, and Civil Liberties Organisation (CLO).

EiE is a coalition of individuals and youth organisations committed to instituting a culture of good governance and public accountability in Nigeria through advocacy, activism and the mobilisation of the youth population as responsible citizens. According to the group's coordinator, Yemi Adamolekun, "we are nonpartisan, neither are we a platform for the actualisation of any individual's political ambitions.

"There are currently 2.84 million Nigerians on Facebook, which is 28 times the reach of the most exaggerated number of Nigeria's most successful newspaper, so the use of technology provides ample access. Our ambitious goal is to mobilise 10 million young people, cutting across religious, ethnic and socio-economic divides in the country to be actively engaged in the electoral process by 2015," she said.

#Occupy Nigeria is a protest movement that began in Nigeria on Monday, January 2,2012 in response to the fuel subsidy removal by the federal government on Sunday, January 1. Celebrities like Banky W, Funmi Iyanda, Seun Kuti, Ras Kimono, 9ice, Dede Mabialoi and others have been at the forefront of #OccupyLagos, as the protests have been referred to.

The Occupy Nigeria protests have also occurred in other countries to show solidarity with the plight of Nigerians back home. The first one was held at the Nigerian Embassy in London on January 6, followed by another at the World Bank complex in Washington D.C. on January 9.. Other countries like Belgium, Ghand, South Africa, Netherland and France joined the protests and occupied the Nigerian embassy in their countries.

Lessons from the Anti-Subsidy Removal

By EmekaNwosu

***ThisDay*, Tuesday January 24, 2012, vol. 17, no. 6119, pg. 14**

Last week Monday, the Nigeria Labour Congress (NLC) and Trade Union Congress (TUC) called off the nationwide strike which the leadership of the organised labour and the civil society groups had staged to protest the unilateral increase in the pump price of petroleum by the federal government. The civil protest which lasted for one week crippled commercial and economic activities throughout the federation and brought the nation to a standstill.

The astronomical increase in the cost of premium motor spirit (PMS) followed the total withdrawal of subsidy on petroleum products by the government on January 1, 2012. The decision which was announced by the Petroleum Products Pricing and Regulatory Agency (PPPRA) took everyone by surprise as it came when many Nigerians were still in their various villages enjoying the Christmas and New Year festivities.

The sudden development resulted in sharp increase in the cost of fuel from N65 to N141 per litre. Transporters immediately responded by increasing transport fare by as much as 200 per cent. The effect was immediate and dramatic. Those who travelled for the Yuletide and New Year celebrations got stranded as they could not afford the hike in the cost of public transportation.

The populace was seething with rage and anger over the policy and the timing which caught almost every one unawares. The public response was swift. Even before the organised labour could declare strike and called workers out, various organised groups and civil society organisations had taken to the streets to demand the reversal of the deregulation policy and re-instatement of the N65 pump price.

It would seem that the government underestimated the resolve of the people when the strike commenced on Monday, January 9, 2012 as no serious efforts were made to dissuade labour from going ahead with the protest. Even the window of opportunity that was offered by the House of Representatives following its intervention in the crisis was not seized by the authorities.

Rather the House resolution which called on the government to suspend the subsidy withdrawal and return to negotiation table with labour was scoffed at by presidential spokesman, Dr. Reuben Abati who issued a statement describing the position of the House as personal opinion which was not binding on the government.

However, labour and the dvil society groups were able to prove to government that they had the capacity to shut down the nation. The public response to the street protests was total. The dtizens in their millions took over the streets and public spaces throughout the country. Offices, banks, markets, shops, schools and in some cases public hospitals were shut down. The airspace was equally shut down with no domestic flights allowed to operate within the country. The effect was crippling.

In many places, the street protests were hijacked by hoodlums who took advantage of the situation to visit terror on innocent Nigerians and dispossess them of their belongings. In places like Lagos, Kano and Kaduna some failed politicians sought to hijack the street rallies to demand for regime change. This was the dangerous dimension which the strike action had assumed before government and organised labour were able to reach a compromise.

From the way and manner the strike was going, there was serious apprehension in the land that the situation might be exploited by anti-democratic elements masquerading as public do-gooders to short-circuit the system. It is against this background that the leadership of labour must be commended for the wisdom in calling off the street protests and going back to the negotiation table with government.

Even though it did not get all it wanted from government, but by its dedsion to deny anti-democratic forces and street urchins the opportunity to harm our hard-earned democracy, labour had shown that the interest of the country is far greater than any other interest in our nation.

For me, the success or otherwise of the just suspended strike action does not lie in the concession labour was able to secure from government which had to climb down from N141 to N97 per litre but the exposition of the high level corruption and sleaze that characterise the operations of the oil and gas industry in Nigeria. Following the expositions and demands of labour, government has committed itself to probing the monumental fraud unearthed in the fuel subsidy regime and sanitising the oil and gas sector to ensure probity and transparency in the management of the industry.

With this development, Nigerians are eagerly looking forward to a forensic investigation of the subsidy fraud and the entire gamut of the oil and gas sector as promised by President Jonathan and the prosecution of members of the cartel that fed fat on the nation.

Indeed, the one week strike action by labour and civil society groups has thrown up many issues which must be squarely tackled for us to make any headway as a nation. Prior to the staging of the protests by labour, the country had been engulfed in serious security crisis which was gradually assuming ethnic and sectarian character. Thousands of innocent people have been killed in. some parts of the North on account of their ethnicity and religion they profess. This has thrown the entire country into fear. We cannot continue that way.

In the aftermath of the labour protests and the continued ethno-religious killings, we must decide as a people whether we wish to continue on the same path that has led us to nowhere or to seek a new and refreshing path that may lead us to a better destination.

Former military President, General Ibrahim Babangida has fired the first salvo in this respect. In a recent public statement, he called on President Jonathan to seize the moment thrown up by the labour protests and ensure enduring changes were effected in the structure of the Nigerian federation which he said was presently skewed.

The former president in the statement noted that "the weaknesses in the present arrangement have since been exposed and have to be discarded to accommodate new thinking in global managerial dynamics." He went further to propose a unicameral legislature, contending that "the cost of running a bicameral legislature has since become apparently unaffordable."

I share the same with Babangida and other discerning Nigerians that President Jonathan has a historic opportunity to ride on the popular crest of the current social struggles to commence the process of restructuring Nigeria for the good of its component parts.

He must demonstrate courage and firmness in this respect. This is what leadership entails in times like this. We desire to live together as one indivisible country. But the terms of such togetherness must be mutually agreed by all the component units of our federation

The many faces of subsidy protest survivors: how traders, artisans lived with the industrial action.

By Geoff Iyatse

***The Guardian*, Sunday, January 22, 2012, pg. 49**

THE nationwide industrial action that trailed the removal of subsidy on petrol may have yielded positive results for some smart businessmen, as some retail traders say they made brisk businesses during the weeklong action, during which the country purportedly lost ₦950d (a figure already debunked by the Finance Ministry in view of the fact that a measure of economic activities took place in South East and South South).

Although turnover was low, it was learnt that many traders on essential communities made huge profits on sales, with most of them raking in more than marginal profit of between 100 and 300 per cent on transactions carried out within the period.

In a perfect market situation, a buyer has opportunity to bargain price with many sellers in a competitive atmosphere. But during the strike and protests that imposed restriction on movement, buyers were compelled to buy from few available sellers who fixed prices for maximum gains.

Victoria Adelabu, a Lagosbased fruit dealer, confirmed this: "It was easy to sell at whatever price you chose, because many sellers could not get stocks, she said.

"Meanwhile, buyers had no other choice than to buy at any rate. The question was not even about price out availability. If you think it is too expensive, another person will pay for the items while you are still bargaining.

"It is just like a war situation; somebody, who takes risk to bring essential commodities to a war zone, can decide to make 500 per cent profit on the cost price. What we experienced was typical of abnormal market; it happens all over the world and people bear it with understanding."

She explained that the fact that most sellers, who traveled for the New Year celebration, were not back before the crisis erupted had affected supply, thereby fuelling the exploitative tendency, especially in Lagos.

Still, evening markets became common sights in Lagos metropolis. Established markets opened about 5pm for the public to restock basic things. However, the market places assumed new character; their hitherto rowdy nature had disappeared, as food became the only item of trade.

Also, they assumed character similar to neighbourhood foodstuff markets, just as most of the traders had nothing to do with other items outside food.

Understandably, many people could not travel far to shop following emerging fear over hoodlum activities.

Reacting to this, Paul Adebayo, a self acclaimed social economist, said: "It is natural to have the kind of market formation we had last week (during the strike). When you are in a battlefield, the only thing that makes sense to you is survival, and you can survive without new clothes or household items. Most importantly, you need food and water.

"This explains why the prices of food stuff and water went up during the protest. At a point, people were becoming apprehensive; it was difficult to plan on what you stocked because you could not tell how long the crisis would last. At that point, no man with his right senses would go shopping for other items you didn't need for immediate survival. Sellers also had this orientation. This informed the kind of market structures we had."

Apart from the designated market places, emergency foodstuff trading centres also sprang up in many parts of Lagos. Items mostly found in the spontaneous markets included vegetables, fruits and yams.

Observers explained that the relaxed regulation of environment and public places and the need to bring market closer to the people had encouraged such formation. Those, who patronised the provisional markets, which have disappeared with the fuel subsidy removal protest, confessed that food items were far cheaper in those places than what obtained in conventional ones.

Nonessential items' dealers were not as fortunate as food merchants. Those who dared to open shop experienced lull, as the cautious customers were nowhere to be found. They acknowledged that sustenance was fundamental concern of an average Nigerian.

"I did not expect to sell; I only opened because this is my life. I have not done any other job in the past seven years. So what was I supposed to be doing at home? For the six days that strike lasted, I can't remember if I sold a yard of cable. I am not sure I did.

"Essentially, people had to eat and drink. Who would be thinking of electrical installation during such a difficult time? Also remember that ATM machines were not dispensing money. Most people were financially stranded, as it were. So, I was not surprised about poor transactions," noted an electrical installation artisan who runs a shop in a Lagos suburb.

While trading shops located on major roads and streets of Lagos closed shops for fear of being attacked by hoodlums, those in obscured areas kept theirs open. This was the situation in many parts of Lagos. But the majority of the traders, according to investigation, were in business.

Those who closed their shops had stayed around for two reasons. First, they needed to protect their investments against mob action. "I may not open but I need to stay close to my business to see how I can protect it in my little way supposing hoodlums visited. You never can tell the form, the protest will assume the next moment," saict Abdulrazak Musa, who runs a supermarket.

Another group that stayed around the location of their businesses, it was gathered, did so for transaction purpose. They sat or stood somewhere behind their shops looking out for customers who could come looking for things to buy. Then, they would approach them to inquire what they needed.

Further findings suggest that this category of traders were among the mass of people that were caught unaware by the strike, and as such were not financially prepared for it. "I need to survive; I don't even know how to survive till next week if the strike is not called off. That is why I come around. It doesn't matter to me if I sell at a loss; all I want is the money," said another trader on the fourth day of the strike.

Ladipo autopart dealers were not excluded from this group. Those whose shops were not located in closed warehouses were in the market to do business. However, they would not open shop until there was a serious customer

"I came to market throughout the period. But I didn't open. I stood at the entrance to the section where my store is. Of course, I know those who are looking for parts when I see them. I still sold, but that was purely for survival not because I was making gains," disclosed Okechukwu Okonkwo.

Artisans said they were the highest losers as the strike worsened the financial position of their clients, who were just resuming from Christmas and New Year holidays. They had depended on telephone communication to keep in touch with those who needed their services, even as they complained that most people were not ready to give fair compensation for their services.

The Monday that Nigeria failed to explode.

By OmololuOgunmade

***ThisDay*, Wednesday, January 18, 2012, vol. 16, no. 6113, pg. 17**

Renewed plans by protesting Nigerians to return to the streets last Monday fell through when the organised labour gave a sit-at-home order while military men cordoned off rally grounds to prevent any further mass protest. Omololu Ogunmade writes on how threats by civil groups to shut down Nigeria fizzled out like mid-night dreams

B eyond the Tsunami rallies witnessed in several parts of Nigeria in reaction to January 1, 2012 removal of subsidy by President Goodluck Jonathan last week, hopes of further explosive protests were dashed on Monday as the organised labour first suspended street protests. And beyond the suspension of street protests by the leadership of both the Nigeria Labour Congress (NLC) and Trade Union Congress (TUC), the government of President Goodluck Jonathan swiftly deployed soldiers across the country to halt any further mass protests and rallies.

Both the suspension of street protests by labour as well as its enforcement by military men put off intensive preparations for bigger, well organised and more effective protests conceived by both leaders of civil society organisations as well as common Nigerians on the street. Leaders of Occupy Nigeria Group which spearheaded last week's protests in collaboration with labour, had resolved to take 6 the Federal Government by surprise on Monday. They had imagined that since Jonathan had remained adamant at the weekend on public demand to revert the pump price of petrol to ₦65.00 per litre, advocates of Occupy Nigeria protests would be left with no option than to exhibit virile, resilient and resolute stance on Monday as a way of telling Jonathan and his executive team that sovereignty actually resides in the people and not in government.

On Friday, when the day's protest was brought to a close in Lagos, organisers had instructed their fellow protesters to spend the weekend (Saturday and Sunday) to refresh themselves, stockpile food and then prepare themselves fit for a long drawn battle of no retreat, no surrender against the Jonathan-led government. To this end, Pastor Tunde Bakare, Convener of Save Nigeria Group (SNG), had told the gathering that they would not be cowed even if the leadership of organised labour failed the masses of Nigeria by backing down in the struggle without achieving the aspiration to compel Jonathan to revert the pump price to N65.00.

According to him, if the organised labour opted to betray the people's trust by calling off the strike prematurely, jobless Nigerians on the street would be encouraged to up the ante of the struggle until justice was eventually achieved. He insisted that the proposal of ₦90.000 or ₦100.00 per litre of PMS was unacceptable as he added that the protesters would move from Ojota this week to "occupy Abuja" as well.

With these words of mobilisation, protesters dispersed one after the other that Friday and with the reported "deadlocked" meeting between labour and Federal Government on Saturday, they looked fired up enough to stage the mother of all rallies with the hope that there would be an explosion in the polity beginning from Monday.

But this was not to be as some protesters who had been angered by Jonathan's announcement of the reduction of pump price of premium motor spirit (PMS) from ₦140.00 to ₦97.00 on Monday morning had headed for the streets to continue with the struggle. But upon arriving at various rally grounds, they got what they did not bargain for.

As early as possible, soldiers had cordoned off the popular Gani Fawehinmi Freedom Park in Ojota, Lagos, where massive rallies which heated the polity were held for five days last week. Besides, those caught by the military men deployed by soldiers to prevent any further protest had severe punishment meted to them. They were not only held under duress but the soldiers also asked them to frog jump. The Ojota rally was led by Bakare, Mr. Femi Faland, Dr. Joe Okei-Odumakin, Dr. Tunji Braithwaite and host of other star actors and musicians.

Prior to events that altered civil groups' plans, on Sunday, Bakare, Convener of Save Nigeria Group (SNG) and a vocal leader of Occupy Nigeria Group, had said he would not be cowed by death threats that he had received on account of the massive rallies he led in Ojota last week. Crowd at the rally had appeared like the sand of the sea with expressions of anger on the marginal hike in the pump price of PMS following the January 1 subsidy withdrawal by the Petroleum Products Pricing and Regulatory Agency (PPPRA).

Bakare, who is the Senior Pastor of Latter Rain Assembly, had told his congregation that protests against the hike would continue on Monday since the meeting between the Federal Government and labour did not yield anticipated response on Saturday night. Bakare had threatened that since the Federal Government was adamant, Nigerians had been left with no option than to intensify demonstrations against what he called injustice against the people.

The activist-politician who alleged that government was after his life, restated the comment he had made last week in Ojota that it was cheap blackmail and misplaced propaganda for Ojota rallies to have been said to be sponsored by certain unscrupulous elements who benefited from subsidy. The cleric who vowed not to succumb to intimidation and blackmail, noted that people stormed the rally without any financial inducement to express their rejection of the subsidy policy. He said the civil groups were not only protesting removal of subsidy but also corruption.

"We are not motivated by another force than the belief that this land must be free and Nigerians must enjoy, if we (SNG) are spon-sored by any political force, you will not see such crowd at Ojota. I was reluctant to protest, we wanted to dialogue. We contacted those in the corridor of power. When the time comes, I will name those I contacted to give the president a soft landing. We are not protesting the removal of subsidy only, but corruption, waste in government," Bakare had told his congregation.

On alleged threat to his life, he said: "In the past one week, there have been threats to my life. My wife was called upon one night to tell me not to sleep at home. While arrangement was made for me to go into hiding, Yinka Odumakin also received an anonymous call, saying 'don't sleep at home this night' but that night, I slept in my bed room. It's only the wicked that flee when no man pursues him but the righteous is as bold as a lion.

"There were threats of death and arrest. The latest one this morning (Sunday) was a text message sent to me which reads: 'you are the one motivating the labour not to accept government offer. We are coming after you. We are going to investigate your early years of legal practice.'"

Bakare, who spoke on the topic titled: "Subsidy Made Easy (SME)" faulted govern-ment claims that ₦1.3 trillion is being spent annually on petroleum subsidy for Nigerians. "Nigerians have been paying ₦65 per litre for fuel. Therefore, cost borne by the consumers is ₦807 billion. Consequently, the true cost of subsidy borne by the government is: ₦943 billion not ₦1.75 trillion."

It was not only Bakare who threatened explosive protest on Monday. The Joint Action Front (JAF), a member of the Occupy Nigeria Group, also said mass action would return to the nooks and crannies of Nigeria through street protests in the entire 36 states of the federation last Monday.

General Secretary of JAF, Abiodun Aremu, had told reporters at the NLC House in Lagos on Sunday that reverting to ₦65.00 as the official pump price of PMS by the Federal Government was non-negotiable. "We want to assure that there is no negotiation than reversal to ₦65. Unless there is overnight reversal, the protest continues," he had said. But on Monday morning, the pump price did not revert to N65.00, yet protests on the streets had suddenly become history as Jonathan had deployed military men on the street to avert any protest.

On Monday morning, Jonathan had in a nationwide broadcast, announced a new pump price for petrol. He said the product would now sell at ₦97.00 per litre instead of the ₦140.00 that PPPRA had fixed on January 1. The new price is N43 less than the ₦140.00 earlier announced by PPPRA and ₦32 higher than the former price of N65 which labour and civil society organizations had demanded as the condition for calling off the strike and street protests.

He said PPPRA had been directed to ensure compliance with this new pump price. He also said in reaction to the cries of Nigerians that his government was working hard to reduce recurrent expenditure and simultaneously cut down the high cost of governance. Jonathan also said the Federal Government had commenced the implementation of Subsidy Reinvestment and Empowerment (SURE) projects which he said included government assisted mass transit programme and job creation for the youth.

Jonathan vowed to tackle corruption in the petroleum industry as well as other sectors of the economy, threatening that "all those found to have contributed one way or the other to the economic adversity of the country will be dealt with in accordance with the law."

He did not hesitate to say: "Government will continue to pursue full deregulation of the downstream petroleum sector. However, given the hardships being suffered by Nigerians, and after due consideration and consultations with state governors and the leadership of the National Assembly, government has approved the reduction of the pump price of petrol to ₦97 per litre. The

Petroleum Products Pricing Regulatory Agency (PPPRA) has been directed to ensure compliance with this new pump price."

"Government is working hard to reduce recurrent expenditure in line with current realities and to cut down on the cost of governance. In the meantime, government has commenced the implementation of the Subsidy Reinvestment and Empowerment projects: including the Federal Government- assisted mass transit programme which is already in place and job creation for the youth.

"Furthermore, the legal and regulatory regime for the petroleum industry will be reviewed to address accountability issues and current lapses in the industry. In this regard, the Petroleum Industry Bill will be given accelerated attention. The report of the forensic audit carried out on the (Nigeria National Petroleum Corporation) NNPC is being studied with a view to implementing the recommendations and sanctioning proven acts of corruption in the industry."

With this broadcast, the rage on the street was arrested while renewed hopes of further protests were later dashed when after 1 pm on Monday, leaders of organised labour, Omar and Esele, announced the suspension of one week of nationwide strike, saying their decision was the output of consultations with relevant stakeholders. They promised to work with the mediating team constituted by the Federal Government.

However, notable Nigerians have said that despite the abrupt end to the strike and nationwide protests, one lesson that has been leant from the entire scenario is that Nigerians can no longer be relegated to the background in matters of governance. According to them, there is increasing awareness about governance, its cost and manners of government operations now than ever before.

NLC Strike: Security chiefs assure protesters, others of safety.

By Terhemba Daka.

***The Guardian*, Saturday, January 7, 2012, pg. 10**

As the Nigeria Labour Congress (NLC) gears up for a nationwide strike action over ,the removal of petroleum subsidy come Monday, heads of the country's security agencies yes-terday met in Abuja and assured the safety of all protesters during the strike action. The security chiefs, including the Chief of Defence Staff (CDS), Air Chief Marshal Oluseyi Petinrin; Chief of Army Staff (COAS), Gen. Azubuike Ihejirika; Chief of the Naval Staff (CNS), Vice Admiral Ola Said; Chief of the Air Staff, Air Marshal Mohammed Umar as well as the Inspector General of Police, Hafiz Ringim met at the Force Headquarters in country's capital.

Others at the security meeting, which lasted several hours behind closed doors, were the Director General of the State Security Service (SSS), Mr. Ita Ekpenyong and the Director General of the National Intelligence Agency (NIA), Mr. Olaniyi Oladeji.

Addressing journalists on behalf of the service chiefs at the end of the meeting, Ringim disclosed that medical services would be on hand for the protesters.

"Motorists, private and public observers plying our roads will be protected. Air travellers, all peace-loving and non-protest participants will be allowed and protected.

"Officers and men of all the security agencies will be on duty 24 hours to ensure non molestation of all citizens.

"Nigerians from all walks of life, who want to continue with their duties, will be protected, traffic and commuters inclusive," he said.

While urging the organisers and participating groups in the strike to be cautious and take charge of their members, and refrain from any acts or conduct that could cause the breach of the peace, he warned that government would deal decisively with acts of brigandage during the strike.

"We believe that the protest will be peaceful, as advocated and promised, by (Abdulwaheed) Omar, Chairman of Nigeria Labour Congress (NLC) and his teams. However, apart from the security arrangement put in place, our medical services, fire brigade service, civil defence, Federal Road Safety Corps (FRSC), National Emergency Management Agency (NEMA and other relevant civil agencies will be on hand to ensure the security of all involved.

"The civil, security and military forces of the country are determined that within the ambit of the law, everybody's wish and rights will be respected. Those that want to protest will be well secured, guarded and protected by the Police in all the nooks and corners of the country. Also those that are not interested in the strike will be well secured."

On the alleged killing of a youth by Police during the protest in Ilorin, the Police boss explained that the operatives or the security agencies did not carry out the killing.

"What happened was that a group of butchers disagreed with one another on the modalities of slaughtering a cattle.

"It was the quarrel among the butchers that led to the loss of life in Ilorin. The medical as well as the post mortem exams is available. The death of the youth was not occasioned by the bullet or weapon of any law enforcement agent.

"The Police and other law enforcement agencies have a duty under the law to make sure that lifeis not disrupted on account of anybody's grievance or decision to protest."

He dismissed the recent call by the Boko Haram sect for Christians residing in the Northern part of the country to return to their states of origin and vice versa, stating that the call was only an attempt to cause panic among the citizenry and disrupt the peace and tranquillity in the country. Ringim, however, warned that the security agencies would not sit back and watch the destruction of government properties in the name of strike action.

He stated: "The Nigerian law does not allow that. And the security agencies of this country will not allow that.

"But anybody that wishes to conduct themselves in an orderly fashion through protests that does not involve violence, the Police and other security agencies will be there to protect them.

"That is why we have asked all those pressure groups including the NLC, Civil Liberties Organisations (CLO), among others to liaise with the various command commissioners of Police to map out the routes, locations and places that they intend to assemble and to march through, so that adequate security will be given to them in order to forestall rogues and vagabonds infiltrating their ranks and causing havoc," he said.

Meanwhile, commuters traversing the Louis Edet House Police Headquarters to various locations in the city centre yesterday had a hectic time due the meeting, as the route was cordoned off, causing a traffic grid- lockon theShehu Shagari Road inAsokoro.

The road is one of the major links to the Eagle Square, the Federal Secretariat as well as other major institutions located in the city centre and the Central Business District (CBD) in Abuja.

Commuters and other pedestrians were diverted by the Police and other security agents to ply the R.B Dikko Road that leads to the city centre.

Passengers stranded as Foreign Airlines cancel flights

By Chinedu Eze

***ThisDay*, Wednesday, January 11, 2012, vol. 16, no. 6106, pg. 9**

Over 500 passengers were stranded yesterday following the cancellation of flights by foreign airlines which were supposed to airlift them on Monday and Tuesday at the Murtala Muhammed International Airport, Lagos.

The passengers who could not go back to town slept at the airport, using their bags as pillows and mattresses, uncertain about when their suffering would be over.

Following the notice to airmen (NOTAM) issued on Sunday by aviation unions, notifying foreign airlines about impending strikes, which started on Monday, some of the airlines, including Delta Air Lines, United Airlines, KLM and Lufthansa cancelled their flights, leaving their passengers stranded at the airport.

The abandoned passengers swelled when more airlines cancelled their flights yesterday and some of them which arrived the Lagos airport were not able to depart as aviation union officials prevented airlines' crew from gaining access to the terminal building.

Some of the affected passengers were those who were billed to travel with Virgin Atlantic, Arik Air, which had South Africa bound flight, Ethiopian Airlines and Emirates Airline.

By 4.pm. yesterday aircraft owned by these airlines were still parked at the international terminal of the Lagos airport, as their tails and livery signal that they were still in Nigeria beyond their departure time.

Some officials of the unions explained that they had to allow the airlines to land in cognizance of the International Civil Aviation Organisation (ICAO) regulation.

The unions include the National Union of Air Transport Employees (NUATE), the Air Traffic Services Senior Staff Association of Nigeria (ATSSSAN) and the National Association of Aircraft Pilots and Engineers (NAAPE).

At the international terminal of the Lagos airport, Comrade Abdulkareem Motajo, the acting Secretary-General, NUATE led other union leaders to foil efforts by the Ethiopian Airlines officials to board their passengers through the back door.

People power and its prospects

By Kayode Komalafe

***ThisDay*, Wednesday, January 18, 2012, vol. 16, no. 6113, pg. 48**

This is certainly not a post-mortem of the popular protests that engulfed this land last week. As a demonstration of the endowed power of the people, the momentum generated by the strike is alive. So we cannot yet be talking of an autopsy. Neither can any judicious evaluation of what happened declare it a failure. Yes, tactical if not strategic errors were committed on both sides of the battle. But significant gains were also amply recorded for the good of Nigeria. It is in this respect that we should ponder on the prospects that the mass action holds for popular democracy.

It is in this spirit that the more than 20 persons killed during the protests would not have died in vain. We commiserate with those who lost their loved ones during the protest while calling for the prosecution of their killers. It is important for the future that we should pay attention to the trend that has emerged from the protest. The contradictions thrown up in the protest movement is particularly worthy of study. The strike was called by the Nigeria Labour Congress (NLC) and the Trade Union Congress (TUC) in collaboration with other civil society organisations primarily to put pressure on government to reverse its policy of removal of subsidy on petrol consumption. It quickly developed into a popular expression of pent-up anger among the people. The agenda quickly expanded beyond the retention of fuel subsidy. While many sat at home as demanded by the strike leaders, millions of protesters took to the streets and peaceful rallies were held at different locations across the country.

The preliminary mistake of officialdom was to treat the protest as strictly an industrial relations problem. The government had a grave socio-politi- cal problem in its hand, but some officials chose to pretend that that they were dealing with a labour dispute. The adventure to the National Industrial Court to stop the action of NLC and TUC should be seen in this light. The issue involved is the constitutional right of citizens to protest; it is never a factory matter.

The civil society organisations have legitimately expressed reservations with the suspension of the strike by the two labour centres, NLC and TUC. Some elements have even made serious allegations of "betrayal" and "sell-out" against the leaders of the organisations. This is unfortunate in the circumstance. For any perceptive student of the history of the progressive movement in this country, the contradiction was easily predictable. However, activists should be sufficiently dialectical about these issues. The structure and method of work of the labour centres are not coterminous with those of their civil society allies. By the nature of their organisations, NLC and TUC could only go as far as asking for policy change. That is their reformist limit. The error made by the labour negotiators in not seizing moments to negotiate with the aim of bringing the price lower than ₦97 may still be corrected using the avenue of the Belgore committee.

For clarity, it was hardly conceivable that a national strike as effective as the one of last week could continue indefinitely in a non-revolutionary situation. It was important for future purpose that labour didn't box itself into a comer. Beyond wild allegations, the security context of the labour's steps at the weekend should also be sympathetically appraised. Organisational errors of omission or commission might have occurred; but this would not amount to a sell-out. Other forces in the immensely heterogeneous protest movement raised more overtly political questions that border on regime change. Now the ready answer to that in a liberal democratic setting is that such agitation should wait till the next election in 2015. It should be assumed that protest leaders would be conscious of the full political implications of the demands they choose to make at any point in time. All told, the organisational bond between labour and its allies in this struggle should not be weakened by undue suspicion. It is in the interest of continued defence of people's interest that errors of that last action be corrected and the spirit of collaboration be consolidated.

The roles of the National Assembly and governors in resolving the issues were a positive response to the popular-democratic impulse that has gripped the polity. The policy debate became more robust as participants came from different classes and generations. The reduction of the price from ₦140 to ₦97 even before the Belgore committee could start work

That is why the deployment of troops in Lagos afterward on Monday should be seen as an egregious assault on popular democracy. Similarly, it was a great disservice to this unity of purpose that in their incoherent efforts, some persons sought to distract attention from the issues in the debate by organising a Niger Delta (or is it an Ijaw?) defence of President Goodluck Jonathan. This is a huge disservice to the stature of the President who won a pan-Nigeria mandate. Those who support the removal of fuel subsidy for technical economic rea-sons are to be found in every section of Nigeria. So are those who oppose the removal. It is a disagreement on policy and not ethnic or regional antagonism. It should not be forgotten so soon that some leaders of the protest were the same persons who went to the streets to protest a governance vacuum and insisted that Jonathan as vice president should act as president while President Umaru Yar'Adua was away for medical reasons. How come the same patriots are now branded "hoodlums" just because they disagree with the policy of the President's government?

The real gain of the struggle is not the reduction in the pump price of petrol fixed on January 1. It is to be found in the socio-political awakening of the citizens for participatory democracy. The anger generated by the fuel price hike was positively channelled in mobilising the citizens to see democracy as transcending queuing up periodically to vote for politicians who may never take their views into account thereafter. Indeed the whole governance process has been put on trial. Pertinent questions have been asked. It is positive that the government is answering them by taking anti-corruption steps, attempting to reduce (albeit cosmetically) governance costs and throwing searchlight into the management of subsidy and indeed the petroleum industry.

In many respects, the people have won this battle but the war for popular democracy in Nigeria will be a long-drawn one. That is why the government and organisations of the people must draw valid lessons from the historic week of protest. The gains of the last few days are a sufficient assurance of the prospects of the exercise of people power for the socio-economic and political progress of Nigeria.

Police battle citizens as subsidy protest spread

By Reporters

***The Guardian*, Wednesday, January 4, 2012, pg. 5, 9, 10, 12**

For the second day running, Nigerians opposed to the removal of subsidy on petrol took to the streets across the country, meeting with mixed 'reception' in the hands of security agencies. While the protests were peaceful in the main, a man in his mid-20s was killed yesterday in Ilorin, Kwara State where protesters put up bonfires on several roads in the state capital, chanting anti-deregulation slogans.

However, the protest turned violent at the Post Office junction at about 10:30 a.m. when the protesters were tear-gassed by armed security agents, causing pandemonium and forcing businesses to close up for the day. It was also gathered that there were sporadic shootings by the law enforcement agents, who came to the scene apparently to discourage the protesters from going towards the Government House Area, along Ahmadu Bello Way, Ilorin. A stray bullet allegedly hit one of the protesters on the chest.

Kwara Police Public Relations Officer, Dabo Ezekiel, however, claimed that the dead man was hit by the protesters for refusing to join in the protest. The Police have recovered the remains of the deceased. Meanwhile, the Special Task Force (STF) in Plateau State has prohibited any unlawful processions especially in four local councils under emergency rule in the state. The affected councils are Jos North, Jos South, Barkin Ladi and Riyom.

The reminder came yesterday as some residents were reportedly poised to protest the fuel subsidy removal announced by President Goodluck Jonathan on Saturday, December 31.

In a related development, the battle against the removal of fuel subsidy may shift to the Judiciary as the Nigeria Laoour Congress (NLC) is set to drag the Federal Government to court over the mandate of the Subsidy Reinvestment and Empowerment Programme Board headed by Nigeria's former High Commissioner to the United Kingdom, Mr. Christopher Kolade.

In a statement signed yesterday by President of the Congress, Abdulwahed Omar, the NLC disclosed that it would seek legal interpretation as to whether any committee has the powers to spend public funds without appropriation by the

National Assembly. The Congress also dismissed the establishment of the Justice Alfa Belgore-led committee to dialogue with Labour as "an after-thought move." It also vowed to hold the Federal Government responsible for any protester killed in the course of the subsidy protest, starting with the Ilorin incident. The NLC also refuted the claim by the government that Labour agreed to the subsidy removal policy, saying the NLC was never a party to the removal of subsidy.

Omar also hinted that organised Labour would take its next line of action over the subsidy removal. He said: "Tomorrow (today) Wednesday January 4th, 2012, the NLC and TUC will issue a clear directive on the date for a coordinated, nationwide general strike."

Also, President, Trade Union Congress (TUC), Peter Esele, told The Guardian on phone yesterday: "I am on my way to Lagos from Port Harcourt now for the TUC meeting. We need to meet to strategise on howto organise the strike but it will not happen this week. Cer-tainly next week, it will happen.'

Though the government has moved to open a line of dialogue witn Labour, The Guardian learnt that Labour has rebuffed these overtures.

Also yesterday, the Department of Petroleum Resources (DPR) raised the alarm over alleged dangers posed to its officials deployed to monitor filling stations across the country in order to enforce the benchmark set by the Petroleum Products Pricing and Regulatory agency (PPPRA). Controller (Operations), DPR, Lagos Zonal Office, Olugbenga Koku, told The Guardian yesterday that the oil regulatory agency has begun monitoring filling stations from Monday, but hoodlums have taken over the stations and are threatening to maim our officials on duty."

In Lagos, (demonstrators yesterday shut petrol stations, formed human barriers along motorways and hijacked buses as they protested the fuel subsidy removal. More than 1,000 people in the main market area of central Lagos sang, chanted and waved placards reading: "No To Fuel Price Hikes" and "We Demand Living Wages." At Ojota in Lagos yesterday, most motorists were forced to turn back after a group of demonstrators set up a roadblock of burning tyres on the highway. Two Toyota Hilux vans loaded with armed police officers drove into the midst of the protesters at Ojota after arresting two persons for burning tyres on the road. The angry protesters quickly held the vans hostage, threatening to set them on fire if the two arrested were not released immediately. When the policemen sensed that the standoff could escalate, they released the two suspects and went their way. But police in riot gear kept watch and the protests were largely peaceful. Our struggle is not just against fuel subsidy, it is against bad governance. Jonathan has shown that he can't be trusted," Issa Aremu, vice president of the National Labour Congress, said at the rally to demonstrators. He added: "He said he was engaging in dialogue and all of a sudden he went ahead and increased the price."

For her part, Mrs. Ganiat Fawehinmi, widow of the late human rights lawyer, said: "The prices of everything will increase, transport, housing, school fees, food, etc. The common man will not be able to survive. We will say no and oppose bad government policies. We will say no and oppose IMF (International Monetary Fund) policies."

Also, Lokoia, Kogi State capital was brougnt to a standstill yesterday as protesters took over the Lokoja- Murtala Muhammed Bridge over the removal of oil subsidy. It was the third time the bridge would be blocked in three months.

The protesters in their hundreds carried placards which read thus, "Jonathan You Are Not A Good Leader," "Resign Now Jonathan," "The Nation Is Heading For Anarchy." Several vehicles traveling through the ever- busy North-South link road were prevented by the protesters who lighted tyres on the main road. Mobile policemen deployed to break up the riot had a hectic time and resorted to firing tear gas to disperse the protesters.

Similarly, hundreds of students took to the streets of Kano metropolis in a peaceful protest over the hike in the price of petrol. In a bid to keep the peace, well- armed policemen and other security agents took positions in strategic parts of the city. Nine students arrested in the course of the protest were later released

Protests reign all over amid desperate search for truce.

By Oghogho Obaywnana and others.

***The Guardian*, Wednesday, January 11, 2012, pg. 1**

The face-off between organised Labour and the Federal Government over the latter's removal of subsidy on petrol entered the second day yesterday with both parties holding on to their own. Labour even went ahead to mobilise more protesters to the streets of Abuja, the seat of power. But hope of an early end to the indefinite strike, rally and protest declared by the workers was raised by the Senate, which resolved to meet with Labour and the Presidency on the impasse.

After a plenary session yesterday, the chamber mandated Senate President David Mark to lead the principal officers of the Senate to meet with the Presidency and Labour to consider national interest and the plight of Nigerians in whatever decisions they make. But Labour declared yesterday that it would not meet President Goodluck Jonathan because it would not serve any useful purpose.

Mark, who spoke on the row, which has paralysed socio-economic activities across the Federation, pledged that the Upper Chamber of the National Assembly would ensure that any'cabal' found culpable by its panel's investigation into the rot in the oil sector and the fuel subsidy management would be prosecuted.

At a rally in Abuja yesterday, the President of Trade Union Congress (TUC), Peter Esele, told the crowd at the "Freedom Square" in Wuse Zone Four that Labour would mobilise 100,000 protesters for today's demonstration. There was an upsurge in human and vehicular move-ments in Abuja, which enabled more Nigerians to join the rally. At Monday's rally, there were about 20,000 demonstrators but the number rose to about 40,000, according to data released by Labour.

Addressing the senators at its first plenary session after the Christmas and New Year break, Mark expressed the concern of the chamber over the lingering crisis in the country, noting that some incendiary comments by some highly placed Nigerians had not helped matters.

"The current security challenge has reinforced the need to aggressively pursue economic development and simultaneously implement the war on terrorism. In this regard, let me caution against reckless utterances by some Nigerians that endanger our national unity. Statements that encourage people to move from one region to another on the basis of faith and ethnicity are unpatriotic. It portends danger to our corporate existence and a clear invitation to anarchy," he said.

Mark said some recent events such as the bombing of some places of worship had further heightened tension and constituted a serious threat to the unity of the country. We have reconvened at a trying period in our nation's history. We are confronted by security challenges in different parts of the country, which are testing our collective resolve to live together as an indivisible nation."

On the subsidy removal, Mark called for honesty of purpose among stakeholders and assured that the Senate would confront the problems and bring sanity into the system. The Senate President said although the economic argument in support of petrol subsidy removal is com-pelling, the political and social imperatives must also be considered. Mark called for understanding among the stakeholders in order to overcome the impasse and directed the Senate Committee on Labour, Employment and Productivity to interface with Labour groups. "I also urged senators to engage with Labour and civil society organisations on the way forward"

Also, yesterday, the chamber resolved to debate the issue of insecurity in the country at plenary today. This followed a motion moved by the Deputy Senate President Ike Ekwere- madu, who expressed fear that the insecurity in the country had led to mass movement of Nigerians on ethnic and religious grounds.

He assured that the Senate would get both sides to shift ground on the matter. "The current position is that Labour is insisting on reversal to ₦65 a litre while government is insisting that subsidy should be removed. The good news is that we have seen some movement on both sides," he disclosed.

The Senate also officially received a communication from the President in respect of the state of emergency declared by President Jonathan in 15 local councils in Niger, Plateau, Yobeand Borno states.

On the ongoing rallies, Esele also said both the NLC and TUC have internal mechanisms to deal with alleged sabotage of the protest by members of the National Union of Road Trans-port Workers (NURTW). "Some of you are agitating about the National Union of Road Transport Workers. We are a democratic organisation. We have a way of taking care of people who go out of the line. Leave that to the organs of the congress to take care off," he said. Esele also discountenanced any planned meeting with the President, saying "some people say we should meet Jonathan but what difference would that make?"

NLC President, Abdulwaheed Omar, submitted that Nigeria is owned by the people, who should take over the land. He said the protest is to force government to reverse to ₦65 a litre.

More security barricades seen in Abuja yesterday emerged unlike on Monday when the major roads to strategic public buildings and the main arteries in the Central Business Districts – Ahmadu Bello and Shehu Shagari ways – had partial barricades. By 130 p.m. yesterday, the crowd had been dispersed leaving behind a mesh of rumpled and sun-beaten green leaves, leaflets, fluffing sheets of paper, polythene bags, plastic bottles and all kinds of fibrous wastes as would be expected of scenes where angry citizens had massed riotously.

A police patrol team, which by while march heated up, remained behind. The security person-nel were still watching happenings at about 2.00 p.m. yesterday. At the popular Banex Plaza in Wuse 2, 10 litres of fuel sold for between ₦2,500 and ₦3,000 as against ₦1,410 at the new benchmark rate of Petroleum Products Pricing Regulatory agency of ₦141 a litre.

Members of the civil society groups, who protested in Lagos yesterday, asked Jonathan to resign. At the Gani Fawehinme Park, Ojota where they converged, their leader and convener of the Save Nigeria Group (SNG), Pastor Tunde Bakare, said sovereignty belongs to the people, and whoever they wish, they give it to. Bakare said Jonathan had not shown the capacity to govern Nigerians and should leave Aso Rock.

President of the Campaign for Democracy (CD) and Founder of Women Arise, Dr. Joe Okei-Odumakin, asked Nigerians to prepare for tough times in their struggle to remove corrupt leaders from office.

Protests suspended as FG cuts petrol price to N97

By Ahamefula Ogbu

***ThisDay*, Monday, January 16, 2012, vol.16, no.6111, pg. 1, 8**

President Goodluck Jonathan, in a nationwide TV address this morning, announced a cut in petrol price from around ₦141 to N97 after prolonged street demonstrations over the deregulation policy. Also, the labour unions told the media early this morning that they were suspending street protests because of the political dimension it had taken but insisted that the strike would go on.

In the broadcast, Jonathan said he had to review the pump price in response to the outcry over the hardship caused by the total subsidy removal and vowed to investigate the subsidy account with a view to punishing those who fraudulently bled the country and nearly destroyed the economy. He also promised a detailed study of the forensic audit of the account of the Nigerian National PetroleumCorporation, (NNPC) with a view to curbing corruption in the oil and gas sector of the economy so as to rid it of corruption. He promised that his government would pursue the passage of the Petroleum Industry Bill with more vigour to ensure it becomes law to regulate activities in the downstream sector.

Jonathan said: "This is the second time in two weeks I will address you on the deregulation of the downstream petroleum sector. In the last seven days, the nation has witnessed a disruption of economic activities. Although, the economic imperatives for the policy have been well articulated by government, the Nigerian

Labour Congress (NLC) and the Trade Union Congress (TUC) went ahead to declare a nationwide strike.

"There was also near-breakdown of law and order in certain parts of the country as a result of the activities of some persons or groups of persons who took advantage of the situation to further their narrow interests by engaging in acts of intimidation, harassment and outright subversion of the Nigerian state. I express my sympathy to those who were adversely affected by the protests.

"At the inception of the deregulation policy, Government had set up the Justice Alfa Belgore Committee to liaise with Labour and other stakeholders to address likely grey areas in the policy, but despite all our efforts, Labour refused the option of dialogue and also disobeyed a restraining order of the National Industrial Court of Nigeria.

"However, following the intervention of the Leadership of the National Assembly, and other well-meaning Nigerians, Labour accepted to meet with government, but this yielded no tangible result.

"It has become clear to government and all well-meaning Nigerians that other interests beyond the implementation of the deregulation policy have hijacked the protest. This has prevented an objective assessment and consideration of all the contending issues for which dialogue was initiated by government. These same interests seek to promote discord, anarchy, and insecurity to the detriment of public peace."

Jonathan however assured Nigerians that he would always respect their right to expression of their minds and commended those who conducted themselves lawfully within the period as well as proffered useful suggestions on the way for and credible alternatives to subsidy removal and acknowledged that he knew it would cause pains which however would be temporary before the gains of the policy. "Government will continue to pursue full deregulation of the downstream petroleum sector. However, given the hardships being suffered by Nigerians, and after due consideration and consultations with state governors and the leadership of the National Assembly; government has approved the reduction of the pump price of petrol to ₦97 per litre. The Petroleum Products Pricing Regulatory Agency (PPPRA) has been directed to ensure compliance with this new pump price. "Government is working hard to reduce recurrent expenditure in line with current realities and to cut down on the cost of governance. In the meantime, government has commenced the implementation of the Subsidy Reinvestment and Empowerment projects: including the Federal Government-assisted mass transit programme which is already in place, and job creation for the youth.

"Furthermore, the legal and regulatory regime for the petroleum industry will be reviewed to address accountability issues and current lapses in the Industry. In this regard, the Petroleum Industry Bill will be given accelerated attention. The report of the forensic audit carried out on the NNPC is being studied with a view to implementing the recommendations and sanctioning proven acts of corruption in the industry.

"Let me assure Nigerians that this administration is irrevocably committed to tackling corruption in the petroleum industry as well as other sectors of the economy. Consequently, all those found to have contributed one way or the other to the economic adversity of the country will be dealt with in accordance with the law.

"My dear compatriots, I urge you to show understanding for the imperatives of the adjustment in the pump price of petrol and give government your full support to ensure its successful implementation. I further appeal to Nigerians to go back to work and go about their normal duties as government has made adequate arrangements for the protection of life and property throughout the federation.

"Government will not condone brazen acts of criminality and subversion. As President, I have sworn to uphold the unity, peace and order of the Nigerian State and by the grace of God, I intend to fully and effectively discharge that responsibility. Let me add that we are desirous of further engagements with Labour. I urge our Labour leaders to call off their strike, and go back to work.

"Nigeria belongs to all of us and we must collectively safeguard its unity," he concluded.

Labour leaders had risen from a meeting with the president last night saying they would go back to meet and decide "on the next line of action" over the proposal by government to cut petrol price.

There were strong indications that the new price might have been accepted by all parties as labour said it was "on the same page" with government which was persuading them to see rea-son for an increase in petrol price or partial deregulation.

Addressing the media after the meeting with Jonathan last night, Nigeria Labour Congress (NLC) President Abdulwaheed Omar said they were persuaded on the position of the president that for the past five years, the price of fuel had been at N65 per litre while the dollar had been rising and stressed the need for a price increase. Sources at the meeting said labour agreed to meet with the Justice Alfa Belgore Committee for two days to work out modalities on the deregulation policy and would, by Wednesday, give their final word on the matter. "We are going to sit down and analyse the position of the president. We will meet and come out with statement today," Omar said.

Those at the meeting include Chairman of the Nigeria Governors Forum and Governor of Rivers State, Rotimi Amaechi, and the Minister of Labour, Chief Emeka Wogu.

Labour had declared an indefinite strike starting a week ago over the January 1 increase in petrol price which used to be ₦65 per litre.

Meanwhile, the Ministry of Petroleum Resources has invited the Economic and Financial Crimes Commission (EFCC) to investigate payments made in respect of the importation of Premium Motor Spirit (PMS) and Kerosene and prosecute anyone found to have been involved in over-invoicing, fraud and any related illegalities.

Also, the Federal Government has ordered an immediate review of the audited report of the Nigerian National Petroleum Corporation (NNPC) and all parastatals under the Ministry of Petroleum Resources with a view to commencing immediate implementation of their findings. These were part of a two-page statement released by the Minister of Petroleum Resources, Mrs. Diezani Alison-Madueke, who also said she had already en- panelled a unit in her office to begin a comprehensive review of management control in all parastatals in her ministry.

Other actions she said she had kick-started included a scheduled meeting with the National Assembly with a view to ensuring the immediate passage of the Petroleum Industry Bill (PIB) on which the comprehensive reform of the oil sector in the country would be anchored.

"With presidential approval, I have written to invite the EFCC to immediately review all pay-ments made in respect to subsidies on PMS and Kerosene and take all necessary steps to prosecute any incidence of malfeasance, fraud, over-invoicing, and related illegalities in open and transparent manner.

"I have set up a unit within my office to be headed by an independent auditor to review the KPMG and other audit reports on NNPC and other parastatals, and immediately begin implementation of their findings, ensuring, at all times, full probity and value for money.

"I am en-panelling another unit in my office to begin a comprehensive review of the man-agement controls within all parastatals in the Ministry of Petroleum Resources, including but not limited to NNPC, PPPRA and DPR. Accordingly, I expect a report in 30 days to enable us take further action in reforming management, personnel and other practices and procedures in parastatals within the Ministry. It should be noted however that this process has already begun in PPPRA and DPR where management changes and reform are beginning to yield desirable results; and I will be meeting with the Senate President and the Speaker of the House of Representatives in the coming week to seek their cooperation and leadership in the quick passage of the Petroleum Industry Bill so that we can anchor the comprehensive reform of the oil industry," Alison-Madueke said in the statement.

In a letter dated January 12, 2012 addressed to the acting EFCC Chairman, Ibrahim Lamorde, with reference number HMPR/EFCC/01/0002, Alison-Madueke wrote that Nigeria had been operating a subsidy regime on import of petroleum products where the difference between the cost of importation and pump price was paid by the government at a pre-approved oil marketing company which she has the approval of the president to investigate.

"Over the years, this bill has grown exponentially to unsustainable levels. As Petroleum Minister, I have become extremely concerned with these figures and following the recent transfer of the PPPRA to my ministry last year, I have moved quickly to change management and inaugurate a comprehensive reform process which include drastic cuts in the list of importer, review of payments and procedures, as well as massive redeployment of staff within the agency.

'To now deepen my reforms and ensure that we root out all forms of corruption and abuse within the subsidy regime. I have sought and obtained the approval of President Goodluck Ebele Jonathan to formally invite the EFCC to immediately review and investigate all payments made in respect of subsidies checked against actual importations and to take all necessary steps to prosecute any person(s) involved in any incidence of malfeasance, fraud, over-payment and related illegalities," she said.

Public space, social media and coming revolution

By Bayo Olupohunda

***The Guardian*, Sunday, January 22, 2012, pg. 14**

The history of strikes and public protests is as old as the existence of ill-thought government policies, poor governance and corruption, which have bedevilled the country. But never in the history of Nigeria has anger over fuel subsidy become story of civil disobedience and public anger directed at perceived government policy been this widespread and profound. The fuel subsidy strike had a different tinge to it.

In line with the wave of protests that swept through the Middle East, which saw the likes of long-standing and feared Hosni Mubarak swept off power through the use of social media, leading to massive and violent protest and sit-ins in public spaces like the Tahir Square in Egypt, the subsidy removal protest effectively imitated the Arab Spring, using the social media for speedy information sharing among Nigerian youth population.

The effective deployment of the social media brought thousands of protesters from the middle class to the lowly mass of the working people throughout the country together in a massive protest that sent the government into a panic mode.

Just like the Tahir Square, the gathering of protesters at the Gani Fawehinmi Freedom Park was symbolic. The park, named after the late fiery human rights lawyer and advocate (whose undying spirit lives on) played host to perhaps, the largest number of protesters ever seen in the history of civil disobedience in Nigeria.

Now, that is the spirit of an emerging revolution from Nigerians across the country. What has changed in the last few years that have made Nigerians often described as docile become activists? What role did the social media play in creating the awareness needed to command government attention to the protesters demands?

Indeed, in the week of the protest Gani Park became a truly public square. Before this, it was merely a big and busy traffic circle until the urban renewal initiated by the government in Lagos few years ago. Perhaps the state government understood the power of a true public square, a place where citizens meet, mingle, gather, protest, perform and share ideas; it understood that a true public park is a physical manifestation of democracy. How has the public space become significant as a battle ground in the quest to achieving a truly democratic society.

Gani Park has thus become a battleground on which the futureof Nigeria is being fought. It is also symbolic in the sense of what the public space can be used when citizens gather to demand for social change. The government felt the pressure of the fury of the people which was beamed on TV stations.

Though one can credit online social network of the country has provided powerful evidence that the virtual is not enough. In Gani Park, it became decisively clear that the occupation of physical urban space was, and continues to be, crucial to the success and continuity of any public protest.

No doubt the initial rush of online tweeting; facebooking and instant blackberry messaging, was critically important; but as we now know, the country was unplugged for six days during which period the protests actually grew larger and the protesters became even more determined not merely to express popular dissent but ultimately to demand sweeping changes in the way we are governed.

Indeed, in the week of the protest Gani Park became a truly public square. Before this, it was merely a big and busy traffic circle until the ur-ban renewal initiated by the government in La-gos few years ago. Perhaps the state government understood the power of a true public square, a place where citizens meet, mingle, gather, protest, perform and share ideas; it understood that a true public park is a physical manifestation of democracy.

When the subsidy strike began, peaceful demonstrators from all over the city converged on Gani Park. It was a magnet partly because of its central location and symbolic name; Gani means "dissent" and also because of the human rights advocate as the symbol of dissent and civil disobedience. The Park became the creation of a dynamic and resourceful community of citizens brought together by the shared goal of bringing true democracy to Nigeria.

The mood in Gani Park ranged from cautious and depressed to celebratory and jubilant. And always there was an amazing cross-section of the society; a mix of class, gender, age, sexual orientation, dress code, ethnicity and religion; strangers who under normal circumstances would never have met. The spirit seemed to break down the longstanding barriers, and to imbue a new sense of solidarity and acceptance.

The Park became a hub for social activity and artistic creativity with placards carrying pro-testers. People sold food and drinks. Protest signs were humorous and creative. Doctors and nurses were providing free healthcare in impromptu clinics. TV stations were interviewing protesters and creating an instant archive, a visual and oral record of history as it was unfolding. There were poets, puppeteers and comedians. Gani Park had been transformed not only into a social and public space but also into the biggest spontaneous event of community- organizing and nation-building the country had ever seen.

The Park took on the atmosphere of a carnival. But the occupation of Gani Park for one week by mass numbers of peaceful protesters, had an over-arching purpose; to bring local and international attention to the demands of the people, the revolution was to force the government to revert the ion that started in Lagos, Abuja and other parts prohibitive price of fuel; to take action and cut government profligacy.

And ultimately, it was this peaceful occupation of an important urban space in the nation's most important city that forced the hand of Jonathan administration. The importance of #Occupy Nigeria became glaring when the government panicked by sending battalion of troops to dislodge protester thus ending the weeWong occupation.

But Nigerians are angry. This was why they were ready to continue the protest even with the truce Labour made with government. The government may have succeeded in using force and subterfuge in cowing the people. Will they succeed in preventing an inevitable future revolution if they don't put their house in order? It is not likely.

Senate Proposes April date for deregulation

By Kunle Akogun and Ahamefula Ogbu

THIDSAY, Wednesday, January 11, 2012, vol.16, no.6106, pg 1, 6

As the anti-fuel subsidy intensified in major cities across the country yesterday, the senate has asked its leadership to meet President Goodluck Jonathan to demand the immediate suspension of the full deregulation of the downstream sector of the oil industry and the associated removal of the perol subsidy. The senators also asked David Mark who was expected to lead other principal officers to the meeting with Jonathan last night to press it on the president to shift the implementation of the subsidy removal to April 1 2012 in light of the prevailing circumstance

On Day Two of the intensified nationwide strike and protests; the Attorney General of the Federation (AGF) and Minister of Justice, Mr. Mohammed Bello Adoke, accused labour unions of disobeying a court order stopping the strike and asked workers to return to their duties or face the 'no work, no pay' rule;

Rivers State Governor Chibuike Amaechi promised to keep petrol price at a maximum of N137 per litre in the state;a situation report on the strike by the Federal Government alleged that the protests have been hijacked by politicians for selfish interest; and Inspector General of Police (IG) Hafiz Ringim warned that government would not allow hoodlums to hijack the protests.

Senators, at the closed door session yesterday immediately after they reconvened after their Christmas and New Year break, mandated Mark to meet with the president to discuss the way forward. Sources at the meeting, which lasted almost two hours, said the senators were concerned about the gridlock and near shutdown of the national economy.

They were also said to have raised the alarm that the announcement of the subsidy withdrawal failed to take cognizance of the prevailing security situation in the country.

Consequently, the Senate suspended other matters for the day's proceedings to allow its leadership to continue the dialogue with organised labour which it started Monday night and also meet with the executive to convey the position of the upper chamber on the fuel subsidy matter. However, the Senate will today debate the state of insecurity in the land and other issues of national importance.

The upper legislative chamber also vowed to use all legislative instruments available to it to penalise "all those found to have abused the fuel subsidy proceeds" within the public service and their private sector collaborators. Mark, who made the pledge while welcoming his colleagues back to the chamber after their Christmas and New Year break, said the Senate was already investigating the management of the N1.3 trillion fuel subsidy scheme through its Committees on Petroleum Resources (Downstream), Finance and Appropriation.

In an apparent reaction to criticisms in certain quarters that the Senate had not been as categorical as the House of Representatives on the fuel subsidy removal by the Federal Government, Mark said the Senate leadership had been interfacing with the leadership of the Nigeria Labour Congress (NLC) and the Trade Union Congress (TUC) as well as the Executive. He disclosed that the talks were on-going, adding: "And I hope that it will lead to an outcome that will be in the best interest of Nigerians." The Senate President said: "In order to overcome the current impasse over the fuel subsidy removal, it is imperative that we engage each other honestly on this issue."

And briefing journalists on the same issue after the plenary, Senate Leader Victor Ndoma- Egba said the Senate's situation was different from that of the House of Representatives, explaining that a motion by Senator Bukola Saraki on the mismanagement of the fuel subsidy fund was extensively debated and following this, a committee was set up to probe the scheme. "So, to start debating the issue now will be pre-empting the outcome of that committee," Ndoma-Egba said.

'NO WORK, NO PAY': In a statement issued last night, Adoke accused labour of dis-obeying lawful court orders which had stopped the unions from going on strike.

He said if workers did not return to their duty posts, government would be forced to apply the 'no work, no pay' rule.

Excerpts from his statement: "Convinced of the unlawfulness of the planned action of the NLC/TUC especially in the absence of any trade dispute with its employees, Government approached the National Industrial Court which is constitutionally vested under section 254 C (f) (c) of the 1999 Constitution of the Federal Republic of Nigeria as amended with exclusive jurisdiction to consider matters relating to the propriety or otherwise of a proposal strike or industrial action.

"The Court in furtherance of government's application, granted an interim injunction restrain-ing the NLC and the TUC from embarking or compelling other persons to embark on a strike action or general strike, mass rallies or street protest pending the determination of the Motion on Notice which will come up for hearing on Thursday 12th January 2012. For the avoidance of doubt, it is necessary to state that the basis of the injunction and the Motion on Notice is that no trade dispute has been declared in consonance with existing laws by the NLC and TUC and a clear distinction between civil protest on one hand and an industrial action or strike on the other.

"The office of the Attorney General of the Federation is therefore dismayed that the NLC and TUC have refused to join issues with the Government in the judicial process and other peaceful initiatives. Rather than obey subsisting court orders, the NLC/TUC have embarked on an indefinite general strike and have pursuant to their threat, forcefully “shut down” all offices, oil production centres, air and sea ports, fuel stations, markets and banks.

“Government wishes to reiterate that the Order of the National Industrial Court (NIC) is a subsisting order and the continuing disregard of that Order is inimical to the public interest as it constitutes an open invitation to anarchy. Respect for the judiciary, particularly, the Orders and Judgments emanating from the Courts is critical to the survival and sustenance of our fledgling democracy.

Government reiterates its commitment to the promotion and protection of the fundamental rights of the people, including the right to free speech, expression and peaceful assembly.

“It is pertinent to remind all Nigerians that the enjoyment of these rights and freedoms must be consistent with the letters and spirit of the Constitution. The current strike by organised labour which has prevented the legitimate pursuit of economic activities across the country in defiance of a valid subsisting order of a superior court of record transgresses the parameters set by the Constitution and extant laws.

“In light of the foregoing, members of the public who are under contractual obligations as employees in the public and private sectors are advised to respect the terms of their contract of service and report to their duty posts. Necessary measures have been put in place to ensure that this is done without any form of molestation or harassment by anyone or group of persons. In the event that public servants continue to disregard the terms of their employment in the absence of any trade dispute and especially in the face of blatant disregard of a subsisting Court Order, the Government will not hesitate to enforce the ‘no work no pay’ policy.

“Finally, Government calls on the NLC/TUC to respect the Orders of the National Industrial Court and engage government in a constructive dialogue with a view to addressing hardships arising from the deregulation in the downstream sector of the petroleum industry.”

RIVERS’ ‘SUBSIDY’: Governor Amaechi has appealed to labour unions in Rivers State to collaborate and work with government to transform the economy while announcing that the maximum price of petrol would be maintained at ₦137 per litre, and not the national average of ₦141.

He made the appeal yesterday, when members of the state branch of the TUC and the NLC led a protest march to the Government House, Port Harcourt over the current removal of fuel subsidy by the Federal Government.

Amaechi, who is also Chairman, Nigeria Governors’ Forum (NGF), said the president’s decision on removal of subsidy is to rescue the economy of the country.

He said in a meeting with the National Union of Road Transport Workers (NURTW), Rivers State Chapter, and with petroleum marketers in the state, of pipelines and depots are strategically located throughout Nigeria to link them.

“With this policy in place, millions of jobs will be created and the economy will become very viable for investment,” Alison-Madueke stated. The minister also explained how the removal of fuel subsidy by the Federal Government would help curb the widely reported incidence of corruption in the downstream sector of Nigeria's oil and gas industry.

She noted that apart from providing the flexibility for reinvestment of key funds into the provision of critical social infrastructure, the removal of subsidy on premium motor spirit (PMS) would help erase corruption which has trailed subsidy claims and counter-claims.

According to her, "It is not possible to have petrol at ₦65 per litre at the pump in Nigeria; in Chad as much as ₦200, in that government had worked out measures to cut the pump price of fuel from the current benchmark of ₦141 to ₦137 per litre.

"As a state government, we will not be willing to go above ₦137 for fuel pump price. We owe an obligation to guarantee the security of your resources under every circumstance. This is why as a government, we cannot stand by and watch while a tiny cabal appropriate your resources to feather their already cushioned nests," he said.

"I have agreed with them (NURTW) that no transport fare should be above N70 apart from fares for Choba and Rumuokoro. We have agreed that the fare from Mile Three to Education bus stop should be ₦50; from Education Bus Stop to Rumuola N50; from Garrison to Park, ₦50," he added.

POLITICAL HIJACK: The Federal Government yesterday reviewed the two-day old strike called by the organised labour and concluded that the action had largely been hijacked by miscreants and politicians still nursing the wounds of their defeat in the last general election.

A government situation report on the strike said: "What is being witnessed in some states is opposition political figures who are trying to campaign even after the general elections."

The report noted for instance that "what is happening in Lagos State as far as the strike is concerned is an opposition political carnival", adding that "Pastor Tunde Bakare, who was defeated by President Jonathan alongside his presidential candidate General Muhammadu Buhari in April was still busy campaigning in Lagos on Monday."

The report continued: "It is becoming clear that the protests we are witnessing is not about subsidy protest but about some opposition political figures trying to fester (feather) their own nets. "What is happening in Lagos and parts of the South West is not protest but opposition political carnival. Or how do you describe a situation where people are being provided with food, music, leaflets, posters and 'T' shirts? Who is paying for those materials and the food?

Who paid the musician who entertained people in Lagos?"

FIGHTING HOODLUMS: President Jonathan yesterday rose from a meeting with security chiefs with a resolve to stop hoodlums and miscreants from hijacking the protests.

Briefing State House correspondents, Ringim said they were impressed with the way labour had so far conducted itself, they were worried about what happened in Government House, Kano where some people attempted to sack the government house where several vehicles were torched by the people whose style was at variance with that of labour.

"This meeting centred on the progress so far made by law enforcement with regard to what has been happening within the last few days and we are satisfied that the NLC on its own has been conducting itself in the best peaceful manner. However, it is also believed that there are miscreants that are trying to hijack this process and make it violent and we here are not going to allow it as law enforcement officers.

"Over 30 vehicles were burnt in Kano Government House. Will you look at this and say this was the work of NLC? No, gentlemen. This was certainly not the work of NLC, this was the work of miscreants who wanted to bum, maim and loot and police have a responsibility to maintain law and order and that was what we did," Ringim said.

He also charged Nigerians who have been fleeing their places of residence to their states to stay on as adequate arrangement had been put in place to protect them but regretted that since they have freedom of movement, no one could stop them from moving to wherever they wanted.

"Unfortunately, some people are feeling apprehensive and there is nothing you can do about it. They have the right to move and we want to give them assurance that we are ready and willing and determined more than ever before to provide them with necessary security to remain wherever they want to remain in this country. However, if they want to move, there is not much you can do about it, you can't stop them," he said. On the number of deaths so far recorded, he said in the record of the police, three people had died.

On the man that was shot dead in Lagos, he said: "I have ordered for investigation and that is what I am supposed to do and after the investigation, I have made a promise that the result will be made public and whoever is found culpable will be charged to court."

Also speaking on some Nigerians fleeing other places to their own areas, Minister of Defence Haliru Bello Mohammed said: "I will like to assure all Nigerians that they should continue living where they are; all arrangements have been made by the security forces to protect all Nigerians to live where they are living."

OPEN TO DIALOGUE: After the meeting with President Jonathan, Minister of Labour Emeka Wogu yesterday said the government was still open to dialogue in spite of the court order stopping labour from going ahead with protests. Wogu said there were three equal parties in the dispute and that in spite of two being on one side of the divide on the issue, the government was willing to dialogue with labour with a view to amicably resolving the issue, pointing out that government or any of the parties would not be persuaded to drop their stance from the streets, hence the need to go back to a round table.

He explained: "When I said that the option of dialogue is still open, it implied that we are exploring that option and labour is equally exploring that option. I don't believe in putting one as a senior partner and the other as a junior partner. In this issue, there are three senior partners within the doctrine and principle of tripartism; the NLC/TUC on one side representing the trade union, government on one side because it could be government at the federal level or state. Then the Employers' Consultative Association (NECA).

"As at today, government has done a policy on subsidy which is a partner in that tripartite arrangement. Then NECA which is an employer consultative assembly has equally supported that removal and the deregulation policy of government on the downstream sector.

"So, in three out of three, it is a question of number and question of democracy and fine aspect of democracy. You know out of three, two agreeing on one issue and one is saying no. So, it means that two is majority and one must have its say. But still, not minding the fact that two out of the three partners have agreed, there is still a room for dialogue; dialogue of persuasion, dialogue of persuading that this is the point."

Wogu pointed out the need to drop adversarial approach on resolving the matter as it would be easier leaving the streets for talks than doing so from violent protests which does not go down well with persuasion, adding: "Despite the fact that there is a court ruling, we are still amenable to dialogue without going into the merit of the case."

STREETPULSE...Our verdict on the strike

By Ejiro Odova

***The Guardian*, Sunday, January 22, 2012, pg. 15**

TO some, it was a soothing relief and to many others, it was an anti-climax. It was a bewildered nation that woke up on the morning of last Monday to the broadcast of President Jonathan announcing a reduction in the pump price of petrol from ₦141 to ₦97. By noon of the same day, organised Labour called off the eight-day nationwide strike and protest over fuel subsidy removal. While the strike lasted, Nigerians demonstrated through rallies, debates, and street protests and the social media that they can no longer be taken for granted and that sovereignty belongs to the people. Some Nigerians believe that the Nigeria Labour Congress (NLC) and Trade Union Congress (TUC) were unduly under pressure to end the strike, while others are of the opinion that the labour leaders might have been compromised to accept government's price of N97. In a chat with The Guardian, some Nigerians expressed their opinion about the outcome of the strike action. Excerpt:

NLC Betrayed Nigerians

JOHN UDENSA, Civil Servant

NIC betrayed Nigerians at a most critical moment. The suspension of the strike without government's reversal to ₦65 is an insult to the psyche of Nigerians. I was alarmed at the abrupt suspension of the strike. I am tempted to believe that NLC is currently being controlled by the people who benefit from the system and who are afraid of the power of the people in the midst of their growing anger against the state and its leaders. I think with the suspension, Jonathan is halfway in the battle to remove fuel subsidy. May God weed out bad eggs in the system.

₦97 Was Govt's Original Intention

Charles Balogun, Journalist

THE initial plan of the federal government was to increase fuel price to ₦100. Mentioning ₦141 in the first place was a subtle strategy. When the issue of subsidy was initially mentioned, the price was pegged at ₦120. Suddenly, it jumped to ₦141, the same way the annual subsidy figure jumped to Nl3trillion. The government knew Nigerians would resist, which was why it pretended to do us a fa the real tare ingthebattliman lives that were lost to tfie struggle died in vain. With this betrayal, I foresee people shunning NLC strike again in the near-est future when the need arise.

Govt Is Insensitive

TAIWO JONAH, Contractor

What NLC/TUC told us was 'no retreat, no surrender,' but labour leaders finally gave in after receiving the normal 'handshake' from government. We are being fooled. Affordable fuel is the only commodity in this country that is being consumed by both the rich and the poor and I don't believe petrol is being subsidized as much as the government claims. This government is insensitive and has nothing to offer but pain and miseries. I urge Nigerians not to give up in the struggle for their rights.

It Was A Successful Outing

BONIFACE UCHE, Contractor

THE strike was successful because it forced government to reduce the pump price to ₦97/litre even though it was made to look like government's unilateral decision. Secondly, government has been made to adopt the policy to drastically reduce cost of governance. The organised Laoour may have called off the strike and demonstration in order to save lives and in the interest of the nation's survival. The third major achievement Nigerians recorded is that the strike got the federal government to decisively move against the massive and crippling corruption in the oil sector. Though Labour may have defaulted in a way, I quite appreciate the successes made in the course of the strike.

Subsidy protest: gains, abuse of technology tools

By Emma Okonji

***ThisDay*, Thursday, January 19, 2012, vo. 16, no. 6114, pg. 26**

Power of Technology Tools amidst Protest

Nigerians who for one reason or the other could not join the nationwide protest over fuel subsidy removal, stayed at home and got every bit of information across the jountry as they unfold, courtesy of modem day technology tools.

Apart from the conventional television and radio gadgets, which relayed live activities of protesters from across the states, Nigerians used heir mobile phones, especially the Blackberry to capture activities of protesters and uploaded hem on Facebook and Twitter, and disseminated the information in pictures and text messages to other Nigerians, just to get them informed. The technology tools, though small and handy, became powerful tools during the protest, as people became fully informed through various medium on why labour had to negate government plea and the National Industrial Court order, to embark on a nationwide strike the crippled commercial and economic activities in the country.

For some, it was time to rest at home and get full information on the activities of protesters, led by the Nigerian Labour Congress (NLC), Trade Union Congress (TUC), Save Nigeria Group (SNG), Religious leaders, political leaders, among several other groups. But for others the information they got through their mobile phones, spurred them into joining the protest, thus increasing the number of protesters on the streets, as the protest enters each new day. Such is the power of technology tools, which Nigerians enjoyed so much during the one week organised labour strike that was suspended on Monday January 16, 2012. During the strike, friends were 'pinging' each other through their Blackberry phones, others were communicating on Facebook, and some on Twitter and Skype, communicating information that turned out to be useful to people.

People used their mobile phones to communicate their families and friends about danger zones, where fighting, shootings and killings were going on in some parts of the country dur-ing the strike. People became informed through the process, and they either resolved to stay indoors, or drive through routes that were less volatile. In so doing, lives were saved, even though some protesters died in the process. Disseminated information was also used to edu-cate Nigerians on the cost of fuel per litre in other countries of the world and how some Nigerians were allegedly defrauding the Nigerian economy through fuel subsidy.

In the face of all these, traders of edible and perishable items were able to get information on the areas where protesters have large concentration of people at various parks and other public places. Traders used the information to target such places of densely populated protesters to sell their goods and make quick money, even though the intention of NLC and TUC was to ground every commercial activity in the country. At Gani Park in Ojota, Lagos, for instance, petty raders were selling bottle and sachet water, cold nineral, Ice Cream, quick food like gala, cakes, Dread, as well as perishable items like vegetable eaves, tomatoes, fruits, among other food items. Protesters and several other Nigerians, who saw die action as opportunity for them to have fun, vere busy patronising the petty traders who seized the opportunity of the strike action to sell at exorbitant prices. A bundle of vegetable leaves that hitherto sells for N20, was sold at V200 at the Gani Park during the strike.

Abuse of Technology Tools

Although Nigerians used their mobile phones to inform people on the activities of protesters across the country, some however used the opportunity to abuse the use of mobile phones md other technology tolls, by sending incorrect information that caused panic to Nigerians at nome during the strike.

For instance, shortly before NLC and TUC declared the strike action, some Nigerians cooked up a story that the Federal Government net with Chief Executive Officers of all elecommunications operators and decided to suspend

Blackberry service across networks, in order to stop people from informing others through their Blackberry phones on the state of country. The information was broadcast through the Blackberry phones, urging Nigerians to rise and resist government on the planned move. With the power of technology tool like Blackberry, the information spread like wildfire and people became angry and started making several calls to friends, Journalists, the Nigerian Communications Commission (NCC), and the telecoms operators, just to confirm the information. Worried by the spread of the false information, the NCC and the telecoms operators, quickly issued press statements to correct the false information.

Again at the peak of the strike, it was alleged through the mobile phone, and via internet, that President Goodluck Jonathan could not bear the heat of the strike any longer and fled to South Africa to cool off. Meanwhile the President was in the country, consulting with labour, through the leadership of the National Assembly, throughout the period.

Other disturbing signals through the abusive use of technology tools, during the strike action, included the purported message that the 'Boko Haram' group was planning to attack Christians during the strike action. Some even alleged that the Islamic Sect 'Boko Haram' would be carrying out a Jihad to kill every Christian in Northern Nigeria, immediately after their Jumat prayers on Friday. The message, which warned Christians to be aware of Muslims during the strike action, sent panic to many Christians, who either locked up themselves at home, or embarked on forced travel from their locations, for those who were mobile.

But on Sunday, few days after the broadcast of the false message, Muslims in Kano, joined Christians to worship in churches, just to prove that Muslims and Christians are of one religious body who serve the same God but in different ways.

Apart from the religious panic created through some false messages, people were broadcasting information through their Blackberry phones, comparing prices of petrol in other countries of the world with Nigeria, without benchmarking their comparisons with other oil producing countries like Nigeria. Such information turned out to be insinuating and created fears in the minds of many.

Abusive Comments

To further instigate the people against govern- ment, some people were using abusive state-ments on President Goodluck Jonathan and other members of his cabinet. Some went as far as calling them names that were unpleasant, all in the name of strike. The office of the President was ridiculed by some group and it was broadcast through some social media.

At some protest points in Lagos, television stations captured and broadcasted the manner in which most people abused the office of the President of Nigeria, and some calling for the outright impeachment of the president just because of his policy, which many regarded as killing and anti-people.

Respect for the office of the President was thrown to the winds and people made derogatory statements, abusing the office publicly.

Counter-reaction

Reacting to the situation that degenerated into abusive use of words on the President of the country, NLC Secretary General, Mr. Owei Lakemfa who spoke in an interview with African Independent Television (AIT), said the essence of the strike was not to attack the personality of President Goodluck Jonathan, nor to ask for his impeachment, but to protect the interest of Nigerians who were insisting on the reversal of Premium Motor Spirit (PMS), popularly known as petrol from N140 per litre to N65 per litre.

Expert Opinion

Taking a holistic view of the whole scenario during the 8 days labour strike, President of the Association of Licensed Telecommunications Operators of Nigeria (ALTON), Gbenga Adebayo said the mobile phones and other technology tools have more advantages than disadvantages. According to him, the mobile phones helped in cushioning tensions during the labour strike. He explained that people were able to communicate with others and informed them on the true position of things in the country especially for those who travelled outside the country and outside their locations within the country and could not return during the strike action.

Adebayo however said anything with advantage must also have disadvantage. He blamed some Nigerians who used the occasion of the strike action to send conflicting and incorrect information to innocent Nigerians that were hungry for information during the strike period. He advised Nigerians not to accept unsolicited messages, especially in times of crises, adding that such messages could cause panic, anxiety and uncertainty among Nigerians who believe in them.

Giving instance of the rumoured information that government and telecoms operators planned to suspend Blackberry services in the country, Adebayo cautioned Nigerians on the rate at which they accept information that has no credible source, and in most cases without name and contact. He said any information that could not be traced to the originator, should be dis-countenanced immediately it is received.

He cautioned Nigerians who hide under the disguise of mobile phone to send information capable of inciting people against government and constituted authority, insisting that mobile phones and other technology tools are essential tools for nation development, and should not be abused.

Why Nigerians Went on Strike

The Federal Government had last year, told the public of its plan to remove fuel subsidy, but the position of government was vehemently rejected by the masses, through the organised labour who threatened to carry out a nationwide strike with street protests across the country.

Government however tried to create awareness on the people, through a town hall meeting organised in Lagos at the instance of the Finance Minister, Dr. Ngozi Okonjo-Iweala, where Nigerians spoke their minds on the planned subsidy removal.

On January 1, 2012, while Nigerians were still celebrating the New Year, government went ahead and announced fuel subsidy removal and the subsequent increase of petrol from ₦65 per litre to ₦140 per litre. Based on the subsidy removal, the NLC and the TUC called for an indefinite nationwide strike action and protest, to contest the fuel subsidy removal. The strike which commenced on Monday January 9,2012, and suspended on Monday January 16, paral-ysed economic and commercial activities nationwide, resulting to pear breakdown of law and order in some states of the federation, with some number of recorded deaths among the Police and protesters. The strike was eventually suspended on Monday January 16, 2012, after government shifted from its initial position of ₦65 per litre of petrol to ₦97 per litre.

Subsidy Protest: the winners and losers

By Ademola Adeyemo

***ThisDay*, Wednesday, January 18, 2012, vol. 16, no. 6113, pg. 16**

For seven days, Nigeria witnessed a nation-wide protest that shook the entire nation. The organized labour and civil societies had called out the people for street protests to register their opposition over the removal of subsidy on the premium motor spirit (petrol) by the Federal Government. Government had on the New Year day, announced that it had decided to deregulate the downstream sector of the oil industry with immediate effect and therefore went ahead to hike the petrol pump price to ₦141 from ₦65. However there were wide outcry and condemnation of the new government policy. Consequently, labour ordered a national strike and protest against the increment. During the one week show of anger the nation was paralysed as social and economic lives of the country were in comatose. However, there were some casualties as some protesters lost their lives to the police bullets. Also some government properties and those belonging to some individuals were destroyed by angry protesters.

As the protest was raising tension in the country, government had to call the labour for dialogue over the crisis. After three consecutive meetings, last Sunday, government reduced the petrol pump price to ₦97 with the assurance to implement the palliatives in order to cushion the effect of the increment in the prices of goods and services occasioned by the removal of subsidy. Besides, government also agreed to carry out reforms in the oil sector and probe the corruption in the sector.

Last Monday, the organized labour after consultation suspended the strike and protest actions; it also agreed to continue dialogue with government on the reforms.

However, there were gainers and losers. After the seven-day protest, while the gainers are savouring their gains, the losers are counting their losses. Here are some of the gainers and losers of the one week national protest.

The Gainers

Nigerians

Nigerians who stood firmly in rejecting the increment in the price of petrol are the gainers of the one week protest as their resoluteness and determination to continue the protest and make the country ungovernable forced the Federal

Government to shift from its rigid position that the removal of subsidy was final and that there was no going back. After shutting down the nation for seven days, government was forced to reduce the price of petrol from ₦141 to ₦97 per litre. Observers said that if not for the protests, the price would have remained at ₦141 with its spiral effect on other goods and services.

Organised Labour

Victory also goes to the organized labour for daring the government and effectively organizing and coordinating the one week protest which eventually forced the government to back down on its earlier position. With the success of the strike action, the credibility and leadership ability of labour have gone up in the estimation of the people.

Civil Society

Another winner of the one week protest against the removal of petrol subsidy is the coalition of the civil society. For effectively collaborating with the organised labour to mobilise the people to resist the imposition of unpopular policy by the government, the civil society groups have demonstrated their patriotism and responsibility as the prorectors of the people.

Democracy

As tension engulfed the country over the removal of subsidy by the government, there were palpable fears that the nation's democracy might be jeopardized if the military seized the opportunity of the logjam to terminate the civilian government in the country. Those who expressed the fear include leader of the Save Nigeria Group (SNG), Pastor Tunde Bakare, leader of Afenifere Renewal Group (ARG), Hon. Olawale Oshun, Lagos lawyer, Femi Falana and Osun State Governor, Mr Rauf Aregbesola. They appealed to the soldiers to remain in barrack, saying that the worst civilian regime is better than the most benevolent military administration.

The opposition

Opposition elements also made some gains during the one week protest; they had to seize the opportunity of the nationwide anger against the government policy to get at the President and the ruling party through crititisms and condemnations. The opposition, eyeing the 2015 election used the mass protest to embark on campaign of calumny against the ruling party.

House of Representatives

Athough, the resolution of the House calling on the Executive to suspend the removal of the subsidy was ignored, nevertheless, the patriotic zeal and sacrifice made by the lawmakers who broke their holiday and resumed on Sunday to play a mediatory role were historical and commendable. It was a huge political point scored by the House of Representatives led by its Speaker, Hon. Aminu Tambuwal. The House by its action has distinguished itself as pro-people parliament.

Senate Leadership

The leadership of the Senate led by David Mark has also passed the patriotic and credibility test by playing a successful mediatory role in making untiring efforts to ensure that they brokered the necessary peace between the government and the organised labour which even-tually culminated in the resolution of the one-week crisis that threatened the unity of the nation and endangered democracy.

Social Media

During the one week nationwide strike, the social media stood with the people in ensuring effective dissemination of news backed with facts and figures, which blew opened what government kept secret from the public. The rage of the people was kept on the front burner in the social media.

People were confronted with pictures of dead protesters, details of the nation's 2012 budget figures, funds allocated to the president and vice president's offices with the cost of living of the average Nigerian.

The Losers

Economy

During the seven-day protest, the nation's ailing economy was shut down as the country lost an average of ₦145 billion income daily to the workers strike action. The protest was total, civil servants stayed indoors, banks closed their doors to customers, aircrafts were not allowed to fly while workers in the downstream petroleum sector also downed tools.

Though, the total loss to the economy is yet to be compiled, analysts were of the opinion that the loss would certainly be in several billions. Indications have emerged that within the five-day strike the nation's downstream sector of the petroleum industry lost over ₦23.265 billion, aside other losses in other sectors of the nation's economy.

This is coming as sources equally disclosed that other countries, which consume Nigeria's crude, had, consequent on this strike on fuel subsidy removal, were shunning Nigerian crude, especially when Petroleum and Natural Gas Senior Staff Association of Nigeria (PENGASSAN) threatened to halt production.

It was learnt that the daily loss on Premium Motor Spirit (PMS) was ₦4.653 billion. This was based on the nation's consumption demand of 33 million per day and the ₦141 per litre, which was the maximum price for PMS during the week, going by the Petroleum Products Pricing Regulatory Agency (PPPRA). Petrol tankers were also unable to deliver supplies to Nigeria because of the striked.

Nigerian Stock Market

The biting effect of the seven-day strike has adversely affected the Nigerian stock market. During the protest, the cash-strapped investors dumped equities, sending the benchmark indices into the negative. With only 12 price changes, there were two losers for every gainer while staff of the NSE said the online trading was becoming challenging with every day of the protest.

Aggregate market capitalisation of all quoted equities dropped to ₦6.579 trillion as against its opening value of ₦6.588 trillion. The benchmark index, All Share Index (ASI), which tracks prices of all quoted companies, relapsed to 20,878.71 points compared with its opening index of 20, 905.35 points.

The decline was orchestrated by highly capitalised stocks, especially in the banking sector which constituted nearly all the losers during the crisis. The NSE 30 Index, which tracks the 30 most capitalised companies and susceptible to banking stocks' positions, dropped from 939.09 points to 937.76 points. The NSE Banking Index nose dived to 269.89 points as against its opening index of 27123 points. The NSE Insurance Index also dropped marginally from 128.86 points to 128.18 points.

Oil Cabals

The cabals are in the centre of the controversy that surrounded the operation of oil sector. Government had claimed that it was spending about N13 trillion as fuel subsidy and that the large percentage of the amount was being lost to the sharp practices and unwholesome prac-tices of some oil marketers who have constituted themselves into a cabal and corrupt the sector in collaboration with the government agencies.

With the crisis over the removal of subsidy, a searchlight has been beamed into the sector with the aim to unmask the corrupt marketers and their official collaborators. Government has ordered the Economic and Financial Crimes Commission (EFCC) to go after the cabal.

Industrialists

Industrialists, Small and Medium Scale Entrepreneurs were also victims of the nationwide strike as they were forced to shut down plants, losing millions of Naira in revenue. The abrupt closure would also affect the machines as some of them would be in a bad shape and may have broken down during the strike. Yet, the owners of the affected companies are expected to pay salaries to their workers for works not done. Also, some of the imported raw materials are laying waste in the Ports due to the strike and are attracting demurrage on a daily basis.

Victims of Police Brutality

Probably, the big losers are the protesters who were victims of Police brutality. They were shot dead by police bullets when the protesters clashed with policemen during the protest. Lives were lost in Lagos, Osun, Ogun, Kwara, Kano States during the one-week protests.

The thrills and frills of subsidy protests

By Olaolu Olusina, Paul Obi, Hammed Shittu and Ibrahim Shuaibu

***ThisDay*, Sunday, January 22, 2012, vol. 17, no. 6117, pg 14, 15, 16**

Mrs. Betty Press will not forget her recent visit to the country in a hurry. Apparently on her maiden trip to the world's most populous black nation, the associate professor of Photo Journalism at the University of Southern Mississippi, USA, was quite excited at the prospect of her visit, during which she was expected as a guest lecturer at the 13th edition of the Professor Bassey Andah Memorial Lecture scheduled to hold in Calabar, the Cross River State capital. But the American professor couldn't make it down to Calabar as she was stranded in Lagos, having been caught in the web of the national strike and protests organised by the Nigeria Labour Congress and Trade Union Congress as well as civil society organanisations against the removal of the subsidy on petrol by the federal government.

For six working days starting penultimate week, the country was practically brought to a halt as economic and other commercial activities were paralysed by national outrage against the withdrawal of the subsidy removal of the subsidy had seen the price of petrol jump from ₦65 to ₦141 per litre. The federal government, however, was forced to back down last week by fixing the price at ₦97 last week, a decision that brought some measure of relief and gradual return of peace to the country.

But beyond the political and economic rationalisations for the controversial subsidy removal, the national strike and protests brought with them some comical and thrilling moments that sustained the momentum, thereby, making the entire exercise not only a success but quite revealing at the same time. From Abuja to Lagos and from Kano to Ilorin, protesters were united as they brought forth the creativity in them for a common cause. And for the first time in recent times, a message was sent to the government that despite the much touted benefits of the subsidy removal, Nigerians would no longer be taken for a ride.

Multiple Freedom/ Liberation Grounds

In Abuja, for instance, many had thought the protests would take place at the Eagle Square but the government had mapped out a plan to prevent the use of the place in view of the incessant cases of bombings in the nation's capital and its environs in recent times. Accordingly, all roads leading to Eagle Square were therefore blocked. But this could not deter the leaders of the labour unions and civil society organisations as they changed their plans by searching for other venues and routes for their rallies.

Multiple freedom and liberation grounds therefore emerged in the city. Labour union leaders had decided to name these locations as such. Berger Junction, where three prominent roads named after three Nigerian nationalists - the Nnamdi Azikiwe Highway, Herbert Macauley Road and Obafemi Awolowo Road converge - suddenly became the epicentre of the protests. For the unionists and protesters, the Berger juction was not only a converging point, but a symbol and cradle of the NLC/TUC battle against the removal of the subsidy.

The Wuse Market Junction was also another focal point that protesters turned into their abode to press home their grievances against the fuel subsidy removal. Chicken House Juction along IBB Boulevard where the road intersects with Ademola Adetokunbo Crescent was the terminating point of the protest from Monday to Wednesday. Area One junction was also another location used by the protesters. Addressing protesters on the first day of the protest, NLC President, Comrade Abdulwaheed Omar, alongside his TUC counterpart, Peter Esele, said Nigerians would not heed to government's position.

Power Bikes

One unique aspect with the Abuja protest was not just the high turnout of protesters but the acrobatic display of the power bikers. As known with such events in recent times in Abuja, renowned musician, Charles Oputa, a.k.a Charly Boy, led the way during the protest.

After the union leaders and protesters had converged and the day's activities were read out as well as the message to the government, the power bikes led the way, where most of the bikers displayed various acrobatic displays to the admiration and applause of on-lookers.

Muslim, Christians Unite

Though the protest might have come and gone, it conquered many grounds and broke religious barriers that were hitherto a-no-go area. One of such was the observation of prayers by both Muslims and Christians and casting out of demons on the same location simulta-neously. As protesters marched along Abuja streets, at each of the meeting points (Wuse 2 and Area One junctions), whenever Muslims started their afternoon prayer sessions with the call to prayer, Allah A'khBar Wu, Christians in return would chant, "Holy Ghost Fire", "Subsidy Removal Fire" and all sorts of incantations. Sometimes, Christians would construct a human barricade to shield Muslims from intruders before they commenced their own prayer sessions and vice versa. It was a rare scene that had not been witnessed in the city for many years.

The Melaye, Igodomigodo Jinks

One man who got considerable mileage in television appearances and newspaper coverage remains former House of Representatives member, Hon. Dino Melaye. First, he was arrested for leading a protest against the subsidy removal which was premised on the fact that he lacked the locus standi to do so.

Then came his decision to ride a bicycle from his house in Wuse to African Independent Television premises in Asokoro. Riding a bicycle by Melaye provided comic relief during the protest, but the symbolism was not lost on the public. Beside the bicycle episode, Dino's numerous stunts added colour to the protest. Though, many accuse him of trying to get cheap publicity, the chants of "Dino, Dino, Dino, Dino" by protesters could not be waved aside.

Another former House member whose appearance also spiced up the protest was Hon. Patrick Obagbion, a.k.a Igodomigodo. His use of grandiloquent words was very entertaining for the protesters, to the extent that many demanded for an encore from the former House member from Edo State. In one of his speeches before the protesters, he described government subsidy removal as a "Cabalocracy." With their presence, the subsidy protest in Abuja was more or less a carnival, as it held the crowd spellbound.

Beggars in Battle for Survival

It was different strokes in Ilorin, the Kwara State capital, a city known as the home of Muslim clerics. While many of the Imams of the various mosques used the opportunity to take a swipe at the federal government in their purported identification with the strike, beggars in the city became aggressive in the battle for survival as they went begging for alms from people already engrossed with the strike.

Many beggars, who were in the habit of staying at particular intersections on the city's streets, resorted to walking about in search of those that could give alms, particularly when they saw some people handling money in public.

Hoodlums Reign Supreme

However, hoodlums hijacked the peaceful protest organised by labour and civil society groups in Ilorin as they reportedly assaulted people, stole and burnt property. Mandate House, the campaign office of all Peoples Democratic Party candidates in the last election located on Western Reservoir Road, Adewole Housing Estate Area, was damaged and burnt, while party foods were also carted away by the oodlums. Goods carted away by the hoodlums at the Mandate House included bags of rice, a large number of mobile phones, and bundles of PDP campaign material, while three campaign buses, party documents and part of the build-ing were also damaged and burnt.

Lagos was not left of the menace of hoodlums and armed robbery attacks. During the strike, crime rose sharply in the city and no party of Lagos was immune from wild-eyed young men, who could not ply their trade for the six days of the strike, and had resorted to setting up barricades on roads to rob motorists or their money and personal belongings. Those that resisted were either molested, beaten or had their windshield or car windows smashed. Similarly, there waS an increase in car snatching in Lagos during the period of the strike.

As if that was not bad enough, public infrastructure such as roads in the state was destroyed as miscreants set up bourne fires on major roads especially in the mainland. Lagos also became particularly filthy as workers of the Lagos State Waste Management Agency were unable to clean the streets for the duration of the strike.

Commercial Sex Workers Show Solidarity

In Kano, commercial sex workers, also known as “run girls”, visibly participated in the protest, on the grounds that the subsidy removal would also affect their business because nobody will patronise them. Speaking to *ThisDay* on the condition of anonymity, a commercial sex worker plying her trade on Enugu Road lamented the effect of the strike on her customers. “We are on strike now because most of our customers are on strike, so we have to suspend the business till when the labour calls off the strike,” some of the girls told this newspaper in an interview. Popular joints in the ancient city such as Enugu, Abedeen, Sani Giwa, Warri, Ijebu Roads all in Sabon-Gari were shadows of their former self, as commercial sex workers also placed a ban on their services during this period.

Song and Dance in Lagos

It was however carnival-like atmosphere in sections of Lagos where “Occupy Nigeria” protesters turned the protest into fun. The Gani Fawehinmi Memorial Park and the MKO Abiola Gardens, all in Ojota, became carnival grounds for Nigerians from all works of life. It was a bie break for many Lagosians, though considered too early in the year. The consensus during the strike was, “If you are not in Ojota, you are not in Lagos,” as protesters trekked long distances from different parts of the city to join in the fun at Ojota. Many cultivated the habit of arriving the parks as early as 5 am to prepare the grounds for the day as many brought mats and beds. Street and food hawkers also had a field day as the made brisk business at the parks. Nolly wood actors and actresses also added glamour to the protests with notable musicians entertaining the protesters alongside the activities lined up by labour and CSO leaders. Some of the leading names in Nolly wood also used the opportunity to test their pub-lic speaking ability.

The artistes that appeared at the protest grounds included Kunle Afolayan, Yomi Blaq, Ufuoma Ejenobor, Toyin Aihmaku, Femi and*, Seun Kuti, Sir Shina Peters, AY.com, YQ, Skuki, Djinee, Saheed Osupa, Obesere, Klint da drunk, Seyi Law and Princess . Others included Eedris Abdulkareem, Olu Maintain, Salawa Abeni, Nigger Raw, JJC, Wasiu Alabi, Gbenga Adeyinka, and Desmond Elliot Popular actor Jide Kosoko, Bimbo Akintola, Ronke Oshodi-Oke, and top musicians like Abolore Akande (9ice), Ras Kimono and KWAM 1, among others were also there. Popular comedian and actor, Babatunde Omidina, a.k.a Baba Suwe, apparently used the opportunity to worm his ways back into the heart of his admirers after his ordeal with the National Drugs Law Enforcement Agency. Like Abuja, Christians and Muslims were united more than ever at the carnival grounds while social media net-working sites such as facebook and twitters were awash with reports on the "Ojota Carnival". On the Island and Ikoyi, protesters gathered in groups at the Tafawa Balewa Square and Falomo Roundabout from where they moved into Ikoyi in a carnival style showing a great deal of creativity and innovativeness as they moved round and popped open bottles of Champagne. Given that protesters from Lagos Island comprise of mostly the well-heeled of the society- it attracted a deluge men and women who seized the opportunity to make new acquaintances and forge relationships. *ThisDay* also learnt that in the Abule-Egba area where the protests became violent and were almost hijacked by area boys and social mis-creants, a woman hawking a local aphrodisiac called agbo offered the protesters free drinks of the product in a rare show of solidarity.

Overstretched Police

It was glaring that the Nigerian Police Force were overstretched and overwhelmed during the rallies and protests as they were unable to contain the activities of the hoodlums who later hijacked the rallies and protests in some parts of Lagos. Police stations were apparent empty throughout the city as personnel had been moved to trouble spots.

Along the Apapa-Oshodi Expressway, Sango-Abule-Egba Road, Lekki-Epe Expressway and Third Mainland Bridge, miscreants mounted their own road barricades, in some instances, about a few metres away from those mounted by the police as they forced road users to part with their money and became violent, smashing vehicles in some instances. But the so-called hoodlums and area boys were discovered to be artisans, street hawkers, bus drivers and con-ductors who normally live from hands to mouth on a daily basis, but had been forced out of business for the six days of the strike. "It's a game of survival as these boys have to eat. It shows the level of poverty in the land," an observer of the development told *ThisDay.*

Lessons Learnt

Many Nigerians believe that the most important lesson learnt from the strike is than Nigerians despite their differences can be united for common purposes, a phenomenon that can be used for forging unity in the country. "Nigerians have never been as united as this," Adekunle Adeoye, a student who was part of the

Ojota rally told *ThisDay*. It also brought the creativity in the citizenry and despite the hardship and incon venience many went through, the expression of hope in the country has never been expressed as during the six-day strike and protests.

The week that change Nigeria

By Chidi Odinkalu

***ThisDay*, Sunday, January 22, 2012, vol.17, no.6117, pg. 24**

The end of the nation-wide shutdown triggered by the New Year's Day announcement of deregulation of down-stream petroleum sector has, predictably, drawn mixed reactions. Organised Labour says government unilaterally dictated an outcome; government complains that the protests against fuel subsidy removal were hijacked by the political opposition; organised civil society stops just short of accusing Labour of selling out All of this misses an important point - that this was a week that changed Nigeria irreversibly and mostly for the better.

The strike may have been triggered by subsidy removal but it resonated so loudly because it was about much more than that. For the first time in Nigeria's history, this was an affirmative protest it was not only the usual protest against something; rather it was a protest for something different - a different way of running government.

Plainly, this was not a protest against anyone. Many of the issues about which people marched pre-date the administration of President Goodluck Jonathan. It is the luck of his government that it has the historical task of addressing them.

In marching, Nigerians asked, quite publicly, whether they get value for money spent by government at all levels. And they asked all in government to demonstrate two things: good faith in sharing the discomforts of the people they serve and honest competence in managing the savings from deregulation for the public good. The strike may be over, but these demands will not go away.

Clearly, the issues have gone beyond whether or not to undertake deregulation. As a policy, deregulation has been championed by Nigeria's governments - military and civilian - for more than a quarter of a century. The full import of this policy has, however, been lost on government and those who run it.

Over the quarter century in which government has pursued deregulation, no government has demonstrated any gains or progress from the things they advertised they would be able to do. This was thus a moment when Nigerian citizens said they wouldn't forgive short memory, nor suffer the old ways gladly anymore.

In the period that government has pursued deregulation and privatisation, the cost and size of government at the federal level has risen exponentially, grand corruption has become endemic in public life, and citizens are unable to see value for the money government appropriates or spends.

Yet, the 1999 Constitution, enacted 13 years after the onset of privatisation, requires government to control the "commanding heights" (whatever that means) of the economy.

There is something profoundly not right about having a smalltime bureaucrat fix the price of petrol and make billions out of doing so in conspiracy with a narrow "cabal". Anyone could agree that this system needs to go. But it is nonetheless possible to profoundly disagree with the New Year's Day policy roll-out.

For a policy with such far reaching consequences for the consumer, citizen and kitchen-table, there was no effort to prepare the public for it, let alone to help them survive it. Having the announcement go out via the website of an agency unknown to most Nigerians was widely perceived as cynical. Senior government officials talked down to citizens with an arrogance that showed they loved the lure of office more than the call to service. At a time that the security situation in the country required optimal harnessing of civic resources, the manner of the announcement risked reckless squandering of vital assets.

But this was a moment when all sides in Nigeria showed that the country has the capacity to grow in its precarious democracy.

There were allegations that the political opposition hijacked the protests. Unquestionably, there was some unprincipled opportunism. Some who had supported and administered deregulation as senior politicians in the past found it convenient to switch sides. That shows lack of character. But they were not the only ones that did. A former Labour leader, now in government also changed sides. Opposition politicians are also Nigerian citizens. They are, moreover, not in the business of making life easy for government. That is democracy. Above all, they did not start the protest; they joined a bandwagon of ordinary citizens. Any other conclusion does considerable injustice to the extraordinary sacrifice of citizens.

The federal government and security agencies largely respected the advisory by the National Human Rignts Commission (NHRC) on the rights to free expression and protest. Tragically, casualties were still reported in some parts of the country. Muyideen Opobiyi in Ilorin, Ademola Aderinto in Lagos and others. Condolences are due and must be offered to all the families who lost these loved ones. Staff of the NHRC monitored the protests. In cooperation with officials in the affected States and the Police, the Commission is investigating all reported violations in the protests and will issue a public report.

By and large, law enforcement agents conducted themselves with commendable restraint. Protest organisers also worked hard to restrain participants. Humour was made and traded with an ingenuity that inspired both civic pride and good neighbourliness. These protests have been a boon for access to information. They have evolved an affirmative agenda for governance, putting corruption and elimination of waste in government at the heart of the public interest. They have given young people huge reason to connect with politics. And they have offered government an opportunity to build a new coalition for governance that can unite the country. These are all positives that must not be squandered.

The end of these protests offers an opportunity to rally the country as never before behind a positive agenda for governance. Three things define that agenda. First, government has shown that it can mobilise security assets when its authority is endangered. Now, it must mobilise those assets and unite the country against the perpetrators of unsolved bombings that threaten insecurity on everyone in Nigeria. Second, as the National Assembly enters into consideration of the 2012 appropriations, the country must rally pressure on the distinguished and honorable members to address the urgent issue of reducing waste in government. The National Assembly should indicate what it must cut to fund better government for a better country. Third, all this will count only if it improves Nigeria's democracy. Everyone who rallied in January 2012 must commit to ensuring that their votes count in 2015. For this purpose, we must all encourage Professor Jega and INEC to improve the voters register. The young people who made such a difference in these protests must keep up pressure. This surely is not a moment to lose hope or focus.

In an article "Who Holds the Power" in the January issue of Prospect magazine, John Chipman offers a piece of pithy insight customized for all in Nigeria at this time: "readiness is all. Power will flow to those who can cope with surprise and shocks, and will be drained from those who resist change rather than shape it In 2012, nominally weak people in badly governed countries still have a chance to shape reform....We must hope that the well intentioned keep up the pace against the more malevolent." To this, there is little to add and nothing to remove.

CBN admits fraud in subsidy scheme, warns of pressure on foreign reserve

By Azimazi Momoh Jimoh and others

***The Guardian*, Wednesday, January 25, 2012, pg. 1, 2**

The Central Bank of Nigeria (CBN) declared yesterday that the total amount of money withdrawn and spent by the Federal Government on petroleum products subsidy was ₦1.763 trillion. The Ministry of Finance had earlier said that ₦1.38 trillion was spent on subsidy from January to October last year.

The CBN Deputy Governor, Dr. Kingsley Morghalu, who represented the Governor of the apex bank, Sanusi Lamido Sanusi, disclosed at the House of Representatives public hearing on subsidy fund management that the huge expenditure on subsidy put too much pressure on the country's foreign reserve. He, however, stated that the CBN was putting measures in place to ensure that the foreign reserve did not go below $30 billion.

Also, Petroleum Resources Minister, Mrs. Diezani Alison-Madueke, at the hearing, noted that the Governance and Control Task Force Team set up by in the ministry would deal with fundamental issues from the audit report, when formally transmitted to her. The minister, who lamented the spate of "sharp practices" in the industry, now- ever noted that Federal Government had started "sweeping reforms" in the oil and gas industry aimed at tackling the menace of corruption, smuggling and manipulations in the subsidy regime. Alison-Madueke who condemned the lapses and rot in the system stressed the need for PPPRA to clarify some issues on payment or certificates for subsidy "before we come to grasp on the actual problem on ground."

The Central Bank of Nigeria (CBN) declared yesterday that the total amount of money withdrawn and spent by the Federal Government on petroleum products subsidy was ₦1.763 trillion. The Ministry of Finance had earlier said that ₦1.38 trillion was spent on subsidy from January to October last year. The CBN Deputy Governor, Dr. Kingsley Morghalu, who represented the Governor of the apex bank, Sanusi Lamido Sanusi, disclosed at the House of Representatives public hearing on subsidy fund management that the huge expenditure on subsidy put too much pressure on the country's foreign reserve.

He, however, stated that the CBN was putting measures in place to ensure that the foreign reserve did not go below $30 billion.

Also, Petroleum Resources Minister, Mrs. Diezani Ali- son-Madueke, at the hearing, noted that the Governance and Control Task Force Team set up by in the ministry would deal with fundamental issues from the audit report, when formally transmitted to her. The minister, who lamented the spate of "sharp practices" in the industry, now- ever noted that Federal Government had started "sweeping reforms" in the oil and gas industry aimed at tackling the menace of corruption, smuggling and manipulations in the subsidy regime. Alison-Madueke who condemned the lapses and rot in the system stressed the need for PPPRA to clarify some issues on payment or certificates for subsidy "before we come to grasp on the actual problem on ground."

While reacting to the report on the sale of oil blocs, Ali- son-Madueke disclosed that, "no oil bloc has been sold since I came into the office

Cost, gain of fuel subsidy removal

By Bukola Olatunji, Uchechukwu Nnaike and Funmi Ogundare

***ThisDay*, Wednesday, January 18, 2012, vol. 16, no. 6113, pg. 34, 35**

Nigerians are still counting the cost of the January 1 removal of subsidy on Premium Motor Spirit (PMS), as the prices of goods and services have shot through the roof across the country. It may be too soon to expect to see the effect of Monday's reduction of the pump price from ₦140 to ₦97. A bag of rice that sold for about ₦7,500 now sells for ₦10,000. The cost of a basket of tomatoes rose from ₦9,000 to ₦19,500; ten litres of vegetable oil from about ₦3, 000 to ₦4,500 and ₦5,000, depending on the brand; while a bag of brown beans is currently sold for ₦17,200, up from ₦15,000. The sellers, expectedly, attributed the increases to the high cost of transportation fares. In most cases, transportation cost has gone up by more than 100 per cent. The immediate impact of this on the education sector is that the prices of exercise books, textbooks and other instructional materials cannot remain the same, although most bookshops remained closed at the time of filing this report. Students who commute to their schools would require more transportation allowance; Feeding allowance will have to increase too.

It is not the beginning of a new session, but private school owners may be forced to increase fees due to the increase in administrative cost. A parent, Mr. John Igwe said, “The fuel price increase has already affected my children’s school fees. The proprietress of their school sent a text message, on January 3, that the school has increased the cost of school bus from ₦13,000 to ₦20,000. The school also increased every other fee by about 60 per cent. The overall effect will be that many parents may withdraw their children from private schools and resort to public schools because there is no indication that there would be a commensurate increase in workers’ salaries.” He said the situation might compel both public and private schools to cut comers in running expenses and overhead costs. The effect of which would be a likely drop in the standard of education across board.

Another parent, who spoke on condition of anonymity, argued that there was need for subsidy in other sectors such as agriculture, education, trade, housing, among others. These he said, would add value to the lives of Nigerians.

“In the US, it is on cotton; in Britain, it is on beef production, while in Singapore, it is on housing. Because of the NHIS in Britain, people are treated free in hospitals. In Nigeria today, many brilliant people are wasting away on the streets because there is no one to fund their education.” A female top civil servant, who spoke on condition of anonymity said, “The increase in the price of fuel will have a multiplier effect on every aspect of our lives. Most of us send our children to private schools. Teachers and other school workers, especially those that have cars, will demand for salary increase because, apart from paying more for fuel, maintenance cost will also go up, though that may be marginal. The demand for higher salaries will be passed on to the students, so everybody should wear their girdle tight, because it is going to be a tight and painful transition. The overall effect to the society is that many more people will drop from the near non-existent middle class.”

International Education Strategist, Prof. Pai Obanya said the increase in the price of fuel would have an indirect effect on the edu-cation sector because it could reduce family and household financial contributions to the education of their children. “However, everything depends on how free government makes ‘free education’ and the extent to which families are able to forgo other things in favour of education.”

A unionist and schoolteacher, Mr. Femi Ogunsiji, was quoted as saying that the fuel subsidy removal would have negative effect on every aspect of the economy, including the education sector.

He said the rate of dropouts would increase, while school enrolment would reduce because most parents would find it difficult to send their children to school as a result of the high cost of living and fee increment. Owing to the rate of school dropout, he said, more children would be engaged in child labour.

In the larger picture, the strike by the labour unions and civil society groups to protest the fuel subsidy removal took its toll on the education sector. But for a few private schools that resumed during the first week of the year, most schools were scheduled to resume on the day strike began.

For public university students, it is a case of double jeopardy because their schools had been shut down since the Academic Staff Union of Universities (ASUU) began its strike on December 4, last year.

Chairman of the Lagos State University (LASU) branch of the union, Dr. Jamiu Oluwatoki, described the removal of subsidy as a coup against the people. Aside the increase in the cost of essential commodities and hardship in the country, he said parents would find it difficult to pay their children's school fees.

'To feed and clothe them may become a challenge. Hungry students cannot learn properly and failure by the federal government to develop human capital means mortgaging the future of the country. Labour has occupied Nigeria and people are saying1 they can no more be made slaves in their own country", he said, stressing the need for government to put the necessary facilities in place to educate the youths properly, if it wants the best for the country.

On the fuel subsidy removal, a businessman, Mr. Segun Omolewu, said it came at the wrong time and that government ought to have provided the palliative measures to cushion the effect and ameliorate the suffering of parents first. 'The removal of the fuel subsidy will increase die overall cost of education, vis-a-vis transportation, feeding and buying of text books because of the over 300percent increase", he said.

On the ASUU strike, Omolewu, a former Director in the Lagos State Ministry of Education expressed regret that "government wants to boast of so many universities instead of providing basic needs and infrastructures that will give the students, sound education. It is a shame that nowadays, students cannot write sound essays. The lecturers are on strike to fight for the improved future and the quality of graduates that they produce from our universities."

He therefore called on the government to increase budgetary allocation to education if, indeed, it wants to be among the first 20 economies in the world by 2020.

The federal government pledged to invest the savings from subsidy removal in providing safety nets for the poor, through various projects. Former Executive Secretary of the National Universities Commission (NUC), Professor Peter Okebukola stressed that whatever would be allo-cated to education would not solve all the funding needs of the sector overnight. Its application should therefore be driven by priorities through a thorough needs-assessment study conducted at the local, state and federal levels. This he said could be done rapidly within a week or two.

According to him, areas needing urgent intervention include the provision of modem facilities and rehabilitation of decayed classrooms, laboratories, workshops and hostels "to ensure that our schools at the basic and higher education levels attain world-class standards." "In four years, let us see the gains of subsidy removal with our 'korokoro eyes' by way of modem, ICT-fitted and learner-friendly facilities in our schools to be named 'Jonathan buildings' at least in one local government in each state of the federation. This has to be a federal institution. The local government chairmen and state governors can also take credit for putting such buildings in place in their domains", he said.

Okebukola also called for massive investment in upgrading the quality and quantity of teachers. "The current mode of massive training of basic education teachers by some parastatals of the Federal Ministry of Education is shoddy and shameful. Our teachers need to be better remunerated to attract quality persons into the profession. In all of these, we should keep in mind that all levels of government will benefit from the fund, hence local, state and federal governments should make provisions for investing the funds to improve the delivery of education at their respective levels."

He warned that ifthe current level of funding recurrent expenditure is maintained and "the corruption monger is not caged, what will remain of the subsidy funds will be too paltiy to make the anticipated impact."

'To be meaningful, we need to cut down the cost of running government by half. It is time for sacrifice at all levels, by the big man and by the poor man. The poor man, who does not have his car fuelled-free by government, should nor be made to carry the pain of subsidy, removal alone. I have no doubt that Nigeria will come-out stronger in the coming years and boast of the best education system in Africa by 2020." A public affairs analyst, Mr. Osize Otsemobor, observed that the sector had been the most neglected over the past few decades, which resulted in the current decay and near collapse of public schools at all levels.

"Some of those yawning needs that are begging for attention include, e-libraries, ICT, laboratories few engineering, medicine, pharmacy and other natural sciences. We need to urgently improve the situation of portable water on our campuses."

He added that a reasonable amount of the money should be deployed to research that would have positive and direct impact on the society. "Our teaching hospitals, most of which have become moribund, must receive sizeable amount of the fund. There is no gainsaying the fact that the recent rejection of graduates from some of the country's medical schools in Britain must be a national embarrassment. This is the opportunity to address the issues."

On his part, Obanya called for emphasis on things that make a difference in education, such as teacher development; provision of infrastructure, textbooks, laboratories and workshops at all levels of education; restructuring of ministries of education, harmonisation of parastatals, among others. "Let's invest in education, rather than merely spending on it. The former has long-term positive multiplier effects, while the latter is mere waste of scarce resources."

The Joint Action Committee of the National Association of Nigerian Students said the yearnings of the masses should be given great priority by the government and not the imposition of unfavourable policies on them. Chairman of the group, Mr. Adeyemi Quam faulted the 2012 budget and called on government to cut down some of its expenses, and approach the issue with dialogue and mutual understanding. "The expenditure of over ₦900 million in the purchase of arms and ammunition for the various security agencies might not be the solution in a country with millions of unemployed, large population of idle youths. The $312.budget has come to show a deficiency in our priority and planning for the future."

A student of Ladoke Akintola University of Technology (LAUTECH), Oyo State. Miss Mopelola Lasisi stressed the need for tHe government to pay more attention to the youths and expressed regret that the precious time that could have been spent in school is being spent to protest on the streets. "Nigerian undergraduates know that the chances of securing jobs after school are close to zero, which has been further compounded by the fuel subsidy removal", she said.

DPO amnestied for kibbling protesters/ arrested for killing protesters

By *ThisDay* Correspondents

***ThisDay*, Tuesday, January 10, 2012, vol.6, no. 6105, pg. 1, 8**

The nationwide strike called by labour to protest the removal of subsidy commenced yesterday on a tragic note in Lagos and Kano States as two persons were killed. In Lagos, the Divisional Police Officer (DPO) of Pen Cinema Police Station, Agege, Mr. Segun Olubunmi, a Chief Superintendent of Police, shot and killed one Ademola Aderinde.

It was an eventful day during which:

- Three persons, described by the police as "hoodlums", were killed in Edo State;
- a protester, Abdulmalik Rabiu, was also shot dead, while 31 others were injured in Kano State;
- the volume of trading on the floor of the Nigerian Stock Exchange (NSE) fell by 82 per cent;
- local flights were grounded;
- lifting of crude oil was hampered by the strike; and
- Coordinating Minister of the Economy and Minister of Finance, Dr. Ngozi Okonjo- Iweala, denied saying deregulation would take off in April;

Beside Aderinde's murder, which happened at Yaya Abatan junction, Ogba, Lagos, the trigger-happy officer also injured four other persons at the scene.

The DPO has been arrested and disarmed and will be charged for murder after preliminary investigations on the orders of the Commissioner of Police, Mr. Yakubu Alkali.

Olubunmi was immediately handed over to the Homicide Division of the State's Criminal Investigation Department (SCID), Panti,Yaba, Lagos. Three of the injured protesters now recuperating at County Hospital in the area are 20-year- old Joel Monday, 40-year-old Alimi Abubakar and 23-year-old Ebujor Samuel. Samuel said when they heard gunshots, they were running away from the scene when they were hit by bullets. The deceased lived at Aderinto Street off Thomas Salako, Ogba, Lagos.

According to reports, the DPO had stormed the area in a patrol pick-up van with registration number RRS 101 LA and allegedly opened fire on innocent persons. His reasons were that they had blocked the road with tyres to play football on the empty street following the total adherence to the strike called by labour leaders. *ThisDay* gathered that Aderinde, who was shot on the thigh, died on the spot, while the other persons were taken to nearby County Hospital for treatment of their injuries.

Alkali said: "I did not send him or others to kill innocent Nigerians and since he has flagrantly disobeyed, he has to face the law." He said the protest in the state was peaceful up "until the moment Olubunmi murdered an innocent citizen and injured others". *ThisDay* gathered that after Aderinde was shot dead, angry protesters carried the corpse to the Pen Cinema Police Station in a wheelbarrow chanting war songs. Olubunmi was the former Officer-in -Charge of the State Special Anti-Robbery Squad (SARS) in Ikeja before moving to Pen Cinema Police Division.

Gains and Loss of subsidy strike

By Cosmas Odoemena

***ThisDay*, Friday, January 20, 2012, vol.16, no. 6115, pg. 15**

After a six-day strike and protests by labour, civil societies and Nigerians, what may be called normalcy has returned as workers have gone back to work following labour's calling off the strike on Monday after government's reduction of petrol price from ₦141 to ₦97. Irrespective of whether labour is satisfied with having won ₦97 instead of ₦65, the gnashing of teeth, the bottled up feelings and the axe grinding, irrespective of what happens after, the biggest winner of all the events of these past days is Nigeria.

Nigerians that are usually divided along ethnic and religious lines were united in anger. Christians and Muslims were seen doing things together, even in volatile states. Even more hope inspiring was a scene in Kano where Muslims were praying and Christians held hands, for protection around them, in oneness. This followed a Covenant that the Muslim protesters shall protect all non-Muslims and escort them to their places of worship and vice-versa. They had vowed that religion will not divide them.

Also, the lethargy that has always held back Nigerians and indeed Nigeria in shaping its future has given way to energy. It says of greater things to come.

A second group of winners is the middle class. In every progressive society, it is the middle class that moves for progress and change. They are in-between the self-satisfied and content rich and the poor suffering masses. Somehow they feel two worlds. It was believed that the present economic situation in the country has killed it and that it no longer exists as an entity, not to talk of it finding its voice. But the controversy found them moving the debate and being actively involved in the protest, and largely making the protest a robust and peaceful event. Kudos!

The next winner is democracy, of which without it perhaps there would not have been any platform for discussion. Nigerians, having experienced long years of military dictatorship should congratulate themselves on having a democracy, and enjoying all the benefits inherent in it. That is what it should be and that is what it is all about.

When I think of the next group I am saddened, yet am filled with hope. I am talking about the people who died in the protests, especially those shot by law enforcement agents. Ademola Aderinto's is most touching for me - and the most terrifying! You would if you were being driven in an ambulance to be assailed with a tragically unnecessary event; talking of being in the wrong place at the right time. He and others who died did not die in vain. They may have lost their lives needlessly, but they have won themselves martyrdom, and are now Nigerian heroes and their names will be remembered whenever the roll call of those who died that Nigeria be saved are mentioned.

The losers are easy to see. Goodluck Jonathan, though has bent backwards a bit, has lost his popularity with the masses. Worse is his deployment of soldiers to stop peaceful protesters in a civilian government. Many now regret voting for him. He missed the opportunity during the negotiations for minimum wage. Nigerian workers would not have complained if (even if it was the paltry ₦18000 a month) he had tied the removal of subsidy to raising the minimum wage. At least he would have had that constituency to himself. You may have a good policy but the way you carry it out could spoil it. The only way of saving his face is to find scapegoats and make their heads roll. And realign himself again with the majority, who after all gave him the mandate to lead. Hopefully, he still has time to make amends. He should start it now. History can be negotiated. Martin Luther King Jr, Mahatma Gandhi, and Abraham Lincoln were all great men. So were Adolf Hitler, Idi Amin Dada, and Sani Abacha. The former were great in the hall of fame, while the latter have theirs in the hall of infamy. What makes the difference is selflessness. It is how you touch the lives of the poor, the helpless, the underprivileged and the silent majority, and not your dalliance with the few you wine and dine with.

Other losers are the bad advisers and sycophants who have surrounded the president. Some of them live double lives and speak from both sides of the mouth. It depends on whether they are on television or in the confines of their homes. Jonathan should do stocktaking, and discard the quislings in his cabinet, and look for better materials. They are all around. Even in the opposition.

Other notable losers are those who sat on the fence. They know themselves. As Karl Marx said, "Every onlooker is either a coward or a traitor". Such people in our midst do not contribute to discussions and ideas to move the country forward. They are treacherous people. And they have constrained themselves on the wrong side of history.

Labour strike: artisans, traders recount tales of woes.

By Festus Akanbi and Malachy Agbo

***ThisDay*, Sunday, January 22, 2012, vol.17, no.6117, pg. 26**

As business activities finally picked up in the wake of the recent six day-olcf strike called by the Nigerian Labour Congress and Trade Union Congress to protest government's attempt to fully deregulate the downstream oil industry, operators in the informal sector have continued to lament the devastating effects of the strike on their businesses.

Although the Central Bank governor, Sanusi Lamido Sanusi, had put the losses incurred from the strike at some ₦600 billion, economic watchers doubt if the informal sector was adequately covered in the figure given the fact that informal sector is hardly captured as a measure of the country's gross domestic product.

ThisDay checks last week showed that apart from the losses suffered by petty traders who could not ply their trade as a result of the strike led by labour and civil society groups, the closure of markets, restriction or movement and pockets of violence in some parts of the countiy during the strike did not only prevent Nigerians from engaging in buying and selling in a free atmosphere, the crisis also kept foreign businesses away from the country.

A random survey conducted in Lagos, for instance, showed that small scale businesses were most affected by the paralysis in the economy. This is because apart from plying their trade, the closure of markets made it difficult for them to justify the huge amount of money paid in rent and taxes for the period of the strike.

Many noted that when the labour leaders were issuing out the strike order to the Nigerian people, very few factored in the effects of the strike on the wage earners who do not depend on salaries unlike the workers on the public and organised private sectors. They maintained that the economic hardship visited on them by the strike can only be imagined.

"The strike is over now and I am sure that the labour leaders will go back to their offices to earn their salaries. But to us, we have no master to run to as what we eat depend on our daily income," said Tayo, a roadside mechanic who was lamenting the effects of the strike on his family.

"The more the strike lasted, the more it affected the downtrodden financially. Though the outcome of the negotiations will still affect them either adversely or positively, in the interim while the strike lasted, they were practically on their knees financially, because many of them live from hand to mouth, lacking in financial planning and savings," volunteered an analyst.

Count the Losses

A communique issued by the PRO of the Association of Tradesmen and Artisans of Nigeria (ATAN), Mr. Isaiah Richard, during the strike-had called on the NLC and TUC to call off the strike which they alleged had crippled the economy; especially its members across the country. The body cried out that thousands of their members nationwide had lost millions of naira during the strike. It said most of its members were dependent on a daily income to take care of their respective families.

According to Mr. Zimaku Anayo, the Public Relations Officer, Alaba Traders Association of Nigeria, the strike was a like sounding the death knell on the lives of Alaba traders because their shops were shutdown for days. "As law abiding citizens of this country, we did not initially embark on the nationwide strike because of the subsisting court injunction at the National Industrial Court, Abuja.

But some hoodlums came and started attacking the traders. So we had to order a complete closure of the market to avoid people breaking into shops and you should know the effects of such action on the life of an average trader," he said.

On the economic loss to the market, Zimaku said it could not be quantified. "You know we service the whole of the West African electronics market from here. And being a multi-rnillion naira market, the loss will run into scores of millions of naira," he said.

Zimako bemoaned the faith of the traders, the strike will still be entitled to their monthly salaries, but whereas traders in Alaba only rely on their daily sales.

"The truth of the matter is that the NLC people will be paid at the end of the month but nobody is going to pay us. We depend on our daily sales. And there was no way we can meet up when our shops were under lock and key. However, the strike was for the good of the country, so we do not regret partaking in it because the fuel subsidy affects all of us irrespective of our different walk of life.

"On whether the prices of goods will increase, definitely it should because when you buy and transport it, you will add the cost of transportation to the cost and now determine the selling price," he said.

Similarly, the director of publicity, Automobile Spare Parts and Dealers Association, Mr. Ozobugha Udoka Bonaventure, told *ThisDay* that the ASPANDA market lost huge sums of money due to the strike. "We lost so much money. In terms of sales, we could not open for days and you know 70 per cent of what we sell here is imported and we control about 30 to 40 per cent of the auto spare parts in the West African subregion. The automobile spare parts market here is expensive. If you ask me, I will say that it should be in the region of a ₦500 million loss.

"We had 100 per cent compliance during the strike because, we did not want a few to start breaking into peoples' shops that was why we ensured that everyone closed shop during this period" he said.

He also lamented that some of their members had their goods undergoing clearing at the ports locked up due to the strike and they will now pay demurrage. Besides the toll of the strike on their lives, the new fuel price regime is also another source of headache for many of them. "As a welder, I rely on electricity for my business and you know that we don't have regular power supply in the country, and it has been affecting our business adversely, making us to rely on generators and petrol.

"Now with the increment, the government which has not given us electricity has increased the pump price of fuel in the country to ₦97. This has compounded the problem and the cost of living will be too high for us," said Sikiru, a welder in a suburb of Lagos.

It was a tale of woe for traders when *THISDAY* visited Computer Village, Ikeja, last week as dealers in computer hardware and software lamented their losses to the strike. Mr. Paschal Andrew of of Gmax Ventures put his loss at several millions of naira during the strike. He explained that apart from his inability to transact sales during the period; his consignments from Europe, which arrived the Lagos port on the eve of the strike, could not be cleared, wondering how he would be able to cope with the attendant demurrage.

"Will my landlord at the computer village not collect his rent for the period of the strike," the angry trader asked. Andrew, who claimed to have borrowed money from banks to run his business, said one of his headaches was how to meet the weekly payments to the bank, given the losses incurred during the strike.

For Mrs. Idowu Oguntoyinbo, a textile material dealer at Balogun Market, Lagos, it was another tale of woe. She disclosed that apart from the direct loss of revenue from sales during the six day-old strike, some hoodlums used the period of the crisis to break into her shop, carting away products worth millions of naira. She also lamented that sales have been very slow ever since the strike was called off, a development she blamed on the increase in the pump price of petrol.

Tourism also Suffers

Findings also showed that the nation's tourism industry was not spared of the losses from the labour strike. Decrying the losses to the strike, CEO, Admiral Tours, Demola Amusan said his company alone lost over ₦50 million on both inbound and outbound tour packages that could not be sold because of the industrial action that paralysed business activities at the airports, destination management offices and related business associates across the country.

"At present, most of our outbound clients are already asking for refunds while our contacts and associates abroad have already collected their fees in advance for hotel bookings, airport transfers and city breaks, among other clients' interest. We are the ones bearing the brunt because it wasn't the fault of our foreign partners. But you must refund the money to maintain credibility and possibly woo back the clients," he said.

Managing director, Empire Travel and Tourism Ltd, Ahmed Ojuolape, said it was only natural for tourists to stay away from trouble spots. According to him, tourism is all about the movement of people from one point to the other and tourists only go to places that are safe, peaceful and secure.

"If as a tourist, you have been patronising a particular destination and all of a sudden there is a problem there, you will divert to other peaceful areas with comparative attractions," he said.

Agriculture Immune to Strike

But one sector that hardly felt the effects of the six-day strike was the'agriculture sector, the nation's largest contributor GDP. Save for livestock farmers who might have suffered supply delays in livestock feed, rural farming went on unimpeded, as the strike and protests were limited to just the cities.

A survey of communities showed that farmers went about their business and were immune to the ruckus in the cities. Also, markets and shops in towns and villages remained unaffected by the strike.

However, farmers who are dependent on intercity transporters to transport their produce from the rural areas to the cities encountered delays, as trucks that normally travel to the communities to transport produce often did not arrive on time.

NNPC created room for subsidy scam, marketers allege.

By Azimazi Momoh Jimoh

***The Guardian*, Thursday, January 26, 2012, pg. 15**

Marketing firms operating in the petroleum industry under the umbrella of the Independent Petroleum Marketing Association of Nigeria (IPMAN) yesterday appeared before the House of Representatives Ad Hoc Committee probing the oil subsidy regime where they alleged that the Nigerian National Petroleum Corporation (NNPC) awarded fuel importation contracts to "portfolio importers," which then created a leeway for sharp practices on the scheme. These "portfolio importers," according to President, IPMAN, Aminu Abdulkadir, neither have depot nor products' retail outlets.

Accusing the NNPC of creating a fertile ground for fraud in the subsidy regime, Abdulkadir stated that instead of the corporation selling the product directly to IPMAN members, it preferred to sell to middlemen, who in turn would sell at premium price to IPMAN members.

He added: "We ought not to be buying at a premium price. We ought not to buy through a third party. When we do, we sell at NllO, N120 because we are in business. If NNPC had been selling directly to us we would have been selling at government-controlled prices".

Abudulkadir noted that rather than commit huge funds to setting up filling stations, NNPC should channel such resources to building refineries. He emphasized that the nation's energy sector would not develop without* functional refineries.

Another Oil firm, OANDO, said the money paid to marketers as subsidy was not a profit or windfall but "under-recovery, arising from the differentials between the landing cost of petroleum products and the official pump price".

The firm's Group Chief Executive Officer, Mr. Wale Tinubu, stressed that subsidy payment was not a special favour from the government but a refund of the actual cost incurred by marketers in the' importation of petrol.

According to Tinubu, marketers spent an average of $30 million to import a 30,000 metric tonnes cargo of petrol but sold the products at $15 million with the balance paid to marketers as subsidy.

"The Petroleum Support Fund (PSF) expected that there would be under-recovery. For example, when the landing cost was higher than the pump price, the government owed us money, which is paid as subsidy. When there is over-recovery, that is, when the landing cost is less than the pump price, we pay back to the government.

"For example, during the Yar'Adua administration, when the petrol price was N65 and the crude oil price dropped to $50 per barrel, the marketers paid back to the fund. I remember that Oando State, most especially now that our nation is experiencing peculiar security chal-lenges.'

According to him, "government recognises the pains Nigerians in general are passing through because of these challenges. The horrors of past crises and the heavy toll paid back Nl.6 billion back to the Federal Government," Tinubu said.

He stated that when the subsidy regime was introduced in 2006, three major marketers - Oando Plc, NIPCO Plc and the NNPC partitipated in the scheme.

Reps uncover eight billion litres fuel subsidy scam.

By Azimazi Momoh Jimoh and Kelvin Ebiri

***The Guardian*, Thursday, January 19, 2012, pg. 1**

IT has been long in coming but it arrived upon us yesterday and Nigerians who long suspected that the nation was oeing bled through the fuel subsidy policy mignt be right after all!

Laying bare the fraud that might have cost the country billions of naira, the House of Representatives Ad Hoc Committee investigating the management of subsidy on petrol learnt yesterday that the Federal Government dutifully paid for 59 million litres or the product on a daily basis throughout year 2011, when the daily consumption capacity for the country was 35 million litres only Shocked by this disclosure, the Committee expressed disappointment that the gap between what was paid for and the consumption capacity - 24 million litres daily - created ample room for all involved in the subsidy regime to rip off the nation.

In a related development, former Petroleum Minister, Prof. Tam David-West, said the disclosures being made before the ad hoc panel on the petrol subsidy ninds were a manifestation that Nigerians have been duped.

David-West, who spoke with The Guardian yesterday in Port Harcourt, Rivers State, said the Federal Government's directives that the Economic and Financial Crimes Commission (EFCC) should investigate fraudulent disbursement of petroleum subsidy showed that government had over the years subsidised "corruption, inefficiency and not petrol."

Also, Nigeria National Petroleum Corporation (NNPC) yesterday differed with the Nigerian Extractive Industries Transparency Initiative (NEITI) over the fuel subsidy figures for the year 2008. While NEITI on Monday put the amount at N360 billion, Group Managing Director, NNPC, Austin Oniwon, yesterday insisted before the Lawan panel of the House of Representatives that the figure was N630 billion.

Oniwon argued that the NNPC at no time provided information to NEITI on its operations. "We have the document for ₦630 billion. . .The ₦1.348 trillion was the reconciled figure be-tween NNPC, PPPRA (Petroleum Products Pricing Regulatory Agency) and Min istry of Finance."

The NNPC chief also warned that the full benefit of the proposed three new refineries and the proposed turn around maintenance (TAM) of the four refineries might not be realised if the spate of vandalism of oil pipelines was not addressed.

However, Oniwon assured that the new refineries would ensure adequate supply of petroleum in the country.

He disclosed that the proposed TAM and rehabilitation of the Port Harcourt refinery would be completed by December 2012, while the TAM of Kaduna refinery would be completed by the end of the first quarter of 2013. The TAM of the Warri refinery would be finished by the last quarter of 2014.

Oniwon stressed that the fund for the TAM for the four refineries would be solely paid by NNPC from its internally generated revenue.

Testifying before the committee Executive Secretary, PPPRA, Reginald Stanley, said that the volume of petrol imported per day in 2011 was 59 million litres. But Petroleum Minister, Mrs. Diezani Alison- Madueke, on Tuesday gave the country's daily consumption capacity as 35 million litres.

Chairman of the Ad hoc Committee, Farouk Lawan, said: "How could the nation be made to pay for 59 million litres daily when we consume only 35 million litres daily?

"The balance of 24 million litres per day might be the area of sharp practices. By making that provision, you are encouraging smuggling because we know that this 24 million litres balance would simply be smuggled out of the country since it has been paid for already and we can-not consume it.

"This is a case of serious economic sabotage because when the daily supply excess of 24 million litres is multiplied by 365 days, you get 8.76 billion litres. This is the volume of fuel that might have been smuggled out of the country in 2011," Lawan lamented.

Stanley also drew the attention of the committee to what he called "serious challenges" facing the oil industry, pointing out that of the 46 depots in the country; only four could accommodate "mother vessels" bringing imported products to the country.

He urged the National Assembly to give accelerated consideration to the Petroleum Industry Bill (PIB) to facilitate the deregulation of the petroleum sector.

The PPPRA chief equally called for the immediate building of strategic fuel reserves saying: "It is very important that we begin to build strategic fuel reserves in the country. In most countries of the world, reserves are built to last for at least one month in case of fuel supply cut, but Nigeria does not nave reserve that can last for one week"

Oniwon, who noted that the refineries on completion would raise the capacity utilisation of the existing refineries from 30 per cent to 90 per cent, however emphasised the need to combat vandals of oil pipelines across the country.

While addressing the public outcry over the deduction of funds in Cash Calls under the joint venture with oil majors as well as fuel subsidy before remittance into the Federation Accounts, Oniwon argued that the National Assembly through the NNPC Act empowered the Corporation to deduct funds from source. He said any attempt to halt the process woula cause a shortfall in the supply of petroleum products in the country.

Strike causes ₦733b loss to economy

By David Ogah *et al*

***The Guardian*, Tuesday, January 17, 2012, pg. 1**

The week-long strike was called off. The streets were being swept of the debris left behind by the protesters as at yesterday. Pockets of disillusionment were being expressed over the stoppage of the protests. But the inventory of losses showed that the country lost ₦733.5 billion at the end of the crisis.

The losses from figures garnered by *The Guardian* from major economic sectors, showed that the banks topped the losers' chart, with about ₦400 billion, followed by the Information Communication Technology (ICT) companies, where operators, especially the telephone com-panies, lost about ₦159.5 billion.

The maritime industry recorded about N96 billion loss, as operators in the aviation sector put their aggregate loss at about ₦18 billion. Losses from the manufacturing companies were estimated at about ₦10 billion, due mainly to assessed low profile of operations at the plants. The aggregate loss figure was rated as conservative, given the non-inclusion of the informal sector, whose operators were less active during the strike.

The conservative profile of the losses was also affirmed from bankers, who said that the figure did not take into consideration such revenue making areas such as turnover changes, money transfer and Automated Teller Machines (ATMs). A renowned banker, who spoke on condition of anonymity, said even though the extent of losses would vary from one bank to the other, the financial institutions would suffer higher losses when necessary reconciliations had been computed.

Indeed, experts concurred that the latent losses could be higher than the current estimates, given un-assessed tangibles from the informal sector.

Strike: Interbank market loses N400 bn in 1 week.

By Obinma Chima

***ThisDay*, Monday, January 16, 2012, vol. 16, no. 6111, pg 26, 27**

Financial market experts at the weekend said the interbank market would have lost a total of ₦400 billion due to the nationwide strike and protest by labour and civil society groups against the removal of fuel subsidy last week.

The interbank market is a short-term market for borrowing among commercial banks to meet their liquidity needs.

A breakdown of the figure, according to a source at the Financial Market Dealers Association (FMDA) showed that the amount of loss suffered at the Nigerian Inter Bank Offered Rate (NIBOR) arm of the interbank market during the five day strike might be about ₦100 billion. He also put the combined amount that would have been lost at the forex, treasury bills, bonds and commercial paper segments of the interbank market at ₦300 billion.

Commercial banks and other institutions across the country, and even Lagos State, were shut down throughout last week as a result of the protest and strike by labour and civil society groups over the fuel subsidy removal. This therefore stalled activities at the interbank market.

The source revealed that even though about two banks participated in Open Market Operations (OMO) deals initiated by the Central Bank of Nigeria (CBN), the transaction could not be settled due to the strike.

The Vice Chairman and Chief Executive Officer, Ancoria Investment and Securities Limited, Dr. Olusola Dada, had said the performance of the economy would be greatly hurt by the industrial action.

Dada who spoke in a telephone interview with *ThisDay*, had urged the federal government to negotiate with labour.

"One would have expected that the president will direct his relevant ministers to go and negotiate with labour. For him to continue to keep silence is not the best for the economy at all. It is not the Senate President that should be negotiating with labour at this time because he does not have the power to implement whatever comes out of the negotiation. We expect the executive to be the one leading on this.

"The current situation implies that the economy is losing heavily. International flights cannot take off or come in, banks other business have been shut since Monday. This is definitely going to negatively affect both domestic and international investments in the country. The impression is that Nigeria is not a stable country," he had argued.

Forex Transactions

Findings from the CBN website showed that the labour strike did not disrupt forex auction at the bi-weekly regulated market as the two sessions were held last week.

At last Wednesday's auction at the Wholesale Dutch Auction System (WDAS), the regulator offered a total of $200 million to dealers. However, it did not reveal the number of demand at the auction. Similarly, at last Monday's auction the CBN offered a total of $250 million.

Cost of Strike to the Economy

CBN Governor, Mallam Sanusi Lamido Sanusi, last week said the nationwide strike was costing the economy about N100 billion ($617 million) daily.

Sanusi had also said he expected inflation to rise to between 14 -15 per cent by the middle of this year, up from its current position of 10.5%, due to the impact of subsidy removal.

"Clearly inflation was always going to go up with the removal of subsidy. I think what we've seen is the immediate shock impact of a sudden removal and things will settle down. It took us two to one and half years from 2009 to come down to single-digit from 15.6%. I think a realistic target if we actually hit 15 per cent, I think we will be looking at end of 2013 before we come back to single-digits," the CBN Governor had explained.

He had added: "I think it's time to make a deal, any kind of compromise should have a final deadline for removal of subsidy," even as he had suggested the option of keeping fuel price at ₦100 per litre and phasing out subsidies.

Phased Subsidy Removal

Sanusi last week called for an agreement between labour and the federal government that would lead to gradual removal of the subsidy.

The banking sector regulator had made this remark on a television programme. He had also indicated that a short-term reversal to ₦65 per litre would not hurt the economy.

He had said: "Look, the federal government can continue paying subsidy at ₦65 per litre for a while. I am not saying that it is not economi-cally possible for that to be done. But speaking as a Nigerian, I will like to see a win-win situation.

"I will like to see a situation in which the government shifts a little and breaks this policy into one or two instalment and I will also like a situation in which Nigerians also shift and understand that we cannot continue to have a Father Christmas kind of situation. If we continue doing this today, our children are going to pay for it."

The CBN Governor had also said the federal government decision was not taken because the country was broke.

"The country is not broke, but a responsible government does not wait for the country to be broke before it can act and that is the point. Do we wait until we are actually broke before we take the right decision?" he had queried.

Cost of Governance

The CBN Governor last week also called for a restructuring of the country's constitution in order to drastically reduce the cost of governance in the economy.

Sanusi had maintained that the President did not have the power to reduce the number of ministers in his cabinet, because of the structure of Nigeria's constitution.

He had described the situation as structural costs that the presidency could not do anything about. "You have a constitution which says you have 36 states and every state must have a minister. The governors have commissioners, they have their aides. You have 774 local governments. First of all, we have to restructure our constitution to reduce cost of governance. Do we need a bi-camera legislature? Do we need 36 states in Nigeria?

Mass Transit Scheme

The finance minister last week said the new mass transit scheme that had been inaugurated by the president would alleviate the pains of the fuel subsidy removal.

Okonjo-Iweala had said that private sector operators who were interested in the policy, would be supported at a zero interest rate to get more of such buses.

According to her, several members of the transport workers' union had agreed to bring down the fare being charged on transportation.

"We are also working to launch a programme to create 370,000 jobs for our youths each year. So if we can use these resources to get our children out of the house to where they can earn money and help their parents," she had added.

Electronic Payment

The CBN last week said that it had commenced full implementation of electronic payment system in all private and public organisations. To this end, the banking sector regulator had directed all Deposit Money Banks (DMBs) in the country to dishonour payment instructions with schedules delivered via unsecured methods.

The CBN had given this directive in a circular addressed to all commercial banks.

It had explained: "In its efforts at enhancing the efficiency and security of the payment system in the country, the CBN hereby sets 9th January 2012 as the commencement date for the implementation of end-to end straight through electronic payments of suppliers, all forms of taxes, salaries and pension by both private and public organisations with more than 50 employees/pensioners in Nigeria.

'To this end, all DMBs are to dishonour payment instructions with schedules delivered via unsecured methods such as Flash Drives, Compact Discs or e-Omail attachments with effect from that data. To support this initiative, DMBs are hereby implored to properly educate and advise their customers on the adoption.

"These are not questions that would be answered by the finance minister, the CBN governor or the president. These are questions that would be answered by Nigerians. I have heard people say they have got 12 ministers in America or elsewhere, the Nigerian president cannot have less than 37 ministers constitutionally. So amend the constitution first!" the CBN governor had argued.

Fuel Subsidy Removal Date

The Co-ordinating Minister for the Economy (CME) and Minister of Finance, Dr. Ngozi Okonjo-Iweala, last week described the allusion that she had said that the fuel subsidy would stay till April this year as false.

The finance minister also made this remark on a television programme. She had said that the federal government was still open for discussion with labour, even as she had maintained that the subsidy removal was beneficial for the economy.

Okonjo-Iweala had explained: "This is a very big puzzle to me because the Newspapers f Proprietors' Association of Nigeria (NPAN) town hall meeting were I spoke is on tape. I never mentioned an April date. I did say we were in discussion, but I never mentioned any April date and it is very puzzling to me that people can say this.

We cannot have conversation in a country, where it is based on lies and deceit.

"You know, the Holy Book -the Quran, says we should run away from falsehood because it leads to immorality. We should be honest because implementation procedures for an end-to-end e- payment."

Okonjo-Iweala Denies Property Acquisition

The minister of finance last week debunked an online media report that she had allegedly acquired a ₦1.2 billion mansion in Maitama, Abuja. She had said that the report was com-pletely false, adding that it had no foundation. Okonjo-Iweala had said that she had no interest in the said property.

"It has been brought to our attention that an online news website (name withheld), has just published a story alleging that the CME and minister of finance have purchased a property worth ₦1.2billion in Maitama, Abuja. According to the disreputable website, the minister paid for the property in November 2011.

"The story is totally false and without foundation. The minister has no interest of any sort in the property in question, ifie story also rehashed some previously published and discredited allegations against the minister and her younger brother. It is simply the latest in a well financed smear campaign against the coordinating minister by persons and groups whose interests are profoundly selfish and anti-Nigeria," a statement from the ministry had added.

Recurrent Expenditure

Okonjo-Iweala last week said that the federal government was seriously working towards reducing the high per cent of recurrent expenditure in the system. She had explained that the issue of ghost pensionersrand ghost workers were being tackled by the government following the introduction of biometric system.

She had restated that«the federal government was also working towards reducing the number of agencies and departments that had duplicating functions, in order to reduce waste in the system.

"Please remember that I came in August 17, 2011, and we did the budget in three months. I was not here last year when there was a salary increase of 53 per cent and increase in the mini-mum wage, although it is not the minimum wage that is the problem. With a 53 per cent salary increase for everyone, what happened was that it increased the salary bill of the government. The salary increase makes up over 80 per cent of the recurrent cost," she had added.

We called off anti-subsidy removal strike in national interest, says Esele What informed Labour's decision to accept N97 per litre?

***The Guardian*, Tuesday, February 7, 2012, pg. 43, 47**

First of all, we didn't negotiate. There was never a time we negotiated. We actually broke fundamental rules. The tool of business for a labour movement is the tool of negotiation. I can tell you that elders in the movement, I got calls from some of them, were very upset, asking why we forgot sucn an important tool and refuse to go through negotiation. I am telling you, we never did. When I look back and start hearing stories about how we sold the masses out, or betrayed them, it is so annoying, because, the first thing is how did it get to ₦65? Before we even talk about the ₦97. The TUC/NLC has been in the forefront of making lives easier for Nigerians. I will take you back down memory lane. In 2007, Obasanjo increased the pump price to ₦75, after protests, he took it back to ₦70 and when he took it back to ₦70, we waited. But when Yar'Adua was elected, we went on a strike and had a meeting with him and he came forward, the gentleman that he was, and said, "Obasanjo was my president and 1 will not do anything to undermine him.

He has moved from ₦75 to ₦70 I am not going to go below that and Labour, also said we can't come to you because you want to deregulate and we can't also come to you and leave empty- handed, so Mr. President, we want you put a tab that there will be no increase for one year.

We had that agreement, signed, sealed and delivered. That agreement expired June 2008. By June 2008, we again (NLC/TUC) went back to the same president and said Mr. President, through his Economic adviser we cannot increase now, because companies, businesses also have their budgets from January to December and once you carry out an increase mid year, what you are going to have is that we also come and ask you for salary increase and you are going to have distortion in your economy.

The president in his wisdom pushed the increase to December 2008. By 2009, the rices of crude oil fell and we rought pressure again to let the President know mat he has to reduce the price. Initially, with deregulation, and by our calculation, we felt the price will be between ₦45 and 51 and they said they want to recover loss and save some money. By his wisdom, the president, after behind-the-scene resolution, decided to move it to ₦65.1 just want to give you a background of what the Labour movement have been doing all these years.

Every year TUC sends people on training on negotiation. But because from day one there were people, who believe Labour will sell out. No matter how, or what we do, we are in a casualty position. There were certain people who have made up their minds to ridicule labour. First, they said we cannot go on strike, stating that by 12 midnight on Sunday night, Omar and Esele will call off the strike. Then, they also said we cannot last more than two days. We went on and on, and you will agree with me that, that became our most effective strike.

All our field commanders were on top of issues. One, we never negotiated and I can say that if we had negotiated, there was no way we would have accepted ₦97 and there was no way we would not have gone lower than that. I can tell you, there are certain pressures that happened on the third and fourth day. All these came because our partners felt there was a sell-out from labour/TUC. If I knew this was how they were going to try and undermine the labour institution, I think I would have done something else with all of them.

You cannot expect me to think like an organisation or a man that is responsible to no one. We are responsible to a group. I am the president of the Trade Union Congress and my bosses are the National Executive Council and the National Administrative Council. Once a decision has been made at that level, as the president, it is my responsibility to carry it out. Regardless of my personal opinion. If I do not accept their decision, the only thing left for me is to resign. As the president I must follow it to the letter. You are based in Lagos and you knew what happened there.

A vice-president of the congress was picked up and had to pay ₦60,000 to get himself off the hands of certain hoodlums. I knew people, who had their cars smashed and we started getting messages that this thing was getting out of hands. We also have people from our state councils, who gave warnings about the state of things and the need for us not to let it get out of hands. In the midst of this, we also had people, who were talking of regime change. We are not comfortable witn this. Labour movement is a democratic institution. If Nigerians, a year ago, were wise enough to elect Goodluck Jonathan as the president of Nigeria, we should also be wise enough to accept the responsibility to face the consequences, for good or for bad. Tnat is life.

So, if change will take place, we believe it must be done constitutionally and any other means by which you want to do that is unconstitutional. We have looked at the people calling for the regime change and other changes. I believe in a movement but that movement must carry out everything in accordance with the constitution. By the time the National Administrative Council met, and came with that decision, I had the task of informing and defending that position. We cannot please everybody, but we will rather make a decision and be criticised than not make any decision at all. If we do not make any decision, that is not leadership.

There are two schools of thought. One believes that labour capitulated because of administration. Another school of thought believe that labour was induced by govern-ment. What is your position on this?

One thing you will always say is that, this is Nigeria and it tells you how deep our feeling of corruption is rooted. Another thing is that, even when you are fighting for a just cause, people tend to believe that there is a religious, ethnic or financial inducement responsible for such fights. That is, people believe you either have ethnic agenda, religious agenda or you want money which is very unfortunate about the way we now think in Nigeria. Do we now have to get to a level where we now keep quiet? There is a Warri saying that "whether you do or you no do, they will say you do." The most important thing is that you do what you have to do because it is what you believe in. It doesn't matter what anyone says. Leaders must make decisions. Whether you say NLC capitulated, you must have Nigerians before you have the Nigerian Labour Congress or Trade Union Congress.

We had to make a decision and with the organs of the congress and once the organs of the congress have given you a go ahead, you have to carry it out. When people come up with stories that A and B have been induced, they nave the burden to make the proof available. Even before you said this, when we started, I had to go on air on AIT, fortunately I have a Facebook page. It was from this page, I read comments about people saying I have collected money until they saw the interview on AIT.

People said we were collecting money from the marketers. I heard tnat we collected about ₦2 billion from the marketers and I had to address this claim by letting them know thafrf we had collected money, why would we be calling for the prosecution of the cabal. One thing I nave also discovered is that no matter the level of education we may have attained, we are also intellectually lazy and most times, we are also ill-informed.

Second thing I will say is that I saw it in the Internet blog that I have been made the chairman of the Petroleum Investment Fund. It was all over the place. I was even wondering that why can't the person even reason that we can't have a

Petroleum Investment Fund without recourse to the constitution or the laws of the land.

The simple thing was the Petroleum Industry Bill. As PENGASSAN president, then, we were part of the people who brought the OGIC, oil and Gas Implementation Committee, which metamorphosed into PIB. And when you are now talking about creating a task force, I was invited for the meeting but I told the minister there are certain things that must be cleared for me to be a part of the committee. I don t want to be a part of committee for the sake of joining a committee and when people were making comments, I said my hands are full.

Some even said government was trying to induce me. I told them I have asked why I was put on the committee and I was told it was because of my experience with the gubernatorial election in Rivers State where I narrowly escaped death and that was it. I have been a board member of NEITI, PPPRA as a result of my experience.

If I have served in all of these places, why haven't they said I have sold out all this while. Suddenly, you now look at things and because you are looking for a scapegoat, you now say I sola out. I still say this irrespective of how people feel; the Labour movement is still the institution of choice for Nigerians. It is still the only movement that can rally people with sachet water.

You know Abuja is divided into two, the poor and the rich and it is always difficult to have such a huge number but the turnout was great. The only thing we had with us was the sachet water. As the PENGASSAN president, I have led several sectors and presently as theTUC president. This means I have chosen to dance naked in the public. So you can afford to throw whatever mud you want to throw at me, but the bottom line is that I could lose this decision, as I wrote on my facebook page to win others. The bottom line is that you do not lose your conscience because if you do, you lose everything.

So, I can tell you that this strike, we gave it everything that we had and it is something that I look back with pride that and say yes, all the plans that we had really worked. We had protests all over the country but the strategic areas of the economy that we planned to shut down, we did, especially the airports. I think this is the first time we had the airports shut down for a whole week. So, the strike was effective in itself. I always tell people that strike protests are a means to an end and not an end in itself. The earlier we know that, the better. You strike and conduct protests to draw attention to certain things that you do not like in the country or environment. By the time you finish, you now have to bring your intellectual capacity to the table to those, who would listen.

In HSE management what is not written does not exist. We could organise our strike on the streets, but we must be able to bring our ideas on paper and let everybody know this is what we are going after and that is what we have just done in the meeting with the Belgore Committee.

So, all in all, the labour movement is important. Irrespective of how people feel, I can give you assurances that we also try to get reports tnat 70 per cent or more of the people do not believe we were very successful in pulling back at that time.

The price of fuel today is ₦97, you said government unilaterally imposed the price, what if tomorrow, or may be in April, government decides to go back to ₦141. What will labour do?

Now, it is time to look at the technical angle. There are two ways to handling issues. Fortunately in the movement, we have insiders. That was why we went the extra mile to make the presentation before the House of Representatives.

The probe committee on subsidy is a fall out of the strike. That would not have happened without the strike. The resolution that was passed at the House would not have been done without the strength of the strike. We had a meeting before the resolution was passed. It is not everything that happens behind the scene that you would reveal in the open. Now, we had that meeting and it is going on.

Now, CBN said the money paid on fuel subsidy is ₦1.7 trillion instead of ₦13 trillion. There are disparities in the figures also being released by the PPPRA and this has further raised questions as regards the amount paid on subsidy. Where and who was the money paid to? Why do we need to have 28 vessels on the high seas that $28,000 is being paid a day as demurrage on, when you can have a bigger vessel that can accommodate the capacity of the 28 and you pay demurrage only on one.

That is wastage. These and other issues of wastage are what we are addressing at the various committees. To change this country, we need a mass movement. The movement we want to have must have a strategy. The movement must not be the type that will destroy the country. I believe in a movement that will respect the rule or law and that will be organized. I am aware about the movement in Lagos and I even called that they should have the names of participants written down. We will create a mass movement that you cannot ignore but it must have a strategy.

When someone said we needed to have a revolution, I asked the person that if we kick this government out, who takes over? The only political structure that has the capacity to take over government right now is the military and God forbid, we do not want the military in our society anymore.

So, how do you now do all these protests and strike and now go and bring in something you don't want in your life?

Create that mass movement that will look towards 2015 and rally round any leader that we think can take the country to the next level. That to me, is it. Some people said, let us create Egypt here, but we are different culturally and in so many ways. The man who was sacked in Egypt has been in power for about 30 years but here you have someone who was elected for a four-year tenure and what do you want to create? The best thing to do if you are not happy, build a base to get ready for the man at the institution either to give him red or green card as you deem fit.

For me, that is democracy and that is what Labour movement will support. We will fight any regime that is unconstitutional. Labour movement has oeen in the vanguard for Nigeria's independence. The June 12 annulment, Labour movement was also very active. We had our leaders in NUPENG and PENGASSAN who were incarcerated.

I am reiterating this, I will not be a party to anything that will be undemocratic, but I will support democratic change in any means and form and I think that is what the movement is all about and stands for. If anybody doesn't like it, we have no apologies.

You have always had your allies in the civil societies. Suddenly, they are now becoming antagonistic of Labour just because they alleged that you didn't cany them along.

I think it is a very sad thing when you say our allies in the civil societies alleged that they were not involved. They are the only people that we nave been dealing with and that is the Joint Action Front (JAF). I was shocked at the letter written by JAF that NLC/TUC betrayed them. I don't expect such to come from JAF. We have had a long-term relationship. In this meeting, the chairman of JAF, Dr. Dipo Fashina was there. He was the one that also said we should let Nigerians know that we were never a part of the negotiation for ₦97/litre. He also said we should go to the Belgore Committee and fight for the reversal to ₦65.1 told him that tactically, we should not raise the expectation because we can surpass the expectation. So, he was part of that meeting and there is no way we would have done that. He was in the meeting that was held at the Villa and even the one that revealed the outcome to the people.

Sincerely, I am also disappointed about that. I believe that we still need each other. But if they choose to go that way, I wish them the best, JAF in particular. However, I know that it is not how to deal with your friends.

If the other stakeholders, even JAF decide to call people to the streets, what will be your reaction?

There are so many ways to a struggle. If in their strategy, they think that that is only way to do, of course, they can. They are free to do so. The first release tnat was made by JAF had TUC and NLC in it. We didn't go to JAF and JAF didn't take permissions from our organs before making that release. We are members of LASCO. I think what we also need to do is to define our relationship so that everyone knows their responsibilities. We are responsible primarily to workers. I think it is nigh time we also drew the lines. In issues like this, the Labour business tool is negotiation. So what happened is a breakdown in communication or lack of understanding of each other's role. As a civil society, there are professional civil society organisations, who are specialists in a particular field. What I think we need is understanding of each other's role and that is the only way the collaboration can get to the top and determine what best to be done. It is not proper for them to issue that release. But they have done that now and we are also saying that they were part of the meeting. Even Abiodun Aremu, the general secretary, I spoke with him on phone and I told him about the challenges we are going through and he said, "Dipo Fashina is in Abuja. He is a very reasonable man. Whatever you think is happening, put it before him and you guys will sort it out and whatever it is, we will understand here in Lagos." That was what he told me on the phone. I saw his missed calland I had to call him back. So sometimes, we have people who react in a different manner in different circumstances. We all cannot be the same. He knows I have also been under tremendous pressure and decided to put that out. We react to pressure differently. However, that is how he chooses to do it. Like I have said, I will not come and destroy any institution. Individuals can carry a country but institutions drive a country. So, the NLC/TUC are institutions that drive the society and they will drive you even if Omar and Esele are apart. NLC/TUC is still the only group that has presence across the local governments. We need each other and the earlier we appreciate each other's will, the better for Nigeria.

Another school of thought presumed that you shouldn't have put your feet down that government should revert back to ₦65 and that was why government was able to boxyou to a comer since you didn't have the tool of negotiation. How true is it?

I am telling you that it is because of this collaboration that we have that make us want to use the tool of negotiation. The union leaders accused us of allowing our tool of negotiation to be in the back burner. They have a point but we had this feeling that, let us sort this once and for all. We didn't deploy the tool of negotiation but we are now doing it in the Belgore Committee.

We could have done that but issues of governance, corruption and politics came into the scene and muddled up the whole issue. The recurrent crises in the states during the strike also made us pull back.

What we have done now is to fight the war in another direction. However, if we had not embarked on the strike, there would not have been a reduction from ₦141.

So what are we expecting from the Belgore Committee?

I don't want to make anything public now because one thing I have also learnt in all of this is that you must have your strategy intact and weigh your options. Whatever will be done will be known later.

Are you still fighting corruption in the oil and gas sector?

Of course we will and that is why we made our presentation. We made a presentation on the technical aspect while NLC did that of the financial aspect. So we have a two-prong approach. On this issue we will not stop.

PETROLEUM INDUSTRY BILL (PIB)

REFINERIES

THE OIL SECTOR

Withheld NEITI report impeding Nigeria's oil sector's growth, say CSOs

By Obiora Aduba and SulaimonSalau

***The Guardian*, Wednesday, September 14, 2011 pg. 42**

CIVIL society organisations with core competencies in extractive industry revenue transparency, have decried Nigeria Extractive Industries Transparency Initiative's (NEITI) continued hold on the audit reports for the nation's oil sector covering 2006 to 2008. While seeking immediate release of the reports, the coalition of 24 civil society organisations abroad, noted that the development was aiding graft and retarding the sector's growth. The demand was one of the six requirements by the board of the Extractive Industries Transparency Initiative (EITI) in Oslo, Norway, for Nigeria's validation as a compliant member. However, in a bid to meet the requirements for validation, the NEITI secretariat set up a task force of Nigeria's EITI validation to meet the core criteria on or before January 15, 2011.

A statement signed by the groups, which was made available to The Guardian on Monday, noted that the group was concerned that such delay in the release of the audit report in the very year of attaining validation, falls far short of what is expected of a compliant nation and would send wrong signals to the international body on Nigeria's commitment to ensuring extractive revenue transparency. According to the group, "this delay runs contrary of the pro-visions in the NEITI Act 2007 of section 14(1), which mandates NEITI to audit the account of total revenue which accrued to the federal government from all extractive industry companies, its receipts, payments, assets and liabilities to be audited not later than six months after the end of the year.

"We are further worried that this report is actually part of a backlog with two other outstanding years and another year is running out. If these repeated delays are recurrent, Nigeria's audit reports may never be up-dated.

"It is unpleasant enough that remediation actions on identified gaps from previous reports are not being implemented and the much desired effects of the reports are therefore yet to be felt in the sector and the lives of Nigerians.

"It is however more unpalatable that almost a year after auditors were engaged and probably paid, the nation is yet to fully see and benefit from the result of services paid for in spite of repeated promises from the secretariat."

The civil society group pointed out that with the seeming delay in the conclusion in this audit report, "we are wondering when NEITI secretariat will present its memo to the Federal Executive Council and subsequent submission of this report to the National Assembly."

Meanwhile, NEITI has adduced reasons for the delay. In a statement by its Director of Communications, Orji Ogbonnaya Orji, NEITI said there was need for due process in its entirety. He said the comprehensive audit had been concluded and approved by the NEITI Board at its meeting held in Uyo, Akwa Ibom State on 27th June, 2011, adding that the approval of the report was on condition that auditors address some key observations before presentation to the Federal Executive Council and the National Assembly as required by law. He stressed that the finalised document was received from the auditors by NEITI Secretariat on Monday 5th September 2011 and a memo to the Federal Executive Council is now ready and is expected to be presented after a meeting of the NEITI Board on the 27th of September 2011. These steps NEITI considers important before dissemination.

Orji, who was reacting to statement issued by some Civil Society Organisations including the CISLAC (Civil Society Legislative Advocacy Centre) urging NEITI to release the 2006-2008 Audit report said, NEITI had released the first part of the 2006- 2008 audit report covering financial flows six months ago, precisely on the 1st of February 2011, and it has been on NEITI website since that date till today. He said: "The media and some civil society organisations have continued to avail themselves of the content of this very important document in their engagement with NEITI, Government and Companies because they have always being in the public domain."

NLC, TUC, PENGASSAN, Others Fault Oil Sector Reform

By Nkechi Onyedika

***The Guardian*, Friday, November 25, 2011, pg. 64**

Stakeholders in the petroleum industry yesterday canvassed a more comprehensive programme of reforms in the sector, with a view to reviving domestic refining and reducing the country's dependence on importation of petroleum products. They were unanimous in submitting that the past and current reform efforts in the oil sector had not worked and that deregulation cannot be import- driven. They also argued that domestic products pricing must not be based on import price parity if the country is to confer on the domestic economy a competitive advantage based on the resource in which the nation is richly endowed.

These formed the fulcrum of submissions at a Stakeholders National Consultation on Petroleum Subsidy organised by the Initiative for Peace and Industrial Harmony, which had in attendance representatives of the Nigerian Labour Congress (NLC), Trade Union Congress (TUC), Petroleum and Natural Gas Senior Staff Association of Nigeria PENGASSAN, Nigeria Employers Consultative Association (NECA) and civil society groups.

Setting the tone for the discourse, convener of the workshop and former Permanent Secretary, Federal Ministry of Labour and Productivity, Timiebi Koripamo-Agary, expressed worry that government had not engaged the stakeholders enough on the proposed removal of the fuel subsidy in order to avert possible crisis that might trail the policy.Koripamo-Agary stressed that government must show "willingness to answer some critical questions being raised by Nigerians on the issue of fuel subsidy."

Acting President, NLC, Kiri Mohammed, noted that the reasons government adduced for its resolve to remove fuel subsidy were untenable. Mohammed charged government to curb corrupting in all sectors of the economy, especially in the oil sector, in order to have more funds for development purposes, instead of milking the citizenry to generate more revenue through subsidy removal without due consideration of the social and economic consequences on the Nigerian people.

He argued that "because petroleum products are inputs in the production process of virtually all sectors of the national economy, the impact of increases in their prices needs to be evaluated on the basis of the overall economy and not just the narrow sector of the downstream and government revenue."

Petrol subsidy removal: the facts, the farce and the fears.

By Dele Fanimo, Obiora Aduba, RoselineOkere, YemiAdepetun and SalaimonSalau

***The Guardian*, Thursday, December 29, 2011, pg. 10,11**

We are at it again. The fierce battle of wits strewn with intrigues is at feverish pitch. The arsenal and arena, over the years, appear too familiar to be mistaken.

Today, subsidy removal is being brandished by government as the only route to balancing next year's fiscal proposal and the cornerstone of the nation's quest towards infrastructure upgrade. At various fora, government officials, particularly the economic team headed by the Finance Minister, Dr. Ngozi Okonjo-Iweala, has had hectic time trying to convince the Labour Movement, civil society groups and opposition parties of the need to raise pump prices of petroleum products through subsidy removal. The reluctance of the latter to go with government was predicated on lack of trust, given their experiences in the past with previous governments.

Indeed, the subsidy removal debate is not novel and did not just start today. Right from the administration of Gen. Ibrahim Babangida, Nigerians have been at the receiving end of either pump price increases through subsidy removal or due to currency devaluation or as a result of lower prices, which have allegedly been encouraging smuggling to neighbouring countries. In 1986, the military administration of Gen. Babangida declared that due to the devaluation of the Naira, the domestic price of fuel had become unreasonably cheap and was therefore burdensome to the Federal Government's purse. The price of petroleum products was thus raised from 23 Kobo per litre through a negotiation process, eventually setting at 70 kobo a litre.

Chief Ernest Shonekan, the brief successor to the Babangida regime, cried out in dismay at the fiscal state of affairs upon taking over. The price of fuel was identified as one of the primary budgetary burdens based on the fact that the currency had further been acutely devalued. In 1993, the price of Premium Motor Spirit (PMS) otherwise known as petrol was therefore increased to N5 a litre.

Shortly after Gen. Sani Abacha grabbed power from Shonekan, he reduced the price of petro-leum products to gain public support: He fixed it at ₦3.25. Just over a year later in 1994, the government announced a sharp increase in the price of petroleum products. PMS would now cost a fearsome ₦11 a litre.

Upon the death of Abacha and the ascension of Gen. Abdulsalami Abubakar in 1998, the price was once again reviewed and increased to ₦25 a litre. An outcry by the public and resistance from the Labour Movement forced the administration to reduce the price to ₦20 a litre in January 1999.

As democracy was ushered in, the newly "rebranded" President Olusegun Obasanjo soon found enough reasons to "remove the subsidy" on oil product prices. Obasanjo would become the president who increased the price of petroleum products three times in eight years. Alongside some other economic indices, this action would bring about a hyper-inflationary trend that remains unresolved even till today. Phrases such as "subsidy removal," "eliminate waste" to "free government funds" and "encourage foreign and local investment in upstream sector," were thrown around with reckless abandon.

In the eight years, the price of petrol went from ₦20 a litre to N30 a litre in 1999 but was reduced to ₦22 a litre because of public resistance in 2000.

In 2002 the price went up to N26 and in 2003, it was increased to ₦40 a litre but reviewed downwards to ₦34 because of another stiff resistance from the public.In 2006 however, the price was revised up to ₦40 a litre again and finally as a parting gift in 2007, the president foisted a sudden increase to ₦75 a litre on the citizens.

For his part, President Umaru Musa Yar'Adua who succeeded Obasanjo, showed some com-passion and reduced the official price of petrol to N65 a litre.

After a mere 18 months in Aso Rocks, the incumbent President, Goodluck Ebele Jonathan declared that the Federal Government could no longer afford to keep paying for the subsidy of oil products, even when diesel had already been surreptitiously deregulated. It was disclosed that government was expending Nl.3 trillion for the fiscal year of 2010 on fuel subsidy. The president further alleged the status quo and current arrangement were painful and debilitating burden on the federal budget and thus unsustainable. He further reiterated that the Federal Government had made a decision to do away with all subsidies and deregulate the domestic petroleum product market - thus opening fuel supply and prices up to capitalistic endeavours and free market forces.

In 2010, Nigeria's domestic market consumed approximately 280,000 barrels per day (bpd), according to official Nigerian National Petroleum Corporation (NNPC) figures. Under the current dispensation, upwards of 92 per cent of Nigeria's domestic demand for finished petroleum products is imported by "independent marketers" through the implementation of contract and licence-based arrangements with NNPC.

The handpicked importers are allocated a proportion oil the domestic demand, which is ex-pressed in weight/volume, upon which the allotted quantity of petroleum products is imported to the nation. The difference in the cost accrued for importation in comparison to the official domestic price of N65/litre (PMS), along with an agreed profit margin for the marketer, is thus calculated and paid out and called reimbursement, which essentially is what is being referred to as "subsidy." This "fuel subsidy" cost has increased dramatically over the years, especially as world crude oil prices have been rising. Other factors that may have contributed significantly to the rising cost are the devaluation of the Naira and the increasing cost of transportation.

However, the primary component of the cost that has caused the greatest uproar is the inordinate "depot" (dock and jetty) charges, best described as very high and unnecessary "demurrage charges" at the ports.

According to information derived from the website of Petroleum Products Pricing Regulatory Agency (PPPRA) - the agency charged with the control and regulation of domestic fuel consumption, petroleum product pricing templates - a formatted and standardised formula for calculating the final landed cost of petroleum products are being used. It was indicated that as of July 2011, the landed cost of PMS was calculated to be ₦142.40 a litre! This suggests that ₦77.40 will have to be "subsidised' by the government in other to sell fuel for ₦65 a litre. A closer study of the underlying component of the cost reveals that "depot - related costs are separately charged to Federal Government account, which amounts to almost ₦50 per litre.

Audit Report Details Graft in NNPC'S Handling of Crude

By John-Abba Ogbodo, Collins Olayinka and Obiora Aduba

***The Guardian*, Monday, January 30, 2012, pg.1**

THE sleaze, incompetence and sloppiness that are commonly cited as the bane of management of the nation's cash cow, the Nigerian National Petroleum Corporation (NNPC), are well documented in an audit report released by the Nigeria extractive Industries Transparency Initiative (NEITI).

It was also learnt at the weekend that the recent choice of auditors for the extractive industries is now mired in controversy. The controversy has even transcended the nation's borders as some foreign elements that are involved have enlisted Nigerian companies to help their case.

The NNPC has however faulted the audit report. The Group General Manager, Group Public Affairs Division of the NNPC, Dr. Levi Ajuonuma, told The Guardian that there was no time NEITI and NNPC undertook audit reconciliation meeting, which is one of the processes required for a comprehensive and acceptable standard.

He also denied an allegation by the House of Representatives Committee on Downstream Sector that the Federal Government is losing about N700 billion due to the non-refining of crude oil by the Kaduna Refining and Petrochemicals Company (KPRC).

His words: "The NNPC is disturbed by the findings of the NEITI report for many reasons. The first is when an audit is carried on any organisation, the organisation is engaged with a view to reconciling the figures; smooth areas of disagreements and agreements. In these processes that are critical aspects of auditing, NEITI did not consult with the NNPC on any of these. We ask: Where did NEITI get its figures from when it is not present at any oil terminal or oil inflow station? All the information they got were voluntarily given and therefore there is the need to cross check their information before going to press." Ajuonuma reiterated the readiness of the NNPC to co-operate with NEITI to midwife a transparent and accountable oil industry.

The NEITI 2011's report prepared by Hart Group of the United Kingdom and S.S. Afemikhe and Co. of Nigeria specifically indicted the NNPC for the mismanagement of the country's crude oil reserve. The report, which has been presented to the Federal Executive Council (FEC), says that there is a rift between NNPC and some parties to the Production Sharing Contract (PSC), which resulted in the presentation of conflicting figures for quantity of oil being lifted. "Production and lifting data reported by the Department of Petroleum Resources (DPR) and other companies (including NNPC) and terminal operators were inconsistent and therefore could not be fully reconciled. This prevented a coherent mass balance being presented by the audit. DPR reported 1.2m barrels less in 2006,0.08m barrels more in 2007 and 1.4m barrels more in 2008 than was reported by companies", the report said.

It added: "There is a long running dispute between NNPC and PSC operators as to the calculation of cost oil, tax oil, and royalty oil under the PSCs. This meant that the parties cannot agree on the entitlements to amounts being lifted by NNPC and the con-tractors. Amounts reported for this reconciliation revealed different interpretations for the same lifting transaction. This issue should be resolved speedily. In view of the values involved, the FEC is advised to request the Hon. Minister of Petroleum Resources to bring the parties to reach a settlement quickly and to agree upon the procedure to be applied in the future."

The reported further said: "The PSCs signed do not make any provision for how the par-ties should treat the gas available for commercial exploitation, except to require that the parties define a separate agreement. No such agreement has been concluded. Where gas is already used in commercial production, such as in Bonga, the absence of an agreement may result in a misstatement of the Federation's income."

According to the report, crude oil from newly producing fields is subject to trial marketing. Cargoes are lifted by both NNPC and the operators. After the trial marketing, NNPC and the operators meet to agree on the pricing formula for the crude. As there appears to be different practices between the PSCs on how the proceeds of sale during the TMP are managed, it is advised that the NNPC should specify a uniform methodology for managing crude sales proceeds during any trial marketing period.

The report says that some data were presented by NNPC and Pipelines Product Marketing Company (PPMC) but there were many inadequacies in them. "NNPC, PPMC provided data on importation and inland distribution but it was not possible to confirm the overall mass balance because of a number of inadequacies in that data," it said. The report added: "Despite extensive reconciliation work, differences remain between receipts reported by government agencies and payments reported by companies on royalties and signature bonuses." The report also showed tardiness in the way NNPC handles proceeds from crude sales, saying: "The credit line for domestic crude payments by NNPC is 90 days from the bill of lading date. However, payment to the Federation Account is delayed in most cases by NNPC. The arrears of payment beyond the authorised period sum up to ₦588 billion as at 31st December, 2008."The report further said: "No standard method of paying the Federation's share of gas proceeds is in place. Some are accounted for by Joint Venture (JV) operators; some are paid directly to NNPC and other equity owners by gas purchasers, while others share the proceeds in terms of equity share of operations. There is need to streamline and standardise the process to ensure that the Federation's gas income is properly accounted for." As part of the efforts to address the matter, the report said: "The Office of the Accountant General of the Federation (OAGF) should make greater use of IT systems to improve controls, to eliminate inconsistencies and to improve transparency by making possible a wider sharing of data on a timeless basis."

Before now, the audits of the extractive industries have always gone the way of foreign firms which always turn around to sublet them to local accounting firms. In most cases, these foreign firms cite insecurity as the reason they could not visit the country physically to execute the job that requires years to accomplish. After the opening of the bid rounds, Sadalaris & Co emerged the company that was chosen to audit the next oil and gas industry audit (2009- 2011) while Haruna Yahaya & Co was hired to audit the first solid minerals sector for the 2009- 2010 period. This is the first time that Nigeria will be auditing its solid minerals' sector. The Guardian learnt in Abuja at the weekend that some foreign companies were working in tandem with their Nigerian counterparts with the help of some civil society groups to discredit the process so as to regain lost ground.

Indeed, it is not only in Nigeria that these foreign firms are battling to be awarded the right to conduct the audit of the oil and gas sector as there are similar squabbles in Ghana, Cameroun and Niger, Liberia and Sierra Leone where local firms have got the nod to carry out the auditing processes ahead of their foreign counterparts. The NEITI has risen stoutly in defence of the processes that led to the emergence of the two local firms. A source told The Guardian that the procurement process for the engagement of consultants to conduct the two industry audits began with advertisement in the national and international media including Daily Trust of June 30, 2010, *ThisDay* of June 28,2010, Vanguard of June 29,2010 and Financial Times of London of July 12010. The advertisement was also on NEITI website as required by Nigeria Public Procurement law.

The source also said Publish What You Pay and Civil Society Legislative Advocacy Centre (CISLAC) were two civil society groups that witnessed the opening of the bids. Others that were present on the occasion included Olusola Adekanolan& Co, Sada Idris & Co, Moore Stephens, Haruna Yahaya & Co, J. K. Randle & Co and George Andrews & Co. The source also submitted that a Due Process Report explaining details of technical and financial scores, financial proposals, technical evaluation using the quality cost base selection method and all the steps taken by NEITI to adhere strictly to all BPP guidelines and the Procurement Act were in the Bureau of Public Procurement.

On why some of the big accounting firms in the country did not participate in the process, The Guardian learnt that they might have been dissuaded by some of the provisions of the section 4(5-6) of the NEITI Act 2007. In a statement in

Abuja yesterday, Ajuonuma said the report of the House Committee which portrayed the 32-year- old company as idle and a drain on government resources was misplaced and uniformed. Ajuonuma insisted that the multi-billion naira complex remains a viable business unit of the corporation that is contributing immensely towards NNPC's operation in the oil and gas industry in Nigeria. Ajuonuma said that though Kaduna Refinery had undergone a quasi-Turn Around Maintenance two years ago by some Nigerian engineers which was generally believed to be inadequate for the refinery, credit must go to the group of local engineers for running the refinery at 60 per cent installed production capacity amid artificially induced challenge of incessant pipeline vandalism.

The NNPC spokesman explained that if not for pipeline vandals, the company could run at 60 to 70 per cent capacity utilisation on a sustained basis, adding that due to incessant pipeline vandalism, the desired production level has remained unsustainable. He dismissed reports that KRPC collects crude oil from PPMC, refines it and hands over the products to PPMC for marketing while the refinery is funded based on cost recovery.

FG begins TAM contract with builders of refineries

By Chineme Okafor

***ThisDay*, Wednesday, January 11, 2012, vol. 16, no. 6106, pg. 1, 6**

Worried by the frequent demand for functional refineries in the country as a way out of petroleum products' importation, the Minister of Petroleum Resources, Mrs. Diezani Alison-Madueke, has disclosed that Nigeria will this week sign a formal contract for the planned turn-around maintenance (TAM) of all its traditional refineries with their original builders. She said in a statement in Abuja yesterday that the contract or agreement for the TAM would be signed by the Ministry of Petroleum Resources, Nigerian National Petroleum Corporation (NNPC) and the original builders of the refineries.

She also said that some other investors from China had also indicated interest to build more refineries in the country. In order to ensure that we get our refineries to 90 per cent utilisation and to show Nigerians that we are serious this time around, we actually went back and brought the original contractors that built our refineries in Warn, Port Harcourt and Kaduna. "Already, they have given us an aggressive timetable and they have assured us that within 24 months all three major refineries will be producing up to 90 per cent capacity utilisation," she said. In the statement that was signed by the Group General Manager, Public Affairs Division of NNPC, Dr. Levi Ajuonuma, the minister assured Nigerians that within the next 24 months Nigeria would become a net exporter of petroleum products, adding that with the removal of fuel subsidy, several investors are ready to invest in the nation's economy.

The four refineries have a combined installed capacity of 445,000 barrels per day (bpd) and a comprehensive network of pipelines and depots are strategically located throughout Nigeria to link them. "With this policy in place, millions of jobs will be created and the economy will become very viable for investment,"

Alison-Madueke stated. The minister also explained how the removal of fuel subsidy by the Federal Government would help curb the widely reported incidence of corruption in the downstream sector of Nigeria's oil and gas industry.

She noted that apart from providing the flexibility for reinvestment of key funds into the provision of critical social infrastructure, the removal of subsidy on premium motor spirit (PMS) would help erase corruption which has trailed subsidy claims and counter-claims.

According to her, "It is not possible to have petrol at ₦65 per litre at the pump in Nigeria; in Chad as much as ₦200, in Ghana at ₦175 and in Niger at ₦190 and yet you expect people not to move the product across our borders? "It is simple economics especially when you consider the nature of our international borders. So in the last 16 months, while we have fought so hard to keep the country wet with petroleum products despite some level of disparity in prices, some people have taken the products to other neighbouring countries where they can sell it for as much as three times the price in Nigeria." Alison-Madueke added: "It is a matter of simple economics that when you have this massive differential in price between you and neighbouring countries, nothing can stop the smuggling of the product."

She noted that it is impracticable for anybody to expect government to stop the incidence of corruption in the downstream sector which is largely due to the subsidy regime and yet expect government to do so without removing the incidence of subsidy which is the biggest incentive for corruption in the sub-sector in the first instance.

"In the bid to sustain the gains of the fuel subsidy removal, a massive transformation and re-organisation is taking place in the Petroleum Products Pricing Regulatory Agency (PPPRA), and Department of Petroleum Resources (DPR) to ensure uniformity of prices of petroleum products in the downstream sector. "We have put in place a much more robust and aggressive transformation in the regulatory agencies of the downstream sector. PPPRA and DPR are being reformed as we speak. Sweeping changes are beginning to go across them as we speak. We have done this so as to tighten the regulatory indices in the oil and gas sector," she said. While suing for understanding from Nigerians, she called on organised labour to reconsider its decision on the strike and return to work.

Alison-Madueke added: "In fact, the policy is a transfer of negativity to positivity in such a way that funds will be put to better use. The subsidy transfer as I choose to call it will lead to a situation where international Trunk A roads will be built for Nigerians. "Major roads such as Abuja- Abaji, Benin-Ore-Shagamu roads have already been earmarked, major railway lines that will help in the freighting of petroleum products and irrigation projects that will help to supply water to Nigerians have already been pencilled down."

Investors seek clarification of profit margin on new refineries.

By Collins Olayinka

***The Guardian*, Wednesday, April 6, 2011, pg. 46**

The inability of government to make categorical statement regarding the profit margin for setting up new refineries has been cited as one of the reasons private investors have refused to embark on the project in the country. Speaking recently in Abuja at a customers' forum on Total Card, a pre-paid card introduced for electronic payment for 'purchase or Total range of products, the Executive Director, Corporate Services of Total, Segun Akpata said though government had made several efforts at ensuring private sector participation in building refineries, the non-disclosure of real profit margin has a proving formidable stumbling block.

He said: 'The country has four refineries, which are government owned and extremely old. Government has tried to invite the private sector into refinery operations but the venture is high capital intensive. Billions of dollars are needed to build refineries and therefore any company, local or multinational, that is ready to go into the business will need to be very certain of its returns on the capital it has committed to the investment. "I think that going forward; government should make it very clear what the profit margin would be. If a refinery operates and its owners are not sure of what the profit would be at the end of day, then it is no longer a business. Therefore, the engagement should be between government and the private sector in real time so that the concerns of the private sector and of investors need to be addressed before they are asked to bring in capital for the building of refineries. I do not believe that engagement has been done in a proper manner."

He insisted that every business needs an assurance of comfort and a clear understanding of what it is going into, saying, "The investor also needs to have a general idea or projection of what he will get out of the business. "Apart from the general problem of investment stability, refinery establishment needs the host country to give very clear guidelines as to what to expect. I do not believe that government has made this clear enough to investors. This is the reason there is high level of hesitation towards the building of refineries by private sector. It is really unfortunate because that is the way it should go."

Akpata pointed out that there is nowhere in the world where petroleum, which is an international commodity is treated like something that is given away. He added that the only way that the operators in the downstream can get profit is for government to keep on losing money by a way of subsidy, which is not the right thing to do. Akpata posited that the anti-deregulation posture of the labour unions is legitimate and that government owns its citizens a responsibility to provide infrastructure that is of international standard before introducing international fuel price. His words: "The arguments of labour and of those that oppose to deregulation also make sense. They argued that government needs to build institutions and that people live at a certain level of comfort before they are asked to pay the international price for petroleum products. Government has to marry these two view points by ensuring that the products are sold close to the international price and not neglecting its responsibilities to Nigerians by providing social amenities to rededicated itself to exploring veritable alternatives, make their lives meaningful and enjoyable."

While pledging Total's continued investment in the country, Card facilities where Total products can be bought and paid for, Akpata identified distribution of petroleum product via trucks as one of the greatest nightmare even as Total has rededicated itself to exploring veritable alternatives. He stated that about 50 TOTAL filling stations have the Total Card facilities where Total products can be bought and paid for via a smart card.

Local refineries contribute 20 per cent of national need, says PPPRA

By SulaimonSalau

***The Guardian*, Wednesday, November 2, 2011, pg. 47**

THE raging deliberations on the proposed removal of fuel subsidy may have further drawn attention to the comatose state of Nigeria's four refineries, which the Petroleum Product Pricing and Regulatory Agency (PPPRA) said have only contributed between four to 20 per cent of the local fuel demand in the past five years.

The Executive Secretary, PPPRA, Goody Egbuji, in a presentation on its position in the deregulation agenda recently, said government's dominance of the downstream petroleum sector has not done much good for the sector, hence the need to encourage private sector participation, particularly to boost refining capacity. He pointed out that the tempo of importation activities has increased over the years due to lack of local refining capacity and the guaranteed cost recovery for importers through the Subsidy Scheme (PSF).

Nigeria has four refineries being managed by the Nigerian National Petroleum Cooperation (NNPC) with combined installed capacity of 445,000 barrels per day, but the PPPRA said even at full capacity, domestic refineries can only meet about 50 per cent of the Premium Motor Spirit (petrol) current demand, hence the need for massive importation. He said: "There has been a noticeable increase in the national consumption of petroleum products. PMS national daily consumption for example currently stands at 35 million litres from the observed 30 million litres in previous years." He gave the production data as, PMS: 18 million litres per day: AGO: 8 million litres per day; HHK: 6 million litres per day. While domestic demand stood at: PMS: 35 million litres per day; AGO: 12 million litres per day and HHK: 8 million litres per day.

He therefore, noted that the supply gap of 17, four and two million litres for PMS, AGO and HHK respectively could be met through investment in additional refining capacity. Opportunities for export particularly abound for AGO and HHK.

He therefore, stated that a creative approach was needed to increase local refining production capacity in order to reduce the volume of product importation. "Emphasis should be on reducing government interference and encouraging private sector participation' he said. Lamenting that current subsidies on PMS and HHK have led to huge unsustainable subsidy burden, he said over ₦3.5 trillion has been spent on subsidy payments since 2006, while the 2011 projected subsidy payments represents about 115 per cent of the 2011 capital budget.

In view of the challenges toward implementing the deregulation policy, he however suggested that all Stakeholders should be engaged with the option of either phasing the proposed deregulation or commencing immediate full deregulation of the sector. He said government and all stakeholders should decide on the appropriate period to commence full deregulation of the sector, while "appropriate measures should be put in place which may include building of adequate fuel reserve, securing and making the pipeline network function optimally, providing various cushioning measures as may be necessary and agreed to by all stakeholders. '

Local refining imperative to Nigeria's petroleum industry growth, say experts

By Sulaimon Salau

***The Guardian*, Wednesday, December 8, 2010, pg. 43**

IRKED by the whooping sum of money gulped by fuel subsidy in recent years, the industry experts, garnering in Lagos at the weekend examined the trend so far and canvassed for subsidy removal and enhanced local refining capacity.

Specifically, the experts, who spoke on the lessons learnt from the history of the Nigerian petroleum industry, had a consensus that government should fast track the deregulation agenda and invite the private sector to take charge of the nation's refineries.

After a thorough evaluation of the fuel importation scenario and the provisions of the Petroleum Product Pricing Regulatory Agency (PPPRA) template, the experts imagined the initial prices of fuel under this anticipated regime, and finally arrived at ₦100 per litre, having taken into consideration all necessary exigencies.

The forum, chaired by the Chairman of the Centre for Petroleum Information (CPI), Chambers Oyibo, however, allayed fears of increasing prices in the regime, assuring Nigerians that competition would regulate the price and even bring it to a rate far below ₦100 in the long run. According to them, the current PPPRA template stated the landing cost of a litre of imported fuel at ₦93, while the marketers are selling at ₦65 per litre, indicating a subsidy of ₦28 on each litre of fuel consumed in the country.

One of the speakers at the forum, a partner in African Capital Alliance, Nigeria, Mr. Afolabi Oladele said deregulation of the downstream sector would help Nigeria to attract new investors and plug back the hole from fuel subsidy. He berated the increasing amount of money spent on subsidy in recent years, giving the step outline of the figures from 2006 when government spent ₦256 billion on subsidy, which was increased to ₦290 billion in 2007. In 2008 subsidy gulped

N654 billion and subsequently ₦680 billion in 2009. "This is a very bad situation. You can imagine where a country is spending more on subsidy than capital expenditure. For example, in 2008, we spent more money on subsidy (₦645 billion). And we spent on capital expenditure (₦420 billion)," he said.

Chairman Afren Energy Resources, Egbert Imomoh advocated for a reformed sector that would ensure more participation of the private sector, especially the local investors. He said: "We need to shake up the system, we need change and the need for dialogue is very important in driving this sector forward." Managing Director of Gladson Petrogas, Godwin Omene backed the motion for privatization of the refineries, noting that the stagnant in investment has led the country to unnecessary shortages of petroleum product she experience today.

According to him, the country could only meet the local demand of about 30 million litres of petrol per day, only if "This is a very bad situation. You can imagine where a country is spending more on subsidy than capital expenditure. For example, in 2008, we spent more money on subsidy (₦645 billion) than we spent on capital expenditure (₦420 billion)" the refineries are privatized and other investor are encouraged to stake funds into the refining sector.

He said: "I can tell you that this country consumes about 30 million litres of Premium Motor Spirit (PMS) per day and the refineries only produce 12 million litres, therefore the remain 18 million litres have to be imported. This trend is likely to continue unabated, unless government gives the right condition to attract private refineries."

For some years now, government has been making moves to woo private operators to build refinery in the country, but this efforts seems to have failed due to some technical differences between it and the prospective investors. Facts from the Department of Petroleum Resources (DPR) indicated that only about two of the private refineries are fast growing and nearing completion, while others are creeping at various stages of construction.

Recounting the experience in the overall industry operations, Omene lauded some achievements like the signing of the local content law, the deep offshore discoveries and the proposition of the Petroleum Industry Bill.

He therefore tasked the lawmakers to adopt fast measure that will ensure that the bill is passed into law in due course. An Executive Director in Total Exploration and Production, Kingsley Ojoh said, "the current status quo may not actualize the Vision 20-2020 aspiration of the country. We have always compared ourselves to other contemporary countries that are doing well, but we are seeing less of action in our own country, so, there is a lot more to do, the PIB has to be thoroughly examined and passed into law."

Mini/mobile refinery for Nigeria's fuel solution

By Nat Cole

***The Guardian*, Monday, January 30, 2012, pg. 13**

NIGERIA may consider allowing the building of mobile/mini-refineries in order to alleviate or reduce the country's dependence on importation of finished petroleum products. It may not be the optimum solution but it will represent a start to move Nigeria gradually from dependence on petroleum subsidy. Waiting to have the optimum solution will further impoverish Nigerians while foreign companies feed fat on us from our oil.

The mini/mobile refinery technology comes in 20 feet containers for easy transportation and mobility; it is made of the best quality materials, for long durability and minimum downtime or loss of production. As an example: As of the time I am writing this in 2006,1 am aware that seven units of mini/mobile refineries have been installed in Russia and Siberia, four units in Papua New Guinea, etc., and currently Democratic Republic of Congo (DCR) is also in the process of installing about 10 of these at the same time.

The manufacturer of the mobile/mini refineries guarantees that under normal circumstances these refineries are the most suitable for remote oil fields that are not commercially viable to be developed, yet they have cities and towns near in need or diesel and other fuels, that do come from far away big refineries and with high transport costs. In the case of Nigeria these mini-refineries will be very useful because of the high cost of building new, big complex refineries, long period of time, i.e. over a few years, or even the lack of the ability to maintain the ones we currently have. These are coupled with the huge cost of importation that helps only to fuel and develop other countries and provide jobs for their citizens while Nigeria is unable to adequately provide for her citizens.

The technology used for the mobile/min refinery can be designed to produce various products including, diesel, naphtha, kerosene, petrol etc., it will depend on the type of crude that the field where the crude oil to be refined comes from.

The cost of the mini-refineries is affordable when compared to the huge cost of building new complex refineries. While the complex refineries are very expensive to maintain, the mini-refineries' maintenance are quite affordable. In addition, a system of mini-refineries such as the ones currently in the process of construction in the DCR, 10 mini-refineries refining crude of about 40,000 barrels a day cannot all be down at once. If one refinery is taken off line for maintenance, the remaining nine continue to refine about 36,000 bpd of crude oil, as they will continue to be in operation.

A 4,000-barrels per day mini-refinery excluding tank farms and generators and the buildings, cost less than $9 million, 10 of such on the same site will cost no more than $90 million as of 2006. The mini/mobile refineries are much easier to maintain and require less effort and technical know to operate. This could easily be operated and maintained 100 per cent by Nigerians after undergoing training that is included in the cost of the refinery. The mini-refineries can also be used to supplement the production of the bigger, more complex refineries when those are down for maintenance or to serve as topping refineries for them. In essence, it is valuable as a stand-alone or as a supplement to the complex refineries. The mobile refinery can be constructed within 12 months and be operational to alleviate the need to import refined petroleum products.

Some of the disadvantages and recommended solutions

One main disadvantage of the mini/mobile refinery is that it lacks a cracking unit that the complex refineries have. This can be added to it but such makes its cost become significant. The mini-refinery lack of a cracking unit to refine die crude oil further does not take away the fact that it is easily set up and would assist Nigeria to curtail dependence on importation of finished petroleum products. Naphtha, one of the main by products can be used to run generators as well as used to power the refineries or used to generate electricity. In addition, it can be sold to industrial firms that can use it in their factories.

Another disadvantage of the mini-refinery is that its cost of production is higher than the cost of production at huge complex refineries that benefit from the economics of scale. However, these costs of production advantage will be reduced when the cost of transportation is factored in. This is because several mini-refineries can be located along the oil and gas pipeline in any locality that investors choose along that path. This will eliminate the cost of transportation for the usual tanker long distance movement of petroleum products to the marketers. This will thereby close the gap in the cost of transportation between complex refineries and mobile/mini refineries.

Creating a viable naphtha market in the West African sub-region

Disposal of one of the main by-products of mini-refineries, naphtha, should be considered. The naphtha can be exported, as there is constant demand for it as a valuable source of energy around the globe.

Currently, while naphtha is traded in other parts of the world, such has not been properly developed in Nigeria or West Africa and this may stem from lack of knowledge. When in essence, almost nothing is wasted and these mini-refineries will alleviate or reduce Nigeria's need to import refined petroleum products.

Crude oil and undesirable components

A straight run mobile/mini-refinery merely fractionates by distillation of the crude oil feedstock into its boiling point components. Distillation does not alter the molecular structure of its chemical components. Therefore, the natural characteristics of the crude oil (or condensate) and the required specification of the final refined products are the determinants of the product yields from the refinery.

To avoid scaling and fouling within a refinery, the crude oil should have a maximum salt content of l kg per 1,000 barrels. Where the salt content exceeds this level, a pre-treatment process may be required. Although adding a de-salter to a mini-refinery is quite feasible, it does require a fresh water supply and a means for disposing of the salt-water waste.

Other undesirable components in the crude oil such as sulphur will carry over into the refined product streams. The maximum allowable sulphur levels for refined products are normally set by government regulations.

Optimizing the use of mini/mobile refineries

There are a number of things that can be considered to improve the mini/mobile refineries project economics:

- In the case where there are a number of possible oilfields to supply crude from, we should choose the oil fields that have the best crude oil qualities, particularly the one with the highest diesel yield in its assay,
- If a crude oil pipeline exists nearby, consider putting the unwanted by-products into the pipeline with an acceptable purchase arrangement for the refinery by-products with the oil company, pipeline company or end-of-pipeline refiner;
- Find local markets for the by-products. For example, naphtha can be considered for turbine fuel or could be used as a solvent or petrochemical feedstock;
- Vacuum distillation will extract heavy diesel (vacuum gas oil) from the residual oil thereby reducing the quantity of residue that ultimately needs to be dealt with; and
- If the naphtha has suitable properties it may be able to be blended with octane improvers such as high-octane gasoline, toluene or oxygenates (MTBE, ETBE, etc.) to produce low octane petrol. However, relatively high volumes of these products are required and may therefore entail significant additional purchase, transportation and storage costs, which may be unnecessary.

The above issues are just for information only, because only the project developer that is familiar with the local territory and markets is well placed to deal with the above issues.

An abridged piece by Mr. Cole, the CEO, Forensics and Compliance Institute based in the United States.

Nigeria loses N700b on Kaduna refinery, pays N12b annually to idle workers.

By John-Abba Ogbodo

***The Guardian*, Thursday, January 26, 2012, pg. 80**

A nerve-racking revelation has come from the Senate Committee on Petroleum (Downstream) that the Federal Government is losing over N700 billion yearly due to the comatose nature of the Kaduna Refining and Petrochemicals Company (KRPC). The chairman of the committee, Senator Magnus Abbe who disclosed this on Tuesday when the committee visited the plant on oversight function added that the Federal Government spends a whopping ₦12 billion yearly on staff salaries in the company. Abbe who spoke after a tour of the plant lamented that instead of focusing on the core mandate of the company which was refining of petroleum products, the company has resorted to producing of drums for oil companies due to decay in its infrastructure. He equally expressed displeasure that the company established over 20 years ago with production capacity of 110, 000 barrels per day could not refine even 30,000 barrels per day.

'We are not happy with the situation in this refinery. It is shocking that the refinery built over 20 years ago with a capacity of 110,000 barrels is operating at low capacity. One appalling thing is that a plant built for refining products is converted to a container- making firm. We are doing this when we are paying ₦12 billion annually as staff salaries. We are going to find out why you are importing crude. It is not that the plant is not working, but there is no immediate plan to revive it", he said. Still counting the losses the Federal Government incurs in the plant, Abbe said the investment in the plant was with the hope that by now Nigeria ought to have received returns on the investment.

He added: "It is more annoying if you consider the investment on the refinery. 110,000 barrels at 90 per cent capacity, we could be making more than ₦719 billion annually. The country would have been able to tackle the problem of infrastructure that we are talking about today. Instead of turnover of over N700 billion, we are battling with obsolete equipment. We are shocked by the obsolete facilities that we have seen here, particularly in the control room. The Nigerian people expect more from this plant."

Expressing dismay over the operations of the plant, Abbe said: "Another baffling issue is that you collect crude from the Pipelines, Product and Marketing Company (PPMC) without proper costing. There is a lot of work to be done here". He asked the management of the plant to submit to the committee the original cost of building the plant, the jobs that the plant has done, and the staff audit.

The Managing Director of KRPC, Bolanle Ayodele, expressed appreciation over the visit of the committee and expressed hope that intervention would come to rescue the plant. He regretted that assets in the plant had been deteriorating over the years because Turn Around Maintenance (TAM) was not carried out on schedule. Ayodele added that instead of the statutory two years period, the plant had suffered neglect.

"Down the line, as the integrity of the assets deteriorated and the company, by virtue of its location, continues to suffer from irregular crude supply owing to pipeline vandalism and inadequate maintenance, it became difficult to sustain steady operations. "Today, the assets require a comprehensive rehabilitation to ensure a strong and healthy business," he said.

Pangs of rots in the petroleum downstream sector on Nigeria's economy

By Sulaimon Salau

***The Guardian*, Wednesday, January, 18, 2012, pg. 46**

Petroleum marketing business in Nigeria is a critical business that remains the strength of the economy, but some unscrupulous activities emanating from the zeal for profiteering has deeply eaten into the effects that guaranteed the sustainability of the nation. Over the years, the inability of the Federal Government to fix the infrastructures needed for smooth flow of petroleum refining and distribution across the country have necessitated improved of involvement petroleum marketers and haulages, thereby creating more avenue for the sharp practices that has taken toll on Nigeria recently.

Nigeria is blessed with vast quantities of oil and is the sixth largest oil exporter in the Organisation of Petroleum Exporting Countries (OPEC). This has generated billions of dollars in revenues over the last fifty years since oil was discovered in Nigeria. However, this has not translated into an improved economy for the country. Instead through inefficiencies, corruption, abuse of natural monopoly powers, mismanagement, smuggling and bureaucratic bottlenecks, the supply of oil in the country has virtually collapsed.

Far from the menace of the refineries, the poor state of the pipelines, which are being vandalised on a daily basis called for concern, while the Jetties and substandard petroleum depots and filling stations are equally sine qua non to the scenario. Nigeria has four refineries including old and new Port Harcourt Refineries, Kaduna and Warri refinery.

Old Port Harcourt Refinery with 60,000 barrels per day (bpd) installed capacity was commissioned in 1965. It is run on a simple hydro skimming plant comprising of three processing units, New Port Harcourt Refinery with 150,000bpd refining capacity, commissioned in 1989, it is a more complex refinery with eight processing units, Warri Refinery and Petrochemical Company Limited - Refinery commissioned in 1978 Petrochemical Plant commissioned in 1988- Petrochemical Plant commissioned in 1988, Kaduna Refinery and Petrochemical Company Limited - Commissioned sequentially between 1978 and 1988, with installed capacity for refining 100,000 bpd.

The refineries have a total installed capacity of 445,000 bpd, which is apparently insufficient to meet Nigeria's demand of about 35 million litres per day, even when fully operational; though they have been operating at between 20 to 30 per cent capacity despite the significant investments over the years.

With a fast growing population, the country was caught in the situation with domestic demand for fuel far outweighing supply, and with corruption, smuggling and mismanagement, the refineries were operating at less than optimal levels. Turn Around Maintenance (TAM) was done on the refineries to improve capacity but this was not getting the desired effect and NNPC had to import heavily from abroad thereby cutting actual revenue derived from oil exports.

Former President Olusegun Obasanjo was estimated to have spent about $800 million on the refineries, while Umar Yar'Adua and Goodluck Jonathan have done the same, yet the refineries are still at their pitiable states. The Minister for Petroleum, Mrs. Deziani Alison Madueke has recently said that original builders of the refineries had been engaged to bring them back to life, analysts believed that only time would tell, saying that one million and one promises of such were not new to Nigerians.

A public analyst, Mr. Adeoye Adefiolu had urged the government to fix the infrastructures in other to ensure smooth operations in the downstream sector. He noted that major producers of oil should be encouraged to refine at least 50 per cent of their products, while other private investors are engaged in the system. He also stated that government should upgrade the railway facilities to complement the pipeline system and reduces road haulage.

In a view to strengthen the refining capacity, private sector operators were licensed in 2002 but very little progress has been made. Mr. Frank Kokori, who was a secretary general of National Union of Petroleum and Natural Gas Workers (NUPENG), admitted that the subsidy issue was all about corruption in the oil industry. He was angry that the masses were made to suffer for the alleged sharp practices of fuel importers. "How can the ordinary people suffer for the ₦1.3 trillion which is going into leakages? The situation is so pathetic that the roads are empty. People are afraid to come out because of what transporters charge now. I am happy that I am in my country home seeing everything that is going on. Obviously, my heart goes out to the people."

He added: "The whole thing is corruption. And the government is not sincere about fighting it, you can recall that Farida Waziri was calling for a special court to persecute corrupt people, and the government turned deaf ear. I am not supporting Farida, but the judicial system in this country is too slow. Any corrupt Big man should be sent to prison for being corrupt." The Finance Minister Dr. Ngozi Okonjo-Iweala and the Governor of the Central Bank of Nigeria (CBN) Mallam Sanusi Lamido Sanusi admitted there was corruption in the oil sector. They said that the government must bring the culprits to book.

The finance minister said that the government was not shying away from auditing the oil sector, stressing that the President himself called for an audit. "We are going to audit this thing but while you are doing that, you don't want the sources of leakages to continue. People are saying we should act against corruption. We are acting but not just acting to stop it but acting to say who are the people responsible and what do we do about it? We have to work on leakages," she said.

However, the Minister for Petroleum Resources, Mrs. Deziani Alison Madueke has invited the Economic and Financial Crimes Commission (EFCC) to review all payment made in respect of subsidies on petrol and kerosene. She said that the EFFC was also mandated to take necessary steps to prosecute any incidence of malfeasance, fraud, over-invoicing and related illegalities in an open and transparent manner. According to her, she had equally set up a unit within the Ministry of Petroleum to be headed by an independent auditor to review the KPMG and other audit reports on NNPC and other parastatals. However, as these promises unfold, stakeholders believed that the suspension of strike by the organised labour movement should not be the end of it all. They called for a thorough probe into all the uncertainties that led the nation to such a critical stage that was experienced last week (during the strike action) and urged that the right peg be put into the right hole, in other to ensure the emergence of an effective and efficient petroleum downstream sector.

Private refineries' scheme not feasible without deregulation, says Oniwon

By Saxone Akhaine.

***The Guardian*, Friday, November 25, 2011, pg. 15**

THE Group Managing Director of the Nigerian National Petroleum Corporation (NNPC), Dr. Austin Oniwon, said yesterday that unless the petroleum downstream sector is deregulated, the prospect of having private refineries established in Nigeria may not be realisable.

Oniwon spoke in Kaduna after delivering the pre-convocation lecture at the Ahmadu Bello University, Zaria. He explained that no businessman can afford to invest in the nation's downstream at the moment because the prospect of making profit will be zero.

While noting that only the government can bear the loss in the industry, Oniwon pointed out that nobody would want to buy crude oil at the international market and earn below the price for the product without profit.

He said: "One of the biggest barriers to any private businessman that is doing investment is if he cannot recover his cost and make profit. Business people survive from the profit they make." A situation whereby you control a price of petroleum products to a point that is below the cost of manufacturing the product, only government can really invest in such sector because it is only government that bear the loss. Anybody you tell to go and pay for crude oil at international price and earn below the international price for the product he is going to bring will not do it

"That is why private refinery licences are stalled. But once we have the courage to deregulate the sector, you will be surprised. The upstream was deregulated. In fact, nobody ever regulated the upstream and you can see how many people are there. The telecom was deregulated; you see how many people are operating there. A lot of mistake we keep making is that oil is God given. It is true, God gives us the oil, but God gave us water, water is all over the place, but once you put an effort to treat water, you have added value, you cannot take it for free anymore. "You cannot take it for free any more. If you want to drink that water, you have to pay for it, and if you say you are going to pay below the cost, the water man will not continue to sell water. So it is the same thing with petrol." Besides, the NNPC boss spoke on the search for oil in the Benue and Chad basins, saying, "the nation has a lot of structures that indicate tapping of hydrocarbon, so all we are going to do is to explore and see whether it is there or not." What we did before was to use old technology in exploring for oil in the Chad basin. But today, we are using more modern technology and we are very sure that if oil is there, we can find it with the technology that we are using now. "Currently, we are very busy in the Chad Basin and when we finish with that one, we will take the data back for full interpretation and once we see anywhere where there is prospect for oil, we will send another team there to go and drill. "And once we drill, we are sure we are going to find oil. We found oil on the other side of Chad, and the formation is the same, so I believe that we might be lucky. But it is not only Chad that is the basin in Nigeria. We have seven basins, which include Niger, Adamawa, Gongola basins among others.

"It is a continuous thing and so, there is no time frame. If I give you a block today, the first oil may not come out until after five years. So you have to persevere and do your studies, and then you have to go and hope that where you drilled is where you find the oil."

Port Harcourt refineries to work at full capacity by November, say NNPC.

***The Guardian*, Monday, January 16, 2012, pg. 15**

Port Harcourt refineries would begin to work optimally from November, after a Turn-Around Maintenance (TAM), the Nigerian National Petroleum Corporation (NNPC) has assured.

Group Executive Director, Refining and Petrochemicals at the NNPC, Philip Chukwu, gave the assurance on Thursday, in Port Harcourt, during an inspection of the refineries alongside officials of MaireTecnimont, the contractors that the Federal Government engaged for the TAM. Chukwu, who decried the lack of maintenance of the twin Port Harcourt refineries in the last 12 years, commended the Federal Government for engaging the original constructors of the refineries for the TAM.

"Everyone knows that the refineries have not been properly maintained over the years and we have had to manage things. What we are doing now is to have the TAM and complete rehabilitation of the refineries by the original contractors," he said.

According to the News Agency of Nigeria the two Port Harcourt refineries, which consist of the old refinery with capacity to process 60, 000 barrels per day and 150,000 barrels per day respectively, had been functioning at very low capacity with the old one not working at the moment because of lack of maintenance. Chukwu explained that the TAM, which would start in October, would require a total shutdown of the plants for between 45 days and 60 days to ensure a thorough job.

He said the TAM and rehabilitation process would also entail overhauling the supply chain and pipelines that bring crude oil and capacity building for staff so as to meet international best practice. He said the NNPC was also working with all stakeholders, including security operatives, to ensure the pipelines were safe and no longer vandalised.

Managing Director, Port Harcourt Refinery Corporation (PHRC), Tony Ogbuigwe, in his remarks after taking the contractors round the plants expressed optimism that the refinery would begin to work at 90 per cent capacity by November.

He said preliminary work on the TAM started since late 2010 and the present stage would signal the return to full production by the refineries. Ogbuigwe said that the NNPC had already placed order for all the equipment necessary for the

TAM, noting that the inspection by the management of the construction company would help to fast-track the whole process.

Managing Director, MaireTecnimont Group of Italy, Roberto Bertocco, said in his remarks that the company, which had been on ground in Nigeria for the last 30 years would be working with the original builders of the refinery. "I can assure you of a very good job on this project. We have been working with JGC in many parts of the world, so we are also collaborating with them on this project because we have been on ground in Nigeria for the past 30 years"

He expressed optimism that the refinery would be working in full capacity by the end of the year. The old Port Harcourt refinery was built in 1965 with an initial capacity of 35, 000bpd which was later expanded to 60,000bpd in 1972. The new wing of the refinery was built in 1989 with a 150,000 bpd capacity to meet local consumption of petroleum products and for export. The management of MaireTecnimont led by the Managing Director is due to sign the MOU with the Petroleum Minister, Dieziani Allison-Madueke and NNPC officials, in Abuja.

Subsidy triggers concern over state of refineries

By Sulaimon Salau

***The Guardian*, Wednesday, January 18, 2012, pg. 18, 2012, pg. 47**

The debate that characterised the removal of subsidy on Premium Motor Spirit (PMS) has largely diverted the interest of Nigerians to the nation's refining capacity, which has been ranked absolutely low in recent times.

Even though the Federal Government had assured that the facilities would soon bounce back to optimal operations, stakeholders believed that corruption and management inefficiencies were among the factors that brought the nation to the poor refining status.'

A member of the Senate chamber, Senator Ayoade Adeseun, who berated government's move on subsidy removal, said it should have advanced to restore electricity and fix the refineries before making such an ill-timed policy.

Giving an example of Venezuela, which is also an oil exporting country, he said: "It is so sad that a single refinery in Venezuela, a country with a population of 28 million, Paraguayan Refinery Complex (PDVSA) refines as much as barrels per day compared to just about 133,000 barrels per day been refined by the four moribund Nigerian refineries with total in-stalled capacity of 445,000 barrels per day.

"No wonder the Nigerian government has increased fuel price over 10 times since 1999 while Venezuelan government has maintained the pump price since 1999."

Speaking from a different perspective, the Vice President of the Nigerian Association of Chamber of Commerce, Industries, Mines and Agriculture (NACCIMA), Bassey Edem was however in support for removal of subsidy, but also clamours for more refineries through private ownership.

He said the removal of oil subsidy was long overdue, adding that no nation could advance to economic greatness without one form of hardship or the other.

Edem said that many prospective investors were given licenses by government to build refineries but they could not operate because of negative business environment caused by oil subsidy.

"A lot of licenses have been driven out for refineries and no businessman will want to set up a business in a situation where there is subsidy. Market forces will not allow you to operate, so for these 20 or more refineries to take off, we need a situation where there is free market," he said.

However, the Federal Government and the Nigerian National Petroleum Corporation (NNPC) have assured that plans are in top gear to ensure that the existing refineries are fixed before the end of this year.

The Minister of Petroleum Resources, Mrs. Diezani Alison-Madueke, said government has invited the original builders of the refineries to carry out complete Turn Around Maintenance (TAM) of all the traditional refineries in the country. She also said that some other investors from China had also indicated interest to build more refineries in the country.

Her words: "In order to ensure that we get our refineries to 90 per cent utilisation and to show Nigerians that we are serious this time; around, we actually went back and brought the original contractors that built our refineries in Warri, Port Harcourt and Kaduna.

"Already, they have given us an aggressive timetable and they have assured us that within 24 months all three major refineries will be producing up to 90 per cent capacity utilisation, she said. Meanwhile the Managing Director of Port Harcourt refinery, Anthony Ogbuigwe has confirmed that a 60-day period of turnaround maintenance will begin on the facility from October 1, 2012 and expected to be completed by November. He said this would be the first of such overhaul of the barrel per day plant in 12 years and that, at the end of it, the refinery should run at up to 90 per cent of its capacity.

The nation's four refineries at Port Harcourt (old and new), Warri and Kaduna have a combined capacity of 445,000 bpd, but now operate at less than a quarter of their potential because of sabotage and poor maintenance.

Also, the Group Executive Director (GED), Refining and Petrochemicals at the NNPC, Philip Chukwu said: "Everyone knows that the refineries have not been properly maintained over the years and we have had to manage things. What we are doing now is to have the TAM and complete rehabilitation of the refineries by the original contractors," he said. Chukwu explained that the TAM, which would start in October, would require a total shut down of the plants for between 45 days and 60 days to ensure a thorough job. He said the TAM and rehabilitation process would also entail overhauling the supply chain and pipelines that bring crude oil and capacity building for staff so as to meet international best practice. He said the NNPC was also working with all stakeholders, including security operatives, to ensure the pipelines were safe and no longer vandalised

Why govt'll build new refineries

By AbiodunFagbemi

***The Guardian*, Thursday, December 29, 2011, pg. 9**

Plans by the Federal Government to build three new refineries in the country are part of the measures to buoy fuel supply and mitigate the effects of subsidy removal, Acting National Chairman of the People's Democratic Party (PDP), Abubakar Baraje, has stated. The refineries, according to the government, would be sited in an unnamed location in Kogi State, Oloibiri, Rivers State and an unnamed state in the North-East.

Baraje, who spoke yesterday in Ilorin, Kwara State capital, added that the new refineries would also complement government's efforts at fixing the existing ones in the country and make petroleum products readily available to Nigerians nationwide.The PDP chieftain disclosed that contractors have been mobilised to pick suitable sites for the refineries and that the facilities would be built through a public/private arrangement. Baraje also disclosed that full railways operations would take off next April across nine Nigerian cities, including Lagos, Abuja, Kano and Enugu.

In yet another official confirmation of the policy take-off, Baraje said fuel subsidy removal would take effect as from next year, even as he disclosed that the government would pursue a public/private transportation initiative, direct release of monthly allocations to local councils and the deployment of the recently trained Nigerian anti-terrorism squad. The PDP leader said the party had endorsed the removal of subsidy as proposed by the Federal Government following "wide consultations with experts who gave us pragmatic examples of the overall benefits inherent in the removal."

Baraje, who also condemned the on-going strike by the Academic Staff Union of Universities (ASUU), hinted that the government had directed that relevant authorities meet most of ASUU's demands, saying that the nation's public universities would be re-opened early next year. His words: "By April 2012, railway operations will begin fully in nine major cities. The idea is to reduce the cost of transportation in Nigeria. Besides, we need to fix our major depots and replace some damaged oil pipes. We shall also establish three additional refineries to support the existing ones. These refineries would also be privatised, knowing fully well that attempts in the past to repair them had defied solutions. "By the year 2013, about 29 major Nigerian roads would have either been renovated or newly constructed. The same thing will happen in the area of power generation and distribution. Definitely, the private organisations are coming on board. We are sure that by the middle of 2012, the effects of all these measures would lead to visible improvement in electricity supply in Nigeria."

Baraje submitted that the various security plans put in place by the PDP-con- trolled government, "with full support of all Nigerians, especially members of the opposition parties", would make the country better secure.

He added: "The security thing is a challenge to all. We need to educate ourselves that the issue of security is not only for the ruling party but also for all, including the opposition. We need to put an end to the spate of bombings in Nigeria. Christmas is a remarkable day not only for the Christians but also the Muslims. The perpetrators of the heinous crime of bombing worshipers in the church are not acting in the name of any religion. They are terrorists and will be treated as such. "We need to assist our security personnel to ensure that their efforts and that of the government do not go in vain."

Challenge of subsidy removal and the transformation agenda: a lawyer's perspective

By Tony Odiadi

***The Guardian*, Tuesday, January 17, 2012, pg. 58**

THIS discussion, I must confess, arose out of some e-exchanges with my friend and colleague Iboroma Akpana, a gifted polemist who with his articulations on the removal of subsidy would have done the Jonathan administration a lot of good pushing their position had he been so engaged. All too often particular public policy initiative fails because it lost necessary buy-in due to ineffective or incompetent advocacy. Iboroma had posted quite persuasively, arguing thus 'The entire subsidy architecture is one that rewards and incentivizes opportunistic behaviour. Given our nature as rational maximizers, we are likely to behave opportunistically and seek to game the system. The mischief can only be solved by removing the structure that incentivizes corruption."

He added: "In any event, given our acceptance of our institutional weaknesses, is it not counter intuitive that we seek the retention of a system whose monitoring is left to the same government?"

To be sure, the main kennel of the subsidy removal issue is the need for government to dislodge the "oil importers cabal" who for years now have a stranglehold on the oil sector. That move it is argued will save Nigeria annually ₦1.134 trillion -although, how this figure was arrived at is another matter. It's been stated that when this trillion naira is shared in line with the existing formula, the FGN will get ₦487.49b, the states will get ₦411.03 and the LGAs will get ₦203.23b. This whole increased revenue will accrue to government once the pump price is taken from current ₦65 per litre to ₦140 per litre. But the arithmetic is not that simple and straightforward.

The whole idea about any government policy is to what extent it helps to deliver common good to the citizens. A policy position, no matter how well conceived and articulated must have an implementation strategy which involves timing and engagement of critical stakeholders as well as a plan B. As in warfare, there is a critical mode and timing of an offensive action for optimum effect which must include strategy rethink. This subsidy removal was very poorly timed, surreptitiously carried out and generally effected to the embarrassment of the entire Nigerian citizen. Quite apart from poor timing, information management has been below par, advocacy poor and you therefore see the aching absence of a think tank in government helping with engaging ideas and response strategies.

Not too long ago the Federal Government set up the NV20 2020 programme. Right from its very inception, the government saw the need to enlighten Nigerians about the programme, workshops, symposia, tours were organised to all the geo-political zones of the country. Representatives were drawn and invited from all the sectors and segments of the economy to make various input. Doubtless that approach worked very well for it helped to sensitize the people, increase the ownership of the final output of the visioning program. This was done and very successfully so by the Yar'Adua/Goodluck administration. What has changed since then?

Nigeria's current architecture of state, most people agree, is more of less resting firmly on a framework of waste and corruption. Resources needed for development initiatives are cornered and hijacked through a system of graft and mindless accumulation by a privileged network of persons. Few people will doubt the need to curb waste which is both a government's duty as well as a vigilant citizen's responsibility. Few people still will antagonize the generation of resources for interventions in critical sectors of the economy, not the least of which is infrastructure repair and development. But most people will resist if there is no proper mobilisation to prosecute a grand that will affect the economic fortunes of a vast majority of the citizens.

This is more so because this President Jonathan was a candidate just a few months that projected himself as an agent with an agenda of transformation. We found no difficulty in buying into the agenda, many as direct volunteers. On the need for change the President had said at the time last year that "Nigeria needs to build a more inclusive society where every Nigerian would have equal access to economic and development opportunities". Along that idea, concerned with increased industrial capacity and employment he then further stated that 'The provision of cheap funding to SMEs will come as a great relief to entrepreneurs who need to reduce their fuel costs as they try to deal with high production costs and provide other operational infrastructure".

How does the removal of subsidy serve as an enabler for the above proposition? That then is the challenge. All policies must be contextualized having regards to the citizens' short, medium and long term interests in mind. Yes, this government indicated its position on the subsidy removal as a way of paying the ₦18, 000.00 minimum wage way back in June, 2011 which many dismissed as a classic case of retrieving with the left hand what had been given with the right. Then again, sometime in October last year the President wrote a letter to the NASS announcing to the policy without widespread consultation. It does not matter that governors have been used to make statements now and again, playing the solidarity game simply believing that the removal of subsidy will deliver fresh financial windfall. These to say the least are sequences of errors.

Policies likely to be precipitously traumatic that will leave vast section of the populace all the poorer in a short spell surely needed a better approach than this government has delivered. I see something of a "you have no choice but take it" attitude here. What is wrong with a phased deregulation after a national mobilisation to contain and control the whimsical profiteering of this national resource by the cabal has been achieved? What is wrong with government demonstrating ample sacrifice in terms of significant reduction in 'comfort' budgeting for the executive and legislative arms with specific cut down in all such budget heads? What is wrong with the government clearly moving for an across the board sacrifice in which the average Nigerian will see that it is not he alone that will bear the burden of an impending hardship through the skyrocketing of prices? The manner of the subsidy removal is bad, the timing is wrongheaded, and this national resistance for now is inevitable.

My friend argued further that the removal of subsidy at this time is a clear demonstration of courage. But I disagree, for courage not supported with wisdom in any circumstance is a misguided risk. So in place of courage, this government seems to be demonstrating that it is a mere political risk taker and this is not good if policies are delivered without critical support framework- something Nigerians generally call 'enabling environment'. The opportunity cost for Mr President is the potential losses of so much political good will needed before and after the elections. Granted this debate about subsidy, deregulation has been on for decades in one form or another, truth is, previous governments were very concerned about social service delivery and so were more circumspect about tinkering wholesale with PMS pricing and its likely devastating effect for the lower classes.

In effect, the refusal or inability to repair the refineries has not been due to lack of funds but due in the main to lack of courage. The continuous smuggling of PMS across Nigerian borders as well is not for lack of security and policing personnel but for want of courage. These points are made here to enable us appreciate areas in which presidential courage can readily be deployed to set the tone and direction for correcting the ills in the sector which will prompt Nigerians immediately to see such efforts and readily identify even with a difficult policy like subsidy removal. Nothing exist now on the card that is reassuring not with the 'cabal' untouched and existing loopholes still firmly in place in the sector, to wit, porous borders, non-functioning refineries, colluding NNPC/CBN officials, etc. With all these, who can therefore bet that the anticipated gains of the subsidy removal will not be lost or frittered away through another corrupt system or a new cabal immediately replacing the old one. This government should know that it is better always to build a bridge before attempting to cross it.

Truth is Mr President is quite eager on his transformation agenda but approach matters. And luckily, that is, if he recognises it as such, the hand of fate has, by default as it were, delivered to him a great transformation opportunity with this national resistance to embark upon and achieve a paradigm shift. This current situation ought to serve as the best adrenaline to directly confront the various mafias as well as every other enclave of waste and corruption in our national scheme of things and save revenue for urgently needed infrastructural development across the country. The coalition of organised labour, civil societies, professional bodies in the vanguard of this resistance have given him very urgent areas Nigerians are angry about. They talked about areas such as jumbo salaries of national legislators and need for part time legislature, bloated structure of the executive arm, other specifics like presidential air fleet, thirty six state governors security vote, overseas medical trips, and several items on the recurrent expenditure list of the federal and state budgets considered wasteful for our lean resources.

What is the way out? With the current logjam it will not be a sign of weakness if the government reconsiders its position and proceed with a plan B which ought really to be on the card from inception. First, immediately concede and revert to the old N65 pump price and set a time say in April for a new pump price already discussed and agreed; second,

announce drastic cut in 'comfort budgeting' across board for all political office holders along the recommended lines of the coalition; third, begin direct engagement through sensitization and cultivation organized labour, professional groups, sections of the civil society, and a broad coalition of Nigerians to meet the April pricing; fourth, immediately begin to sign MOUs with companies to effect the refurbishment and turn around maintenance of the four refineries in Port Harcourt, Warri and Kaduna and give each refinery complete autonomy; fifth, begin immediately to demonstrate fresh efforts in deploying security agencies to monitor and police the borders. Finally, invest more in information dissemination and management. Then and only then can the subsidy removal initiative become truly an enabler for transformation.

Odiadi, (LLMf BL) practices law in Lagos

The hoodwinking of Jeffery Sachs

By Olu Akanmu

***The Guardian*, Monday, February 6, 2012, pg. 51**

Professor Jeffery Sachs, the progressive and well respected development economist from the Columbia University wrote an Op-ed in the New York Times on January 10 defending the removal of oil subsidy by the Nigerian government. His arguments were the familiar usual, that oil subsidy benefits the rich more than the poor and that the subsidy when removed would be used in targeted investments that serve the poor and more meaningful social investments. For Sachs, the current Nigerian government is one of the best things that could ever happen to the country. According to him, "President Jonathan is giving Nigeria a chance to cast off the instability, poverty and corruption that have long plagued the country". Professor Sachs visited Abuja, met the Nigerian government and was obviously impressed by the claimed intention for the oil subsidy removal. He must have felt the compelling need to do policy advocacy for Nigeria's much misunderstood government.

Another well respected development economist, Professor Paul Collier of the Oxford University Centre for Study of African Economics writing in the *Financial Times* few days later, virtually lambasted the protesters on the streets of Nigeria. To him, if they have been more economically literate, they should be jubilating and celebrating the Nigerian government. He pushed the same arguments as Professor Sachs on the need to remove oil subsidy. Collier believes that the oil subsidy when removed could be used to give bursaries to poor people to attend school! He cautioned that it is entirely possible that populist rhetoric could be used to seduce people into fighting against their own true interest.

The economic arguments adduced by Sachs and Collier are very sound and are difficult to fault. They however wrongly assume that sound economic policy and intentions automatically translate to sound economic actions. Economics does not exist in the abstract. It exists within the institutional context of politics. The implementation of economic policies cannot be devoid of its institutional context. A better appreciation of Nigeria Political Economy would have made Sachs and Collier to appreciate that this "Jonathan's oil subsidy removal" is not the first time Nigeria would be having a sound economic policy. Why has previous government's good policy intentions not translated to sound economic actions? What guarantees that when government makes promises to the people that it will follow through on its commitments? How would or how could people trust that their elected government will do what it claims it would do? These are more than economic questions. They are political questions. They are questions of governance of society, of trust between government and the people. They are questions of whether society has strong institutional mechanisms that help the people to hold their government to their commitments. They are questions of whether society has strong institutions that guarantee that government will be accountable to the people. And in particular, in a democracy that the government will truly rule on behalf of the people and not on behalf of itself.

If Sachs and Collier have situated their sound economic policy suggestions within Nigeria's weak institutional political context, they would have better appreciated the skepticism and the protests of the Nigerian people to oil subsidy removal.

Professor Sachs wrote in his essay "when Nigeria won relief on its external debt in the mid- 2000s, the savings on debt service were actually redirected to meaningful social investments in states and local governments..." He opined that we can therefore trust that this would happen again with the oil subsidy removal. As a Nigerian, I wonder where those so called investments from debt reliefs are. I can't see them and many Nigerians cannot. What we can see is the fact that billions of dollars of Nigeria's Excess Crude Account, a future savings for our children, have been depleted with no improvement in infrastructure, school or education to show for it in all tiers of our government. What we can see are expensive governments, expensive legislature in which public cost per legislator is nearly two million dollars per annum. Why would this time then be different? Why should we trust government if it has not previously won our trust? Economic history has shown that where there are wide social and income inequality and people do not trust government, people tend to refer short-term, immediate income redistribution programmes even if it will hurt long term economic growth, since they do not believe that the benefit of economic growth will reach them. Unlike Collier claimed in his essay that the masses are economically illiterate, the masses are actually rational beings! This is the challenge of our fiscal reform and providing a broader context to understand why people were on the streets and will not support what seems like a good economic policy.

The oil subsidy protests are watershed moments for Nigeria. We have had a most rigorous public polity discourse. The gains must be consolidated via the building or strong political and social institutions that will ensure that government will be more accountable and will deliver on their commitments to the people. Civil society must keep up the pressure for a more transparent government. We must strengthen the institution of a free press as an alternate public parliament to debate public policy. Civil society activism should not just be for human rights activists. Our town unions, religious, trade and professional associations should become more active in how they are governed at state, local and federal levels. More civil organisations should use the Freedom of Information Act to demand a higher level of transparency of public expenditure from our governments. States who do not pass their own version of Freedom of Information Act should be publicly shamed. Peaceful protest as a legitimate democratic right of the people must continue to be formally protected.

We must also strengthen our electoral institutions to ensure free and fair elections. When there are no free and fair elections, governments have no incentives to be accountable to the people as they know they cannot be voted out of power. Political parties as the foundation of our electoral process must become more democratic to reflect the true will of their rank and file and offer the electorate real electoral and ideological options. We must also reform electoral campaign financing to limit the influence of money or at least compel political parties and contestants to publicly declare their size and source of funding. If we can develop the institutional mechanisms that will limit corruption in our elections, we will significantly limit corruption in our governments.

We must also strengthen the rule of law and the institutions of law enforcement. Unless crime can be punished, there will be no incentive to avoid committing it we should consider separating the office of the Attorney General from the Justice Minister. The office of the Attorney General should be non-political, independent of the executive, with a fixed tenure that ensures it cannot be removed by a sitting President. Such Attorney General working with the Financial Crime Commission would be better able to prosecute high level politicians who have committed economic treason and bring them to justice. Even Collier in his essay implicitly recognized this, adducing reasons why Germany is the best managed economy in Europe. Quoting Collier "Germans are locked into sound decision making by a combination of legal rules, dedicated institutions and a critical mass of ordinary citizens who understood why the rule and institutions mattered and so defended them". It is those rules and the strong institutions that can enforce them that are missing in Nigeria. That was why the people were on the streets.

Akanmu is an executive in the financial service industry

Pains, gains of subsidy removal by stakeholders

By Obiora Aduba and SulaimonSalau

***The Guardian*, Wednesday, January 11, 2012, pg. 45**

The issue of fuel subsidy removal may have put the nation to a state of stand still, with stake-holders becoming increasingly worried over the economy.

The ongoing struggle was believed to be a challenge that Nigerians need to face and completely overcome. However, stakeholders have been proffering antidotes to the issue through various reactions, allegations and explanations.

Among them was the Deputy President of the Nigerian Labour Congress, Isa Aremu, who alleged that there is a lot of inefficiency in the system and such weakness should be removed to make the refineries functional so that Nigerians should not be made to suffer unnecessarily, "Fuel subsidy removal will result in inflation; it will worsen the poverty situation in the country and the government knows this. We will resist it," he said.

The son of the former 'Senior Advocate of the Masses', Mohammed Fawehinmi was also quite active in the scene, he said: "We are all opposed to removal of fuel subsidy. Petrol must be sold at ₦65 per litre. Nigeria is rich enough. Let the government start working. No more tightening of belts, we are tired. We have suffered enough as Nigerians. Our money is being used to buy houses and businesses in London, Dubai, United States of America, South Africa and other developed countries.

President Goodluck Jonathan who deemed it necessary to announce palliatives to tackle the removal of subsidy, said: 'To save Nigeria, we must all be prepared to make sacrifices. On the part of government, we are taking several measures aimed at cutting the size and cost of governance, including on-going and continuous effort to reduce the size of our recurrent expenditure and increase capital spending.

"In this regard, I have directed that overseas travels by all political office holders, including the President, should be reduced to the barest minimum. The size of delegations on foreign trips will also be drastically reduced; only trips that are absolutely necessary will be approved," he said. Jonathan stated that for the year 2012, the basic salaries of all political office holders in the Executive arm of government will be reduced by 25 per cent adding that government is also currently reviewing the number of committees, commissions and parastatals with overlapping responsibilities. The Federal Government had however, approved the procurement of 1,600 mass transit buses, as part of the long term plans to cushion the harsh effects of the increase in pump price of petrol, that this will form part of the N10 billion revolving loan set aside by the government to address problems of the transport sector in the country.

In a quick reaction to this pronouncement, the Acting General Secretary of NLC, Comrade Owei Lakemfa said the claim by government that it was importing 1,600 buses into the country was false, stressing that the buses in question belong to the Trade Union Congress (TUC). Lakemfa said the decision by government was an afterthought, arguing that the Presidency should have put the measures in place before coming out with the policy decision.

"The announcement is laughable because if divided by the 774 Local Governments in the country, it amounts to 2 buses per Local Government. Thirdly, one would have thought that the Presidency would put these "cushioning effects" in place before the unreasonable hike in petrol price," he said.

In his usual dramatic way, the Governor of Edo State, Adams Oshiomhole, asked the Labour unions to allow the Federal Government continue with the removal of petroleum subsidy, noting that it is the only way the economy could be saved from possible collapse.

"The question is what are we subsidising and what are we not subsidising. Today, we are not subsidizing cost of production. We are not subsidizing employment but we are subsiding cost of consumption. I think we should credit both Yar'Adua and Jonathan for not taking arbitrary position as it affects subsidy removal by throwing it to public discourse. If it is about five years ago, we all know what would have happened, even though I won't like to mention name.

"If President Jonathan does not take the decision to do the right thing now, Nigeria will crash in no distant future,' he said. The former Labour leader advised the unions against pushing people to do what they are not capable of sustaining, but that they should consistently ensure that the additional revenue realised from the removal of the subsidy is not pocketed by a few individuals.

While advocating that government should jail those that are responsible and who have benefited unjustly from the fuel subsidy, he argued: "Don't push the people to do what they are not capable of sustaining. Allow the Federal Government to move forward in the direction it has chosen," Oshiomhole said.

Olisa Agbakoba, a human right activist and lawyer, argued that there is nothing bad about removing subsidy, saying: "Nobody is against government removing the subsidy, but that government should put in place institutional legal framework. "It is unfortunate. I am highly disappointed that government disregarded public outcry against fuel subsidy removal. There are ongoing public consultations on this issue and it was even debated at the National Assembly without any conclusion. "I expected! President Jonathan to have waited for the legislators to return from their Christmas break before taking any action on the issue," he said.

The Minister of Finance, Ngozi Okonjo-Iweala agreed that the cabals accused in the fuel subsidy saga should be made to face punitive measures so as to deter others from doing such things in future. Okonjo-Iweala said, it has become imperative to remove the subsidy if the country is to guard against some of the situations that some European countries are facing.

She said the price of PMS in the country is currently not determined by the forces of demand and supply. The current landing cost of PMS, she said, is about \$133 per a litre with additional N15.72. "Between 2006 and 2011 over ₦3.7 trillion was spent on subsidy which is about 30 per cent of the capital expenditure. The revenue realised from the subsidy would be ploughed into maternal/health care, public works, youth employment, urban mass transit scheme, vocational training scheme and social safety net programme.

"The Federal Government is desirous of discontinuing the subsidies on prices of petroleum products because of the huge financial burden on government, it disproportionately benefits the wealthy, it is inefficient and diverts resources away from potential investment in critical infrastructure," she said

Governor of Central Bank, Sanusi Lamido Sanusi, stated that the situation in the sector has encouraged corruption to thrive and warned that, "we must free our resources if not, government would have incurred so much debt to the extent that the next government after 2015 may not be able to operate when it comes on stream."

The Executive Secretary of Major Oil Marketers Association of Nigeria, Mr. Obafemi Olawore said: "We have a strong feeling there will be more serenity in the market place after deregulation because we will have competition and more investments. We will be deceiving ourselves if we keep opposing deregulation. "We want to see a dynamic downstream sector where the consumers are free to choose who and where to buy products from, for us it is not whether deregulation is desirable but how government will spend the savings from it and that is what we must all come together to do.

"I told labour to rather than oppose the plan, form a committee that will monitor government's plans for the savings, if they say they are building roads with the money, monitor its progress periodically and hold them accountable, if possible shut down the country if there are no signs of their promises.

The Chairman/Managing Director, Integrated Oil, Emmanuel Ihenacho, said: "Subsidy must be removed because there is a lot of money trapped there. If we deregulate the market the government will not be compel led to pay subsidy. The subsidy that are currently paid are meant to be targeted in alleviating the condition of the masses but that is not happening be-cause that subsidy has been appropriated by parties other than those who are supposed to get it.

"I have read in newspapers where they said NNPC and marketers share so much money in subsidies that is not true. What happens is that marketers make out money to pay for imported petroleum products because they buy a liter of petroleum product for about ₦140 and the government then compel them to sell it at ₦65, which means the government has to refund the difference of ₦75 to them.

The Minister of Petroleum Resources, Deziani Allison-Madueke stated that to mitigate the immediate impact of the petroleum subsidy discontinuation on the population, government has mapped out a programme tagged: Subsidy Reinvestment and Empowerment Programme (SURE Programme).

She pointed out that this will accelerate economic transformation through investments in critical infrastructure projects to lay a foundation for the successful development of a national safety net programme that is better targeted at the poor and most vulnerable on a continuous basis.

On the selected power projects, the minister noted that the component would improve generation capacity through hydro and coal power plants and also provide counterpart funding for the construction of the large Mambilla hydropower project that will generate an additional 2,600 megawatts of electric power. According to her, "there is also the petroleum project, which will restore and improve domestic refining capacity and prevent shortfalls in supply of petroleum products. The integrity of the petroleum pipeline systems will also be enhanced through additional investments and protective security. The targeted projects under this component are Greenfield refineries and pipeline reinstatements.

Three new refineries will be built under a counterpart funding arrangement with the private sector in Bayelsa, Kogi and Lagos States with the following processing capacities," she stated.

Rising from an extraordinary emergency session, members of the House of Representatives asked the executive arm of government to suspend the removal of subsidy on petroleum products in appreciation of the mood of the nation and to allow for more consultations.

Other decisions arrived at by the House also were the setting up of the two ad hoc commit-tees, one to mediate between the executive and organized labour and the other to verify and determine the actual subsidy requirements and monitor the subsidy regime.

The decisions were arrived at following the adoption of a Motion on the Removal of Fuel Subsidy by the executive Arm of government, sponsored by Hon. Yusuf Tajudeen and 60 others.

People power!

***The Guardian*, Tuesday, January 10, 2012, pg.2-4**

In compliance with the directive of organised Labour and its allies, Nigerians yesterday took to the streets to protest removal of fuel subsidy by the Federal Government, which has led to astronomical increase in the price of petrol.

During the action which paralysed socio-economic and educational activities across the country, Labour leaders and members of civil society organisations spoke vociferously against the removal of the subsidy urging the government to reverse it and work out other strategies to take the country out of the woods.

Meanwhile, the Federal Government has said dialogue remains the best option to resolve the deadlock between it and the labour unions over the implementation of deregulation policy in the downstream oil sector.

It therefore appealed to labour unions call off the strike and support government's efforts to move the country forward. Minister of Information, Mr. Labaran Maku, who stated this while reacting to the protest, reiterated government's commitment to civil liberty and protection of human rights of all Nigerians. He said security agencies have been directed to enforce the fundamental human rights of all.

The Minister assured that the Federal Government would continue to implement policies that will expand the economy in order to improve the social well-being of Nigerians and create more job opportunities for the teeming unemployed youths. According to him, Nigerians would soon begin to feel the impact of the deregulation policy. Maku urged Nigerians to support government in its determination to return Nigeria to the path of sustainable development and economic growth.

On his part, Governor Chibuike Rotimi Amaechi met with independent petroleum marketers in Rivers State yesterday to discuss ways of reducing fuel price and getting the products easily and readily available to end-users. At the meeting were members of the state branch of the Independent Petroleum Marketers Association of Nigeria (IPMAN) and officials of Nigerian National Petroleum Corporation (NNPC) area office/depot.

According to Amaechi's Chief Press Secretary, Mr. David Iyofor, "also as part of the governor's effort to see how he can bring down the price of petrol in the state below the N141 benchmark, he will be meeting with other groups in the sector." "Governor Amaechi will be meeting with the National Union of Road Transport Workers (NURTW), major oil marketers, oil farm tank and depot owners, between today and tomorrow and to also ensure that the cost of public transportation does not escalate too much."

In Ondo State, it was total paralysis of social and economic activities in Akure the capital and other major cities. Ail the major streets in Akure were completely deserted as residents obeyed the stay-at- home order while Labour leaders, rights activists and irate youths who had earlier gathered at the State Secretariat of the Nigeria Labour Congress (NLC) at Alagbaka took to the streets in a peaceful demonstration.

In Kaduna, an unprecedented number of youths, market women, labour and human rights activists came out to the streets to protest. The action which was led by the officials of the NLC, Kaduna branch, was later hijacked by thousands of hoodlums who carried fresh leaves and placards, chanting anti-government songs, just as most residents in the metropolis stayed indoors. Former Governor of Kaduna State, Abdulkadir Musa Balarabe, human rights activist, Festus Okoye as well as the President, Civil Rights Congress of Nigeria Shehu Sani led the protest to major public places in the city as early as 8.00 a.m.

All public and private institutions in Ekiti State were under lock in total compliance with the directive for strike. The peaceful protest in the state was led by the Catholic Bishop of Ekiti, Felix Femi Ajakaye, who said he had to identify with the people to protest what he called insensitivity of President Goodluck Jonathan in handling the welfare of Nigerians.

The Bishop, who dressed in his cassock, joined other protesters from Ajiiosun Area of Ado Ekiti, marched through some major streets in the state capital and stopped at Fajuyi Park where the protesters were addressed

Attempts by security operatives to forcefully open the gate of the Rivers State secretariat in Port Harcourt were resisted by the workers enforcing the strike. Economic and social activities were grounded in Port Harcourt as hundreds of residents took to the streets. Primary and secondary schools that were billed to reopen after the Christmas and New Year holidays could not do so. Officials of the

Trade Union Congress (TUC) and NLC stormed the Port Harcourt International Airport, Omagwa, to prevent take-off and landing of aircraft.

In Benue State, all banks, shops, markets and business centres as well as hospitals were shut down. The State Radio as well as FRCN stations that started offering skeletal services at dawn were later shut down by officials of the NLC.

In Abeokuta, the Ogun State capital, the protest was total. All shops, markets, business centres and mechanic workshops were completely shut as the streets were taken over by protesters.

But for the timely intervention of armed policemen and other security agents, the NNPC filling station along the Western Bye-pass in Minna, Niger State capital would have been set ablaze by protesters. Also all billboards with President Good luck Jonathan's pictures in Minna and its environs were pulled down and set ablaze by protesters. Trouble started at the NNPC station when the protesters discovered that the attendants were selling fuel to motorists and immediately ordered them to close business, but the station's managers resisted as the attendants continue the sales.

Reacting to the nationwide protest, the chairman of the Northern Governor's Forum, Alhaji Babangida Aliyu, yesterday in Minna said the government had no choice than to listen to the voice of the people over the subsidy removal.

Speaking while receiving members of the NBA who were in the Government House to present their position on the fuel subsidy removal, the Niger State helmsman said what influenced the decision of the 36 governors to support the subsidy's removal was to stop illegal deductions being made in the name of subsidy by the Federation Allocation Committee.

The protest in Edo State almost turned violent. Some persons sustained various degrees of injuries while at least four persons were rushed to the Central Hospital, Benin City where doctors were seen attending to the victims. Suspected hoodlums infiltrated the ranks of the organisers and ransacked some business premises in Erie along Sakpoba and Mission roads.

They also ransacked parts of Third Junction and set bonfires in major junctions across the state capital. But law enforcement agencies drawn from the Army, Police and Nigerian Security and Civil Defence Corps, were quickly mobilised to the hot spots.

Governor Adams Oshiomhole expressed solidarity with the labour unions and the civil society groups, saying they have a right to stage peaceful protest against any policy they feel ag-grieved about. Speaking during the procession to the Government House, Benin City yesterday by the NIC Chairman, Emmanuel Ademokun and TUC Chairman, Joe Aligbe, the governor who said government feels the pains of the people as a result of the subsidy removal, assured that the issues would eventually be resolved through dialogue.

Over 2,000 non-indigenes were yesterday evacuated from their various places of residence to the State Command Headquarters of the Nigerian Police and the 4th Mechanised Brigade of the Nigerian Army for fear of attacks by suspected hoodlums who seemed to have hijacked the peaceful protest in the morning.

Some vehicles as at the time of filing this report were being mobilised to transport these victims to their zones. *The Guardian* also gathered yesterday that three persons were reportedly shot dead while attempting to loot shopping complexes and business centres.

Removal of oil subsidy (3)

Editorial

***The Guardian*, Wednesday, January 11, 2012, pg. 14**

Thorny as it may seem, the crisis arising from the surreptitious removal of fuel subsidy by the Federal Government on New Year Day, is not beyond solution. It only needs the government to muster the political will to implement them. For this to be done, it is important to go back to basics. The issue of subsidy on locally consumed petroleum products rests on the assumption that there is a shortfall between the cost of import and local selling price but does not address the causes of importation. Indeed, the need to surmount the vagaries of international pricing led government to establish more refineries and supply networks across the country from 1970 onward. The country's refineries have a processing capacity of 445, 000bpd and the original vision is to satisfy domestic demand, deepen self-reliance and avoid a situation in which oil companies and marketers would enslave the country.

This vision worked up to 4 point in which a group of speculators took over importation of refined products as a result of the massive devaluation of the naira by the Gen. Ibrahim Babangida administration. This happened against the backdrop of low capacity utilisation, bloated overheads, inadequate technology for process upgrade and outright sabotage. These conditions have been entrenched and successive governments have not had the courage to address them.

Ironically, Nigeria is the 6th largest oil producing country in the world and in other oil producing countries; consumers enjoy a great deal of good pricing. For example in Algiers, Algeria, a litre of fuel sells for 20p; in Muscat, Oman it is 20p per litre; in Egypt's Cairo it is 19p per litre. In Doha, Qatar, it is 15p per litre; in Kuwait City it is 14p per litre; in Manama, Bahrain, it is 13p per litre; in Ashgabat, Turkmenistan, it is 12p per litre; in Libya's Tripoli it is 9p per litre; in Riyadh, Saudi Arabia, it is 8p per litre and in Caracas, Venezuela, it is 2/3p per litre. At the current price of N141 per litre, or about 60p, the price of petrol in Nigeria will be the highest among oil producing countries. There is no reason why Nigerian consumers cannot enjoy price advantage like other oil producing countries.

But this cannot happen until the refineries are repaired and new ones built. As knowledgeable and other well-meaning Nigerians have observed, the issue of subsidy arose in the first place because the refineries are down; and some people are profiting from the situation. The information that the original builders have been invited to do the turnaround maintenance is not a guarantee that they will work in an environment of intrigues. More private firms should be encouraged to set up refineries with lesser bottlenecks and devoid of the deliberate scare tactics of government officials which many of them have complained about.

The oil majors should be called upon to build more refineries which should be amortised over time. Refining Nigeria's sweet crude is not rocket science and local refineries in the Niger Delta should be encouraged for focal consumption.

Government should also look at short term measures such as refining petrol in neighbouring West African countries where they would be required to pay only shipping and refining cost and where costs are almost at par with Nigeria. At the same time, government should work earnestly to resuscitate the comatose refineries as well as ensure the building of new ones within a specified period.

Besides, government should implement a repayment strategy with major buyers, which frees the entire industry from the meddlesomeness of Bretton Woods's institutions as practised under the Buhari administration.

Like it or not the state would always be a major player in the energy sector. Elsewhere, it is tied to the military-industrial complex and guarded by the amour of the state for the larger interest of the citizenry. Therefore, a responsive government does not wait for resources from subsidy to implement capital projects like road construction and rehabilitation, railway and electricity. After all, government does budget for these projects yearly without results. Government divert resources to other important areas.

The President said the other day that he was ordering a 25 per cent cut in the basic salaries of public officials in the executive arm of government He should go further than that and secure the consent of the National Assembly, State governors and their officials, to cede a pro-portion of their emoluments to the national purse. He should also initiate and enforce such measures as a ban on all officials from embarking on all but the most essential foreign travels which the government said will gulp ₦11.25 billion in the budget this year. The Nigerian National Petroleum Corporation (NNPC) should be overhauled to enthrone transparency and accountability. A government that seeks the trust of its citizens should not shy away from confronting corruption of the magnitude reported in the petroleum sector, and making an example of those responsible for the rot.

Rather than dismiss the resolution of the House of Representatives at its extraordinary session, as a mere opinion, and presumably consider the on-going efforts at the Senate as an irritation, the government should turn to the nation into a comer with very little room for manoeuvring. It found it difficult to forge a national consensus on the fuel subsidy issue and the need to remove it but in the event it has created the opportunity for ordinary Nigerians to construct a national consensus against the government's policy, leaving it very vulnerable and weakened.

The situation cannot be allowed to continue. The National Assembly should insist on the President reverting to the old price of fuel, and more intensive consultations should be carried out While this is afoot the government should begin implementing some of the palliatives it has outlined in the SURE document This will reassure the public, earn their trust and create the conducive environment for the government to eventually withdraw the subsidy.

Reforming the petroleum industry in Nigeria through the Petroleum Industry Bill (PIB)

STOCKWATCH

***The Guardian*, Monday, January 30, 2012, pg. 52**

Introduction

A week of protests over fuel prices has put Nigeria's government under more pressure than ever to make good on long-unfulfilled promises to reform its notoriously inefficient and corrupt energy sector, and this time it will be harder not to act. CIVIL society organizations across the country have urged the Federal Government to attach the removal of the fuel subsidy to the argument for the passage of the Petroleum Industry Bill, PIB, as proof of its commitment to the development of the industry and the economy at large.

The President, Association of Registered Insurance Agents of Nigeria, Mr. Kingsley Obuvie, has urged the Nigerian Labour Congress to ask the National Assembly to pass the Petroleum Industry Bill. The bill, according to him, is to establish the legal and regulatory framework for operations in the Nigerian petroleum industry. The bill, when passed into law, is expected to provide guidelines for the operation or the upstream and downstream sectors of the industry.

Despite being among the world's top 10 oil producers, Nigeria relies heavily on imported fuel as its own refineries are dilapidated, so the subsidy has become a cash hand out of billions of dollars to a cartel of wealthy fuel importers. Investment on refining and developing further oilfields for production hinges on passing a wide-ranging Petroleum Industry Bill (PIB) that has been stuck in parliament for more than four years, costing Nigeria billions of dollars in lost investment The Petroleum Minister Allison-Madueke also promised that she would meet legislators to try to speed up this massive bill aimed at changing everything from fiscal terms to the state oil company. On the same day, her ministry announced that it had set up a committee designed to facilitate this.

The Senate has also said all interests in the controversial Petroleum Industry Bill (PIB) should be articulated in a bid to secure a quick passage of the Bill. Chairman, Senate Joint Committee investigating the management of fuel subsidy regime, Senator Magnus Abe, disclosed this. He noted that if key actors in the oil industry, the Federal Government, National Assembly and other Nigerians put the interest of the country first, finding a common ground to pass the PIB would not be difficult.

Why PIB?

The proposed Petroleum Industry Bill (PIB) represents the most radical, comprehensive and pro- Nigeria law in the industry. It came into being following the attempt by the present administration to undertake a reform process of the oil and gas industry in order to improve on the general efficiency of the sector. It seeks principally to overhaul the clutter of numerous laws in the industry, establish a new framework for good governance and best practice, enhance government revenues through better tax codes and undo the harm done by the profit sharing contracts of 1993 in which the then regime seemed to have generously given out the nation's wealth, to the oil majors.

In summary, Key proposals of the bill include: measures to ensure the government increases its take from a growing number of deep-water developments, review of the royalties on gas production. increasing the tax take from gas by creating a new fiscal regime separate from rules governing oil, changes to the way tax breaks are applied for new developments, oil companies will be encouraged to refine at least 50 per cent of their production in Nigeria by the end of the decade, new rules to boost employment of Nigerians in the oil industry, incentives to encourage development of marginal fields, improved community programmes in the Niger Delta. The central plank of the reform strategy is to restructure joint ventures between the NNPC and Western majors to allow them to raise private capital, rather than rely on a notoriously unreliable annual injection of cash from the government.

KEY FEATURES OF THE PIB

Necessity

The reform process of the oil and gas industry would require a holistic approach. This, in effect, means that the existing laws governing the administration of the industry in the country would have to be repealed or reviewed. The present Petroleum Legislation and especially, the fiscal regimes are no longer in tune with the current realities of Nigeria and international best practices in the oil and gas industry.

Major Changes

The changes to the existing laws are specific as well as diverse in many instances. For example, the laws seek to create a much more transparent administrative system where all interested parties could assess information and indicate interests on a given venture/projects in the oil and gas industry. It attempts to amend aspects of the Petroleum Profit Tax Administration, PPTA, which treat information relating to the chargeable profits of companies as confidential and secret. The new laws also clearly state procedures for bidding processes and retention of licenses' and leases which were hitherto, not the case in the old laws. It also simplifies collection of petroleum revenues by emphasizing on rents and royalties and less on taxes.

Participation by Nigerian Entrepreneurs

The PIB will encourage the development of small fields with significant low tax incentives having a bottom level of 5 per cent royalty scale, based on daily oil production. This provision is a deliberate effort to encourage Nigerian entrepreneurs to partake in the oil and gas sector business. In addition, the local content provision has been incorporated into the new law which would require all projects and procurements to have Nigerian content elements in them. By this, all purchase of local goods and services in the oil industry will receive a significant boost, given that the new PIB makes only 80 per cent of foreign costs deductible for Nigerian Hydrocarbon Tax purposes. The deregulation of the downstream sector coming alongside the reform is also expected to stimulate economic activities in the country as new areas of local entrepreneurship skills will be promoted to enhance the operation and management of the downstream assets under a deregulated regime.

Gas Flaring and Local Utilization of Our Gas Resources

The provision of the new bill provides adequate incentives to promote domestic gas utilization in Nigeria. This is consistent with the National Gas Master Plan. Article 282,335,404 - 410 of the Gas Master Plan highlighted the significance of encouraging the use of gas in domestic markets as well as ending gas flaring.

Institutions

Under the proposed law, institutions would have distinct roles and responsibilities, in order to avoid duplications of functions. The separation of the oil and gas value chain into Upstream, Midstream and Downstream, with clear demarcation of boundaries among the segments ensures that the institutions function properly without any recourse to overlapping responsibilities. The number of institutions being created is linked to the oil and gas value chain. Indeed, most of the institutions are already in existence, namely the Inspectorate, the Authority, the Fund, the Frontier Service and the Centre. In technical terms, therefore, only two new institutions are being created; The "Agency" and Directorate" all of which have clearly defined roles.

Funding the Institutions

In order to ensure prudent management of resources and accountability, the institutions' running cost will be tied specifically to the sectors that they regulate and will not unduly put burden on Government finances. For example, the "Authority" would derive their fund from fees and levies on Petroleum Products and Gas sales. Decentralization of the NNPC The policy and regulatory roles of the NNPC is to be excised and transferred into three regulatory entities for effectiveness and efficiency. Therefore, government will still have strong oversight and control of the oil and gas industry. NNPC would not be privatized. It will be fully commercialized. The reform will rather see the present NNPC transit from being a statutory Corporation into a Limited Liability Company under the Companies and Allied Matter Act It will function as a purely commercial business entity but wholly owned by Government It would have freedom to enter into commercial ventures within and outside of Nigeria and pay taxes on its profit to the Government

Directorate of Petroleum Resources

The PIB provides for the current Directorate of Petroleum Resources (DPR) to be transformed into the National Petroleum Inspectorate, NPI, which is an autonomous regulatory body empowered with financial and operational independence to regulate the activities in the upstream petroleum sector.

Downstream Integration

All the provisions in the previous downstream gas bill have been incorporated in the PIB. The Gas sector will be regulated by the three regulators: Agency, Inspectorate, and Authority.

Access to New Oil Acreage

The new law also proposes to remove a major bottleneck that impedes new investments: lack of access to new oil acreage. The normal international practice is that a petroleum producer must return unutilized acreage (or oil block) to the government after a specific period of time, usually 10 years. This creates constant acreage turn over with opportunities for new comers. The relinquishment provisions also encourage the oil companies to explore the areas actively; otherwise they may end up forfeiting acreage that could contain important oil and gas field. It is not clear why these general international practices are not timely implemented in Nigeria. As a result of the delay, petroleum companies are sitting on idle acreages on existing joint ventures and production sharing contracts, thus denying the nation new investment opportunities. The PIB is addressing this by demanding that the idle acreage would be given back for another round of bidding in a timely manner. This may free up as much as 30% of the nation's prospective petroleum area for new investors, according to official estimates.

Employment opportunities

The reform process of the oil and gas industry is more or less about creating opportunities for Nigerians. The various institutions to be created would seek to engage Nigerians from all walks of lives to be involved throughout the entire value chain of the oil and gas industry. Moreover, the bill compelled Oil and Gas Companies to employ host community members in their employments and contract awards, especially on community related development projects.

Host communities

The Bill mandates oil and gas companies operating in Nigeria to be guided strictly by the PIB Local Infrastructural Development and Maintenance Guidelines. It also stipulates for a Mandatory Consultation with host communities in the development of infrastructure and all related development initiative under Social Corporate Responsibility (SCR) to be undertaken by company operating in an area. The bill mandates that all Oil and Gas companies must ensure support for educational and skill acquisition training programmes for indigenes of the host communities. The sole aim is essential to create a highly skilled manpower as well as provide the unskilled persons with skills that would provide employment for them, especially, in the operational segments of the oil and gas industry.

Reactions

Like most new things and changes, the immediate reaction was resistance and criticism that the bill was too far-reaching to be effective and successful. The international or multinational oil companies cry, "Foul! Nigerian government is trying to run us out of business," but the proponents of the bill retort, "No! It is the law worldwide and you have been cheating us all these years."

Having gone past the second reading at the House of Representatives and now awaiting public hearing, various interests groups, the National Assembly, labour unions, civil society groups and indigenous operators began to scrutinize the bill to ensure their interests have been protected. However, the multinationals, either through individual spokespersons or their trade group, the Oil Producers

Trade Section of the Lagos Chamber of Commerce, have refused to comment on the bill. Rather they have been making representations to the government to get some sections changed to protect their interests.

But the fact is that now, with the incidence of dwindling resources being experienced by the federal government, there is increasing pressure on finances and the need to increase revenues to meet capital budgets, notwithstanding the fact that majority of government funds are frittered away through political frivolities.

Strengths

- Seems to have to give Nigeria and its people sovereign control of petroleum resources which had hitherto, been controlled by the multinationals - oil majors
- Provides a robust legal framework for increased Nigerian take and higher level of value addition
- Also, industry operators believe that its ability to capture operations, either technical or commercial in both the upstream and downstream oil and gas, is quite commendable.
- Furthermore, it provides for the incorporation of the Nigerian National Petroleum Company Limited as an independent limited liability company, and also provides guidelines for the incorporation of Joint Ventures, which is expected to free government from cash calls and other funding constraints.

Weaknesses

- Most of the criticism against the bill relate to the fiscal terms as it relates to the multinationals - they argue that the terms being proposed by the bill will reduce their take to a point where their investments become unattractive
- Some top petroleum experts argues that the fiscal terms proposed by the bill would be inimical to government in the long run and a disincentive for further investments.

Previous incentives like those contained in the 2003 production sharing contracts led to the huge investments in the nation's deepwater region, which resulted in the big discoveries like Shell's Bonga, ExxonMobil's Erha, Chevron's Agbami, Total's Akpo and Agip's Abo. There should be a way of ensuring that government gets more revenue as oil prices rise. As prices go up companies' share of the economic rent reduces in favour of government. But if left as it is in the bill, when prices go below $35 per barrel, as we have witnessed since the global crises, then the companies would gain more."

Conclusions

The Petroleum Industry Bill may not be a perfect work of legislation, but as one industry executive puts it, 'its nationalistic focus is not in dispute'. It is now up to our law makers in Abuja to stay above board and give this proposal urgent and fair consideration.

Subsidy crisis through a creative theory

By Simon Emeje.

***The Guardian*, Thursday, February 2, 2012, pg. 68**

Development crisis is a common phenomenon in Nigeria and other developing countries of the Third World. Some schools of thought have viewed it in different ways. For instance, the modernisation school sees it as a crisis of backwardness resulting from unending and abundant traditional structures which should move to modernity because they have vehemently withstood development. On the other hand, the underdevelopment school perceives it as a crisis of development which has direct relationship with the expansion of global capitalism. The dependency school views it as a dependent, distorted and conditioned development between the Third World countries (including Nigeria) and the advanced industrialized countries. However, the mode of production school looks at it as a crisis of articulation of capitalist and pre-capitalist modes of production and feels that attention should be given to the dialectical relation between the internal and external process.

Based on the above perspectives of development crisis, the case of Nigeria particularly, can be divided into various crises of poverty, leadership trust, technological artefacts, education, industrialization, health, transportation, governance, welfarism and the general social and economic dimensions. Some people have viewed development in Nigeria as that which should be seen as an effort to catch up with the Western World and an increasing acquisition of artefacts as found in developed countries. Such artefacts include cars, roads, hospitals, houses and others. What then is development in Nigerian perspective? I will come back to this. But let us understand what this creative theory is. Our understanding of this theory will settle the development crisis and set an adequate growth template for Nigeria.

The creative theory is called Creative Autolytic Destruction. Please do not be scared of these seeming high sounding words. Do not also view this theory from a negative perspective. Look, it is positive. I will explain. "Autolytic" is a scientific term from "autolysis." Autolysis is the destruction of tissues or cells of an organism by enzymes that are produced within the organism. It is the self-destruction of the tissues or cells within the living body. An enzyme is a protein produced by any organism that behaves as a catalyst. A catalyst is a substance that causes speedy chemical reaction without being changed itself; it causes a change. Enzymes are cleaning agents that remove stains. Protein is an essential component of muscles, skin, bones and the whole body, required for the structure, function and regulation of the body's cells, tissues and organs. Tissue is any group of cells meant to perform specific functions like bone marrow tissues and others. Please do not be bored. What is the relevance of autolysis to a nation like Nigeria?

The living body or organism is Nigeria, policies and programmes. The enzymes are pressure groups and individuals. The enzymes are divided into two. One set of enzymes is positively directed to work on policies and programmes that will bring positive change or development to the country. Any visionary political leadership, groups or individuals belong to this set. The activities of such ones are targeted at bringing change and development. The second set of enzymes are negatively directed with activities to hit the polity, policies and programmes in such a manner that such policies and programmes will become disarticulated, distorted and crushed to possible total extinction. Consequently, development will become disillusioned, distorted, weak and retarded. For further explanation, it will be expedient to define creative destruction. This will explain the whole creative theory.

Creative destruction is derived from the economic theory of Karl Marx. It is the linked processes of the accumulation and annihilation of wealth under capitalism. Marx and Engels described this in the Communist Manifesto in 1848. Creative destruction describes the way in which capitalist economic development arises from the destruction of some prior economic orders. Marx further explains that creative destruction does not only imply that capitalism destroys and reconfigures previous economic orders, but also that it must ceaselessly devalue existing wealth either through periodic economic crisis or otherwise in order to clear the ground for the creation of new wealth. The German Marxist sociologist, Wermer Sombart corroborated this and said, "from destruction, a new spirit of creation arises." Joseph Schumpeter popularised it and used it to describe the disruptive process of transformation that accompanies radical innovation. In Schumpeter's view, innovative entry by entrepreneurs was the force that sustained long-term economic growth, even as it destroyed the value of established companies and labourers that enjoyed some degree of monopoly power derived from previous technological, organisational, regulatory and economic paradigms.

A combination of autolysis and creative destruction is what has brought about what I call the theory of Creative Autolytic Destruction. This is a self-destruction that brings about a new creation of better life. It is an evolvement of new policies and programmes as new orders over the old ones to produce higher and better development. This definition is also biblically credited from the injunction that when you put the new wine into an old wine skin, it will burst. The old order must give way for the new order to be able to achieve effective sustenance. Though creative autolytic destruction can cause temporary economic distressor severe hardship in the short term, which is the price it carries, the economy will eventually generate new opportunities for workers or the citizenry to participate in more creative and productive enterprises. For example, it was reported that 90 per cent of Americans were farmers in 1790, and 2.6 per cent of Americans were farmers in 1990. Over the 200 years, farm jobs were destroyed by exponential productivity gains in agricultural technology and replaced by jobs in new industries. Present day farmers and non-farmers alike enjoy much more prosperous lifestyles than their counterparts in 1790.

The whole human society has been going through creative autolytic destruction in the process of development consciously and unconsciously from the beginning of creation to date. Various nations have been undergoing this process over time. Every epoch that gives way to another is a manifestation of creative autolytic destruction. The development process of Nigeria from pre-colonial time to date is the process of creative autolytic destruction. The various regimes from Governor General Nnamdi Azikiwe to President

Goodluck Jonathan has experienced creative autolytic destruction to come to the current stage of development. The downstream petroleum sector has been experiencing creative autolytic destruction. Corroborating the facts published by Punch Newspaper, fuel price has changed from one regime to another. Under the administration of General Yakubu Gowon (rtd), the fuel price was changed from about 3kobo to 6 kobo. Under Shehu Shagari, it was from about 9 kobo to 15 kobo. Under General Ibrahim Babangida (rtd), it was from 15 kobo to 70 kobo. Under Chief Shonekan, it was from 70 kobo to ₦5.00. Late General Sanni Abacha changed it from ₦5.00 to ₦11.00. General Abdulsalam Abubakar moved it from ₦11.00 to ₦20.00. President Olusegun Obasanjo moved it from ₦20.00 to ₦70.00. While late President Musa Yar'Adua moved it from ₦70.00 to ₦65.00, President Goodluck Jonathan moved it from ₦65.00 to ₦141.00. Other changes had occurred in various sectors in Nigeria over time. The educational system was changed from 7-5 system to 6-3-3 system. Reflect and you will be able to count many of such changes. The various changes in the price of fuel over the years were marked by different percentages. These changes were meant to usher in new life and better development based on the theory of creative autolytic destruction.

One of the major factors that makes creative autolytic destruction to succeed as a development paradigm is leadership trust. The electorate must trust the leadership. The current situation of the deregulation of the downstream petroleum sector should be weighed on the platform of creative autolytic destruction. The best way to assess a regime is to allow it to implement its policies. If the performance is less than the content of the policies, the electorate could hold the regime responsible for failure. But where there is no implementation of policies and programmes, there will be no basis for assessment. Besides, every regime should be evaluated on its own right. Every regime is different from the other. Every regime has its own vision. There will be a misjudgement in a situation where a preceding regime is used to judge the performance of its successor. In fact, such judgment is against the principle of creative autolytic destruction which even sees the preceding regime as inadequate to cope with the upcoming policies and programmes of the successor.

The key to successful development is Leadership Trust The initial agitations are natural and are expected in creative autolytic destruction process. But trust should neutralize the tension or pressure or uncertainties. The enzymes that are otherwise minded should embrace trust to prove the worth or reliability of the leadership. The opportunity to perform is enhanced by trust. The crisis of development in Nigeria will, therefore, become a thing of the past if this theory of creative autolytic destruction is understood, considered and applied. Development should, therefore, be understood as the effort of the people, promoted by government, in applying their creative energies to transformation of the local, physical, biological, socio-cultural, economic and political environments for their own betterment. **Dr. Emeje is Senior Assistant. Postmaster General and Head, Courier Regulatory Department of NIPOST**

The subsidy on our democracy

By Emmanuel Badejo

***The Guardian*, Monday, January 23, 2012, pg. 51**

"Sorrow, tears and blood"! President Goodluck Ebele Jonathan did a stealth act on Nigerians by removing alleged subsidy on fuel on January 1, 2012. Nigerians would have none of it! Certainly not at the beginning of a New Year in which they were trying to forget how the last one ended with Boko Haram mass-murders especially the bombing on Christmas Day of worshippers at St. Theresa Catholic Church Madala, Niger State. It was an insensitive move by government, worsened by woeful timing. The invectives poured on the president and his cabinet was so scathing that some state governors who were among the initiators of the removal of fuel subsidy, could not own up to their role in it. Angry Nigerians berated President Jonathan for his insensitivity, naivety and inexperience. Others regretted voting for him. Some even asked him to resign.

The Catholic Bishops Conference of Nigeria CBCN, which much earlier had asked government to be extremely careful with the removal of subsidy, disapproved of its style. The Conference acknowledged the eventual benefits of fuel subsidy removal, but questioned the timing, having listed a number of things which government should have done to pre-empt the pains of the decision. The action of the president gave good led labourers, professionals, academics, clergymen, politicians and even the unemployed masses to protest the decision! Then followed a gruelling week of fierce public discourse, crowded street protests at times accompanied by freestyle banditry and some hard negotiations! The president finally reduced fuel price. Labour and company called off the strike just as it went into the second week, ostensibly due to security concerns. By then some protesters had gone wild provoking damage and loss of lives. Such deaths, especially by the security forces, add to the long list of condemnable wastage of human lives and point to the weakened state of public order and security in Nigeria. The government put up a brave face but, any careful observer could see how unsettled it generally was, as it made far-reaching concessions to placate the public.

Yet, President Jonathan could still emerge Nigeria's "best President ever" for his brusque reawakening of the patriotic Nigerian in most of us. For too long, like zombies, we have wallowed in corruption-induced pacifism, hallucinatory complacency while claiming to be the most resilient people on earth. We celebrated the dubious honour of being the most religious people on earth, filling the mosques, churches and shrines on prayer days and then doing dirty business as usual. We tolerated just about anything, even the abuse of our rights and demeaning of our esteem by the very officials whom we armed and elected to defend and govern us. We wallowed in self-deceit, with the false hope that somehow, someday, something would change.

Yes indeed President Jonathan did us a favour. Once, when faced by some burning national issues, he told Nigerians that he could never be a "Lion President". Those who took his words for weakness were in for a rude shock!

Convinced that he was doing Nigeria a world of good by removing fuel subsidy the president proved tough as a nail. Who could have predicted that level of toughness from a man who in popular judgment had refused to be a lion against corruption? His stubbornness made Nigerians to realize even more how high their stakes in the democratic project really was. Many who would normally shrug off important national issues threw their hats in the ring. Oh, happy fault! By his mistake, President Jonathan forced Nigerians to speak in unison, probably as never before, against endemic national ills and insist on it. Comrade Abdulwaheed Omar, the NIC president may have been right in saying that no government would ever take Nigerians for granted again in policy implementation.

Indeed, more questions were asked and more answers proposed during the months of the Jonathan administration. So much "secret" data, figures and information about governance, which was uncovered, could never have been publicized in peace time, never mind the Freedom of Information Act. Nigerians put government under enough pressure to compel most government officials to actually work for the bizarre salaries they receive. Thank God for our "Lion President", public discourse has become far more participatory than ever before. Methinks that this is a democratic springtime to appreciate and uphold for accountability and integrity" in our country. Our democracy will not be productive without the active, responsible and selfless involvement of everyone though with diverse talents and competencies. We must change our lackadaisical attitude to public issues for nothing will positively change if we don't.

Meantime, the street battle has ended with all arms of government demonstrating uncharacteristic seriousness of purpose. Now we need selfless Nigerians to analyseand process the mass or information generated by this crisis so we can turn this knowledge into people power. Despite the sorrow, tears and blood, we may yet have good cause, I believe, to thank the man who removed the subsidy on our democratic participation, President Goodluck Ebele Azikiwe Jonathan. **Bishop Badejo is of the Catholic Diocese of Ovo**

Subsidy outside the neoliberal box

By Ayo Olukotun

***The Guardian*, Monday, February 6, 2012, pg. 52**

A nation cannot be delivered from political and social afflictions outside of its ability to conceptualise and contextualise her problems and come up with ingenious solutions to them. The policy universe in this country is dominated by neoliberalism which in its globalised form privileges an unrestrained free market and the nostrums of the Washington Consensus. Never mind that as one scholar has famously quipped there is no longer any consensual support for the Washington Consensus even in Washington itself and that influential mainstream economists such as apostate World Bank chief economist Joseph Stiglitz as well as Dani Rodrick have openly challenged the key assumptions of neoliberalism.

In the aftermath of the traumatising alleged subsidy removal and the accompanying volcanic protests, it is urgent that we begin to interrogate the policy arena and ask why it has become a pitiful clone of the jaded economic ideology imposed by the IMF, the World Bank and other international financial institutions often with disastrous results on the developing economies. Anyone in doubt of the preceding statement should merely recall the woes of neoliberalism in Pinochet's Chile when the Chicago School of Economics turned the country into a seminal experimental ground for their mathematical models as wen as the virtual destruction of the Bolivian mining economy under the so-called expert tutelage of Prof. Jeffrey Sachs who along with Prof. Paul Collier of Oxford University have offered intellectual support for the removal of the phantom petroleum subsidy in Nigeria.

Of course Nigeria lacks a political class with a national project while the country itself under the assault of centrifugal forces is better considered more of a market than a nation; if it were otherwise it ought to have been possible for such a class to avail itself of a policy document such as the African Alternative to Structural Adjustment Policy whose guiding inspiration was Nigeria's Professor Adebayo Adedeji who is living in dignified retirement in Ijebu-Ode. That document pinpoints the harshly inappropriate nature of the neoliberal paradigm for African countries and comes up with several policy suggestions for charting a gender and kinder roadmap out of the woods of underdevelopment. That apart, it is remarkable that the Nigerian ruling class perhaps out of intellectual laziness is unwilling to engineer policies outside of the controversial neoliberal straitjacket in spite of the proven deleterious effects of these policies especially on the poor and the disappearing middle class. Why is it for example that as a nation we are not interested in the exciting developments on the Latin American continent where a clutch of left leaning governments have been voted into power featuring a fair share of female presidents with many of them speaking and acting boldly against neo-imperialism and neoliberalism?

Take for example the oil producing country of Venezuela where the leftist government of Hugo Chaves is concluding its second term in office this year; the country boasts of close to 40 refineries, it is an exporter of crude to Nigeria's Kaduna refinery and has not increased oil price since Chaves came to power in 1999. Notwithstanding Chaves' demonisation by the western media as a demagogue, Venezuela's leader has made a clear dent on poverty in his country through such programmes as free higher education to two million adult citizens, mounting a programme of remedial education for over four million school dropouts, the provision of sundry medical clinics targeted at the poor as well as the grants of food and housing subsidies for socially excluded Venezuelans among other initiatives along the lines of social and economic transformation. Internationally and in the context of what has been described as a pink tide involving other socialist governments such as Brazil, Bolivia, Ecuador and Nicaragua among others, Venezuela using oil resources is midwifing a Bank of the South projected as an alternative to the IMF and the World Bank whose policies are considered extremely harmful for the developing countries. Interestingly, the wave of pro-poor reforms in Latin American is coming after the wasted decades of the 80s and 90s in which neoliberalism severely eroded and sapped the economic potential of many Latin American countries; indeed the ascendancy electorally of leftist governments on that continent is directly traceable to the extremely poor showing of neoliberal economic prescriptions with their fallouts of growing squalor.

Nigeria does not have to follow the contemporary Latin American path to development but it certainly needs to broaden its policy and ideological purview beyond the current one- dimensional fixation on the discredited Washington Consensus which even former British Prime Minister Gordon Brown described at a G20 meeting in 2009 as effectively dead. For this to happen we must encourage unconventional thoughts and intellectuals who are Nigerians and stop relying on foreign experts and consultants who if their advice leads to disasters simply move on to the next consulting job leaving the country to bemoan its tragedy. Part of the problem is that Nigerian leaders have become more steadily anti-intellectual overtime and as a consequence are easily awed by the prestige of international experts forgetting that expertise is often not a neutral technocratic activity but an ideology in the service of hegemonic interests. Indeed, the concept of counter expert which consciously opposes itself to receive knowledge suggests the imperative of rigorously interrogating established authorities especially in the context of subalterns or victims of the global neo-imperial order such as Nigeria is. An illustration of this hypothesis is provided anecdotally in an account of a meeting between World Bank experts and the ANC government in South Africa. As a participant from the ANC reported it: "Each time we made a suggestion the World Bank experts would open their laptops and predict its negative effect on the economy; shake their heads and blow us away". This by no means apocryphal story points up the difficulty of arguing or debating with experts who respond to every challenge to their knowledge base by referring to their established profiles. One encounters this kind of dogmatism in the cock sure and know it all approaches of Prof. Paul Collier and Jeffrey Sachs in their analysis of the effect of the removal of the alleged subsidy on the poor in Nigeria. As many have observed there is no shred of truth in their interpretation that it is the rich rather than the poor that benefits from relatively low petroleum prices in a country where basic infrastructure and social safety nets are tragically absent or exist only in the most rudimentary forms.

True, corruption on a monumental scale, mediocrity of vision and the paucity of reliable data on such basic things as the volume of petrol consumed in Nigeria are very much part of our governance woes as we are learning from the ongoing legislative probes of the subsidy racket. Beyond that however and in the context of the Jonathan government's promise to transform the economy even if that promise leaves unanswered the question of transforming from what to what, there is a need for our leaders across the political parties to broaden their ken by entertaining development alternatives beyond those prescribed by international financial institutions and their acclaimed technocrats. Our universities, think-tanks and policy research institutes in spite of their well-known disabilities can catalyse this process of reformulation by tilting the current debate on governance options in the directions suggested above. **Olukotun is a Professor of Political Science at Lead City University, Ibadan.**

Subsidy removal crisis in perspective (1)

By Bukar Usman

***The Guardian*, Wednesday, February 1, 2012, pg. 51**

The most surprising thing about the wholesale fuel subsidy removal announced by the Petroleum Products Pricing Regulatory Agency (PPPRA) on January 1, 2012, was that it was contemplated at all. The second surprising aspect of the entire drama was that the removal became so urgent a policy thrust that development could not wait for the year-end holiday season to pass but was compelled to announce it on New Year day! This overview, in appraising the many issues thrown up by the crisis, hopes to identify policy areas which require urgent attention to ensure that the gains of the crisis are maximized for the benefit of the people. From about ₦141 per litre pegged by the PPPRA on January 1, 2012 (thereby abolishing the then prevailing price of ₦65 per litre), the pump price of "petrol" was reduced by President Goodluck Jonathan, 15 days later, to ₦97 per litre. It was a welcome relief, al-though none of the nationwide protesters was relieved enough to thank the president or the labour leaders who capitulated without achieving the set goal of making government revert to ₦65 per litre.

Indeed, many protesters were disappointed by the Nigeria Labour Congress and the Trade Union Congress (NLC/RJC) decision to call off the strike. Their explanation that they would

press further for their demands to be fully met through the forum of the committee chaired by former Chief Justice of Nigeria, Justice Alfa Belgore, impressed very few people.

I think both government and the protesters should take solace in the fact that each side got 50% of what they had wanted. But beyond this compromise is the floodgate of open enquiries into the hitherto secretive goings-on in the downstream sector of the petroleum industry. This, for me, far more than the "palliatives" and the Subsidy Reinvestment and Empowerment programme (SURE), is the greatest achievement of the mass protests. And I hope the enquiries, especially that of the House of Representatives committee chaired by Hon. Lawan, should be carried out to its logical conclusion and the findings made public.

The public began it all and deserves to know the findings unearthed by its representatives. While it was labour which initiated the protest, it developed into a mass protest as non-wage earners equally participated while other interest groups expressed solidarity with the labour cause. Some saw the protest as their round of "harmattan" protest akin to the "Arab spring."

Such was the far-reaching impact of the protest! It afforded Nigerians the opportunity to vent their pent-up feelings and for government to feel the pulse of the people from whom it appeared to have alarmingly drifted within so short a time after the general elections. Otherwise, how did a civilian administration imagine it would succeed in pushing through a one-time, wholesale removal of fuel subsidy, a long-standing temptation even past military administrations were sensitive enough to avoid? It was mere upward adjustments of the pump price of "petrol" that elicited serious protests in the past. What made the state and federal governments appear so insensitive this time around?

The question is: what pushed us to this subsidy removal crisis. Looking back at the road leading to the fuel subsidy removal policy would help us understand where we are coming from and where we might be headed. It has become even more compelling to so reflect in view of the recent accusations and counter accusations as to who was responsible for the policy. For sure, it was a government decision and not an individual's. But that would not explain it all. How the idea of subsidy removal come about; and now did it crystallise as a compelling policy of government?

Before the subsidy removal, government had dropped the hint of its intention to remove fuel subsidy, estimated at ₦13 trillion for the period January-August, 2011. It followed up by entering into discussion with various interest groups, including Labour which quickly indicated its intention to oppose it. Socialist-oriented, Labour had taken such principled stand over the Structural Adjustment Programme (SAP) and the on-going deregulation of public enterprises.

The first hint that government was determined to remove fuel subsidy emerged when it submitted to the National Assembly the 2012 national budget without making any provision for the subsidy. This put Labour, the civil society and, indeed, the entire nation on the alert. But since government gave the impression that it was committed to its on-going consultation with interest groups on the matter, all adopted a wait-and-see approach. Following the decision to raise the national minimum wage to ₦18, 000 per month, about the middle of 2011, state governors, fresh from elections, raised issues with the federal government about their inability to meet up with the financial burden of the new wage bill. They asked for an upward review of the revenue allocation formula or some other source of money to augment their revenue.

They also raised issues about "illegal" deductions from what was due to them from the Federation Account and, in protest, refused to come forward to collect their regular allocations on at least two occasions. They further objected to the Excess Crude Account (ECA) and the Sovereign Wealth Fund (SWF) which affected the quantum of money in the Federation Account available for distribution to all tiers of government.

With some dialogue, the governors somehow patched up their differences with the federal government. The SWF which was already signed into law would stand while money in ECA would be transferred into the SWF after some were released to the states. In effect, ECA gave way to the SWF with hopes raised about more money coming from the fuel subsidy removal. Meanwhile, the implementation of the minimum wage was stalled, with some states making some token gestures, here and there, amidst threats by the labour unions to embark on strikes to back up their demand for immediate implementation.

All these took place under the tense atmosphere of continual Boko Haram attacks in some parts of the federation, resulting into massive destruction of lives and properties. There was widespread panic when the group ordered some religious groups to relocate from their normal places of abode. Towards managing the crisis, government announced the imposition of state of emergency in some affected local government areas in Bomo, Yobe, Plateau, and Niger states.

It was against this background that the public received the shocking announcement on January 1, 2012, that fuel subsidy had been removed. Most Nigerians were still in holiday mood and had travelled to various places for the holidays. Suddenly their calculations for the cost of their return journey to their destinations were thrown into disarray as prices of goods and services immediately shot up, with some prices doubled or tripled to match the percentage of the subsidy removal.

Labour was immediately up in arms. Within a few days, it put its scheme in place and commenced strike with effect from Monday January 9, 2012. As at January 14, the strike had entered its 5th day with government and labour yet to arrive at an amicable solution. The Senate President, Senator David Mark, turned out to be the honest broker between the executive arms of government and labour while the president walked a tight rope ensuring that he carried the governors, the formidable power brokers and international creditors who favoured zero subsidies, along.

The protests and measures taken by government to forestall or abort the labour-led mass protests brought out the worst and the best in both parties. That government waited till Friday to move an ex parte motion leading to the National Industrial Court order stopping a strike that was scheduled to start on Monday was very curious, to say the least. Conveniently, too, labour claimed not to have been served with the order, and went ahead with the strike.

The use of the security agencies, particularly the police, resulting into deaths, here and there, inflamed the situation. In some states, curfews were imposed to check violence. Public servants were ordered to resume work or lose pay. Labour replied with "work-to- rule" threat.

Having come under heavy barrage of protests against what had turned out to be an unpopular policy, government officials embarked on the blame game. The Minister of Finance and Coordinating Minister of the Economy, Mrs Okonjo-Iweala, tried to absolve herself, stating that the decision to remove oil subsidy was taken before her arrival into the country. She pointed to the state governors as being the catalysts. Governor Babangida Aliyu of Niger State, on his part, kicked the blame ball in the direction of the Governor of Central Bank, Sanusi Lamido Sanusi. Some ministers placed the burden on the Minister of Petroleum Resources, Mrs Alison-Madueke, who was alleged to have given the final directive to PPPRA to make the subsidy removal announcement on New Year eve. The Petroleum Minister maintained that it was a "collective decision," in other words, the collective responsibility of the federal executive council members. **Usman, retired federal permanent secretary in the Presidency, lives in Abuja**

Subsidy removal crisis in perspective (2)

By Bukar Usman

***The Guardian*, Thursday, February 2, 2012, pg. 68**

There were also denials over accusations that, in removing the oil subsidy, government were merely implementing World Bank/IMF programme. The visit of the IMF Managing Director to the country shortly before Nigeria took the final decision on the subsidy removal tended to lend credence to this belief. But Izielen Agbon, in his article, "IMF and 'Fuel Subsidy* Removal" (*The Guardian*, January 12/13, 2012), amply traced the conception and crystallisation of the fuel subsidy removal policy to documents prepared by high- ranking IMF officials dating back to 2002.

Some of the documents include IMF Working Papers 02/140, 03/42, 06/247, 07/71, IMF Public Information Notice (PIN) No.08/135 and IMF Staff Position Note 10/05 all of which were debated in Washington and at the G-20 meeting before adoption as a policy for implementation.

Reportedly, in IMF Public Information Notice (PIN) No. 08/135 of October 10, 2008, the IMF and World Bank pushed for the adoption of their fuel subsidy removal policies in the September 2009 G-20 leaders meeting in Pittsburgh, USA. The G-20 supported fuel subsidy removal worldwide, calling on the International Energy Agency (IEA), Organisation for Petroleum Exporting Countries (OPEC), Organisation for Economic Cooperation and Development (OECD) and the World Bank to provide an analysis on the scope of the energy subsidies and suggestions for the implementation of the initiative.

To advance their price-gap methodology campaign, and using Nigeria as a test case, IMF officials, as far back as 2003, prepared a paper which developed policies "to stop any strong protest and social unrest after subsidy removal. Further IMF policy papers developed similar strategies aimed at selling the bitter pill to make it palatable for interest groups to swallow.

Agbon, earlier mentioned, had pointed out that "in 2011, the Federal Ministry of Finance carried out a review of the economy based on the IMF price-gap methodology. The Federal Government insisted that the fuel subsidies must be passed on to the consumers. It advocated fuel subsidy removal and the implementation of the IMF plan." Part of the IMF plan was the necessity of a proper management of the pre- and post-subsidy removal publicity. It was apparently that plan which inspired the various publicity stunts generated by the NNPC, the Ministry of Petroleum Resources, the Federal Ministry of Information, state governors and establishment NGOs.

According to Agbon's research, even the much- promoted Subsidy Reinvestment and Expenditure Programme (SURE) of the federal government was not home-grown. It was IMF-inspired. For sure, SURE shares the same origin as the Structural Adjustment Programme (SAP), Millennium Development Goals

(MDGs), and the SWF. Such terminologies point to their external roots in today's global village in which some transnational organisations and foreign powers lord it over others. SWF and the fuel subsidy removal especially are programmes primarily targeted at OPEC member countries to recycle their enormous petro-dollar, a task OECD was charged with by the West since the energy crisis of1973.

It could be seen that the formulation and implementation of fuel-subsidy removal was scripted over a long period of time at the IMF and in Nigeria. Considering her exalted position in the World Bank, a major player with the IMF in shaping the economies of developing countries and the world, it would be difficult to accept Mrs Okonjo-Iweala's claim that she had no prior knowledge of the policy or that the IMF has no connection with it.

It was a well-packaged policy which was poorly executed because the product was unsalable. If subsidy-removal as a concept is such a worthwhile policy, why are some developed countries, notable for administering heavy subsidies to their people, not adopting it even when such countries are currently known to be facing serious budget deficits? Some of those countries for decades subsidised farm products, such as wheat and butter, and are still doing so with no sign of discontinuing.

If you discount the corruption which bloated the actual subsidy amount, fuel subsidy may not be the heavy burden the government wants Nigerians to believe it is. Since government has traced this corruption to "a cabal," why should it, rather than deal with the "cabal" and their official collaborators, toe the line of least resistance by depriving Nigerians the subsidy they rightly feel entitled to? The people are not convinced that if the regular annual budgets of the federal, state and local governments had not appreciably delivered jobs and social amenities, denying them oil subsidy would make these governments overcome corruption and do more.

From the pieces of information passed through internet social media during the protests, corruption emerged as the number one problem, not oil subsidy. Unlike past protests against fuel price increases, social media was fully utilised by the intelligentsia, the political elite, civil society, opinion-moulders and Nigerians abroad to exchange information and effectively mobilise public opinion.

The CBN Governor's position, which was well articulated and freely circulated in the internet, cuts both ways to the cause of the subsidy removal policy. It made a strong case for subsidy removal while throwing up issues of monumental fraud, thereby making many to believe that government did not do enough to check glaring abuses in the disbursement of the funds. How aid ₦246 billion subsidy budget for 2011 rise to ₦13 trillion within eight months when the annual average for preceding years was at worst ₦400 billion? That was and still remains the big question yet to be answered. Could we not have cut down such wastages and the enormous perks of public officers before embarking on subsidy removal?

The circulation of the list of beneficiary organisations, which list was associated with who's who in the society, merely compounded the situation, as it made people to make insinuations and resolve that before we could proceed any further there is need to first sort out the rot so that the sacrifices the generality of Nigerians are being asked to make could be justifiable and better appreciated. Even now, government needs to reassure people by indicating on project-by-project basis how the "subsidy" removed would be applied, as the public remains highly sceptical and do not seem ready to give a blank cheque.

In summary, the agenda for items requiring government attention may be short but critical as it includes looking into financial leakages in the NNPC and the maritime industry, perks of public officers, corruption, devolution of powers, review of the revenue sharing formula, and internal security without which the SURE programmes cannot even be implemented. It is advisable for the authorities to quickly sort out these issues for the genuine transformation of our beloved country. **Usman, retired federal permanent secretary in the presidency lives in Abuja.**

Subsidy Scam: How Saraki's motion opened Pandora box

By Davidson Iriekpe.

***ThisDay*, Friday, January 27, 2012, vol. 17, no. 6122, pg.17**

The strike and protests that greeted the removal of petrol subsidy by the Federal Government might have come and gone but it was perhaps an opportunity to engage in a post mortem reflection on the unfortunate saga with a view to extricating useful lessons.

The nationwide strike, which witnessed street protests of a disturbing kind, was primarily intended to register the Nigerians' displeasure over removal of subsidy on Premium Motor Spirit (PMS) otherwise known as petrol by the Federal Government. From the pump price of ₦65 per litre, the commodity officially sold at ₦141 per litre while Nigerians in some parts of the country spent between ₦250 and ₦300 to buy a litre of petrol on account of the artificial scarcity created by marketers.

To many observers, the success or otherwise of the just suspended strike action does not lie in the concession labour was able to secure from government which came down from ₦141 to ₦97 per litre but rather the exposition of the high level of corruption and sleaze that characterise the operations of oil and gas industry in Nigeria. Following the expositions and demands of labour, government has committed itself to probing the monumental fraud unearthed in the fuel subsidy regime and sanitising the oil and gas sector to ensure probity and transparency in the management of the industry.

With this development, Nigerians are eagerly looking forward to a forensic investigation of the subsidy fraud and the entire gamut of the oil and gas sector as promised by President Goodluck Jonathan and the prosecution of members of the cartel that fed fat on the nation. Indeed, the one-week strike action by labour and civil society groups has thrown up many issues which are expected to be squarely tackled if Nigeria must make any headway as a nation.

The week-long protest has put Nigeria's government under more pressure to make real its long-unfulfilled promises to reform its inefficient and corrupt energy sector. This includes the assurance to implement the KPMG audit report engineered by the Minister of Petroleum Resources, Diezani Alison-Madueke.

For many Nigerians, one issue that kept reverberating during the protests against the removal of fuel subsidy was the need for the Federal Government to tackle the menace of corruption head on if the country is to ever move forward. For^ them, they don't understand why President Goodluck Jonathan-fed administration lacks the courage or political will to tackle hydra-headed malaise that has eaten deep into the country's foundation.

Speakers upon speakers who mounted the podium to speak at the various rallies held across the country either lambasted the president for allegedly lacking the courage to arrest and prosecute those who have been looting the country dry or accused of complicity. Most of the speakers, particularly those at the Lagos rallies all themselves adorned T-shirts with the inscription: "Kill Corruption Not Nigerians."

Even the ordinary man on the street knows that nothing works in the country because of the corruption in high places. To them, that these people still walk the length and breadth of the country displaying their ill-gotten wealth is provocative. What really fuelled the protests was the revelation that the government spent N1.3 trillion on fuel subsidy in 2011 when only N240 billion was the actual amount budgeted for the project in the 2011 Appropriation Act. The difference would have gone a long way in fixing the country's dilapidated infrastructure. And yet, nobody was told how this came to be.

However, not many Nigerians would remember that it was the former Governor of Kwara State, Dr. Bukola Saraki, that actually blew up the sleaze in the fuel subsidy regime when he sponsored a motion in the Senate, calling for an investigation into the management of petroleum subsidy in the 2011 budget. Saraki, who is currently representing Kwara Central senatorial district in the Upper House, was merely acting pursuant to Sections 88 and 89 of the 1999 Constitution, which empower any chamber of the National Assembly to probe any sector of the nation's economy, with a view to exposing corruption and waste of public funds.

For those who followed the debate on fuel subsidy removal then, the Federal Government had been inundated with calls to institute a probe into the activities and operations of the Nigerian National Petroleum Corporation (NNPC). The calls were predicated on the fact that nobody knew the exact amount the country was earning from the sale of crude oil. Every attempt to know this had often been frustrated through alleged manipulation. Knowing the consequences of conducting such a probe, each time the calls came, those who think that such action was targeted at them would do everything to frustrate it.

But Saraki decided to take the bull by the horns in his motion by seeking Senate's permission to set up a committee to investigate how the funds were sourced, saying he feared it might have been misappropriated. He further expressed worry that during the first three months of the year, both NNPC and independent oil marketers did not exceed ₦62 billion monthly, but wondered that within July and September 2011, figures had ranged between ₦159 billon and N186 billion.

The motion, which instantly generated interests on account of its timeliness and importance then, was uncertain if it would see the light of day following allegations that some powerful business and political interests who benefited from the opaque management of fuel subsidy infiltrated the National Assembly to stop it from seeing the light of day. For about five weeks, the motion was listed for consideration but unfortunately, like a plague, each time; it was carefully dropped and avoided under one pretext or the other.

As the debate opened, most senators commended Saraki for the motion. For those who sought to know the motive, the senator representing Kwara Central explained that the fuel subsidy was becoming a fraud which needed to be looked into. According to him, so much had been spent on subsidy without tangible results. In the motion, the former governor noted that he was propelled by the need to make fuel subsidy scheme more transparent, corruption-free and competitive within an appropriate legislative framework and in compliance with the Appropriation Act.

He noted that ₦240 billion was appropriated in the 2011 budget to implement fuel subsidy. He said of the ₦20 billion monthly allocations, ₦11.2 billion was approved for domestic fuel subsidy while ₦8.8 billion was for domestic fuel subsidy (market) as stated in the Appropriation Act. Stressing the need to make the scheme more transparent and competitive within an appropriate legislative framework, he noted that although ₦20 billion was set aside for subsidy on monthly basis in the budget, in August 2011, ₦165 billion was expended of which the amount for NNPC was ₦88 billion and independent marketers, ₦77.7billion.

The former governor observed that as at the end of August 2011, ₦931 billion had been spent, although ₦240 billion was budgeted for the entire year. This he said was ₦771 billion or 700 per cent above the budget. He was worried that in the first three months of 2011, NNPC and independent marketers did not exceed ₦62 billion monthly expenditure but by July and September, the figures were between ₦150 billion and ₦186 billion.

According to him, going by this trend, by the end of 2011, the nation would have a fuel subsidy bill of over ₦1.3 trillion as against the ₦240 billion budgeted in the Appropriation Act. This expenditure would be treated as a first line charge and the implication, according to Saraki, would be that "all other expenditures including capital expenditure and even distributions to the states and local councils, which we represent, is secondary."

He contended that the implementation of 2011 Budget would run into troubled waters if a variation of ₦1.3 trillion arises as a result of the expenditure incurred on fuel subsidy so far. He noted that while the National Assembly, spent time to conclude a capital budget of ₦1.1 trillion, one agency of government could incur the same amount without approval of the lawmakers. This he said posed a challenge and an urgent need to review the subsidy scheme, noting that otherwise, the implementation of the 2011 budget would be hampered.

The former governor had barely finished his explanation when it struck his colleagues that a strong cartel was milking the nation dry of its hard-earned revenue through the fuel subsidy policy of the Federal Government. They all commended him and agreed with him that the management of fuel subsidy had been shrouded in secrecy and that it was time to carry out an inquest on the matter.

In unison, the senators directed the Senate Committees on Petroleum Resources (Downstream), Appropriation and Finance to investigate the fuel subsidy scheme.

Many analysts believe that in what has turned out to be a vindication for Saraki, his innocuous motion has thrown up a lot of issues leading to probes by the House of Representatives and the Economic and Financial Crimes Commission (EFCC). From the testimonies of stakeholders at the public hearing by the House on fuel subsidy, not only are Nigerians inundated with damning revelations, more questions have remained unanswered. It also signposts the obvious disarray in the management of the nation's petroleum sector.

Even the proceedings of the ad-hoc committee have revealed quite disappointingly, that the long spell of direct headship of the Ministry of Petroleum Resources by presidents led the NNPC to exploit the resultant close working relationship with the number one citizen to avoid observing due process. It also revealed that the degree of manipulation and level of sharp practices over petrol subsidy, which appears to be officially engineered are altogether appalling. The Executive Secretary of the PPPRA, Reginald Stanley, testified before the ad-hoc committee that the volume of petrol imported per day in 2011 was approximately 59 million litres. The figure has been faulted. The Central Bank of Nigeria (CBN) added more to the revelations when it disclosed that it was ₦1.7 trillion that was expended on the subsidy and not the bandied ₦1.3 trillion.

While speaking to journalists in in Calabar, Cross River State last weekend, Senate Majority Leader, Senator Victor Ndoma-Egba, acknowledged that Saraki's motion on the fuel subsidy regime, exposed the graft in the industry. He promised that the Upper House had committed itself to working with the executive arm of government to wage war against the worrisome corruption in the oil sector. Ndoma-Egba said the lawmakers had already demonstrated their resolve to move against corruption by asking the EFCC to probe the alleged mismanagement of fuel subsidy funds and endemic corruption in the oil sector. He added that since the oil sector was very critical to the Nigerian economy, the Upper House felt that it was imperative to sanitise it by asking the EFCC to check the questionable activities of all the stakeholders.

"Every year, they exhaust their recurrent budget but they never get up to 30 per cent of capital budget which is always less than 30 per cent of the yearly budget. We debated the motion that was brought by Senator Bukola Saraki about the management of the subsidy regime and one of the calls was for the EFCC to investigate the management of the subsidy regime.

"There must be a comprehensive audit of the subsidy regime. As a Senate, we are committed to seeing the oil sector becoming more transparent because it is the most critical of all sectors. We are committed to a more accountable oil sector in the country. The current situation where nobody gets to know what is happening there is unacceptable," he said.

Former NUPENG president opposes proposed policy

From AlemmaOziomvaAliu, Benin City

***The Guardian*, Tuesday, October 11, 2011, pg. 48**

THE FORMER president of the National Union of Petroleum and Natural Gas Workers (NUPENG) and now a member of the House of Representatives, Peter Akpattasson over the weekend in Benin City expressed his opposition to the planed removal of fuel subsidy by the Federal Government.

He said if implemented, the removal of fuel subsidy would lead to "inflation, penury, poverty, crisis and violence." Instead, Akpattasson said the Federal Government should embark on a phased removal of fuel subsidy and then liberalisation of the sector and full commercialisation of the Nigerian National Petroleum Corporation (NNPC). He spoke to journalists at the Benin Airport over the weekend.

"Liberalisation is good what is important is to make sure that NNPC as a government representative in the industry should be fully commercialised and should operate as a commercial business entity fully funded for a take off so that it can operate as a separate entity that does not have to wait for politicians before business decisions are taken. In such a way, it will now be in a position to compete with other private investors in the industry and then at that point, refineries will spring up, our local refining capacity will increase because NNPC will not be their regulator, will not be their monitor but a competitor, a more efficient organisation and that is provided for in the Petroleum Industry Bill. If only they can wait for expediting the passage of the bill to create the enabling environment for competition, for commercialisation for effective takeoff of whatever policy they then propose." The lawmaker representing Akoko Edo Federal

Constituency under the platform of the Action Congress of Nigeria (CAN) also insisted that organised labour has not sold out on their stance in the proposal of government. "I have been in this struggle for a long time and our position has not changed, if it has changed, I will find out. The position has always been that there are conditions before deregulation and those conditions have to be achieved before you deregulate. I will personally subscribe to a phased removal after attaining some level of competition."

He said the timing for the planned removal of the subsidy was wrong because the right investment climate in the sector that would help regulate pricing "Liberalisation is good, what is important is to make sure that NNPC as a government representative in the industry should be fully commercialised and should operate as a commercial business entity fully funded for a take-off so that it can operate as a separate entity that does not have to wait for politicians before business decisions are taken. In such a way, it will now be in a position to compete with other private investors in the industry and then at that point, refineries will spring up, our local refining capacity will increase because NNPC will not be their regulator, will not be their monitor but a competitor, a more efficient organisation and that is provided for in the Petroleum industry Bill" has not been created.

"What is important at this point in time is to start working towards achieving such economic environment where the level of manipulation will be curtailed, where investors will be encouraged to come in and set up refineries and it is important that why doing this, plans should be on to investigate those shortcomings that have been identified in the present regime of subsidy. As they are complaining now that this money is not getting to the right people, why is it not getting there? Deal with those who are manipulating the process and until that is done; it is totally uncalled for, for anybody to insist on removing fuel subsidy. Secondly, the argument that the money will be used for development is not tenable because over the years, they've been telling us this same story all the way from the time of Abacha that if they increase generated will be used to build schools, roads all the rest of them, the whole thing has turned like the magic year 2000 where we expected that we will become adequate in health, in education and everything but look at where we are. The same thing will happen when they remove subsidy and there will be high inflation, which will make life unbearable for Nigerians, which will reduce the already abysmally low purchasing power of the ordinary Nigerian."

Good fate for the PIB

By Charles Soeze

***The Guardian*, Thursday, January 19, 2012 pg. 52**

Now that the federal legislators have finally agreed to pass IN the Petroleum Industry Bill (PIB), one can boldly and proudly say that there is now good fate for the PIB which would e for the benefits of all Nigerians. In the past, the PIB suffered from legislative delays and special attention from the relevant authorities to make it a reality. Since the importance of the bill has received or arrested the attention of the lawmakers, it may be appropriate to say 'kudos' to all Nigerians and other well- wishers internationally.

It is obvious that the PIB is mainly to increase government revenue with minimal or no extra expenditure. In the words of Dapo Falade in the Nigerian Tribune of Friday, October 28,2011 ' page 28, "Among the fundamental objectives of the bill is the vesting of petroleum and natural gas, in property and sovereign ownership of petroleum within Nigeria, its territorial waters, the continental shelf, the Exclusive Economic Zone and the extended continental shelf shall vest in the Nigeria for and on behalf of Nigerians; and allocations of acreage, licence, lease or contract for the exploration and production of petroleum to any qualified company under terms and conditions prescribed from, time to time by the relevant institutions."

Whatever the case may be, the PIB is mainly to increase government revenue with minimal or no extra expenditure. In the words of an oil administrator cum technocrat and one-time oil Minister, Alhaji (Dr.) Rilwanu Lukman, "The PIB represents the largest overhaul of the government Petroleum revenue system in the last four decades through four control objectives, to simplify the collection of government revenue; to cream off windfall profits in case of high oil prices; to collect more revenues from large profitable field in the deep offshore waters; and finally to create Nigerian employment and business opportunities by encouraging investment in small oil and gas fields. As a result, the willingness of the legislation to pass the proposed bill soonest possible should be seen as a welcome rarity because it would place Nigeria in putting oil affairs in the current and national perspectives. A careful study of the bill reveals at a glance that it establishes the legal and regulatory framework, institutions and regulatory authorities for the Nigerian Petroleum Industry (NPI). It went on to stipulate guidelines for operations in the upstream, midstream, and downstream sectors and for other purposes relevant to same.

With the PIB in place, the texts of all licences, leases and contracts and any of the changes that got such documents will no longer be confidential. I think that was why the Minister bellowed "Nigeria will move in one step from one of the most opaque petroleum nations in Africa, to one of the most open and transparent in the world". This is because payments to the government of Nigeria will be through public information. It will not be through secret or hidden agenda.

According to President Umaru Musa Yar'Adua (of blessed memory) the Bill will form foundation for a revival of an industry where attacks on pipelines and constraints on investment have fuelled a growing sense of crises among energy outfits. It is flabbergasting to say that the executives, from Nigeria's biggest producers, which include Exxon Mobil, Royal Dutch Shell, Total and Chevron, said the prepared new terms were so stringent that they risked deterring investment rather than encouraging it. Where do we go from here, according to a popular musician? Happily, it is pertinent to state that the Bill would definitely inject new vigour in the NNPC by reforming its opaque, octopus like structure to create discrete units to handle essential tasks based on training, professionalism and experience (putting federal character principle in oblivion) such as exploration and production, regulation and research. From my own point of view, the PIB would restructure joint ventures between the NNPC and Western majors to allow them to raise private capital, rather than rely on a notoriously unreliable injection of cash from Nigeria's government at the expense of poor, frustrating and worried Nigerians who are living under hard economic conditions, in other words, abject poverty.

Furthermore, the benefits of the bill include making the government to increase its take from a growing number of deep- water developments. Review of the royalties on gas by creating a new fiscal regime separate from rules governing oil. Changes to the way tax breaks are applied for new developments. To this end therefore, oil companies will be encouraged to refine at least 50 per cent of their production in Nigeria by the end of the decade, and in addition, new rules to boost employment of Nigerians in the oil industry will take effect The issue of incentives to encourage development of marginal fields as well as improve community programmes in the Niger Delta region, the goose that lays the golden eggs.

Importantly, the PIB would restructure, repackage and revolutionise the oil industry in a system that would guarantee more returns on investment for Nigeria, which currently relies immensely on oil for 90 per cent of its foreign exchange earnings. The Bill combines sixteen (16) different Nigerian Petroleum Laws like the existing legislations as the Petroleum Act 1969; the Petroleum Profits Act 1959 and the Nigerian Petroleum Corporation Act of 1977. Other existing laws to be affected include the Petroleum Profit Tax (PPT) Act of 1959; the Petroleum Act 1969; the Petroleum Technology Development Act 1973; theAssociated Gas Re-injection Act 1979; the Petroleum Equalization Fund Act 1989; the Oil Pipelines Act 1990; the Nigerian National Petroleum Act 1997; and the Petroleum Products Pricing Regulatory Agency Act2003. The Oil Producing Trade Section (OPTS) which made a submission before the Senate public hearing in July 2009 also highlighted the importance and fate of the Bill.

Writing on 'What Fate Awaits the Petroleum Industry in the *ThisDay* newspaper of Sunday, October 30, 2011 page 109, Mr. Onwuka Nzeshi, traced the journey of the bill through the sixth session of the parliament. According to him, the petroleum industry Bill was one of the most important, yet controversial that was presented during the sixth session of the National Assembly. His words, "The much politicised bill is geared towards enhancing greater transparency and accountability in oil and gas industry in Nigeria. It seeks to introduce a wide range of reforms in the petroleum sector and evolve a set of new regulations to govern the operations of oil companies, local and foreign, doing business in the country. It was introduced by the government on the premise that the existing laws in the sector were old, archaic and had undermined transparency and accountability in the sector for several decades."

Interestingly, the Minister of Petroleum Resources, Mrs. Diezani Allison-Madueke, sometime acknowledged that the signing of the Bill into law will move Nigerian businessmen and women into the commanding heights of the oil and gas industry, while the oil bearing communities could attract incentives as much as $1.1 billion from oil revenue if the law comes into effect. What a bonanza and improvement on the standard of living of Nigerians! She specifically pointed out that the Nigeria's annual oil revenue is expected to rise to about $680 billion when the Petroleum Industry Bill is passed into law. Another bonanza for Nigeria, Nigerians indeed!

Finally, as part of efforts to boost the activities of the oil industry, the Bill should be passed without further delay to give the NNPC (currently funded by the government) the opportunities to create a viable and self-financing oil companies for the good and betterment of all Nigerians.

Soeze is a Mass Communications Scholar cum Professional Public Relations Practitioner and Head, Academic and Physical Planning; (A&PP) of the Petroleum Training Institute (PTI), Effurun, Delta State.

Imperative of incorporating costing capacity in subsidy re-investment

By AgeleAlufohai

***ThisDay*, Wednesday, January 25, 2012, vol.17, no. 6120, pg. 37**

The Nigerian Institute of Quantity Surveyors (NIQS) has consistency encouraged the Federal Government of Nigeria to prioritise investment in infrastructure development. We firmly believe that this will boost productive activities and provide a basis for economic growth and structural economic diversification. Nigeria spends more on recurrent expenditure than on capital projects by a ratio of 3:1. This means that we give preference to consumption over durable investment in social and economic assets like schools, hospitals, residential and commercial buildings, roads and other inter-modal transportation systems, hydroelectric power plants, petrol-chemical plants and refineries - assets that will enhance the nation's ability to produce goods and services for domestic consumption and export.

The Federal Government of Nigeria, according to its estimates, spent ₦1.134 trillion on petroleum subsidy in 2011. The Government attempted to eliminate the subsidy, promising to "reinvest" it in infrastructure. While this move is welcome, despite temporary rise in the prices of goods and services it may cause, Nigerians are highly and rightly sceptical about the ability of the Government to judiciously invest the savings from the fuel subsidy removal. For its part, the Federal Government has put in place a Subsidy Reinvestment and Empowerment (SURE) Programme to manage the investment of its share of the subsidy savings (₦478.49 billion). A board comprising prominent private sector and civil society representatives that will monitor and evaluate the expenditure of the savings on identified projects by Federal Government Ministries, Departments and Agencies has been set up.

The SURE Programme will increase FGN expenditure on infrastructure by around 50%. States and Local Governments too are expected to invest an additional ₦411.03 billion and ₦203.23 billion respectively in social and educational infrastructure, thus raising the potential increase in infrastructure expenditure in Nigeria by 100%. These sums are likely to reduce given the reinstatement of a part of the subsidy.

The Nigerian Institute of Quantity Surveyors (NIQS) is of the opinion that the Subsidy Reinvestment and Empowerment (SURE) Programme could POTENTIALY contribute to closing Nigeria's crippling infrastructure gap and lay the foundations of strong economic growth and diversification. This positive outcome depends both on government sincerity and more importantly, the vigilance of civil society groups such as professional associations, labour unions, the media, and student unions. As a body of professional cost economists, the NIQS enjoins both the Government and these society groups to embrace the discipline of costing that utilises appropriate costing methodologies and planning, value studies, value management, value engineering and reporting, to ensure rigour and transparency in the reinvestment of the subsidy savings.

This is a discipline that we have urged, unsuccessfully, on successive Nigerian Governments. It is imperative that costing practices and standards, which are routine and mandatory requirements in public construction works in all well-governed countries, are incorporated into the monitoring and evaluation of the Subsidy Reinvestment and Empowerment (SURE) Programme. This will ensure a high degree of public confidence, and guarantee that the economic and social goals of the Programme are delivered. We call on President Goodluck Jonathan and Dr. Christopher Kolade, the Chairman of the Board of the Sure Programme, to make sure that subsidy reinvestment funds are not spent before rigorous costing procedures and capacities are fully in place. Let's seize the opportunity to rescue billions of our national resources from the cesspit of waste and corruption by insisting on and winning hard guarantees that the fuel subsidy savings will be judiciously used. Given the inclement international economic climate and its potential negative effects on Nigeria's earnings, it is imperative that we conserve and prudently use our resources in order to avoid the painful economic chaos that attended the decline of international oil prices in the early 1980s.

Subsidy Reinvestment and Empowerment Programme - Target Areas of Expenditure

According to the "Economic Team" of the Federal Government, the Federal Government's share of the subsidy savings over the next three to four years will be invested in: Social Safety Net Programmes, Niger Delta Developmental Project, Road Infrastructure Projects, Rail Transport Projects, Water and Agriculture Projects (encompassing irrigation projects, rural, urban and regional water supply projects.), Selected Power Projects, Petroleum/NNPC Projects, and ICT Projects.

An in-depth look at the proposed Subsidy Reinvestment and Empowerment Programme in the Agriculture, Education, Health, ICT, Petroleum, Power, Water Supply, Road and Rail Transportation Sectors, as well as Public Works and Youth Empowerment Programmes shows that it will not only lead to the transformation of public infrastructure in Nigeria, but will also ensure the gainful employment of millions of Nigerians.

Governance of the Subsidy Reinvestment and Empowerment Programme

The Federal Government's share of the funds that will become available through the subsidy reduction will be spent on projects in the sectors indicated above by the relevant Federal Government Ministries, Departments, and Agencies (MDAs). But there are three critical differences in how the SURE Funds will be spent:

1. The Ministries, Departments and Agencies (MDAs) will spend Subsidy Reinvestment Funds only on projects identified under the SURE Programme
2. The Ministries will set up special Project Implementation Units (PIUs) to manage the projects

The governance structure of the subsidy reinvestment programme should be extended to the State and Local Governments who will also have a substantial portion of the savings transferred to them. The leadership of Nigerian political parties should take the lead in urging and assisting States and Local Governments in replicating this governance structure. Civil society groups should monitor and ensure compliance at different levels of government, demanding modifications to the design and operations of the SURE Boards as may be required.

Composition and Mandate of the Subsidy Reinvestment and Empowerment Programme Board

The Board, which has the responsibility to ensure that the subsidy savings is utilised judiciously, is composed of:

a. A Chairman, who must be an experienced person of excellent reputation and integrity, who shall be appointed by the President of the Federal Republic of Nigeria

b. A Deputy Chairman, who shall be a person with the same qualities as the Chairman;

c. Six (6) reputable individuals; one from each of the six (6) geo-political zones of which three (3) must be women

d. One (1) Representative of Civil Society Organizations

e. One (1) Representative of the Labour Union

f. One (1) Representative of Nigerian Women Groups

g. One (1) Representative of Nigerian Youths

h. One (1) Representative of the Nigerian Union of Journalists (NUJ)

i. Coordinating Minister for the Economy/Honourable Minister of Finance

j. Honourable Minister, National Planning Commission

k. Honourable Minister of Petroleum Resources

l. Honourable Minister of State for Health

m. Special Adviser on Technical Matter.

Terms of Reference of the Board

The Board will have the following responsibilities:

a. Determine in liaison with the Ministry of Finance and Ministry of Petroleum Resources, the subsidy savings estimates for each preceding month and ensure that such funds are transferred to the Funds' Special Account with the Central Bank of Nigeria.

b. Approve the annual work plans and cash budgets of the various Project Implementation Units (PIUs) within the Ministries, Departments and Agencies (MDAs) and ensure orderly disbursement of funds by the PIUs in order to certify and execute projects.

c. Monitor and evaluate execution of the funded projects, including periodic Poverty' and Social Impact Analyses (PSIA).

d. Update the President regularly on the programme.

e. Periodically brief the Federal Executive Council (FEC) on the progress of the programme.

f. Appoint Consulting firms with international reputation to provide technical assistance to the Board in financial and project management.

g. Appoint external auditors for the fund.

h. Do such other things as are necessary or incidental to the objectives of the Fund or as may be assigned by the Federal Government.

i. The Board will be supported by a Secretariat. The Secretariat will also be responsible for communication and press briefing.

The Nigerian Institute of Quantity Surveyors' Opinions and

a. The reduction of the subsidy on fuel and the investment of the associated savings in social and physical infrastructure that could make our economy more productive, assist the creation of jobs and improve the incomes and livelihoods of poor Nigerians is welcome.

b. This, to a significant extent, reverses the severe neglect of infrastructure that is inherent in budgets that allocate up to 74 % of expenditure to consumption and involve borrowing: 'most 25 % of all government expenditure to fund the waste and corruption the fuel subsidy promotes.

c. While the benefits of the fuel subsidy is concentrated in a few cities and amongst more privileged socio-economic class, the benefits of investing in roads, bridges, railways and other modern mass transit systems, agricultural infrastructure, etc. will greatly ease the transportation of goods and people all over the country, thus making the economy much more productive.

d. While these infrastructure investments, if closely monitored and transparently implemented, will enhance access to the products of rural areas and boost incomes, we call on the Federal Government of Nigeria and the Board of the Subsidy Reinvestment and Empowerment (SURE) Programme to go further and specifically design and fund social interventions in health and education for rural dwellers and the urban poor.

e. Since the success of reinvestment of the fuel subsidy (which has promoted waste and corruption) depends on absolute transparency, we call on all civil society and professional groups to demand iron-cast transparent mechanisms to ensure that subsidy reinvestment funds are used to transform Nigeria's infrastructure rather than the fortunes of people who are close to the Government.

f. We believe that the SURE Programme Design and Governance Structure offers a realistic opportunity for civil society and professional groups to engage the Board, which has the mandate of monitoring and evaluation, and ensure that the subsidy reinvestment is used to impact the lives of our long suffering citizens.

g. We also call on the Government to make serious efforts to cut waste and excess in government while seriously tackling corruption so that Nigerians can see it to be sharing in the sacrifice to invest more in closing our infrastructure gap.

h. The Institute (NIQS) and its regulatory Board Quantity Surveyors Registration Board of Nigeria (QSRBN) will stand and enter into professional indemnity with the SURE Programme Board to guarantee the quality, diligence and professional integrity of the Registered Quantity Surveyors that will be appointed to render professional consultancy technical services in the area of financial and project management in the SURE Programme; while we encourage Nigerian professional and regulatory bodies to also join us in this as a means of fostering the local content agenda.

i. As cost economists and specialists, we note that Governments in Nigeria have shied away from incorporating cost and value engineering in the operations of Ministries, Departments and Agencies; while multinational companies from jurisdictions that have value, transparency, value-for-money, fairness and social harmony operating in Nigeria unfailingly incorporate it in all capital projects.

j. The Subsidy Reinvestment funds should not be spent BEFORE the design of appropriate costing methodologies, value studies, value management, value engineering and value reporting which represents an objective tool to secure transparency and accountability which is far superior to guarantees provided by the reputations of individuals, no matter how distinguished. This is particularly critical for core civil engineering projects such as roads, ports, and railway construction, if Nigerians are to regard the promise of insulating SURE funds from corruption as a sincere one which symbolizes a total departure from the business as usual.

k. While we do not object to appointing external auditors for the SURE Fund (item g of the Terms of Reference of the SURE Board), we note in the most emphatic terms that a major factor that aids and abets corruption in heavy engineering and construction project initiation and implementation in Nigeria is lack of "Construction Contract Auditing".

l. It is unfortunate that the Nigerian Government has not seen the need and necessity of post-construction "Contract Auditing" which is a global mandatory best practice for ensuring checks and balances in the construction project delivery system and in obtaining value-for-money.

m. The much-advertised fight against corruption will continue to be a myth until Construction Contract Auditing is embraced by the Government to eliminate fraud at the pre-contract and post-contract stages of Construction Project Delivery.

n. Nigeria lacks standards and consistency in the development of budget estimates for construction works across MDAs. The Institute as a matter of public concern will devise and publicise a set of cost benchmarks for construction works for use across Ministries, Departments, Agencies MDAs, starting with SURE Funds projects, which will take into cognisance project specifics such as design, location and site conditions. These cost standards will be reviewed on an annual basis to guide the MDAs in their Budget preparation for appropriate appropriations.

o. The Federal Government and the National Assembly should work to pass the Petroleum Industry Bill by the second quarter of 2012 at the latest so as to clarify the fiscal and regulatory basis of the oil industry and stimulate investment in the sector. This will also satisfy calls for increased transparency and the separation of operational, commercial and regulatory roles in the industry.

Legislators need courage to pass PIB, says expert

By SalaimonSalau

***The Guardian*, Wednesday, September 24, 2011, pg. 42**

For the umpteenth time, the National Assembly has been urged to put up courage and pass the Petroleum Industry Bill (PIB) to law, to revive the stagnant petroleum sector.

The Chairman, Global Ocean Engineering Nigeria Limited, Mr. Vincent Ebuh made this call during a ceremony to receive an international award on quality management system from Bureau Veritas in Lagos recently. Ebuh, who described the company's feat as an indication of a growing local industry, said that the oil and gas industry would flourish if the PIB were passed into law.

"For this generation to leave a lasting legacy for the future, we need to act now. Nigeria must come to terms that nobody can develop this country for us except Nigerians themselves. Let us therefore leave out names in the history book.

It is not just courage that matters, but the courage you put into life, so I am urging the National Assembly to put courage into life and pass the PIB," he said.

Commenting on the ISO 9001:2008 certification on Quality Management System by Bureau Veritas, Ebuh said that certification was an affirmation that the Nigeria's drive to develop local content was actually working, and a proof of promise delivered.

"Five short years ago, I told the world that we could start an engineering design company that would deliver work at a standard of quality that will be comparable with that found in any developed country in the world. I said that we would employ Nigerians and would grow them to do what their counterparts were doing elsewhere in the world. It sounded like it was ambitious to even think it was possible given the lack of skills that many International Oil Companies (IOCs) said was evident in Nigeria. This ISO 9001:2008 certification by Bureau Veritas is therefore confirmation that we have delivered." Acknowledging the contributions of its technical partner, Subsea 7, the chairman said: "Oceon means a lot to us. It is more than just an engineering design company. It is a vehicle for growing indigenous participation in Nigeria's oil and gas industry. It is a company for developing leaders in engineering that will position Nigeria on the global stage. We are very pleased that we have started, and we want to assure you that we will not stop. We will continue to provide you the industry with quality services that you can rely on and trust."

The Executive Secretary of the Nigerian Content Monitoring Board (NCDMB), Mr. Ernest Nwapa, however, applauded the firm for the certification and enjoined other Nigerian firms to emulate the feat. Nwapa, who was represented by The General Manager NCDMB, Mr. Chizoke Okorie, said: "They have done well, they deserve the certification and this is a symbol of encouragement for Nigerian companies."

The Managing Director of the company, Mr. Seun Faluyi said that the company had significantly invested in human capital development to achieve the milestone.

Nigeria risks N15tr investment over non-passage of PIB

By Obiora Aduba and Taiwo Hassan

***The Guardian*, Wednesday, July 13, 2011 pg. 45**

The non-passage of the Petroleum Industry Bill (PIB) by the National Assembly, may have taken its toll on the oil and gas service operations in the country, as the effect has stalled the over $100 billion (about ₦15 trillion) oil investment in the petroleum industry by local operators.

Chairman, Lagos Deep Offshore Logistics Base (LADOL), Ladi Jadesimi, who made this disclosure, bemoaned the non-passage of the bill, stating that, if care was not taken, the country may lose a lot of fabrication projects worth billions of dollar to other neighbouring African countries.

A coalition of civil society organisations in the country had said recently that the non-passage of the bill will impact negatively on the fortunes of the oil and gas sector, which accounts for the bulk of government's revenues and foreign exchange earnings, noting that most responsible foreign investors would be scared to invest in an uncertain business environment, which the bill sought to address.

Also, the Director-General, Nigerian Economic Summit Group (NESG), Frank Nweke has said that Nigeria's economy is under threat with the foot-dragging on the PIB, warning that the non-passage of the bill will undermine growth.

Jadesimi, however, stated that Nigeria still needed to fast track its development in the offshore sector, by increasing local participation of Nigerians to enhance their local capacities, adding that the process had taken place in other countries in Africa.

According to him, "We've seen huge developments take place in recent years in Angola, South Africa, Ghana, but development and investment in Nigeria has been stagnant.

"If the bill is not passed now, it will be a significant blow to Nigeria, because Nigeria is not the only oil producer in this sub-region. Investment will be diverted to Ghana, Angola and elsewhere as it's already moving to Ghana.

"We are all hopeful and praying that the PIB would be passed, so as to fast track the huge investment being held back in the sector," Jadesimi added.

The Ladol's boss explained that the offshore sector may have witnessed a rapid development recently, but there was need to change the Status-quo, if the country hopes to make a giant stride in the sector.

"U.SA Korea, Europe and even other African nations will continue to get these projects and jobs and the resultant economic boost, while Nigeria continues to foot the bill."

The chairman noted that various policies of the government had benefited the multinational oil companies operating in the Nigerian Upstream sector, thus, prompting the countries to imports goods and services into Nigeria, worth $300 billion in the last 30 years.

According to him, "Ironically, importation from these continents, such as: United States of America (U.SA), Europe and Asia, had created huge jobs and grew the Gross Domestic Product (GDP)'s of these foreign economies, while draining Nigeria of her developmental growth.

"Over the years, government thought its policies in the oil and gas sector, were meant for the country's developmental plan, but Nigerians working in the multinational oil companies have cornered government officials to ensure that those policies favoured the foreign firms at the expense of indigenous operators, because of the royalties and levies at the doorstep of government officials, he stated.

He stressed that the deep offshore market was a time-limited opportunity for the country to overcome the 'Natural resource curse' and turn it into a blessing,' stressing that over $100 billion, will be spent on deep offshore projects in West Africa, in the next five years.

According to him, the country needs to demonstrate its dominance in the sector, because of its vast development and huge investment in the offshore sector, adding that the expansion of the deepwater sector has undoubtedly been constrained in the recent years by the lack of yard availability, equipment, engineering contractor capacity and experienced personnel.

He emphasised that operators are now expecting the supply of these products and service to come into line with demand.

Petroleum Industry Bill and Nigeria's Capital Market

By Goddy Egene

***ThisDay*, Wednesday, February 15, 2012, vol.17, no. 6141, pg. 29**

There is high optimism that the nation's capital market will witness a growth this year having closed last year on negative note. Analysts from three leading investment bank and research firms have already projected a positive 2012 for the market. Specifically, Meristem Securities Limited, FSDH Securities Limited and FBN Capital Limited have already projected a growth of between 13 and 14 per cent in the Nigerian Stock Exchange (NSE) All-share Index this year.

While FSDH and FBN Securities had made their forecast in January, MLS early this month, said the index would close 2012 at 23,532.91, representing 13.5% over the 2011 close of 20,730.63. MSL was among the top 10 stock broking firms that led equities transactions on the floors of the NSE in 2011, and noted their expectation was being driven by the bullish outlook on the financial service (majorly banks), Nigeria's stable foreign exchange market, expected downward trend in yield on fixed income instruments and anticipated positive macroeconomic performance.

"Our valuation suggests a robust 2012 return of 22.53% for the NSE index, which we believe is justified by the attractive valuations of our coverage companies (which represent 90 per cent of the entire market). However, we are inclined to adopt a conservative outlook. This is informed by the outlook on global economy and the increased possibility that the Nigerian market might witness reduced foreign participation in 2012. We therefore discount our forecast by 40 per cent to arrive at an adjusted 23,532.91 index level," they said.

The analysts explained that their sectoral returns distribution showed their upside bias for the financial service sector particularly the banks, given their fundamentals, weight and volatility.

"We expect the sector to dictate and lead market performance in 2012. Our 22 per cent target return is 82 per cent overweight on the financial sector particularly the banks. We will however, subject our forecast and underlying assumptions to testing and review as events in both the economic and financial markets warrants. Our understanding of market performance and returns distribution is that market returns are always skewed towards a short period of time, and this is expected this to play out in 2012. Though we remain watchful on the economic climate given the increasing level of uncertainties that overshadow 2012, we anticipate a fragile first quarter rally and a much stronger rally in the second half of 2012," they said.

Market operators said that while the Nigerian market is expected to bounce back, noted that there should be efforts to deepen the market so that investors would have enough securities to patronise.

According to them, getting more firms from critical sectors of the economy such as oil and gas and telecommunications to list their shares on the NSE is a good move in that direction.

They stressed that the passage of the PIB, particularly, would boost the capital market as it would encourage companies in that sector to access the market.

The PIB is an ambitious attempt to comprehensively reform the Nigerian oil and gas sector. It is intended to correct most of the defects in the oil and gas industry, introduce new fiscal regime and enhance transparency. The bill proposes to ensure that government increases its revenue from a growing number of deep-water developments; review royalties on gas production, increase revenue accruable from tax charges and change the way tax breaks are applied to new developments.

However, many operators in the industry said that the delayed passage of the bill had remained a big blow to the industry and that it was already taking a toll in terms of investment in the upstream. Most international oil and gas companies refused to invest because of the uncertainty in the fiscal regime brought about the bill not having been passed into law.

The Controversial Issues

The first draft of the PIB was presented in 2008. Since then, the bill has passed through many amendments as government sought consensus among various stakeholder groups. Those amendments gave rise to opinions that different drafts of the PIB were in circulation. The 6th session of the National Assembly in its final days tried to speed up passage of the bill but did not succeed until the April 2011 general elections.

There are strong indications that one of the reasons International Oil Companies (IOCs) are opposing the PIB is the lack of guarantees to existing investors. Holders of existing joint- venture and Production Sharing Contracts (PSC) licenses and leases would be required to re-apply for their respective contracts within a year of the PIB's passage.

No guarantees of renewal is said to have been provided to the existing license holders. Analysts said that by imposing such terms on both the prospective and existing operations, the bill threatens contract sanctity and would increase the risk premium applied to future investment decisions. This, along with stricter fiscal provisions, has put the IOCs, a critical stakeholder group, in opposition to the bill's passage.

The PIB plans to separate oil and natural gas licensing. Current legislation provides for combined rights for exploration and operation. By separating the contracting frameworks, the on-going development of associated fields would become more difficult, since the operator would be required to hold two licenses. The measure is intended to re-open the natural gas licensing field, but in practice, it would likely increase bureaucratic obstacles and the cost of the licensing process.

PIB and the Capital Market

In 2008 when the Federal Government asked the IOCs to get listed on the Nigerian Stock Exchange, operators cited non-passage of the PIB as major hindrance. One of the most important aspects of the PIB is the concept of the Incorporated Joint Ventures (IJVs).

Over the last 30 years, most of Nigeria's oil concessions have been held in Unincorporated Joint Ventures between the IOCs (Shell, Total, Mobil, Agip, Chevron, Mobil) and the Nigerian National Petroleum Corporation (NNPC).But analysts contended that these unincorporated JVs, controlled by NNPC, always had their share of problems, principally because of the government's inability to meet funding obligations.

The IOCs always believed that if these JVs could be turned into normal companies - that is, incorporated - then the funding would become much easier, as capital could be raised from the capital market. Hence, capital market operators said that listing NNPC and other IOCs would not only impact the capital market positively but would also change the way business was done in the oil and gas sector in Nigeria.

The Chinese Example

To better appreciate this, let's look at how the industry reform and capital market revolutionised the Chinese oil and gas sector.

In 1998, the Chinese oil and gas sector underwent comprehensive reorganisation. Under the reforms and re-organisations, the Chinese government directed the three major Chinese petroleum companies- China National Petroleum Corporation(CNPC), China Petroleum and Chemical Corporation (SIMOPEC) and China National Offshore Oil Corporation (CNOOC) to embark on increased structural reforms and pursue listings on overseas stock markets after successfully being listed on the domestic stock exchange.

By April 2000, CNPC listed PetroChina on the Hong Kong and New York stock markets. SINOPEC Corp. in October of the same year got listed the on the Hong Kong, New York and London stock markets. CNOOC followed PetroChina's and Sinopec Corp.'s listings by being listed on the Hong Kong and London stock.

Through initial public offerings (IPO), the three Chinese oil firms raised vast funds totalling more than $7.8 billion.

Almost all of this was achieved through large-scale financing by the majors. The IPO financings, strategic tie-ups with major corporations led to various collaborations on projects.

In upstream exploration and development activities, CNOOC received IPO financing from Royal Dutch/Shell, and by making use of those funds and technological/management know-how from the European oil giant, the two are working together on upstream exploration and development activities. In the same vein, SINOPEC made a strategic alliance with US oil major, ExxonMobil at the time of SINOPEC's IPO. The Chinese energy firm has made use of its partner's technology and funds to plan oil refinery expansions in the Guangdong Province in southern China.

Since China's three major oil companies were listed on overseas stock markets, they have recorded tremendous successes. The three firms' stock prices enjoyed price rallies after listing. The stocks of PetroChina, Sinopec and CNOOC Limited rose 88.2%, 103.4%, 78.1% respectively at some point.

Market Operators' Views

Capital market operators believe that a quick passage of the PIB will pave way for Nigeria's firm like NNPC and the IOCs to be listed on the Exchange."Getting these oil and gas firms on the capital market will not only rejuvenate the market but also impact greatly on the economy and the way the oil and gas sector operates," a stock deals said.

The Chairman, Association of Stockbroking Houses of Nigeria, Mr. Emeka Madubuike, said since the PIB would lead to streamlining and better regulation of the industry, it we'd attract more investments that would in turn boost the economy

"Since the capital market is part of the economy, it we'd benefit from the growth expected from that sector of the economy. The bill will open up the sector for more investments to cc ne in because there would be a supervisory and regulatory body Li the industry. Once it is opened up and more investors come in, the impact will be positive for the entire economy and the capital market will also benefit," Madubuike said.

Speaking in the same vein, the Managing Director/Chief Executive Officer of Investment Centre Limited, Mr. Ifeanyi Odunwa, said the PIB provided the legal frame work for the deregulation of the oil and gas industry. He added that it also encouraged indigenous investors in the industry whose businesses were bound to rapidly grow and ultimately have multiplier effect on the Nigerian economy.

Apart from heralding a new era of due process and transparency in the conduct of business by companies and government agencies connected to with oil, the PIB is expected that our capital market will benefit from this bill as oil majors and several indigenous companies in the related business may raise funds from the market to fund their increased operations. With the implementation of PIB, I foresee the "new" NNPC listing its shares on the NSE and elsewhere abroad to raise huge funds for aggressive business expansion similar to its other counterparts like Petrobras(of Brazil) Petronas of Malaysia the Chinese national giants," he said. According to Odunwa, the expected listing would deepen the market and raise the market capitalisation tremendously.

Apart from the expected passage of the PIB bill, some market operators last week renewed calls for the listing of leading telecommunications and multinational oil producing firms operating in the Nigerian economy.

The Chairman, House of Representatives Committee on Capital Market and Institutions, Herman Hembe, was already sponsoring a bill that would make it mandatory for the companies to be listed on the NSE and the President, Chartered Institute of Stockbrokers (CIS), Mr. Mike Itegboje, said the National Assembly should use the doctrine of necessity as the major reason for such legislation.

"It is in the mutual and collective interest of all stakeholders for this to be done. The local investors will ensure that their investments in the companies are protected since they will also share in the dividends and other benefits. The foreign stakeholders and shareholders will be at peace. The market capitalisation will increase in real terms. It will attract more international investors for equity and debt instruments to be issued by these companies. Now is the time," Itegboje declared. Also, a capital market analyst and investor, Mr. Abiodun Hakeem, said that getting the telecoms and oil and gas multinationals to list on the Exchange would boost liquidity that would transform the fortunes of the capital market and in turn restore the much needed investor confidence.

Hakeem cited instances of some African countries that had legislation in place mandating multinationals to list on the host countries' exchanges.

He said that in 2002, Kenya enacted the Foreign Investor Regulation, which compelled multinationals operating in the country to list in the capital market.

He added that similarly, Tanzania parliament in February 2010 passed a Communication Bill which made it mandatory for mobile telecommunications companies to be listed on the Dar es Salaam Stock Exchange.

"In Kenya for instance, the legislation provided for a minimum of 25 per cent reserve of the issued share capital for local investors while the balance of 75 per cent was left for other categories of investors. The legislation made it possible for Kenyan citizens to invest in companies like Nation Media, a regional media player; TPS East Africa, a tourism operator and Safaricom, a mobile telecommunication company amongst others," he said.

On his part, Odunwa noted that the telcos and oil firms do highly profitable business and repatriate the profits to their home countries.

"It is unfair that more than 40 years for oil majors and 10 years for telcos respectively, they remain unwilling to create wealth for local investors through the listing of their shares on the NSE," he said.

According to the stockbroker, the eventual listing of their share s will deepen the capital market as there would be a quantum leap in the market capital market and all-share index.

"Furthermore, the seeming apathy of the Nigeria of Nigerian investors in the market presently will suddenly disappear as everybody will confidently want to invest in shares due to their track record of profitability," Odunwa said.

He explained that the appreciation in share prices of these companies, dividend payment out among others would no doubt create wealth for investors.

The petroleum industry: challenges and achievements in 2011

By MuhyideenJimoh

***The Guardian*, Monday, January 16, 2012, pg.17**

Perhaps, the most criticised and sensitive sector in the Nigerian economy in 2011 is the petroleum sector. The sector has been facing severe criticisms in spite of its huge contributions to the national economy. Analysts contend that the thorny issue of fuel subsidy removal and the deregulation of the downstream sector of the petroleum industry and its envisaged effects on the economy and the citizenry have been a veritable source of concern for all and sundry.

The Minister of Petroleum Resources, Mrs Diezani Alison-Madueke said during the launch of the gas revolution agenda in March, that Nigeria ought to deregulate the downstream oil sector and remove fuel subsidy so as to fast-track the country's development and end the perennial fuel scarcity in the country.

She said that the move would enable the government save about N13 trillion annually, adding that the savings would be ploughed into infrastructural development projects, while creating the enabling environment for the growth of the oil and gas industry.

Sharing similar sentiments, Dr. Levi Ajuonuma, the group general manager (Public Affairs) of NNPC, stressed that the deregulation of the downstream oil sector would instil efficiency in the sector and fast-track the country's development.

In spite of the arguments in favour of the deregulation of the petroleum sector, some stakeholders, including the organised labour, are also quick to point out that the plan will negatively affect the living standards of the average Nigerian.

Such dissents notwithstanding, the Federal Government insists that the benefits of the subsidy removal include the accumulation of more resources for the country's development, the elimination of cartels, which have been holding the country to ransom and the promotion of the sector's efficiency.

The President of the NLC, Mr. Abdulwahab Omar has repeatedly condemned government's plans to remove the fuel subsidy, insisting that the labour movement would resist the policy, as it would engender widespread poverty because of the resultant increase in fuel prices.

In line with its threats, the NLC and its sister organisation - the Trade Union Congress (TUC) - called a nationwide with effect from Monday, Jan. 9, to protest against the government's removal of the fuel subsidy on January 1.

The labour unions and civil society organisations are particularly worried that the snowball effects of the subsidy withdrawal include hikes in transport fares, commodity prices and the attendant increase in inflation. The problem is compounded by the inability of the counties four refineries to function at full capacity, while the Turn Around Maintenance (TAM) of the refineries has for a long time been enmeshed in a lot of controversy.

Analysts believe that the only panacea to the bleak oil situation entails the refurbishment of the refineries, saying that tangible efforts should also be made to establish Greenfield refineries.

Such comments notwithstanding, the contribution of the oil sector to the national economy is quite substantial, while Nigeria's crude oil is highly rated in the international oil market. Nigeria is also recognised as a key player in the affairs of the Organisation of Petroleum Exporting Countries (OPEC), a group or oil producers and exporters. Ironically, while some citizens view the petroleum sector as a blessing for the country, some cynics say that the sector has induced some national drawbacks, particularly with regard to the fading interest in agriculture - the erstwhile mainstay of the national economy.

No doubt, the significant earnings from crude oil exports have catalysed the country's infrastructural development, while improving the citizens' living standards.

Many critics, nonetheless, argue that Nigeria would have experienced a remarkable development if the oil revenues had been judiciously utilised by the country's successive leaders, particularly those that governed the country during the oil boom years.

The critics particularly bemoan the perceived neglect and the environmental degradation of the Niger Delta area, where the vast majority of the country's oil wealth is derived, saying that the development somewhat reflects the ineptitude of the country's leaders.

Analysts note that the Niger Delta situation has led to widespread discontentment among the people of the area, manifesting in the menace of youth restiveness, insecurity and all kinds of social upheavals, which plagued the region until very recently.

These social conditions have adversely affected Nigeria's oil production, thereby provoking a downward trend in the country's revenue earnings.

The precarious situation compelled the administration of the late President Umaru Yar'Adua, to initiate the Amnesty Programme for Niger Delta militants and the policy, which is still subsisting, as been able to provide some kind of succour to the aggrieved youths and communities in the area.

Although oil production in the region has picked up since peace and stability returned to the Niger Delta area, the price fluctuations in the international oil market have often created some economic problems for OPEC member nations, including Nigeria. The price instability and security threats in the Niger Delta have created serious economic challenges for the country, even as some economists have been urging the Federal Government to diversify the economy by giving priority attention to the development of the agricultural sector.

"The epileptic shifts in the international oil prices and instability in the Niger Delta region have made the nation's economy very vulnerable," says Dr. Johnson Abejide, an economist.

Concerned citizens also note that in spite of the rising oil resources of Nigeria, the country s poverty index reveals that a significant proportion of the citizenry still lives below the poverty line.

They partly attribute the development to wide-scale corruption and inefficiency in the petroleum industry over the years, stressing that the current situation largely negates the people's development expectations in spite of the huge proceeds from crude oil sales.

"There has been lack of transparency and accountability. This, coupled with the non-implementation of oil sector reforms over the years, had limited the people's potential benefits from the sector," says Abejide. However, Nigeria's adoption of the Extractive Industries Transparency Initiative has been adjudged by many observers as a good development. The Nigeria Extractive Industries Transparency Initiative (NEITI), the Nigerian subset of the global initiative is aimed at upholding the due process and achieving transparency in payments by Extractive Industry (El) companies to the government and its agencies.

Besides, many observers commend President Goodluck Jonathan for signing into law the Nigerian Local Content Development Bill in April 2011. The new law partly seeks to develop local competence in the oil industry, while promoting technology transfer, use of local manpower and local manufacturing.

"'Expenditure in the industry must transcend returns in terms of revenue and it should also translate to improved local capacity, technology growth and increased job opportunities for Nigerians," Jonathan said when he signed the bill into law.

Senate reviews acreage, bidding process in oil sector

By John Abba Ogbodo

***The Guardian*, Wednesday March 23, 2011, pg. 1, 2**

The Senate has introduced new ways of doing business and managing Nigeria's oil resources to enhance openness and transparency in the industry.

After a scrutiny of the recommendation of its Committee on Petroleum Resources that worked on the Petroleum Industry Bill (PIB), the Senate endorsed the proposal that a new system of acreage management, licensing, and leasing be introduced in the sector.

Consequently, the Upper House inserted Clause 195 in part three of the PIB, which states that the National Petroleum Inspectorate, to be established under the planned law, will adopt a national grid system for petroleum acreage management. According to the panel, "the basic unit for the national grid shall be a parcel of two- By-two kilometres, subject to adjustment zones and the Consequently, the Upper House inserted Clause 195 in part three of the PIB, which states that the National Petroleum Inspectorate, to be established under the planned law, will adopt a national grid system for petroleum acreage management.

According to the panel, "the basic unit for the national grid shall be a parcel of two- By-two kilometres, subject to adjustment zones and the national boundary, in which case a parcel shall be the part in the adjustment zone or on Nigerian territory". The Senate had last Wednesday considered the bill but suspended action on it because of the one-month break to enable its members go on campaigns for the 2011 elections. A principal officer of the Senate told The *Guardian* in Abuja that the chamber would pass the bill as soon as it reconvenes in April. He said "Our Committees on Petroleum (Upstream and Downstream) have worked on the bill and brought a report, which we have no problem passing the bill."

The clause further provides that the grid system shall also be used for the definition of licence and lease areas. "The grid system shall be used for the definition of licence and lease areas, relinquishments, bid procedures, identification of well locations, petroleum conversation measures and such other regulatory and acreage management procedures as are applicable in the opinion of the inspectorate". On classification of licences and leases, the proposed law says: "There shall be the following licences or leases - (a) a licence to be known as petroleum exploration licence to carry out exploration on a non-exclusive basis (b) a licence to be known as Petroleum Prospecting Licence (PPL) to prospect for petroleum, and (c) a lease to be known as Petroleum Mining Lease (PML), to search for, win, work, carry away and dispose of petroleum."

The clause also defines the process of issuance of licence and lease to thus: "In accordance with the provisions of this Act and with respect to acreage vested in the commission and subject to the approval of the President, the minister on the recommendation of the commission, may grant a Petroleum Prospecting Licence or Petroleum Mining Lease and where the commission decides to grant such licence or lease, (a) it shall be to the winning bidder pursuant to bid process prescribed in section 214, provided the bid winner has complied with all requirements specified in the bid process."

On the issue of confidentiality clause, section 198, which the Senate panel included, provides that "subject to the provision in subsection (3) of this Act or the provisions of any other relevant law, confidentiality clauses or other clauses contained within any licences, leases, agreements or contracts for upstream petroleum operations that are for the purpose of preventing access to information and documents by third parties in respect of any payments of (a) royalties and (b) fees and bonuses of whatever sort, shall be null, void and of no effect." The bill restricts a petroleum exploration licence to a period of three years. "A petroleum exploration licence shall be for not more than three years and shall not include any right or option to win, get, work, store, carry away, transport, export or otherwise treat petroleum discovered in or under the said area."

The bill defines the duration and area of petroleum prospecting licence in clause 200 as a petroleum prospecting licence shall be (a) with respect to onshore and shallow water areas, for a duration of not more than seven years consisting of an initial period of three years and a possibility for appraisal of any discoveries until the termination of licence or such later period as may be granted by the Inspectorate following due representation of lease and the initial petroleum prospecting licence area shall not be more than 500 square kilometre and not to be one parcel and (b) with respect to deep water areas and inland basin for a duration of not more than 10 years, consisting of an initial period of five years, a renewal of three years and a possibility for appraisal of any discoveries until the termination of the licence and the initial petroleum prospecting licence area shall not be more than 1,000 square kilometres and not less than one parcel."

www.ingramcontent.com/pod-product-compliance
Lightning Source LLC
Chambersburg PA
CBHW050522240926
51846CB00003B/656
9789785193275